The Tyndale Old Testament Commentaries

General Editor:
PROFESSOR D. J. WISEMAN, O.B.E., M.A., D.Lit., F.B.A.,
F.S.A.

1 and 2 KINGS

1 and 2 KINGS

AN INTRODUCTION AND COMMENTARY

by

DONALD J. WISEMAN, O.B.E., M.A., D.Lit., F.B.A., F.S.A.
Emeritus Professor of Assyriology in the University of London

INTER-VARSITY PRESS
LEICESTER, ENGLAND
DOWNERS GROVE, ILLINOIS, U.S.A.

Inter-Varsity Press
P.O. Box 1400, Downers Grove, Illinois 60515, U.S.A.
38 De Montfort Street, Leicester LE1 7GP, England

© *1993 by Donald J. Wiseman*

InterVarsity Press®, U.S.A., is the book-publishing division of InterVarsity Christian Fellowship®, a student movement active on campus at hundreds of universities, colleges and schools of nursing in the United States of America, and a member movement of the International Fellowship of Evangelical Students. For information about local and regional activities, write Public Relations Dept., InterVarsity Christian Fellowship, 6400 Schroeder Rd., P.O. Box 7895, Madison, WI 53707-7895.

Inter-Varsity Press, England, is the book-publishing division of the Universities and Colleges Christian Fellowship (formerly the Inter-Varsity Fellowship), a student movement linking Christian Unions in universities and colleges throughout the United Kingdom and the Republic of Ireland, and a member movement of the International Fellowship of Evangelical Students. For information about local and national activities in Great Britain write to UCCF, 38 De Montfort Street, Leicester LE1 7GP.

Text set in Great Britain
Printed in the United States of America ∞

UK ISBN 0-85111-645-0 (hardback)
UK ISBN 0-85111-846-1 (paperback)
USA ISBN 0-87784-259-0 (hardback)
USA ISBN 0-8308-1430-2 (paperback)
USA ISBN 0-87784-880-7 (set of Tyndale Old Testament Commentaries, hardback)
USA ISBN 0-87784-280-9 (set of Tyndale Old Testament Commentaries, paperback)

Library of Congress Cataloging-in-Publication Data

Wiseman, D. J. (Donald John)
    1 & 2 Kings: an introduction and commentary/by Donald J.
Wiseman
        p.   cm.—(Tyndale Old Testament commentaries; 9)
    Includes bibliographical references.
    ISBN 0-87784-259-0 (cloth).—ISBN 0-8308-1430-2 (pbk.)
    1. Bible.   O.T.   Kings—Commentaries.   I. Title.   II. Title: 1
and 2 Kings.   III. Title: First & Second Kings.   IV. Series.
BS1335.3.W574   1993
222'.507—dc20   *93-3484*
                                                                            CIP

British Library Cataloguing in Publication Data

A catalogue record for this book is available from the British Library.

16	15	14	13	12	11	10	9	8	7	6	5	4	3	2	1
06	05	04	03	02	01	00	99	98	97	96	95	94	93		

GENERAL PREFACE

THE aim of this series of *Tyndale Old Testament Commentaries*, as it was in the companion volumes on the New Testament, is to provide the student of the Bible with a handy, up-to-date commentary on each book, with the primary emphasis on exegesis. Major critical questions are discussed in the introductions and additional notes, while undue technicalities have been avoided.

In this series individual authors are, of course, free to make their own distinct contributions and express their own point of view on all debated issues. Within the necessary limits of space they frequently draw attention to interpretations which they themselves do not hold but which represent the stated conclusions of sincere fellow Christians.

The Books of Kings continue the history of God's people from the united kingdom under David and Solomon to the tragedy of its division into the realms of Israel and Judah until their respective downfall and exile. Here is portrayed those kings who sought to govern according to the divine law and with the encouragement or rebuke of a long line of prophets from the renowned Elijah to Jeremiah. The historian concentrates on Solomon, Hezekiah and Josiah of Judah and on Ahab of Israel, and in this unique piece of history writing we are introduced to the lives of many individuals whose part is faithfully recorded for our learning.

This commentary is based on the New International Version, though other translations are frequently referred to as well, and on occasion the author supplies his own. Where necessary, words are transliterated in order to help the reader who is unfamiliar with Hebrew to identify the precise word under discussion. It is assumed throughout that the reader will have ready access to at least one reliable rendering of the Bible in English.

Interest in the meaning and message of the Old Testament

continues undiminished, and it is hoped that this series will thus further the systematic study of the revelation of God and his will and ways as seen in these records. It is the prayer of the editor and publisher, as of the authors, that these books will help many to understand, and to respond to, the Word of God today.

D. J. WISEMAN

CONTENTS

AUTHOR'S PREFACE

THE Books of Kings are a unique source for the history of Israel from the last days of the united monarchy under David to the fall of the subsequently divided kingdoms of Israel (with the capture of Samaria in 722 BC) and of Judah itself (with the sack of Jerusalem in 587 BC). Without these books, and the partly parallel account in the Chronicles, our knowledge of God's dealings with his peoples throughout the first millennium BC would be severely limited.

It is not possible in the brief space allowed to quote the many scholars to whom I am indebted. We are today well served by recent full-scale commentaries in English, to which reference is made here by the author's name (*e.g.* Jones (1984)). In these more extensive works will be found much of the detailed argumentation, theoretical speculations about editorial redactions and some conjectural emendations of the text which abound in such studies today. While this study notes some of their conclusions, it is itself based on the final text of Scripture as it has come down to us today. The overall aim of this commentary, as of this whole series, is to make the text better understood by lay people. There is, however, a sense in which any comment on a historian who is himself commenting on events closer to his time may be thought superfluous.

I have included emphases which will betray my own personal preferences. Among these are aspects of archaeological discovery which relate to the Bible, for this has been my lifelong interest and work. Also I have not attempted, except where essential for clarity, to render the ineffable divine name (in Hebrew consonants 'YHWH', commonly interpreted as 'Yahweh' but unpronounced and unpronounceable) as other than 'LORD'. This follows the ancient practice by which the vowel signs for 'Lord' (*adonai*) were added (hence the interpretation 'Jehovah'). The One God is unquestionably and unmistakably identified.

9

All readers today need to study this history, which is largely biographical and gives us a vivid picture of national and individual life and the way God was working in both. Its frank statement of the triumphs and tragedies of God's people has a relevance for us today. These things were recorded as examples to keep us from setting our hearts on things as they did. They were written also as warnings, so that when we think we are standing firmer than they, we must be careful not to fall (1 Cor. 10:6, 11). At the same time they were written to help us, as also the original readers, to endure in times of testing and to encourage us to trust and hope in the same unchanging God. Many of the events and characters here portrayed are taken up in the New Testament and so have ongoing significance.

My thanks are first and foremost to my wife Mary for her long-suffering patience and understanding over more than forty years. Much of this time has been occupied with my own academic work, Bible translation and the editorship of this series. Throughout I have sought to support the Inter-Varsity Press, whose staff have always been helpful and encouraging to me. Thanks also to Mrs Ruth Holmes for easing my burden by deciphering my manuscript and bringing it to typescript, and to Alan Millard and Bruce Winter of Tyndale House for help in bibliographical references.

This book is sent out with the prayer that, despite its many deficiencies, it may help us all to be loyal to the LORD and his word.

DONALD J. WISEMAN

CHIEF ABBREVIATIONS

ANEP *The Ancient Near East in Pictures*, edited by James B. Pritchard (Princeton: Princeton University Press, 1954).

ANET *The Ancient Near Eastern Texts Relating to the Old Testament*, edited by James B. Pritchard (Princeton: Princeton University Press, ²1955, ³1969).

AOAT *Alter Orient und Altes Testament.*

ARAB *Ancient Records of Assyria and Babylonia* by D. D. Luckenbill, 2 vols. (Chicago: University of Chicago Press, 1926–1927).

BA *The Biblical Archaeologist.*

BASOR *Bulletin of the American Schools of Oriental Research.*

BDB F. Brown, S. R. Driver and C. A. Briggs, *Hebrew and English Lexicon of the Old Testament* (Oxford: Oxford University Press, ²1952).

Bib. *Biblica.*

Bi.Or. *Bibliotheca Orientalis.*

BSOAS *Bulletin of the School of Oriental and African Studies.*

CAD *The Chicago Assyrian Dictionary.*

CBQ *Catholic Biblical Quarterly.*

DOTT *Documents from Old Testament Times*, edited by D. Winton Thomas (London: Nelson, 1958).

EI *Eretz Israel.*

EQ *Evangelical Quarterly.*

Exp.T. *Expository Times.*

HUCA *Hebrew Union College Annual.*

IBD *The Illustrated Bible Dictionary* (Leicester: IVP, 1980).

IDB *Interpreter's Dictionary of the Bible* (Nashville: Abingdon, Vols. I–IV, 1962; Supplement, 1976).

IEJ *Israel Exploration Journal.*

IJH *Israelite and Judaean History* by J. H. Hayes and J. M. Miller (London: SCM Press, 1977).

JANES	*Journal of the Ancient Near Eastern Society of Columbia University.*
JBL	*Journal of Biblical Literature.*
JCS	*Journal of Cuneiform Studies.*
JEA	*Journal of Egyptian Archaeology.*
JNES	*Journal of Near Eastern Studies.*
JQR	*Jewish Quarterly Review.*
JSOT	*Journal for the Study of the Old Testament.*
*JSOT*Supp	*Journal for the Study of the Old Testament*, Supplements.
JSS	*Journal of Semitic Studies.*
NBD	*The New Bible Dictionary* (Leicester: IVP, ²1982).
Or.	*Orientalia.*
PEQ	*Palestine Exploration Quarterly.*
POTT	*Peoples of Old Testament Times*, edited by D. J. Wiseman (Oxford: Clarendon Press, 1973).
RA	*Revue d'Assyriologie et d'Archaeologie.*
RB	*Revue Biblique.*
SOTSM	Society for Old Testament Study Monographs.
TynB	*Tyndale Bulletin.*
TDOT	*Theological Dictionary of the Old Testament*, edited by G. I. Botterweck and H. Ringgren, Vols. I–VI (Grand Rapids: Eerdmans, 1977–1990).
TOTC	*Tyndale Old Testament Commentary.*
TWOT	*Theological Wordbook of the Old Testament* by R. Laird Harris *et al.*, 2 vols. (Chicago: Moody, 1980).
UF	*Ugarit-Forschungen: Internationales Jahrbuch für die Altertumskunde Syrien-Palästinas.*
VT	*Vetus Testamentum.*
*VT*Supp	*Vetus Testamentum*, Supplements.
WHJP	*The World History of the Jewish People: The Age of the Monarchies* Vols. IV–V, edited by A. Malamat (Jerusalem: Massada Press, 1979).
ZA	*Zeitschrift für Assyriologie.*
ZAW	*Zeitschrift für die Alttestamentliche Wissenschaft.*
ZDPV	*Zeitschrift des deutschen Palästina-Vereins.*

TEXTS AND VERSIONS

Akkad.	Akkadian (Assyrian and Babylonian).
AV	Authorized (King James) Version, 1611.

DSS	Dead Sea Scrolls (Qumran).
EVV	English versions.
GNB	Good News Bible (Today's English Version), 1976.
Heb.	Hebrew.
JB	The Jerusalem Bible, 1966.
LXX	The Septuagint (pre-Christian Greek version of the Old Testament).
LXX(L)	Lucian recension.
M. Heb.	Modern Hebrew.
MT	Massoretic Text.
NASB	New American Standard Bible, 1960.
NEB	New English Bible, 1970.
NIV	New International Version, 1984.
NKJV	New King James Version, 1982.
NRSV	New Revised Standard Version, 1989.
OG	Old Greek translation.
REB	Revised English Bible, 1989.
RSV	Revised Standard Version, 1952.
RV	Revised Version, 1881.
Syr.	Syriac.
Targ.	Targum.
Ugar.	Ugaritic.
Vulg.	The Vulgate (the late fourth-century Latin translation of the Bible by Jerome).
5QK	Fragment of DSS Kings from Qumran Cave 5.
6QK	Fragments of DSS Kings from Qumran Cave 6.

COMMENTARIES
(referred to by author's name only)

Burney	C. F. Burney, *Notes on the Hebrew Text of the Book of Kings* (1918: repr. Oxford: Oxford University Press, 1983).
Cogan	M. Cogan and H. Tadmor, *II Kings*, Anchor Bible (New York: Doubleday, 1988).
DeVries	S. J. DeVries, *1 Kings*, Word Biblical Commentary 12 (Waco: Word, 1985).
Gray	J. Gray, *I & II Kings: A Commentary*, Old Testament Library (London: SCM Press, ²1970).
Hobbs	T. R. Hobbs, *2 Kings*, Word Biblical Commentary 13 (Waco: Word, 1985).

Jones
: G. H. Jones, *1 and 2 Kings*, Vols. I–II, New Century Bible Commentary (London: Marshall, Morgan & Scott, 1984).

Keil
: C. F. Keil, *The Books of Kings* (1872: repr. Grand Rapids: Eerdmans, 1954).

Long
: B. O. Long, *1 Kings with an Introduction to Historical Literature*, The Forms of O.T. Literature, Vol. IX (Grand Rapids: Eerdmans, 1984).

Montgomery
: J. A. Montgomery and H. S. Gehman, *Commentary on the Books of Kings*, International Critical Commentary (Edinburgh: T. & T. Clark, 1951).

Nelson
: R. Nelson, *First and Second Kings*, Interpretation (Atlanta: John Knox Press, 1987).

Noth
: M. Noth, *Könige*, Biblischer Kommentar: Altes Testament IX/I (NeuKirchen-Vluyn: Neu-Kirchener Verlag, 1968).

Provan
: I. W. Provan, *Hezekiah and the Book of the Kings*, Beihefte zur ZAW 172 (Berlin: De Gruyter, 1988).

Robinson
: J. Robinson, *The First Book of Kings, The Second Book of Kings*, Cambridge Bible Commentary (Cambridge: Cambridge University Press, 1972, 1976).

Slotki
: I. W. Slotki, *Kings* (London: Soncino Press, 1950).

INTRODUCTION

Some modern readers may hesitate to approach the Books of Kings, for it is not easy for all to bridge the gap between our day and the first millennium BC through which the history of the ancient kingdoms of Israel and Judah is traced. The narrative covers almost five hundred years from the initiation to the eclipse of their kingship. It is the story of the rise and fall of kingdoms, of high promise and abject failure, of tragedy and yet of hope. God's chosen people seem to lose out because of the tendency to trust in themselves and so break away from the service of God to worship others rather than follow the LORD God himself.

I. THE VALUE OF THE BOOKS OF KINGS

The history opens with the end of the reign of David as he controls from his capital Jerusalem a region stretching from Syria to the Philistinian city-states on the south-west Palestinian coast, to the transjordan border states of Ammon and Moab on the east and Egypt's borders to the south. This was largely due to the weakness of the major powers of the day. Assyria had not yet expanded westwards to make the small city-states of Aram (Damascus) join with Israel to resist Shalmaneser III at Qarqar in 753 BC. It was to be more than a century later that the Assyrians took Damascus and then gradually dominated and incorporated the city-states as vassals until Israel itself was taken in 722 BC. Soon thereafter Judah was invaded (701 BC) and put under pressure until it too fell to the Babylonians, as heirs of Assyria, and the people were carried off into exile. Throughout this period Judah had had to withstand incursions from Egypt. The history of Kings is in no small measure that of relations between God's people and their neighbours around and within their land.

The history of Kings does not set out to be a complete and

exhaustive portrayal of the period but rather a selection made to illustrate God's overall control of history, even when this is not obvious to observers. The historian does this by a judicious use of his sources and by highlighting the lives of certain individuals. Thus David, king of Judah, is the ideal or model ruler and Jeroboam son of Nebat is typical of those kings of Israel who lead the people into sin. Ahab and Jehu are singled out as those who began well yet, despite the admonishments of contemporary prophets, did not carry reforms to a final conclusion and thus influenced even Judah to err and ultimately to suffer the same fate as their northern neighbours.

One result of this selectivity (a common method in historiography) is that there is also emphasis on Solomon, Hezekiah and Josiah ('the new David') of Judah and on Ahab as the hoped-for reformer of Israel, while others are treated in a summary fashion. Thus the distinguished ruler Omri of Israel, renowned according to contemporary documents (*e.g.* The Moabite Mesha' inscription and Assyrian references to the 'House of Omri'), is passed over in only eight verses (1 Ki. 16:21–28) and Manasseh's long reign occupies less than a chapter (2 Ki. 21:1–18).

Kings is a unified work and, as argued here, probably and largely the work of one historian. The purpose for which the book was written is nowhere explicitly stated and must be deduced from the history as it now stands. It serves for all time as a warning of the inevitable retributive judgment brought on themselves by those who deviate in worship and practice, yet as an encouragement to follow God and receive the blessings promised for those who are obedient to his law even through times of exile. It is also a reminder of God's persevering love and grace despite his being rebuffed. Most space is given to those who, at least initially, were viewed as 'doing the right in the LORD's sight' and thus as practically keeping his law.

Kings then is not just a chronicle, political or religious, but 'sacred' history with appropriate theological comment, that is, a religious commentary on history (see Themes and Theology, pp. 18ff.). Without the details given, little would be known of the outcome of the experiment in kingship following the promise given to David of an everlasting dynasty. Nor would the wisdom and splendour of Solomon, the exploits of the prophets Elijah and Elisha, the event and explanation of the exile of Israel and of Judah, to all of which reference is made elsewhere in Scripture, be known or understood. All peoples since the earliest societies using writing, have given an account to themselves of the principal events known to them for the benefit of subsequent generations.[1]

Kings, as part of the continuous history of Israel from the time of the exodus from Egypt when they were designated 'God's people' as a nation until their downfall and dispersal into exile, is no exception. Claims are made that it represents also the earliest continuous and genuine historiography.[2] Many of the literary forms employed are known to have been in use among contemporaries in the ancient Near East. In common with them, facts are drawn from diverse yet authenticated sources. While it may not be possible at this distance to distinguish in detail the historian's primary sources (see Sources, pp. 40–46) there is no reason to deny that he could well have had access to objective and reliable records as usually kept in official archives of a capital city at this time. These included lists of kings, officials, reports of civil and military activities, personal biographies and the like. Attempts are today made to distinguish other genres, *e.g.* popular narratives, story, legends and memoirs, but there is no unanimity in this.[3]

Kings also contributes to our understanding of the cultural milieu of the period. It tells something of the learning, writings and wisdom (1 Ki. 3; 4:29–34), law and justice (1 Ki. 3:16–28), as well as injustice (1 Ki. 21); palace and temple building (1 Ki. 5–7); dedication and upkeep (1 Ki. 8); and the dangers of interfaith and mixed marriages (1 Ki. 11:1–13; 2 Ki. 8:18). There are details about international trade (1 Ki. 5:1–18; 10), the problems of kingship and succession leading to palace intrigues, rebellions (1 Ki. 12:16) and frequent recourse to murder and assassination to remove rivals, especially in the Northern Kingdom (*e.g.* 2 Ki. 8:7–15; 9:14; 30–37; 10:18–19; 15:30). The frequent episodes of famine (1 Ki. 18:2; 2 Ki. 6:25–33) and the sieges of Samaria (1 Ki. 20; 2 Ki. 6:20 – 7:10) and Jerusalem (2 Ki. 18:17) as well as the wars against neighbouring Moab and Edom (2 Ki. 14:7) and

---

[1] *Cf.* J. H. Huizinga in R. Klibansky and H. J. Paton (eds.), *Philosophy and History: Essays Presented to Ernst Cassirer* (Oxford: Oxford University Press, 1936), p. 9.
[2] DeVries, p. xxx.   [3] Long, pp. 4–8, 249–264.

Aram (1 Ki. 20; 22:29–36) may distance the reader from the sad events but it must be remembered that, though portrayed according to the setting of their time, many of these would be classed today as 'colonial expansion' (of Israel into Aram/Syria) or as border raids or even as the liberation of areas under a tyrant, developments not unknown in the same regions still. These, and the mafia-like vendettas and family feuds, raise moral questions no less for us today than they did for God's people in Old Testament times.

II. THEMES AND THEOLOGY

Appreciation of Kings may vary with the standpoint taken by a commentator or reader with reference to the purpose, period and place assigned to the historian or editor(s). If the book is taken only as a late reworking of some earlier facts to encourage exiles in Babylonia to understand the just fate of God's people, then the emphasis varies, depending on whether the book is thought to see the whole history as pessimistic or to contain, and end with, a note of the hope of restoration. In consequence differing themes are considered dominant. However, the view taken here is that there is no single overriding theme, but the whole selection of events and the theological comment on them carries forward the historical story of God at work and relating to his people just as they had experienced earlier.

Many themes of theological import are discernible throughout the book. Some will be seen as recurrent phrases already known from the law (especially Deuteronomy) or in the recurrent experiences recorded in the lives of a number of kings and prophets. Those theological emphases as commonly described are cited here for study.

(a) God in history

God is referred to frequently but most often here as the LORD (Yahweh) God (over five hundred times). He is the Sovereign LORD (1 Ki. 2:26), the LORD Almighty (1 Ki. 18:15; 19:10, 14; 2 Ki. 19:31). He is declared to be the one true God (1 Ki. 18:24), incomparable (1 Ki. 8:23), the creator (2 Ki. 19:15) and giver of life (1 Ki. 17:21). He is living (1 Ki. 18:15 and often in the oath formula 'As the LORD lives', 1 Ki. 17:12; 18:10, 15; 22:14; 2 Ki. 2:4, 6; 3:14). God is especially thought of as the God of the fathers (1 Ki. 18:36) and God of Israel

18

(1 Ki. 1:30, 48, *passim*). So he is the God of David (2 Ki. 20:5) and Solomon (1 Ki. 3:3, 7; 5:4; 8:28) who refer to him personally as 'My God/LORD' as the people do of him as 'our God' (1 Ki. 8:59, 61, 65; 9:9; 10:9). He is transcendent (1 Ki. 8:27; 2 Ki. 2:1–12), omnipresent (1 Ki. 8:27; 20:28) yet with his people (1 Ki. 8:3, 12, 57), thought of as invisibly enthroned in his temple (2 Ki. 19:15) which bears his name (1 Ki. 5:3, 5; 8:43), where he is to be worshipped (1 Ki. 18:12, *cf.* 2 Ki. 17:32–34, 39, 41) and praised (1 Ki. 1:48; 8:15, 56; 10:9). His name is to be made known to others (1 Ki. 8:60; 2 Ki. 19:19). As the God of law he commands (1 Ki. 9:4; 13:21) and requires trust and obedience (2 Ki. 18:5–6). He shows himself in deeds, some thought miraculous (2 Ki. 20:11), and reveals himself in words through his spokesmen the prophets (see Prophetic narratives, pp. 23–24, 44–46).

In history God is conceived as ruling over the kingdoms of men (2 Ki. 19:15), raising up kings (against Solomon, 1 Ki. 11:23) and controlling the turn of events (1 Ki. 12:15; *cf.* 3:13). He drives out some nations (2 Ki. 16:3; 17:8) or reduces their territory (2 Ki. 10:32), rejects others, removing them from his presence into exile (2 Ki. 17:20–23; 23:27) when they stubbornly fail to serve him. It is God who sends enemies to punish his people (2 Ki. 24:2) and strikes Israel (1 Ki. 14:15). Indeed God can be provoked to anger (1 Ki. 11:9; 16:7, 13, 26, 33; 2 Ki. 17:11, 18). To him is attributed disaster (1 Ki. 9:9; 2 Ki. 6:33), tragedy (1 Ki. 17:20), disease (2 Ki. 15:5),[1] famine (2 Ki. 8:1) and even sudden death by fire (2 Ki. 1:12). Yet at the same time God is the one who hears and answers prayer,[2] and the prayers of Solomon (1 Ki. 8:22–54) and Hezekiah (2 Ki. 19:14–19) are recorded. God gives deliverance (2 Ki. 13:5; 18:30–35; 19:6–7, 35–37), victory (2 Ki. 5:1), forgiveness (2 Ki. 5:18), wisdom (1 Ki. 3:28; 4:29; 5:12; 10:24), his Spirit (1 Ki. 18:12; 2 Ki. 2:16) and power (1 Ki. 18:46; 2 Ki. 3:15).

(b) God in judgment
    (i) Failure to worship God and keep his law inevitably led to

---

[1] The historian's interest in various diseases is consistent for king Jeroboam I (1 Ki. 13:4–6), Asa (1 Ki. 15:23), Azariah/Uzziah (2 Ki. 15:15) and Hezekiah (2 Ki. 20:1–8), as well as other individuals such as Naaman (2 Ki. 5) and the Shunammite's son (2 Ki. 4:8–36). Similar detailed interest in disease is observable in the writings of Isaiah and Jeremiah.
[2] 1 Ki. 8:22–54; 19:4; 2 Ki. 6:17; 13:4; 20:2, 11.

the tendency to worship other gods and to break the first commandment (Dt. 5:7). For many the denunciation of idolatry together with innovation, or non-removal, of high places is a characteristic theme of the narrative.[1] It is certainly a much emphasized reason for the judgment that fell on both Israel and Samaria and Judah and Jerusalem.

(ii) The example of kings whose deeds affected both the well-being of their own families and that of their successors is cited, *e.g.* Jeroboam of Israel (1 Ki. 12:26–33; 21:21–22) and Jehu, the effect of whose sin lasted through three to four generations (Dt. 5:8–9) and led to the fall of Israel (2 Ki. 10:30–31; 14:6).

(iii) The theme of the law prevails as the standard by which kings were judged and their reigns assessed as to whether they did 'good' or 'evil' in the sight of the LORD (see theological appraisal in the regnal formulae (pp. 47–50). The historian assumes throughout that the law was known or knowable, even though periodically forgotten (2 Ki. 17:13, 35). The law played a significant part in the coronation of kings (2 Ki. 11:12), and the covenant was reaffirmed at times of national crisis (2 Ki. 11:17; 2 Ch. 29:10) or breakdown (2 Ki. 23:3) as well as after changes in the national leadership (*cf.* Jos. 8:30–35; 1 Ch. 11:3).

(iv) Failure to keep the law and way of God is frequently alluded to. Even the most devout were no exception. So David erred and was responsible for the eventual schism begun with Solomon's reign (1 Ki. 15:5; 22:43, Heb. *raq*, 'except'). Jehu's temporary reintroduction of the worship of Yahweh in Israel failed in that he himself did not follow the law (2 Ki. 10:28–31). Earlier Jehoshaphat, though judged righteous, is criticized for his connivance with Ahab and his son Jehoram and his unsuccessful joint enterprises with them (1 Ki. 22; 2 Ki. 3). Hezekiah, though trusting in God and delivered from the hands of the Assyrians, saw his new reforms marred by his show of subservience to another world power, Babylonia, which was eventually to end the kingdom of Judah (2 Ki. 20:12–18). Josiah's hard-won reforms were soon terminated by his death at the hand of Egypt at Megiddo (2 Ki. 23:28–30). Overall the fate of Israel is traced in such a way as to foreshadow that of Judah.

[1] DeVries, p. xlvii.

(v) Retributive judgment follows from this theme of failure to keep the law. This is foretold for all who reject (1 Ki. 19:10; 2 Ki. 11:12; 17:14–20) and violate the covenant (Dt. 29:25; 31:6–8, 16; 32:26–27; 2 Ki. 18:12). It is a strong note throughout the prophetic narratives. The result is the separation of God's people from the land demonstrated in their exile (2 Ki. 17:20, 23).

(c) God as deliverer: hope and restoration

Kings is not entirely a picture of tragedy, failure and unrelieved pessimism (against Noth). The same divine covenant which invokes judgment also promises hope and restoration for those who are obedient, turn from sin and repent and humble themselves (1 Ki. 8:33–34). It holds out also the potential of redemption (*cf.* 2 Ki. 25:27–30) and God in his long-suffering mercy preserves a remnant of the faithful (1 Ki. 11:34; 2 Ki. 11:12). The happier note is attributed to God's promise to David of an established throne (1 Ki. 8:25; 9:5), a strong ruling house (1 Ki. 11:38) and an everlasting dynasty (1 Ki. 2:4, 45). As will be shown, several interpreters see the optimistic ending of the history (*e.g.* 2 Ki. 25:27–30) as introduced by a later editor into the narrative as part of the preaching to the exiles (von Rad, Wolff). Commentators are divided in holding a view of the promise to David as conditional or unconditional and this colours their understanding of the outcome of the history as favourable or failure and of the composition of the book (see also p. 22).

(d) God's promise to David

The original promise to David of an everlasting dynasty was that his house and kingdom would endure and his throne be established 'for ever' (*ʿaḏ ʿôlām*; 2 Sa. 7:11–16; 1 Ki. 9:5). In this way he would reflect God's eternal rule and kingdom on earth (*cf.* Dn. 4:3). This was reiterated to his son Solomon in the form that he would never fail to find a man (someone) on the throne of Israel (1 Ki. 8:25). The original word 'for ever' was not repeated to Solomon who, however, was told that after him, when the kingdom was wrenched away, there would remain a part or remnant 'tribe' for the sake of God's servant David and Jerusalem (1 Ki. 11:32, 34–36). The enduring nature of the family was symbolized as a lamp burning 'for the sake of David' (see on 1 Ki. 11:36; *cf.* 1 Ki. 15:4; 2 Ki.

8:19). David was well aware that the promise was conditional on the faithfulness and way of life of his successors (1 Ki. 2:4), as was Solomon himself after receiving the divine word (1 Ki. 8:23; 9:4). David was the ideal king only in so far as he too kept the law. He became the symbol of divine favour and acceptance in Judah, whereas Jeroboam and those kings of Judah who followed in his way were rejected.

Thus many see a contradiction between the promise and the fact, and find that the original promise must have been unconditional and was only made conditional by reinterpretation after the fall of Judah when those in exile required an explanation of the breakdown (so Noth). Others would explain this conditionality as a much later theological trend, while Nelson (pp. 100 ff.) argues that the condition of obedience was never intended to be applied. It has been suggested that the 'for ever' of the promise must not be taken literally as in contemporary royal treaties, grants and appointments where the 'for ever' is part of the language of royal legitimization (Long, pp. 16–17; *cf.* the use of peace for David and his descendants 'for ever', 1 Ki. 2:33).

The frequent references back to David are to him as a model (2 Ki. 14:3; 18:3) or as the founder of the City of David.[1] The promise of 2 Samuel 7:4–16 as seen in 1 Kings 2:4 is not evidence of a different source but the implicit unfolding of what is explicit in the divine promise in the covenant and is henceforward qualified for both Israel and Judah.[2] Conditionality is present throughout the history (Nicholson, Wolff, Tsevat) and is an integral part of the theology of retribution for failure. It will be seen as the introduction by a later editor only if the Deuteronomy law is considered post-exilic. God's promise not to destroy utterly or abandon his people is rooted in the covenant promise made to Abraham, Isaac and Jacob according to the historian (2 Ki. 13:23). Later Jewish and Christian tradition sees that, despite the conditionality, God kept a remnant of his people alive, including the line of David to whom they look back as the founder of their kingdom rather than to Saul. Through this line was to come the Messiah who would rule over all his people for ever (*e.g.* Rom. 1:3; Rev. 22:16). Thus Kings ends,

[1] 1 Ki. 2:10; 8:1; 15:8; 2 Ki. 8:24; 9:28; 12:21; 14:20; 15:7; 15:38; 16:20.
[2] Hobbs, p. xxiv; J. G. McConville, 'Narrative and Meaning in the Book of Kings', *Biblica* 70, 1989, pp. 31–49.

as it began, with David's line still established in and through the exile (2 Ki. 25:27–30).

(e) Prophecy

Prophecy is a history-creating force (von Rad, p. 221; Long, p. 29) and runs through the narrative of Kings more extensively than is often recognized. The word of the LORD comes to the nation through statements by prophets, often directed to its leaders.[1] In each period there were one or more spokesmen in God's name who played a significant part in reminding king and people of God's requirements. Named prophets include Nathan intervening at the end of David's reign (1 Ki. 1:22). Ahijah of Shiloh foretold the division of the kingdom after Solomon to Jeroboam of Israel, as well as announcing that king's death (1 Ki. 11:29–39; 14:1–18).[2] At the same time Shemaiah's intervention with Rehoboam of Judah delayed that final breakdown (1 Ki. 12:21–24), while two unnamed prophets spoke of the coming desecration of Bethel (1 Ki. 13:1–32). Jehu son of Hanani warned of the end of Baasha's family for following in Jeroboam's evil ways (1 Ki. 16:1–4).

Extensive narratives concerning the prophets Elijah (1 Ki. 17–19; 21; 2 Ki. 1) and Elisha (2 Ki. 2:1 – 10:36) are grouped together (see below Sources, prophetic). Their ministry alone spanned almost a century from the reign of Ahab to Jehoash, the grandson of Jehu,[3] and occupies about a quarter of the Books of Kings. At the same time Micaiah, son of Imlah, and an unnamed prophet withstood large groups of false brethren advising Jehoshaphat of Judah and Ahab of Israel (1 Ki. 22:8; 20:35–43). In Israel Jonah, son of Amittai, foretold the restoration of lost territory to Israel during the time of Jeroboam II (2 Ki. 14:25).

Another outspoken prophet with influential court connections was Isaiah, who was at work throughout the reigns of Uzziah, Jotham, Ahaz and Hezekiah of Judah (*i.e. c.* 740–686 BC; Is. 1:1). Yet other prophets were present in the long but perverse reign of Manasseh (2 Ki. 21:10–15) and a prophetess

[1] See R. E. Clements, 'The Messianic Hope in the Old Testament', *JSOT* 43, 1989, pp. 13–14.
[2] G. A. Auld, 'Prophets and Prophecy in Jeremiah and Kings' *ZAW* 96, 1984, pp. 66–82 argues that the favourable attitude towards prophets is always the result of late editorial additions, but this is not proven.
[3] Cogan and Tadmor, p. 11, n. 21.

Huldah urged the message of the newly rediscovered book of the law which led to Josiah's reforms (2 Ki. 22:14–20). During his reign Jeremiah was active.

The rôle of these prophets was primarily to convey 'the word of the LORD' which through them came to rulers and people alike.[1] The historian specifically states when events fulfilled the word of the LORD given them or which happened 'according to the word of the LORD',[2] thus authenticating their messages in accord with Deuteronomic tradition (Dt. 18:21–22). Their words were sometimes demonstrated with signs like the torn cloak of Ahijah (1 Ki. 11:30) and the split altar (1 Ki. 13:3), or were accompanied with music (2 Ki. 3:15) or symbolic actions (2 Ki. 4:41; 5:27; 13:17–19; 20:9–11). Their statements are remarkably constant throughout for, as the historian himself comments, 'the LORD warned Israel and Judah through all his prophets and seers' (2 Ki. 17:13, 23) against the punishment which would inevitably follow their forsaking the true God and worshipping false gods (1 Ki. 11:31–33; 16:3, 7, 13). The warnings not only told of judgment to come (1 Ki. 16:3; 2 Ki. 21:12; 22:16) but gave advice not to go to war against their fellows (1 Ki. 12:24, 22:6–23), or to prepare to resist attacks (1 Ki. 20:22). Their words spoke of God's mercy in preserving the remnant of the faithful (2 Ki. 14:25), promising deliverance or victory (2 Ki. 3:17; 13:17) or healing (2 Ki. 8:10, 19:10, 34). Theirs too was the call to repentance and to turn back to God (1 Ki. 11:11–13, 38–39; 2 Ki. 17:13; 19:10). Their denunciation of idolatry was no mindless polemic and sometimes included the merciful act of God in delaying retribution (1 Ki. 11:4–13).

The cost to a prophet of his outspoken testimony is noted. He was often shunned and his message rejected. So Elijah was hunted nationwide and driven out of the land with a price on his head and this led to deep depression (see on 1 Ki. 19:3–9). Yet throughout the LORD preserved and provided (1 Ki. 18:4). Other prophets were publicly rebuked (1 Ki. 22:24), seized (1 Ki. 13:4) or imprisoned (1 Ki. 22:27). Tradition has it that Isaiah was put to death and sawn asunder (*Martyrdom of Isaiah*, ch. 5; *cf.* Heb. 11:37).

[1] 1 Ki. 6:11; 12:22; 13:20; 16:1, 7; 17:2, 8; 18:1, 31; 19:9; 2 Ki. 3:12; 9:36; 15:12; 19:21; 20:4, 6, 19.
[2] 1 Ki. 2:27; 8:20, 56; 12:24; 13:2, 5, 9, 26; 14:18; 16:12, 34; 17:5, 8, 16; 22:5, 19, 38; 2 Ki. 1:7; 4:44; 7:16; 9:26; 14:25; 23:16; 24:2.

(f) Other themes

(i) *Models.* The historian's style gives rise to a number of paradigmatic models which run through the book. This has already been shown under (d) above, on the promise to David who is referred to as the ideal king. Similarly the rôle of Jeroboam ben Nebat in leading Israel astray (1 Ki. 15:34; 2 Ki. 17:7–23) is taken as a yardstick to measure Israel's subsequent sin on twenty-three occasions. He is followed by Ahab as an apostate who in turn became the model for Manasseh (2 Ki. 21:3) – Judah's 'Ahab' (*cf.* 1 Ki. 16:31–34). In like manner Elijah is portrayed as the 'new Moses'.

(ii) *The centrality of worship.* Jerusalem was the place God chose (1 Ki. 11:13, 32, 36) for his name and for the temple towards which worshippers pray (1 Ki. 8:30, 42, 44, 48; *cf.* 2 Ki. 19:1, 14; 20:5). Some look to this centralizing of worship there as another theme of the book. A central sanctuary, though envisaged in Deuteronomy (*cf.* Jos. 22:27), was never there explicitly stated or located. In ancient experience the main cultic centre was usually at the seat of power, but the national deity was equally revered in holy places in other cities.[1] Under David Jerusalem was the key-point of the royal legal powers and court, and the temple and its ancillary buildings were made to serve as the treasury (1 Ki. 15:15–18; 2 Ki. 14:14) from which state disbursements were made in time of need (2 Ki. 12:16; 22:4–9; 24:13). The temple was a place of pilgrimage and sanctuary (2 Ki. 11:13), but in this rôle was referred to only when access to it was thwarted during inter-kingdom and tribal conflict when a substitute was set up at Bethel and Dan (1 Ki. 12:29–30). In fact, little is said about the Jerusalem temple after the details of its construction and dedication (1 Ki. 3 – 10) have been given. There is periodical concern for its repair (2 Ki. 12:4–16; 15:35; 22:4–7) and only a brief mention of its destruction (2 Ki. 25:9). Temple worship is not therefore a main theme in comparison with the detail given on the condemnation of worship at the non-Yahwistic shrines.

(iii) *Kingship.* The historian appraises individuals rather than the institution of kingships. That was considered as sacral in that it derived from the divine initiative reaffirmed by the people. Apart from an instance of coronation or covenant

[1] M. Weinfeld, 'Cult Centralisation in Israel in the Light of Neo-Babylonian Analogy', *JNES* 23, 1964, p. 205.

renewal (2 Ki. 23:1–3), Kings does not, like the surrounding peoples, celebrate the New Year Festival or declare its king the son of its god. Indeed, apart from David, kings like Solomon were considered the antithesis of the ideal king (*cf*. Dt. 17:14–20). There were tensions between central authority and tribal independence and this underlies much of the local disturbance which led to the break-up of the kingdoms of Israel and Judah. Neither the kingship itself nor the land ruled and lost is a major theme of the book.

III. CHRONOLOGY

The historian extends his selectivity to a discrimatory use of sources to group together events within a single reign or relating to an opposing people (such as Aram or Edom) without the necessity to present them in a strict chronological order. Similarly he felt free to vary the repetitive formulae which served as the framework within which he wrote up the whole (see Sources and Literary Form, pp. 46–52) and to introduce his own personal review or comment at different points in the composition.

The break in the history between 2 Samuel and 1 Kings is arbitrary. 1 Kings 1 – 2 concludes the throne-succession narrative of David from 2 Samuel 20. The mention of David is essential to the theme of dynastic succession. Similarly, the break between 1 Kings 22 and 2 Kings 1 is of little significance. There is no break in the Hebrew text itself to support an interruption in the accounts of the reign of Ahaziah and the ministry of Elijah. The usual reason given is that later translators needed to divide the text into scrolls of roughly equal length either for lectionary purposes or to mark the end of David's reign (itself concluded in 1 Ki. 2:11) or the point of Solomon's succession (2:46).

In reading this history, note must be made of ancient conventions. One source is placed following another even if referring to the same time or event. There was no easy way of indicating contemporaneity. Here the longest reign in one kingdom is followed by the accounts of rulers in the other kingdom whose lives overlapped or coincided.[1] Adequate cross-reference is, however, provided by synchronisms with

---

[1] *Cf*. also the juxtaposition of more than one account of creation in Gn. 1–2; and the overlap in lists in Gn. 5, 10.

others ruling at the same time. These are given in the introduction to each reign and, occasionally where significant, to
rulers in external countries by name and by the event by
which they impinged on Israel and Judah.[1] These incidentally
provide valuable referents to the history of Assyria,
Babylonia, Syria and Egypt and a check on the chronology.
They also serve to remind the reader that the events discussed
here occurred on a real world stage.

The close chronology and synchronisms given in Kings are
remarkable. Though these are interpreted in different ways,
the figures assigned to individual rulers from the time of
contemporaries such as Jeroboam I of Israel and Rehoboam
of Judah down to the death of Ahaziah and Jehoram differ by
only two to three years even when converted to our modern
Julian calendar. By the standards of ancient historiography
such differences are minimal, yet numerous solutions are
proposed to attempt harmonization. Some variants between
the MT, LXX and LXX (L) texts may be in part a later attempt to
achieve this. The chronology most widely accepted today is
one based on the meticulous study by Thiele.[2] The chronological table given on pages 28–29 is a modification of his
tables. For the later kings reference to extra-biblical sources
enables checks to be made, so that there is virtual unanimity in
datings, bearing in mind that the ancient New Year commenced in spring. This means that regnal years should often
be indicated as, *e.g.*, Omri 886/5–875/4 BC where the precise
month of accession is not known. There are many claims to
present a precise chronology according to our modern calendar, and methods of harmonization include the following:

(a) Approximation
Tadmor thinks that some figures have been rounded off.[3]
This was not the practice in contemporaneous Assyria, and
against it is the careful noting of reigns of less than one year,
as Zimri (1 Ki. 16:15). Others suggest that an artificial structure has been employed, based on a total length for the
monarchy of 480 years, equal to the time from the Exodus to

[1] See p. 51, *cf*. pp. 32–35.
[2] E. R. Thiele, *The Mysterious Numbers of the Hebrew Kings* (Grand Rapids: Zondervan, [2]1983).
[3] H. Tadmor, 'The Chronology of the First Temple Period', *WHJP* V, pp. 51–56.

Chronology in Kings

Bible refs.	Kings of Judah/Israel		Contemporary prophets	BC	Kings of Assyria:	Babylonia:	Egypt:
	UNITED KINGDOM						
1 Sa. 16:1 - 1 Ki. 2:10	**David** (40) (1010-970)		Nathan	1010	Ashur-rabi II (1010-970)		Dynasty XXI
1 Ki. 1 - 11	**Solomon** (40) (970-930)*		Gad	970	Tiglath-pileser II (966-935)		
	DIVIDED KINGDOM						
	JUDAH	ISRAEL					
1 Ki. 12:1-24; 12:25 - 14:20	**Rehoboam** (17) (930-913)	**Jeroboam I** (22) (930-909)		930	Ashur-dán II (934-912)		Dynasty XXII
1 Ki. 15:1-8	**Abijah** (3) (913-910)						
1 Ki. 15:9-24	**Asa** (41) (910-869)						
1 Ki. 15:25-31		**Nadab** (2) (909-908)					
1 Ki. 15:32 - 16:7		**Baasha** (24) (908-886)		900			
1 Ki. 16:8-14		**Elah** (2) (886-885)			Ashur-nâsir-apli II (883-859)		
1 Ki. 16:15-20		**Zimri** (7 days) (885)					
1 Ki. 16:21-22		**Tibni** (5) (885-881)					
1 Ki. 16:21-28		**Omri** (12)+ (885-874)	Elijah				
1 Ki. 16:29 - 22:40		**Ahab** (22)+ (874-853)		870			
1 Ki. 22:41-50	**Jehoshaphat** (25) * (872-848)				Shalmaneser III (858-824)		
1 Ki. 22:51 - 2 Ki. 1:18		**Ahaziah** (2) (853-852)					
2 Ki. 1:17; 3:1 - 8:15		**Jehoram** (12) (852-841)	Elisha	850			
2 Ki. 8:16-24	**J(eh)oram** (8-)* (853-842)						
2 Ki. 8:25-29; 9:27-29	**Ahaziah** (2) (842-841)						
2 Ki. 9:1 - 10:36		**Jehu** (28)+ (841-814)					
2 Ki. 11:1-16	**Athaliah** (7) (841-835)						
2 Ki. 11:17 - 12:21	**Joash** (40) (835-796)			800			
2 Ki. 13:1-9		**Jehoahaz** (17)+ (814-798)					

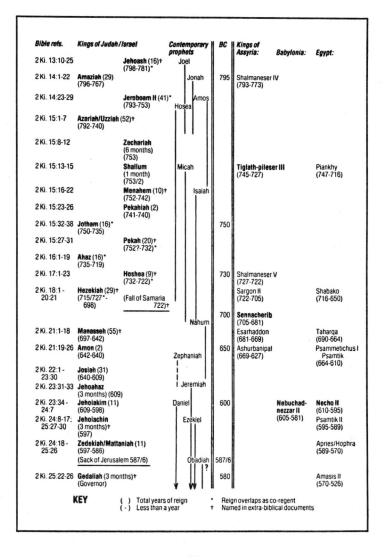

Bible refs.	Kings of Judah / Israel		Contemporary prophets	BC	Kings of Assyria:	Babylonia:	Egypt:
2 Ki. 13:10-25		Jehoash (16)+ (798-781)*	Joel				
2 Ki. 14:1-22	Amaziah (29) (796-767)		Jonah	795	Shalmaneser IV (793-773)		
2 Ki. 14:23-29		Jeroboam II (41)* (793-753)	Amos Hosea				
2 Ki. 15:1-7	Azariah/Uzziah (52)+ (792-740)						
2 Ki. 15:8-12		Zechariah (6 months) (753)					
2 Ki. 15:13-15		Shallum (1 month) (753/2)	Micah		Tiglath-pileser III (745-727)		Piankhy (747-716)
2 Ki. 15:16-22		Menahem (10)+ (752-742)	Isaiah				
2 Ki. 15:23-26		Pekahiah (2) (741-740)					
2 Ki. 15:32-38	Jotham (16)* (750-735)			750			
2 Ki. 15:27-31		Pekah (20)+ (752?-732)*					
2 Ki. 16:1-19	Ahaz (16)* (735-719)						
2 Ki. 17:1-23		Hoshea (9)+ (732-722)*		730	Shalmaneser V (727-722)		
2 Ki. 18:1 - 20:21	Hezekiah (29)+ (715/727*- 698)	(Fall of Samaria 722)+			Sargon II (722-705)		Shabako (716-650)
			Nahum	700	Sennacherib (705-681)		
2 Ki. 21:1-18	Manasseh (55)+ (697-642)				Esarhaddon (681-669)		Taharqa (690-664)
2 Ki. 21:19-26	Amon (2) (642-640)		Zephaniah	650	Ashurbanipal (669-627)		Psammetichus I Psamtik (664-610)
2 Ki. 22:1 - 23:30	Josiah (31) (640-609)		Jeremiah				
2 Ki. 23:31-33	Jehoahaz (3 months) (609)						
2 Ki. 23:34 - 24:7	Jehoiakim (11) (609-598)		Daniel	600		Nebuchad-nezzar II	Necho II (610-595)
2 Ki. 24:8-17; 25:27-30	Jehoiachin (3 months)+ (597)		Ezekiel			(605-581)	Psamtik II (595-589)
2 Ki. 24:18 - 25:26	Zedekiah/Mattaniah (11) (597-586)						Apries/Hophra (589-570)
	(Sack of Jerusalem 587/6)		Obadiah ?	587/6			
2 Ki. 25:22-26	Gedaliah (3 months)+ (Governor)			580			Amasis II (570-526)

KEY

( ) Total years of reign   * Reign overlaps as co-regent
(-) Less than a year   † Named in extra-biblical documents

the building of the Temple, but the interpretation of this figure is open (see on 1 Ki. 6:1).

(b) Regnal years

The introductory formula for individual kings gives the total years of his reign (*e.g.* 1 Ki. 15:2), or, if less, by months (2 Ki. 15:8, 13) or days (1 Ki. 16:15). A synchronism between one royal accession is made with the regnal year of the contemporary ruler in another kingdom, *e.g.* 'In the eighteenth year of the reign of Jeroboam son of Nebat, Abijah became king of Judah, and he reigned in Jerusalem for three years' (1 Ki. 15:1–2). Sometimes cross-reference is made to contemporary events in other nations (1 Ki. 14:25 *etc.*, see pp. 32–35). There is, however, difficulty in interpreting some of these references, should different systems of dating be used in the two states involved. An *ante-dating* system was used, as in Egypt, where the period between an accession and the next New Year's day is claimed as the king's first regnal year.[1] This system is said to have been used in Israel from Jeroboam I to Jehoahaz. Thereafter (Jehoash–Hoshea) a *post-dating* system similar to that used in Judah, in which the first regnal year was counted from the first New Year's day after accession (as commonly in Babylonian texts),[2] was employed. Such changes could have been the result of an imposition of the Mesopotamian style as the western city-states became vassals of their powerful Assyrian and Bablylonian conquerors.

Another solution commonly proposed is to assume that Israel's New Year began with a spring (Nisan) calender while, until the eighth century BC, Judah followed a calendar commencing in the autumn month of Tishri (September/October; Wellhausen, Mowinckel, Jones). Yet others believe that the Northern Kingdom used the autumn New Year under Canaanite influence (Talmon).[3] Some even apply this argument to Judah, but evidence for an autumnal New Year is highly questionable.[4]

---

[1] A. Gardner, *Egypt of the Pharaohs* (Oxford: Clarendon Press, 1961), pp. 69–71; *cf.* 2 Ki. 25:27.

[2] S. Talmon, 'Divergences in Calendar-reckoning in Ephraim and Judah', *VT* 8, 1958, pp. 48–74.

[3] *Ibid.*

[4] D. J. A. Clines, 'The Evidence for an Autumnal New Year in Pre-Exilic Israel Reconsidered', *JBL* 93, 1974, pp. 22–40.

(c) Co-regencies

In his well-argued reconstruction of the chronology, Thiele advocates the acceptance of the principle of overlapping reigns explained by the existence of demonstrable co-regencies.[1] Some such arrangement has long been proposed, since the coinciding reigns of Omri and Tibni (1 Ki. 16:21) are clearly stated; for Jotham and Uzziah, Jehoram and Jehoshaphat they are indicated (2 Ki. 8:16, *cf.* 1:17; 3:1), and for Jotham and Uzziah/Azariah reasonably assumed because of the latter's leprosy (2 Ki. 15:5). In addition Thiele proposes other co-regencies between Jeroboam II (793–753) and Jehoash (798–781); Pekah (752–732) and Menahem (752–742) for Israel, and between Azariah (792–740) and Amaziah (796–767); Ahaz (735–715) and Jotham (750–732); Manasseh (697–643) and Hezekiah (716–687) for Judah. Other co-regencies have been proposed for Ahaziah (853–852) and Ahab (874–853); Joash (749–781) and Jehoahaz (813–797); Amaziah (798–767) and Jehoash (835–796). Thiele considered the chronology could thus be shown to be consistent with the integrity of the Hebrew text. However, he thought that the editor in 2 Kings 17 – 18 was in error over the reigns of Jotham of Judah and Pekah of Israel resulting from the interpretation of Ahaz' twelfth year, which coincided with the year of the accession of Hoshea in Israel (2 Ki. 17:1), as relating to his sole reign rather than dating from his earlier co-regency with his father Jotham. This led to the untenable proposal of 710 BC for the fall of Samaria, contrary to all other, including external, evidence. This confusion is obviated by the proposal that the system of co-regencies continued with Ahaz co-regent with Jotham for twelve years and Hezekiah with Ahaz. From the days of David and Solomon this use of co-regencies contributed much to the stability of Judah and a relatively untroubled line of succession.[2] Certainly such co-regencies are well attested for Mesopotamian kings during this period and harmonization of the data in Kings is possible

---

[1] E. R. Thiele, 'Co-regencies and Overlapping Reigns among the Hebrew Kings', *JBL* 93, 1974, pp. 174–200.

[2] The co-regency of Hezekiah and Ahaz was first proposed by K. A. Kitchen and T. C. Mitchell, *NBD* (1962 edn.), p. 217; *cf.* 1982 edn., p. 193; *cf.* L. McFall, 'Did Thiele overlook Hezekiah's Co-regency?', *Bibliotheca Sacra* 148 (Oct./Dec. 1989), pp. 393–404, esp. n. 29. E. Ball argues for 'The Co-regency of David and Solomon', perhaps under Egyptian influence, in *VT* 27, 1977, pp. 268–279.

using such methods. Precise correlation with our Julian-based calendar is not possible until the reigns of the last kings of Judah. Prior to that, years need to be indicated as, *e.g.*, 722 BC by indicating 723/2 or 722/1 according to whether the ancient year is conceived as commencing in the spring (March) or autumn (September). Later dates than these, where the royal year is indicated by precise day, month and regnal year, can be converted to our calendar within twenty-four hour limits (the latter necessary because the day was then taken as beginning at sunset). For instance, the fall of Jerusalem on the second of the month Adar in Nebuchadnezzar's seventh year occurred on 15/16 March 597 BC.[1]

(d) Extra-biblical references

At a number of points the history in Kings can be verified or complemented by comparison with extra-biblical, mainly Assyrian and Babylonian, sources. These dates are derived from king lists, chronicles or other documents which are checked by more than one source, often including astronomical data.[2]

(i) Omri and his son Ahab are mentioned in the Mesha' Inscription (Moabite Stone) dated *c.* 830 BC. This is a valuable source for the study of the relations between Israel and Moab and for religious beliefs there at the time (*cf.* 2 Ki. 3:1–27).[3]

(ii) On the battle of Qarqar in the sixth year of Shalmaneser III, king of Assyria (853 BC), the Assyrians record the contribution of Ahab of Israel (*Ahabbu (māt) Sir'ilaia*) with two thousand chariots and ten thousand men to the coalition led by Hadadezer (*Adad-'idri*) of Damascus which opposed them.[4]

(iii) Jehu of Israel is named in the caption, and probably depicted on the Black Obelisk from Kalhu (now BM. 118885,

---

[1] R. A. Parker and W. H. Dubberstein, *Babylonian Chronology 626 BC–AD 75*, Brown University Studies XIX (Providence, Rhode Island: Brown University Press, 1956).

[2] H. Tadmor, 'The Chronology of the First Temple Period. A Presentation and Evaluation of the Sources', *WHJP* IV/I, 1979, pp. 44–60; Cogan and Tadmor, pp. 4–5; pp. 330–340 for selected translations; J. Reade, 'Mesopotamian Guidelines for Biblical Chronology', *Syro-Mesopotamian Studies* 4/1, 1981, pp. 1–7; *cf.* W. Hallo, 'From Qarqar to Carchemish in the Light of New Discoveries', *BA* 23, 1960, pp. 34–61. The absence of extraneous records for the reigns of David and Solomon may be largely explained by the paucity of extant contemporary texts for that period in all neighbouring countries.

[3] *DOTT*, pp. 195–198; *IBD*, pp. 1016–1018.

[4] *DOTT*, pp. 46–48; *ANET*, p. 279.

dated 841 BC reading *Ya'ua mār Humri* ('Jehu of the Omri dynasty').[1]

(iv) Jehoash of Samaria (*Yu'asu samerināya*) is named by Adad-nērāri III of Assyria as bringing him tribute from Israel in 796 BC.[2]

(v) Tiglath-pileser III, king of Assyria (745–727), mentions a number of kings of Israel in his inscriptions. Among tribute exacted from Israel (*Bīt-Humri*) was that from Menahem of Samaria (*Menihimme samerināya*) in 738 as also recorded in 2 Ki. 15:19 f.,[3] and from Pekah (*Paqaha*) whom he deposed in favour of his own nominee Hoshea (*Ausi'*) who also paid tribute to him in 731 BC.[4] It is possible that his reference to one *Azriau māt Yaudi* is to Azariah of Judah (see on 2 Ki. 15:1–7),[5] as is his telling of *Yauhazi (māt)yaudāya* becoming a vassal in 734 BC.

(vi) Shalmaneser V of Assyria claimed the capture of Samaria in his Eponym List (and the Babylonian Chronicle) and is the 'king of Assyria' who attacked Hoshea in 723/2 BC (2 Ki. 17:3–4) in a three-year siege and initiated the final blow. He appears to have died before the city finally fell.[6]

(vii) Sargon II of Assyria is not named in Kings (*cf.* Is. 20:1), but his annals hail him as the conqueror of Samaria who took the Israelites into exile (2 Ki. 17:6). He claims in 722 to have deported as prisoners '27,290 of the people ... and the gods in whom they trusted' and to have been 'the subjugator of the land of all Israel' (*Bīt-Humria*) and 'conqueror of Samaria' (*Samerina*).[7]

(viii) Sennacherib of Assyria in his annals for his fourteenth regnal year (701 BC) describes his siege of Jerusalem when he 'shut up Hezekiah the Judean (*Hazaqia yaudāia*) ... like a caged bird within his royal city (Jerusalem)' as well as the tribute exacted from him.[8] His palace sculptures in Nineveh

---

[1] *DOTT*, p. 48; *ANET*, p. 281; *IBD*, p. 1427.

[2] The Rimah stela, *Iraq* 30, 1968, pp. 139–153; A. Malamat, *POTT*, p. 145; *IBD*, p. 790.

[3] *DOTT*, p. 54; *ANET*, p. 283.

[4] *DOTT*, pp. 56–57; *ANET*, p. 284; Cogan and Tadmor, p. 5.

[5] H. Tadmor, 'Azriyau of Yaudi', *Scripta Hierosolymitana* 8 (Jerusalem: Magnes Press, 1961), pp. 232–271; *ANET*, p. 282.

[6] *DOTT*, p. 85.

[7] *DOTT*, pp. 59–62 (Annals 12); *ANET*, p. 284; C. J. Gadd, 'Inscribed Prisms of Sargon II from Nimrud', *Iraq* 16, 1954, pp. 173–201.

[8] *DOTT*, pp. 67–69; *ANET*, pp. 287–288.

show Sennacherib before the conquered city of Lachish (2 Ki. 19:8).[1]

(ix) Manasseh, a tributary of Assyria *c.* 674 BC, is named by king Esarhaddon of Assyria (680–669 BC) as 'Menasē, king of Judah' (*me-na-si-i šar (āl)ya-ú-da-a-a*),[2] and by Ashurbanipal of Assyria (668–627 BC) as 'Mīnsē of Yaudi' (*mi-in-se-e šar (māt)ya-ú-di*).[3]

(x) The important series of Babylonian Chronicle tablets for the years 625–595 give background details for the history of this time. They provide evidence for the fall of Nineveh in 612 BC, and of the Assyrians on whose behalf Egypt intervened with military forces, marching to relieve Harran in 609 BC. In the course of that intervention Josiah met his untimely death, an event thus firmly dated to that year (2 Ki. 23:29). The same source records the battle of Carchemish in 605 BC and the first attack by Nebuchadnezzar II on Jerusalem, when 'in his seventh year, month Kislev, the king of Babylonia moved his army into Syro-Palestine, laid siege to the city of Judah (*Yāhudu*) and took the city on the second day of the month Addaru. He appointed in it a (new) king of his own choice, took heavy tribute and brought it into Babylon.' Thus the fall of Jerusalem can be dated precisely to 15/16 March 597 BC, and the accession of Zedekiah/Mattaniah in Judah following the capture of Jehoiachin happened in that year. The commencement of the Judeans' exile is thus fixed. Jehoiachin king of Judah (*Ya'ukīn šar (māt)Yaudaya*) is named on several tablets found in Babylon as receiving rations from the royal stores there. These tablets are dated to 592–569 BC (*cf.* 2 Ki. 24:8).

This written evidence, predominantly in the cuneiform script, is valuable not merely for the correlation of events between Israel and its neighbours but also for their interpretation. Regrettably few native Palestinian inscriptions have as yet been found.[4] It is likely that the kings of Israel and Judah

---

[1] *ANEP*, pp. 371–374; *IBD* pp. 865–868.

[2] R. Campbell Thompson, *The Prisms of Esarhaddon and of Ashurbanipal* (London: British Museum, 1931), v. 55, pl. 11; *ANET*, p. 292; *DOTT*, p. 24.

[3] Prism C ii. 27; M. Streck, *Assurbanipal* II (Leipzig: Hinrich, 1926), p. 138; *ANET*, p. 294; *DOTT*, p. 74.

[4] *E.g.* the stone found at Gezer listing agricultural operations throughout the year and dated by its script to the tenth century BC is the only extant Palestinian inscription from the period of the united monarchy (*DOTT*, pp. 201–203; *ANET*, p. 321; *IBD*, p. 224).

recorded events on more perishable or limited materials. This is indicated by the ostraca, seals and bullae from the time of the monarchy.[1] The names on some of these can be identified with persons named in Kings or they at least show that the name was used at the time. Seals of an official of Hezekiah (*hzqyhw*), the name Pekah (*pqh*) written on an ostracon (2 Ki. 15:27),[2] and the seals of Gedaliah (*gdlyh*)[3] and of Jaazaniah (*ya'azanyh*) who supported him at Mizpah (2 Ki. 25:23), are among the survivors. A rare reference to a woman is the seal naming Jezebel (*yzbl*).[4] Sufficient remains to indicate that writing was in use at different levels and for different purposes throughout this period.[5]

The chronological table on pages 28–29 is based on the above observations and allows for the flexibility in dating of reigns to include the co-regencies for which there is evidence.

IV. ARCHAEOLOGICAL EVIDENCE

While the extra-biblical inscriptions which relate to the history of the times of the monarchy are a useful correlation with the chronology of Kings, excavations at Palestinian sites provide useful evidence for the cultural situation in this same period. By this means some characteristic architectural features have become well defined. High standards in construction, with solid masonry of fine drafted ashlar stones carefully laid, mark royal buildings of the tenth to ninth centuries. This, like the Phoenician (Canaanite)-type monumental structures with columns bearing proto-Ionian (Aeolian) capitals found at Jerusalem, Samaria, Hazor and Megiddo, passed out of fashion by the late ninth century BC. Similarly, the type of fortification introduced during the united monarchy, with its unfilled casemate walls which could be used for storage and which were quickly erected with an adjacent 'six-roomed' gateway building with towers, proved effective until the late

---

[1] *E.g.* for the Samaria inscribed sherds see on 2 Ki. 14:28; the Arad ostraca *c.* 598/7 BC; *BA* 31, 1968, pp. 2–32; *ANET*, pp. 568–569.

[2] Fragment of a store-jar inscribed *lpqh* (*IBD*, p. 1181).

[3] Described as 'son of Ahikam, who is over the House' (*'šr 'l hbyt*); 2 Ki. 25:22; *IDB*, p. 545.

[4] N. Avigad, 'The Seal of Jezebel', *IEJ* 14, 1964, pp. 174–176.

[5] *E.g.* a letter from the time of Josiah (*ANET*, p. 565); the Lachish letters *c.* 590 BC (*ANET*, p. 322; *DOTT*, pp. 213–215); the Tel Hinom (Jerusalem) find of the priestly blessing (Nu. 6:24–26) dated to the sixth to seventh century BC.

tenth century. The advent of Assyrian siege equipment and battering rams[1] led to the adoption of massive (4 metre thick) solid walls, as at Dan, Hazor, Megiddo, Lachish, Tell en-Nasbeh, Arad, Ashdod and Beersheba. In a few places which were perhaps not considered 'defendable cities' (2 Ch. 11:5) the casemate system continued in use for many decades at Tell Beit Mirsim (Debir?) and on the acropolis at Samaria which lay above the main line of fortifications. At Beersheba the lack of Egyptian siege equipment precluded the need for such massive structures.

The characteristic 'six-room' gate-buildings with twin towers and heavy defences are found in the time of Solomon at Hazor (Level X), Megiddo (IVB) and at Gezer, which were all planned by the central government (1 Ki. 9:15). By the ninth century the main city gateways were reduced to 'four-room' and then by the eighth to 'two-room'-type entrances. Associated with changes in fortification techniques was the need by the eighth century to ensure sufficient water supplies within a city to withstand a long siege. Thus the earlier conduits bringing water from springs outside the walls were as at Megiddo (VB) with its 285 metre deep shaft and 307 metre tunnel, Gibeon and possibly Jerusalem (Warren's Shaft), replaced by deep shafts and steps down to ground water inside the walls.

Another general feature of the monarchy is the typical 'four-room' building consisting of three long rooms, the central one probably open as a courtyard, and one long room with an upper storey. This became the basic plan for both wealthy and poorer houses and even for the ground floor of large citadels. Large public buildings also took the form of three long rooms with two intervening rows of columns with capitals. An upper storey was sometimes added to this structure (Hazor, Ramat Rahel), the pillars enabling the roof to be of short span and, in part, load-bearing. Some served as stores (*miskenōt*) for grain or wine in large pots. In some, holes in the pillars, and shallow feeding troughs, may show that they served as stables in what were 'chariot-cities'. No certain traces of 'high places' remain except at Dan where a raised platform with access up large steps was found. Other sites with such ritual places have been said to include Megiddo and

[1] D. J. Wiseman, 'The Assyrians' in Sir John Hackett (ed.), *Warfare in the Ancient World* (London: Sidgwick & Jackson, 1989), pp. 36–53.

Beersheba, where a horned altar was found. Aharoni considered the cult centre at Arad, with a niche in the west wall with incense burners, to be a temple on the same plan as that built by Solomon at Jerusalem (itself influenced by Syrian structures found at Tainat and Alalah) with a columned porch, main room and inner sanctuary, but this has been questioned by Yadin.[1]

As well as these characteristic architectural features, other archaeological finds enable the cultural background to be traced in some detail. In the early days of the united monarchy the presence of 'Philistines' (Egypt., *prst*) associated with other colonists depicted in wall paintings of Rameses III at Medinet Habu) in southwest Palestine, is shown by their polychrome pottery at Sharuhen, Gezer, Debir and throughout the Shephelah north to Joppa. There are signs of their trade as far inland as Tell Deir 'Alla in the Jordan valley, Gibeah, Jerusalem and Beth-zur. The main Philistine strongholds were at Gath, Ashkelon, Gath (Tell el-'Areini or Tell en-Nagila) and Ekron. Their unique temple at Tell Qasile (IX) shows that the roof supports were wooden columns set on stone plinths. The Philistines occupied Shiloh (Khirbet Seilūn) in the Early Iron Age but soon thereafter it was destroyed (Je. 7:12). The repair to walls at Beth-Shemesh (Tell Rumeileh IIA), Tell Beit Mirsim and Megiddo (VB) has been explained as defensive activity in the days of David.[2] Beth-Shemesh lost ground when Rehoboam restored Zorah nearby using casemate walling (2 Ch. 11:10).

By the reign of Solomon there is increased use of iron (IA II) and improved techniques and activity. His central palace appears to be modelled on the Syrian *bīt-hilāni* type. This included walls constructed with layers of wood between courses of stones (see on 1 Ki. 6:36). In Jerusalem the Millo or 'Fill' may be represented by the walled terraces and building found on the slopes of Ophel.[3] Jerusalem at that time covered about the same area as the other Palestinian large cities. Bronze working of this reign may be seen in the numerous

[1] Y. Yadin, 'The Archaeological Sources for the Period of the Monarchy', *WHJP* V, 1979, p. 219.
[2] The javelin found at El-Khadr, between Bethlehem and Hebron, may have belonged to a soldier following David into exile.
[3] K. Kenyon, *Jerusalem* (London: Thames & Hudson, 1967), pp. 50–51; *BAEHL* II, 1976, pp. 595–596.

open smelting pits with their surrounding slag and ore at Zarethan (Tell es-Saidiyeh), east of Jordan and at Ezion-Geber (I). He also built new palaces at Megiddo and at Beersheba (Tell es-Saba' III/II) which appears to have been destroyed, as was Ashdod (VI), by raids by Siamun of Egypt early in his reign. Traces of imported Egyptian labour and residence have been found in the Tel Mor (Aqaba) mines.

In the early divided kingdom the raid by Shishak (Sheshonq I) against Rehoboam *c.* 928 BC (1 Ki. 14:25–6) is shown in his triumphs depicted on the walls of the Karnak temple of Amun in Thebes, which lists 150 towns in Phoenicia, Judah as far as the Esdraelon valley, and into Edom and south Syria. Megiddo was invaded (so a broken stele there) and destruction levels at Beth-Shemesh and Tell Beit Mirsim (Debir or Kirjath-Sepher) attest the raid, after which the Egyptians renewed the defences of Sharuhen, Gezer, Tell el-Ajjul and Tell Jemneh to maintain a strong presence against which Rehoboam reacted by strengthening Lachish and Azekah. Meanwhile Jeroboam I reinforced the gate of Dan, built at Shechem, Gibeah, Bethel and Tell en-Nasbeh (Mizpah?) which became the northern boundary of Judah in subsequent clashes with Israel (*cf.* 1 Ki. 15:15–22). About this time Dan was destroyed (1 Ki. 15:20), but soon thereafter the city gate and fortifications were rebuilt. The massive (4 metre wide) walls and towers and finely preserved city gate at Tell en-Nasbeh appear to be the work of Asa (*cf.* 1 Ki. 15:22).

During the ninth century, buildings at Ramat Rahel (VB) south of Jerusalem, indicate a royal citadel there and the possible remains of a 'House of Baal' which Yadin attributes to the time of Athaliah.[1] A later building there (VA), once thought to be the 'separate house' used to isolate the leprous Uzziah (2 Ch. 26:21), is now assigned to the reign of Jehoiakim.

The activities of Omri and Ahab are best seen in the former's work at Shechem and at Tirzah (Tell el Far'ah) eleven kilometres to the northeast, which he made the new capital of Israel. There he built over a pre-existing settlement and, as shown by pottery and other remains, left several major buildings unfinished when he transferred the capital to yet another site at Samaria, fifteen kilometres to the west. There he built

---

[1] Y. Yadin, *op. cit.*, p. 211.

splendid buildings in good Israelite architectural style, using some pottery from the earlier settlement as fill in the floors (*cf.* 1 Ki. 16:23–24). Ahab extended the top of the hill with retaining casemate walls and infill as the base for a large palace (I), monumental buildings and administrative stores in which inscribed ostraca were later found. Ahab's love of luxury can be seen in the colonnade leading to the city gate and the ivory furnishings (fragments of which were found similar to those from Arslan-Tash and Nimrud) which were renowned (1 Ki. 22:39; Am. 6:4). A large cistern (10m × 20.6m) may be the pool in which his chariot was washed down (1 Ki. 22:38). The 'House of Baal' set up by Ahab (1 Ki. 16:32) could well have been located outside the acropolis, for it is referred to as 'the city/built-up area' (NIV 'inner shrine') of the House of Baal, 2 Ki. 10:25. Ahab also refortified Megiddo (IVB: four-room gateway), Dan, Hazor and Tell Qasileh. These towns remained in poorer occupation until eventually destroyed by the Assyrians (*e.g.* Megiddo III).

Sargon II, in revenge for the rebellion by Yamani of Ashdod, besieged and sacked Gezer (shown as *Gazru* on his palace reliefs) and Ashdod where a fragment of his inscribed victory stela was found (*cf.* Is. 20:1). Sargon also destroyed Hazor (V), Tell Qasileh (VIII) and Tirzah (II) at this time.

Archaeological evidence for the time of Hezekiah includes the development of Jerusalem from Ophel across to the western hill. A massive seven-metre-wide wall discovered by Avigad in his excavation of the Old Jewish Quarter may mark his (or Manasseh's) enclosure of this 'second city-quarter' (*mišneh*). The new water supply brought in by the Siloam tunnel to resist the Assyrian siege in 701 BC (2 Ki. 20:20; *cf.* 2 Ch. 32:30) was protected by an extended wall. Rock-hewn tombs north of the temple in a Phoenician style found by Mazar and dated to the ninth century to eighth century may well be among those used as burial places for the kings of Judah. Sennacherib's successful siege of Lachish may be marked by the large siege-ramp, inner counter-ramp, mass grave for 1,500 bodies and fragmentary Assyrian remains found there with the destruction level (III). Some, however, argue that this may be the result of Nebuchadnezzar's first campaign in the area in 598/7. If so, the sack of the city associated with the Lachish letters must refer to a later destruction level after a second Babylonian campaign in 588/7 BC. Archaeology shows that Tell Beit Mirsim thirteen kilometres southeast of Lachish was partly destroyed in 701 BC, as was Beersheba (II). Archaeological support for the final sack of Jerusalem is difficult to find because of the subsequent rebuilding. However, some badly destroyed and burnt houses on the eastern side may be attributable to this event. Certainly, destruction levels at Lachish, Ashdod, Azekah (2 Ki. 24:7), Gezer, Tell el-Hesi (VII/VI), Beth-Shemesh (II), Tell Beit Mirsim and Ramat Rahel show that they never recovered.[1]

V. SOURCES

In all large ancient Near Eastern societies of the period of the Hebrew kings a variety of chronographic sources were available to the historian. For more than two millennia records of a high order were kept in royal or temple archives in the form of king lists, annals and chronicles, royal inscriptions, historical epics as well as pseudo-epigraphical autobiographies, texts which gave a generalized description of periods in a 'prophetic' form, as well as numerous historical allusions in a wide range of literature.[2]

Annals gave details of genuine royal campaigns and were usually composed soon after the event as part of the report by a king to his national deity on how he had exercised his divine commission.[3] Annals, attested from the second millennium and well used by the Hittites also, would cover operations and events in one or more years or in an area and, like those kept in Egypt, were based on diaries or records kept by the king or

---

[1] The archaeological data is summarized in D. J. Wiseman, 'Archaeology and the Old Testament' in D. J. Wiseman and E. Yamauchi (eds.), *Archaeology and the Bible: An Introductory Study* (Grand Rapids: Zondervan, 1979), pp. 3–59; *cf.* F. Gabelein (ed.) *The Expositor's Bible Commentary* (Grand Rapids: Zondervan, 1979), pp. 309–335; Y. Yadin, *op. cit.*, pp. 187–235.

[2] A. K. Grayson, *Assyrian and Babylonian Chronicles* (Locust Valley, New York: J. J. Augustin, 1970), pp. 1–5; *Babylonian Historical-Literary Texts* (Toronto: University of Toronto Press, 1975), pp. 13–37 (Akkadian prophecies), 41–45 (historical epics).

[3] D. J. Wiseman, 'Law and Order in OT Times', *Vox Evangelica* 8, 1973, pp. 10–11; F. Thureau-Dangin, *Une relation de la huitiéme campagne de Sargon* (Paris: Paul Geuthner, 1912) for the account of Sargon II's wars in 714 BC reported to Ashur; H. Tadmor and M. Weinfeld (eds.) *History, Historiography and Interpretation: Studies in Biblical and Cuneiform Literatures* (Jerusalem: Magnes Press, 1983), pp. 58–75, discuss some of the complex problems resulting from variant readings of a single campaign.

a secretary on his behalf. A few royal biographies were compiled from royal inscriptions and some pseudo-autobio-
graphical narratives were collected, relating to a person who
had by then become 'legendary'.[1] Chronicles are found from
the early Sumerian period down to Hellenistic times. These
are interrelated with king lists and annals and should not be
too closely distinguished. They were frequently compiled in
Babylonia where some covered a long period. An example is
the Neo-Babylonian Chronicle, with yearly entries running
from the time of Nabonassar in the eighth century down to
the fall of Babylon in 539 and on into the Achaemenid era.
Such chronicles are briefer than annals and follow a strictly
chronological form according to regnal years, with references
to principal events including accession, military campaigns,
rebellions, internal and foreign affairs, economic and
religious happenings and the death of a king and his succession. Other chronicles are based on special extracts, such as the
Synchronistic Chronicle of Assyro-Babylonian relations *c.*
1550–783 BC, where each paragraph deals with one king and
his contemporaries where they had any dealings (usually wars)
with each other. Another lists market prices (*c.* 1800–750 BC)
or gives an eclectic resumé of events *c.* 1100–722 BC.[2]
Babylonian chronicles have been shown to be contemporary,
accurate, objective and reliable sources which may originally
have been extracted from astronomical and other diaries.[3] All
this is of interest as the background to the work of any major
Hebrew historian. It would be surprising if the narratives of
Kings, unique in their clarity, style and range, do not reflect
these contemporary literary forms and draw on similar
indigenous sources. Indeed Kings does make reference to
sources to which the original reader was directed for additional information (see Concluding Formulae below, pp.
50ff.), and these must have been available in the writer's day.

---

[1] *E.g.* legends of Sargon, *ZA* 42, 1934, pp. 62–65; Naram-Sin, *Anatolian
Studies* 5, 1955, pp. 93–113; *JCS* 11, 1957, pp. 83–88. These, like Akkadian
prophecies, *JCS* 18, 1964, pp. 7–30, set out to show a ruler as 'good' or 'evil'.
[2] See A. K. Grayson, *Assyrian and Babylonian Chronicles* (Locust Valley, New
York: J. J. Augustin, 1975), Chronicle P, pp. 51–65.
[3] D. J. Wiseman, *Chronicles of Chaldaean Kings (626–556 BC) in the British
Museum* (London: British Museum, 1956), pp. 1–5; A. K. Grayson, *Assyrian and
Babylonian Chronicles* (Locust Valley, New York: J. J. Augustin, 1970), pp. 1–5.

1 AND 2 KINGS

(a) The Book of the Acts of Solomon (1 Ki. 11:41)
This palace or court record forms the basis of much of this reign, and the Jerusalem-held administrative documents included lists of court officials (4:2–6) and district-governors (4:7–19, 27–28), as well as the arrangements for provisioning the court (4:22–23) and for royal revenues (10:14–29). As with other state archives,[1] it was customary to house duplicates of texts concerning international affairs, both negotiations and treaties (*cf.* Solomon and Shimei, 1 Ki. 2:43; Egypt, 1 Ki. 3:1; Philistines, 1 Ki. 4:21; Solomon and Hiram of Tyre, 1 Ki. 5).[2] Similarly trade (1 Ki. 10:10) information could have stemmed from this same source. It is not likely that the details of the building of a major temple and palace were derived from temple records rather than Solomon's annals, for such were commonly preserved in a precise literary structure in which ancient kings include (*a*) the commissioning of a building enterprise at the behest of a national deity; (*b*) the preparations for the building (*cf.* 1 Ki. 5); (*c*) the actual building process (*cf.* 1 Ki. 6 – 7), (*d*) praise of the construction, usually in the form of a hymn (*cf.* 1 Ki. 8:15–21); (*e*) the story of the dedication of the completed building (*cf.* 1 Ki. 8:22–66) and (*f*) the blessing and reward of the king by the national deity (*cf.* 1 Ki. 9:1–9).[3] In Kings the historian follows a similar pattern. The same archive kept by state scribes would be concerned with the ability of the king as judge and administrator (1 Ki. 3:16–28) displayed in 'wisdom' (1 Ki. 11:41 and see p. 85).

With this source (*sēper dibᵉrē*; 1 Ki. 11:41) the historian lays more emphasis on the building of the temple than on the construction of the royal palaces which took more time and money. This source may differ from any 'book of the annals of Solomon' (*sēper dibᵉrē hayyamîm*) which could well have been available for additional reference.

---

[1] *Cf.* Ras Shamra, J. Nougayrol, *Ugaritica* III–V (1956–68); *Le palais royal d'Ugarit* III–VI (1955–70); A. Malamat, *Mari and the Early Israelite Experience* (Oxford: British Academy, 1989), pp. 8–9.

[2] The historian in Kings is consistently interested in such international agreements made by Asa with Benhadad II of Damascus and with Baasha (1 Ki. 15:19–20); Ahab with Benhadad (1 Ki. 20:33–34) and with Moab (2 Ki. 1:1); Jehoshaphat and Joram (2 Ki. 3:7); and between Assyria and Judah (2 Ki. 18:23, 31).

[3] V. Hurowitz, *Temple Building in the Bible in the Light of Mesopotamian and North-West Semitic Writings* (University of Jerusalem: Doctoral thesis, 1983). *Cf.* *'I Have Built You an Exalted House'* (Sheffield: *JSOT*Supp 115, 1992).

(b) Annals and chronicles

For the Kings of Judah and Israel annals were available for reference and were used as sources.[1] The historian of Kings therefore frequently refers the reader to the appropriate 'annals (= 'book/record of the affairs of the days') of the kings of Judah'[2] or to the 'annals of the kings of Israel'[3] as the source for additional information. It can be assumed that, like the counterpart Assyrian Annals and Babylonian Chronicles, he considered these sources as complete ('all he did'), or as the source for unspecified actions of 'what he did', or as containing notes of special 'achievements' including military exploits (1 Ki. 22:45; 2 Ki. 14:28). For these annals are said to have included details of wars (1 Ki. 14:19; 2 Ki. 13:12; 14:15), rebellions (1 Ki. 16:20) and conspiracies (2 Ki. 15:15). Notable building and construction activity was recorded in them (1 Ki. 15:23; 22:39; 2 Ki. 20:20). These documents were not compiled by the kings themselves, for they tell also of the rôle of the prophets and the sins that kings such as Manasseh committed (2 Ki. 21:17). It would be expected that the last kings of Judah would have used the contemporary Babylonian Chronicle type of record, for Mattaniah/Zedekiah is referred to by Nebuchadnezzar II in his chronicle entry for his seventh year as 'a king after my heart'.[4]

(c) Other unacknowledged sources

(i) *The 'Succession' narrative.* 1 Kings 1:1 – 2:46 continues the 'court history' of King David from 2 Samuel 9 – 20 and presupposes knowledge of the earlier events. This is commonly called the 'Succession Narrative' as it concludes the story of David with details of the struggle for succession which ended with the throne firmly in the hands of Solomon.[5] The narrative forms a unity with consistent treatment of the

---

[1] Except that nothing is said about Jehoahaz. The later reference to Asa's reign is that from beginning to end it was written in 'the book of the kings of Judah and Israel' (2 Ch. 16:11), a general reference to the use of these sources.

[2] 1 Ki. 14:29; 15:7, 23; 22:45; 2 Ki. 8:23; 12:19; 15:6, 36; 16:19; 20:20; 21:17, 25; 23:28; 24:5.

[3] 1 Ki. 14:19; 15:31; 16:5, 14, 20, 27; 22:39, 45; 2 Ki. 1:18; 10:34; 13:8, 12; 14:15, 18, 28; 15:11, 15, 21, 26, 31, 36; 16:19.

[4] D. J. Wiseman, *op. cit.*, pp. 72–73 (BM. 21946, r. 13 'a king of his own choice').

[5] L. Rost, *Die Überlieferung von der Thronnachfolge Davids* (Stuttgart: W. Kohlhammer, 1926); G. von Rad, *The Problem of the Hextateuch and Other Essays* (Edinburgh: Oliver & Boyd, 1966), pp. 189 ff.

43

complex characters and themes which pervade the whole. The story appears to have been compiled early in Solomon's reign when the historical facts were still verifiable.[1] Most commentators consider this section to be pro-Solomonic but the author is unknown. The narrative forms a significant link with David and serves as an introduction to the following account of Solomon's reign. The whole is a skilful product of a literary genius.[2] There is no agreement on whether it may contain later additions or editorial comments and none have been traced in it with proven certainty.[3] It is possible that literate court circles, including Nathan the scribe, may be responsible here, as for the following chapter with its assessment of Solomon's wisdom.[4]

(ii) *Prophecy sources.* Kings includes many narratives about named prophets, including Ahijah (1 Ki. 11:29–39; 14:1–18); Shemaiah (1 Ki. 12:21–24); Jehu, son of Hanani (1 Ki. 16:1–16); and Micaiah, son of Imlah (1 Ki. 22). Other prophets are unnamed, though with indications of where and when they were active (1 Ki. 13:1–32 and a man of God in Judah, an old prophet from Bethel), working in the time of Ahab (1 Ki. 20:35–43) or of Manasseh (2 Ki. 21:10–15). The historian throughout puts emphasis on how 'the word of the LORD came to' rulers, prophets and people.[5] He specifically states when events fulfilled the word of the LORD or happened 'according to the word of the LORD'.[6] This theme runs through the whole history more frequently than is often recognized.

[1] R. N. Whybray, *The Succession Narrative: A Study of II Samuel 9–20 and I Kings 1 and 2* (London: SCM Press, 1968), pp. 19–47; though some argue that it is a neutral and objective report (*cf.* D. M. Gunn, *The Story of King David: Genre and Interpretation* (Sheffield: *JSOT*Supp 6, 1978), pp. 23–24), the interpretation of it differs widely (see n. 66).

[2] Von Rad, *op. cit.*, pp. 176, 192, takes it as 'the oldest specimen of ancient Israelite historical writing' yet classes it as 'political propaganda' while being 'genuine historical writing'; W. McKane (*I & II Samuel*, London: SCM Press, 1963, p. 19) takes it as 'national epic' and O. Eissfeldt (*The Old Testament, an Introduction*, Oxford: Basil Blackwell, 1965, p. 141) as a 'good historical novel'.

[3] Jones, pp. 48–51, for a survey of numerous theories and additions; *cf.* M. Noth, *The Deuteronomic History* (Sheffield: *JSOT*Supp 15, 1981), pp. 8–13; Gray, pp. 14–22.

[4] J. L. Crenshaw, 'Methods in Determining Wisdom Influence upon "Historical Literature"', *JBL* 88, 1969, pp. 129–142.

[5] 1 Ki. 6:11; 12:22; 13:20; 16:1, 7; 17:2, 8; 18:1, 31; 19:9; 2 Ki. 3:12; 9:36; 15:12; 19:21; 20:4, 6, 19.

[6] 1 Ki. 2:27; 8:20, 56; 12:24; 13:2, 5, 9, 26; 14:18; 16:12, 34; 17:5, 8, 16; 22:5, 19, 38; 2 Ki. 1:7; 4:44; 7:16; 9:26; 14:25; 23:16; 24:2.

More extensive narratives concerning Elijah (1 Ki. 17–19; 21; 2 Ki. 1) and Elisha (2 Ki. 2:1 – 10:36) are grouped together. Hence these are often designated 'the Elijah cycle' and 'the Elisha cycle'. They are placed within the last decade of the Omri dynasty (Jehoram–Joash) with the end of Elisha's ministry extending to the successors of Jehu.[1] In a variety of incidents which could well have been treasured memories retained by groups of prophets and recorded in prophetic memoirs, as for Samuel, Nathan and Ezra, a vivid and memorable picture is portrayed.

(a) *Elijah* is presented as Moses *redivivus*[2] fighting for the purity and continuance of the worship of the LORD amid idolatry and the intrusive syntheistic acknowledgment of foreign gods. The demand for a consistent faith and practice contrasts with the polytheism of the many Baal cults and their lack of ethical concern.[3] The miracles performed, five by Elijah and ten by Elisha, cluster here, as at the exodus and later at the resurrection of Jesus and the birth of the church, at a time when the faith of God's people is being severely tested. They are not directed to emphasize the personal greatness or charismatic prestige and power of the prophet himself so much as to encourage the faithful by the demonstration of divine power.

The relation of these events, often dismissed as legends, sagas or popular miracle stories, to history has been much discussed with little enlightenment. At this distance it is impossible to distinguish between historical narratives and legend and the whole cannot be summarily dismissed as hagiology. Much depends on the reader's attitude to the supernatural and miracle. The circumstantial evidence provided by the detail of place, persons and event (*e.g.* drought, Naboth, Mount Carmel, Zarephath, the revived child (1 Ki. 17:17–24) and the arrest of Elijah (2 Ki. 1:9–16) were all among the many happenings which were witnessed, remembered and recounted (*e.g.* 2 Ki. 8:4–5). The historical kernel is firm, which cannot be said for the evidence ranged against these traditions. The stories, like the history as a whole, are given a theological emphasis and do not read as a deliberate

[1] Cogan and Tadmor, p. 11, n. 21.
[2] R. R. Carroll, 'The Elijah–Elisha Sagas', *VT* 19, 1969, pp. 408–414.
[3] L. Bronner, *The Stories of Elijah and Elisha as Polemics against Baal Worship* (Leiden: E. J. Brill, 1968).

polemic against popular Canaanite mythology,[1] even though they could serve as such.

(*b*) *Elisha* also took an active part in politics in the time of Jehu and in many ways shows a similar stance and sense of the divine mission as Elijah (1 Ki. 17:1; 18:15; 2 Ki. 3:14, 16). It has been noted that frequent mention is made of holy places such as Carmel (2 Ki. 4:8–37), Dothan (2 Ki. 6:8–23) and Gilgal (2 Ki. 4:1–7, 38–41; 6:1–7), as earlier to Bethel (1 Ki. 12:33 – 13:31) and Shiloh (1 Ki. 14:1–18), and these were associated with prophetic circles who might have preserved the narratives. The commentary will point to questions of similarity and difference between the deeds of Elijah and his disciple Elisha.

(*c*) *Isaiah.* The historian includes matter (2 Ki. 18:17 – 20:19) which is also found in shorter form in Isaiah (36 – 39). Most consider these sources to be independent, with priority given to Kings. On the other hand the appendix (2 Ki. 25:27–30) which is also found with little change in Jeremiah (52:31–34) may be drawn from a later source common to both.

VI. THE LITERARY FORM

The historian arranges the material he has taken from the various sources in a distinctive way. For each reign described he uses an obvious and convenient literary framework of regnal formulae or resumés (Long), to mark both the beginning ('Introductory Formulae') and termination ('Concluding Formulae') of each royal reign.

(a) Introductory formulae

These are found except where details of a struggle for the throne take their place in a longer narrative which provides the same data (*e.g.* for Solomon, Jeroboam and Jehu).[2] This information includes:

(i) *The king's name* and relation to his predecessor, usually father, by direct succession.[3] The same sentence adds:

---

[1] Against Bronner, *op. cit.* p. 139.
[2] The formulae are also omitted for Athaliah, who was not considered a legitimate ruler.
[3] The father's name is absent where he was a usurper, thus Zimri (1 Ki. 16:15) and Omri (1 Ki. 16:28).

(ii) *The date of accession* with a synchronism with the corresponding contemporary ruler in the other kingdom, Israel or Judah (see Chronology, pp. 28–29), and also:

(iii) *His age* on coming to the throne (given only for the kings of Judah).[1]

(iv) *The length of reign* is recorded in total years, with months and days where less than a full year,[2] for all rulers of both of the divided kingdoms. The rounded figures include any time the king acted as co-regent with his father (see also p. 31). That no ruler is omitted may well be added testimony to the existence of king lists in Judah and Israel.

These details (i–iv) follow a form for Israel already used in Judges (9:22; 10:2–3; 12:7, 11) and, for Judah, that employed in Samuel (1 Sa. 13:1; 2 Sa. 10:5; *cf.* 2 Ki. 12:1, 2; 21:1; 22:1).

(v) *The place of reign* is given. For the kings of Israel this was initially Tirzah until the capital was relocated at Samaria under Omri (1 Ki. 16:24, 29). For Judah it was always Jerusalem as the city where God had chosen to put his name (1 Ki. 14:21).

(vi) *The mother's name* is added for kings of Judah only. The exceptions of Jehoram (2 Ki. 8:17) and Ahaz (2 Ki. 16:2) may be due to the mother having died before the accession or having married into an opposing Israelite family. Usually the mother's parentage[3] or place of origin,[4] or both, as for the last six kings of Judah,[5] are given. The only exceptions are Rehoboam's mother Naamah, noted as an Ammonitess (1 Ki. 14:22), and the omission of any name for the mother of Ahaz (see on 2 Ki. 16:2), or matronym for Hephzibah (2 Ki. 21:1). This concern that the Davidic line should be fully recorded through both parents is also to be seen in the note concerning Abishag (1 Ki. 1:3–4), the naming of Solomon's mother's parents (2 Sa. 11:2), and in the colophon at the end of the book of Ruth (4:18–22).

(vii) *A theological appraisal of each reign.* The initial verses always include a statement judging the reign as 'right' or 'evil'. This is not simply a judgment as 'good' or 'bad' as in some Mesopotamian chronicles. It is an evaluation of the whole of the individual's life, for the criteria are theological and specific

---

[1] As earlier given for Saul (1 Sa. 13:1) and David (2 Sa. 2:10).
[2] 1 Ki. 16:15; 2 Ki. 15:8, 13.
[3] 1 Ki. 15:2; 22:42; 2 Ki. 15:33; 18:2.   [4] 2 Ki. 12:1; 14:2; 15:2.
[5] 2 Ki. 21:19; 22:1; 23:31, 36; 24:8, 18.

in the Hebrew phrase 'in the eyes/sight of the LORD' which includes the moral and practical aspects of daily life. These judgments are couched as summary verdicts in clear, unequivocal sayings (sometimes called 'judgment formulae') in one of the two following ways.

1. *He did (the) right in the eyes of the LORD.*[1] This is said of only ten kings of Israel including, initially, Solomon (1 Ki. 3:3, *cf.*, 11:6).[2] The reference is by comparison with the fathers, especially the 'ideal' King David as founder of the dynasty who was himself similarly assessed (1 Ki. 15:5). It is noteworthy that the historian says that Asa 'did right as had David' (1 Ki. 15:11; 1 Chr. 14:12). So did Hezekiah (2 Ki. 18:3) and Josiah (2 Ki. 22:2). Others who 'did the right' are compared with their immediate forefathers who had done the same, thus Jehoshaphat as Asa (1 Ki. 22:43), Azariah as Amaziah (2 Ki. 15:3) and Jotham as Azariah (2 Ki. 15:24). It is remarkable that the parental influence was reinforced by the encouragements and warnings given by contemporary prophets (to Asa by Azariah and Hanani the seer, 2 Ch. 16:7; to Jehoshaphat by Jehu the seer and by Micaiah, 2 Ch. 18:8; 19:2; to Jehu by an unnamed prophet, 2 Ki. 9:1–10; and by Jehonadab, 2 Ki. 10:15; Joash encouraged by Jehoiada the priest, 2 Ki. 12:2; and rebuked by Zechariah, 2 Ch. 24:20). The same is true of Amaziah (2 Ki. 14:3; 2 Ch. 25:7 ff.), Azariah (2 Ki. 15:3; 2 Ch. 26:5), Jotham (2 Ki. 15:34). Hezekiah was spoken to by Isaiah (2 Ki. 19:1–2; 20:1, 14) and Josiah by the prophetess Huldah (2 Ki. 22:14, 20).

The verdict of 'doing the right' implies that the reader would recognize that the king was being measured against the standard of the divine law – 'the law of Moses' (*cf.* 1 Ki. 2:3; 3:14; *cf.* Dt. 6:7–10) – and God's covenant with his people (Dt. 12:28; 13:19).[3] This judgment is not confined to those who are said to have initiated reforms demanded in the Deuteronomic law, such as the removal and destruction of the high places, votive poles (Asherah), cult prostitutes or pagan priests, though such actions are noted in the case of those who won or lost this verdict on their careers. Nor is the judgment

---

[1] *Cf.* Dt. 12:25, 28 and the Chronicler's 'just and right' (1 Ch. 18:14).

[2] Jehu of Israel may have been so classified initially since he brought the house of Ahab to an end (2 Ki. 10:30).

[3] D. J. Wiseman, 'Law and Order in OT Times', *Vox Evangelica* 8, 1973, pp. 5–7.

specifically related to the king's pursuance of the temple services in Jerusalem.[1] However, it is clear that those who 'did the right in the LORD's eyes' committed righteous acts. For all of them it is stated that they did so except in certain incidents. Thus even the ideal king David did so 'except in the matter of Uriah the Hittite' (1 Ki. 15:5). The judgment appears to result from an attitude of heart in full commitment, devotion and obedience to the LORD and to his ways and word mediated through the prophets,[2] and from a willingness to seek the LORD's will.[3]

That they 'did the right' did not of itself protect the kings from disaster or distress, though the Chronicler notes that Asa (2 Ch. 14:6–7; but *cf.* 1 Ki. 15:16) had peace within the land and Jehoshaphat peace with the surrounding territories. Joram and Jotham had to endure wars (2 Ki. 15:23, 37). Even 'good' kings suffered misfortune: Asa with foot disease (1 Ki. 15:23); Jehoshaphat the wreck of his fleet (1 Ki. 22:48) and Azariah/Uzziah leprosy (2 Ki. 15:5). Joash and Amaziah were assassinated. It has been noted that the average reign of the ten 'good' kings of Judah (33.1 years) was much greater than that of the thirty-three 'evil' kings of Israel (13.3), a fact which stands apart from any editorial influence. It is said of only one king, Ahaz, for whom no mother's name is given, that 'he did not do the right in the eyes of the LORD' (2 Ki. 16:2; *cf.* 2 Ch. 28:1). The expression that 'everyone did the right in his own eyes', *i.e.* anarchy, used where there is no-one upholding the law (Jdg. 21:25) is not found in Kings.

2. *He did evil in the eyes of the LORD.* This, the only alternative judgment, is the verdict passed on all the kings of Israel, as well as on some in Judah. For the rulers of the Northern Kingdom the evil is usually described as following 'the ways (manner of life) of Jeroboam son of Nebat and the sins he caused Israel to commit'. His division and disruption of the unity of God's people led to their turning away from the LORD and his law (*cf.* Ps. 18:21–2). Jeroboam is taken as the

[1] *Contra* von Rad.
[2] So Joash did so only while Jehoiada was alive (1 Ki. 12:2); Amaziah 'not wholeheartedly' (2 Ch. 25:2) and Azariah only while Zechariah was his advisor (2 Ch. 26:5).
[3] The overall attitude of life is characterized by 'walking in the ways of the fathers and not straying from them ' and seeking God: so Asa (1 Ki. 15:14; 2 Ch. 14:4); Jehoshaphat (1 Ki. 22:43; *cf.* 2 Ch. 17:6); Azariah (2 Ch. 26:5); Hezekiah (2 Ki. 22:43; *cf.* 2 Ch. 17:6) and Josiah (2 Ki. 23:25).

prototype apostate, though early kings of Judah who failed are compared with others who had sinned. So Joram did not act as his fathers had done (2 Ki. 3:2), whereas Jehoram did 'as the kings of Israel' (2 Ki. 8:19); Ahaziah acted as Ahab, through a bad marriage (2 Ki. 8:27); and the last king Zedekiah is compared with his uncle Jehoiakim (2 Ki. 24:19). Here again family influence is shown to be as strong for evil as it could have been for good. The last kings of Judah were all compared with Manasseh, whose sin in the Jeroboam tradition is specifically listed (2 Ki. 21:2–6). It included detestable Canaanite practices, rebuilding high places, erecting altars to Baal and Asherah poles, astrology, and introducing non-Yahwistic features into the Jerusalem temple.[1] No judgment of any kind is passed on Shallum who ruled but one month before his assassination.

In all these introductory sections to a reign it will be noted that, alongside the more stereotypical formulae, several variations and additions are to be found. These would indicate a fluid style of writing related to actual historical conditions.

(b) The history
As with the introductory formulae, the history which follows shows a great variety of treatment. Much space is devoted to the figures who form the major emphasis of the history and are, in a way, its heroes – Solomon, Hezekiah of Judah and Ahab of Israel. Other long-reigning monarchs are passed over briefly (*e.g.* Omri, 1 Ki. 16:21–28; and Manasseh). For most others only a few highlights of their reign are given, while for some no details are given between the introduction and the concluding formulae. This may well be due to the historian's selectivity rather than to any absence of available data.

(c) Concluding formulae
Following any historical details or episodes recounted for each reign the account is usually terminated by a series of statements arranged in a common order, and often with a common terminology. These 'concluding formulae' include:
   (i) *Citation of sources.* These provide additional information

---

[1] As did Amon (2 Ki. 21:21–22); Jehoahaz (23:32) and Zedekiah (24:19).

on any reign to which the reader is referred (see above on Sources, pp. 40–46).

(ii) *Additional historical notes*. These appear to have been added by the same historian to give an overall perspective. These are usually references to wars (Abijah, Nadab, Jehoshaphat, Ahaziah, Jehoahaz, Jehoash, Jotham, Josiah) or to the recovery of lost territory (Jeroboam II) or to architectural exploits such as Hezekiah's tunnel. Where a king rebelled or was assassinated some details are given here.

(iii) *Notice of death*. This is introduced by 'X rested/slept with his fathers'. It has the force of 'died naturally' since it is not used of anyone who met a violent death[1] and is immediately followed by a notice of burial.

(iv) *Notice of burial*. David and the succeeding kings of Judah were buried (*wayiqqābēr, i.e.* given a grave) 'in the city of David'. These graves lay to the southwest of the temple mount and west of Ophel. Hezekiah is said to have been buried 'on the hill where the tombs of David's descendants are' (2 Ch. 32:33), which, if not in the city of David royal necropolis, may show that that was now full. Manasseh and the remaining Judean kings were buried in Iron Age caves (Josephus, *Wars* v. 147) on the Shechem (Nablus) road (now part of the monastery of St Etienne).[2] This area may have included the 'garden of Uzzah' used for the burial of Manasseh and Amon (2 Ki. 21:18, 26). Josiah, killed in battle at Megiddo, was buried in his own tomb in Jerusalem (2 Ki. 23:30). No reference is made to the death and burial of Jehoiachin since he was presumably still alive when the final verses of Kings were added.[3]

The kings of Samaria were buried in Samaria after its foundation by Omri; those who died by assassination (Nadab, Pekahiah and Pekah) have no notice of death or burial place given.[4] Again the variations from the pattern seem to be

---

[1] Omission of this notice for Jeroboam II (2 Ki. 14:29) is not explained. Zimri, following suicide (1 Ki. 16:18) is just said to have died (*wayyamôt*).

[2] A. Kloner, 'The Cave of the Kings', *Levant* 18, 1986, pp. 121–129; A. Nazar, 'Iron Age Burial Caves North of the Damascus Gate, Jerusalem', *IEJ* 26, 1976, pp. 1–8.

[3] *I.e.* 561 BC. See on 2 Ki. 25:27.

[4] No burial place is given for Jeroboam I (1 Ki. 14:20), Jeroboam II (2 Ki. 14:29); Menahem (2 Ki. 15:22) or Jehoiakim (2 Ki. 24:6).

historical and conditioned by the actual burial.[1]

(v) *Succession.* The name of the successor, usually the son, who 'reigned as king in his place' (*i.e.* 'succeeded him') concludes the closing regnal resumé. Obviously, where a king was assassinated, taken prisoner, a substitute put on the throne (*e.g.* Jehoahaz, 2 Ki. 23:24) or the people chose to set another on the throne, this is told in detail (2 Ki. 14:21; *cf.* precisely as in Assyrian annals (1 Ki. 12:20; *cf.* 2 Ki. 14:21; Assyr. *ušeššib*). Again the varied details accord with historical reality. Occasionally the historian adds an additional sentence to reinforce the link with a successor.[2]

(vi) *Postscripts.* In a few instances what appears to be an addendum or postscript has been added after the concluding formula, with its detail of the succession, has been ended. These vary from the explanatory 'there was war between Asa and Baasha ... throughout their reigns' (1 Ki. 15:32) to 'the time that Jehu reigned over Israel in Samaria was twenty-eight years' (2 Ki. 10:36). One explanation may be that the order of the closing formula was varied as in each instance assassination precluded the normal details of death, burial and succession being provided. The illegitimacy of Athaliah's reign may have rendered the introductory and concluding formulae inappropriate or even unrecorded. The absence of final formulae for Hoshea (1 Ki. 17:1–6), Jehoahaz (2 Ki. 23:35), Jehoiachin (2 Ki. 24:8–17) and Zedekiah (2 Ki. 24:18–19) can be best explained by invasion, capture and deportation.

VII. COMPOSITION AND AUTHORSHIP

Theories abound as to who wrote or compiled the Books of Kings. Most start from a view that the additions or comments added to the standard framework of the history reflect a distinctive viewpoint of the editor(s). While the outline pattern of the book with its repetitive formulae and selection of data are commonly accepted, there is a wide difference of acceptance, and no agreement, on what may be post-exilic additions or reworking.

---

[1] E. J. Smit, 'Death and Burial Formulas in Kings and Chronicles relating to the Kings of Judah', *Biblical Essays* (Potchefstroom: Die Outestamentiese Werkgemeenskap, 1966), pp. 173–177.
[2] *E.g.* 1 Ki. 15:38; 2 Ki. 16:36.

(a) A single historian

This commentary takes the minority view that there was a single author/compiler/editor who selected from pre-existing historical sources (see pp. 40ff.) and let them carry his interpretation of events. He occasionally interpolates his own comments (*e.g.* 2 Ki. 17:1–23), but treats his sources reverently as trustworthy and uses them objectively.[1] It is noteworthy that the history from David to the fall of Judah forms a unity. Since the author's aim is to give an interpretation of that history as showing God at work, blessing, warning and judging his people according to their recorded obedience or disloyalty to his revealed and knowable law, he omits many political, military, economic and personal details which a modern reader might expect or desire. The historian selects his materials in accordance with this specific aim. Thus, for example, the record of the internationally renowned king Omri is reduced to a mere six verses in 1 Kings 16 and the long reign of Jeroboam II to seven (2 Ki. 14:23–29).

For long this view of a single authorship held sway and Jewish tradition attributed the books to Jeremiah (*Baba Bathra* 15a). Indeed Kings has much in common with Isaiah and Jeremiah in theological perspective, language and purpose.[2] The view may not simply reflect an early tendency to believe that all Scripture was penned by a prophet. Nor is it a mere reflection of the identical ending of Jeremiah and Kings. It is not improbable that Jeremiah, with his close association with court and thus scribal circles in Jerusalem, had access to the earlier state archives of both Hebrew kingdoms prior to the fall of the city in 587/6 BC. It has been suggested that the history was written up *c.* 580 BC from existing records by Jeremiah or a companion then residing with Gedaliah in Mizpah before Jeremiah and his party withdrew to Egypt.[3] Against this it is usually surmised that the author must have been someone in exile in Babylon at least twenty years later after 561 BC, the year in which the closing reference to the release of Jehoiachin into a more favourable refugee status

---

[1] *Cf.* Long, p. 21.

[2] And of course with Dt. Note that extensive use of medical terminology is found also in these three books.

[3] This is basically also the view of Montgomery, p. 45; *cf.* S. R. Bin-Nun, 'Formulas from Royal Records of Israel and Judah', *VT* 18, 1968, p. 415, after Noth.

there was made. However, if the final three verses of the book (2 Ki. 25:27–30), which are almost identical with those that conclude Jeremiah (52:31–34),[1] are to be understood as an *appendix* added to both books, this in itself would form no argument against an earlier date for the completion of the book.

The major exponent of the case for a single author is Noth, though he viewed him as at work in the mid-sixth century BC, with the closing verses of the book written by a pessimist,[2] whereas von Rad interprets the same passage as optimistic.[3] There does not seem evidence to warrant reading the final verses of the 'appendix' as expressing any specific theological outlook which would require a later editor to recast the earlier history. For Noth the single author (commonly called the 'Deuteronomist' and his work 'Deuteronomistic', since it shares the ideals, outlook and language[4] of Deuteronomy) wrote a work that forms part of a continuous narrative from Deuteronomy to 2 Kings. In that sense Kings is part of the Hebrew 'Former Prophets' (Joshua – Kings). The whole nation was the covenant people of God, called to be holy and distinctive. The monarchy was the political means whereby the whole could be held together, though the nation was always in danger of judgment if the people succumbed to the evil influences of their polytheistic neighbours or re-emerging Canaanite practices.

The bearing of Deuteronomy on Kings must dominate views on the period in which Deuteronomy influenced Kings. Those who consider Deuteronomy to have been the book found at the time of Josiah's repair of the temple in 622 BC see it as composed shortly before that time and assign the book to that period. They assume that the earliest possible time it could have influenced Kings would be early in the following century. There is, however, no certainty that the 'Book of the Law' discovered by Hilkiah (2 Ki. 22:3 ff.) was Deuteronomy

[1] The only verbal variants are 'twenty-fifth' for Kings' 'twenty-seventh' day (2 Ki. 25:27) and 'as long as he lived' (v. 30) for Jeremiah's explanatory addition 'until the day of his death' (52:34).

[2] M. Noth, *The Deuteronomistic History* (Sheffield: *JSOT*Supp 15, 1981), pp. 75ff. *Uberlieferungsgeschichtliche Studien* (Tübingen: Mohr, 1957, 1943) pp. 1–110.

[3] G. von Rad, *Studies in Deuteronomy* (London: SCM Press, 1953), pp. 90–91.

[4] M. Weinfeld, *Deuteronomy and the Deuteronomic School* (Oxford: Clarendon Press, 1972), pp. 320–365.

as we now know it, though it contained such provisions as would have encouraged Josiah's reform (see commentary). The view taken here is that the rediscovery included documents of the Pentateuch written down early in the monarchy and which form the basis of any evaluation throughout the history of the Hebrew kingdoms. The choice of Israel, the fulfilment of prophecy, the exercise of divine justice, and the understanding that the principal shrine of a national deity was to be found in the capital city, were old ideas. Nevertheless, the equation of Jerusalem as the only central and legitimate place that God had chosen (1 Ki. 11:13, 32, 36) with the requirement of Deuteronomy 12 as a 'Deuteronomistic' marker, is not so easily substantiated, since Deuteronomy neither names Jerusalem nor stresses such centralization.

(b) A staged redaction

It must be noted that the majority of scholars today do not accept the concept of a single author proposed above. They opt for a 'dual redaction' of Kings, whether one basic work to which another later hand has made moderate changes or a drastic 'second edition' reworking of the earlier core, substantially changing the viewpoint. The literature on this is immense but may be briefly summarized as follows.

1. A first pre-exilic edition of the Deuteronomic history (D(tr)H) prepared in the reign of Hezekiah (Weippert, Provan) though with additions to the end of Judah, and the whole revised with some changes in the original purpose (von Rad, Wolff).

2. The structural framework carried as far as 2 Kings 16 forms a history down to the time of Josiah (2 Ki. 23) to emphasize the fulfilment of the promise made to David's dynasty and the judgment on the Northern Kingdom following the sin of Jeroboam. Thereafter additions and a post-exilic reworking of the whole (some say as a 'second editon') extol Josiah as the ideal 'new David' (Gray, Cross, Nelson, Robinson, Mayes).[1] Some of these scholars contend for more than

---

[1] A. Šanda, *Die Bücher der Könige* (Münster: Aschendorff, 1911), pp. xxxvi-xlii, thought the 'second edition' consisted only of minor additions and corrections. However, this is not attested in ancient Near Eastern literary practice (Long, pp. 18–19).

one redaction.[1]

3. Some argue for a three-staged redaction (Veijola)[2] and seek to identify the different strands with precision *e.g.* Smend (source R I, the work of a priest connected with the temple in early exile, and source R II which later still reinterpreted the earlier attitude to 'high places').[3] Some emphasize the basic DtrG(eschichte) = DtrH(istory) as showing a positive view of the Davidic dynasty whereas DtrN is diagnosed as a source interested in the law and obedience to it.[4] DtrP(rophetic) is said to be yet another hand who later inserted the words of prophets into the history to emphasize the theme of fulfilment.[5] This is to be distinguished from those who find a didactic priestly style (from Jerusalem?) in some passages (von Rad). Early attempts to find a P(riestly) source in Kings, as postulated for the Pentateuch, have long been contradicted.[6] This supposed discernment of differing post-exilic editorial hands reworking or adding to the history appears to rely upon:

(i) Passages (especially 2 Ki. 17:7–25) said to presuppose the exile of Judah and which must therefore be post-586 or 561 BC (Gray) or imply an exilic situation. However, 'other passages are totally unaware of the exile' or the destruction of the temple, as in the requirement to pray towards it (1 Ki. 8:21–64). Exile, however, was a common experience in the ancient Near East following foreign invasion, and ever present in the Hebrew mind following the Assyrian incursions into Syria in 853 and the fall of Samaria in 722 BC.[7] Unless the Kings references can be shown beyond question to be

[1] F. M. Cross, 'The Theme of the Books of Kings and the Structure of Deuteronomy' in *Canaanite Myth and Hebrew Epic* (Cambridge, Mass.: Harvard University Press, 1973), pp. 274–289.

[2] T. Veijola, *Das Königtum in der Beurteilung des deuteronomistichen Historiographie: Eine redaktionsgeschichtliche Untersuchung* (Helsinki: Academia scientiarum fennica, 1977).

[3] R. Smend, 'Das Gesetz und die Völker: Ein Betrag zur deuteronomistichen Redactionsgeschichte', *Probleme Biblischer Theologie* (Festschrift von Rad, ed. H. W. Wolff, Munich: Kaiser Verlag, 1971), pp. 494–509.

[4] E. W. Nicholson, *Deuteronomy and Tradition* (Oxford: Basil Blackwell, 1967), pp. 58 ff. *Cf.* also above, 'prophetic sources', *e.g.* Abijah (1 Ki. 14:7–14), *etc. Cf.* Ki. 3:4–15; 9:1–9; 11.

[5] *Cf.* also 'prophetic sources' (above), *e.g.* Abijah (1 Ki. 14:7–11).

[6] I. M. Kikawada and A. Quinn, *Before Abraham Was* (Nashville: Abingdon, 1985) remains a provocative challenge to the documentary hypothesis.

[7] K. A. Kitchen, 'The Concept of Exile' in J. B. Payne (ed.), *New Perspectives on the Old Testament* (Waco: Word, 1970), pp. 5–7.

applicable only to a later Babylonian situation their value for dating purposes is limited.

(ii) Passages in which the attitude to the Davidic dynasty is said to change. The original DH was optimistic that this would be eternal ('for ever', 1 Ki. 11:34–36; 15:3–4; *cf.* 2 Sa. 7:11–16); his optimism came to a climax in the reign of Josiah. A later editor, it is surmised, in a more pessimistic setting, made permanence conditional upon obedience to God. Similar phraseology ('for ever') is found in many ancient Near Eastern treaties, decrees and royal grants which did not outlast 'all the days of the king' who made them (*cf.* 1 Ki. 9:3). The expression is commonly used for royal appointments to office which may be hereditary (*cf.* 2 Sa. 19:13; Je. 35:18–19). This is not to say that the tradition of an everlasting line for David was only a theological concept.[1]

(iii) Passages which are said to show a change in structure and thought can be indicated by the briefer regnal formulae used for the last four kings of Judah.[2] This would imply that 'annalistic'-type sources were not available during the exile, but that is precisely the time when increasing numbers of such varied chronicles have been found in Babylonia.

(iv) Such expressions as 'unto this day'[3] are used of situations which it is said are appropriate only to an exilic editor. Most of these occurrences indicate a source within Palestine and most are unquestionably taken from the historian's sources (*e.g.* 1 Ki. 9:13), though it is not always clear whether others are from similar material or are the historian's own comment. The phrase is no reliable indicator of post-exilic authorship.[4]

(v) Some passages are said to show an ambivalent attitude to places of worship. Kings frequently refers to worship at 'hill shrines' (*bāmāh*, AV 'high places', Montgomery 'heathenish shrines').[5] Their removal is favoured and taken as a mark of a

---

[1] Long, pp. 16–17. For the Assyr. *ana ūmē ṣâti*, 'for time to come', see D. J. Wiseman, *The Vassal-Treaties of Esarhaddon* (London: The British School of Archaeology in Iraq, 1958), pp. 51, 57 (ll. 289, 384, 393).

[2] Weippert assigns these to editor R III.

[3] 1 Ki. 3:6; 8:8, 24, 61; 9:13, 21; 10:12; 12:19; 2 Ki. 2:22; 8:22; 10:27; 14:7; 16:6; 17:23, 34, 41.

[4] Nelson, pp. 23–25.

[5] 1 Ki. 3:2, 3, 4; 11:7; 12:31–32; 13:2, 32–33; 14:23; 15:14; 22:44; 2 Ki. 12:4; 14:4; 15:4, 35; 16:4; 17:9, 11, 29, 32; 18:4, 22; 21:3, 5, 8, 9; 23:13, 15, 19, 20.

ruler doing what is right (as Asa, 1 Ki. 15:11–15). Yet Provan has recently suggested that the judgment formulae show tolerance which were 'provincial yet Yahweh sanctioned'. For him a later editor sees the shrines as places of Yahwistic worship which was 'correct in content but illegitimate in terms of where it was practised'.[1] Such a view argues from silence, for the text nowhere explicitly confirms it.

Thus it will be seen that there are a number of views without agreement on what form any late editing takes. Some contend for a continuous redaction (Jones), though most assume a kernel of pre-existing material on which such redactors worked.[2] Literary analysis is insufficiently exact and often subjective, so that the different stages in the evolution of any document cannot now be distinguished with any certainty. Contemporary historiography shows that repetitions, digressions and variety of expression and outlook are to be found even in one document. The details of all the proposed interpolations and editorial glosses are well summarized in recent major commentaries (Jones and Long). Since insufficient is yet known of differences in late pre- and early post-exilic Hebrew literary style for any given passage to be assigned to one or other period with confidence,[3] only where they may seriously affect interpretation are such points discussed in this brief commentary.

VIII. TEXT

The Books of Kings terminate the section of the Hebrew Bible called 'The Former Prophets'. The Massoretic Hebrew text (MT) is remarkably smooth and clear.[4] A few small scattered fragments dated to the late second century BC are among the Dead Sea Scrolls found in Qumran caves 5 and 6. Leather

---

[1] Provan, pp. 57–91. He thinks that Hezekiah's reform was to concentrate the worship in Jerusalem and that 1 Ki. 3 – 2 Ki. 18 betrays different views and hands with perhaps a north-south divide on the subject.

[2] But not van Seters, who opts for the whole being post-exilic. J. van Seters, *In Search of History: Historiography in the Ancient World and the Origins of Biblical History* (Chicago: Yale University Press, 1983).

[3] *Contra* Nelson.

[4] K. Elliger and W. Rudolf (eds.), *Biblia Hebraica Stuttgartensia* (Stuttgart, 1967–71) depend on the recensions of Ben Naphtali and Ben Asher preserved *c.* 1008 AD. The current Hebrew University Project is based on the damaged Aleppo codex (8th century AD).

fragments 5QK give the text of 1 Kings 1:3, 12, 22 and generally support the proto-MT, as do the oldest fragments of 4Q Sam[b] of the third century BC.[1] Papyrus fragments (6QK) show only slight differences with a shorter text of 2 Kings 8:1–6 and these take us back to the time the Hebrew text was first translated in the Septuagint (LXX). The primary text behind this commentary is the Hebrew.

The Greek translations of Kings have different readings in various recensions. In these, following the books of Samuel, 1 and 2 Kings were designated 'Third and Fourth Book of Kingdoms' or Reigns (*Basileiōn* A, B, C, D; 1 Kings = '3 Reigns'; 2 Kings = '4 Reigns'). The Old Greek (OGr) translation was probably originally based on an Egyptian Hebrew text of the fourth century BC and is reflected in the Codex Vaticanus (sixth cent. AD) and used in many revisions. The Lucian text (LXX(L)) is generally considered Old Palestinian of the third century BC, while Origen's Hexapla *c*. AD. 240 sought to make his translation conform to the then fixed MT. There is no agreement on the significance or development of the variant LXX texts.[2] Gooding argues that the text shows a deliberate attempt to reorder the material and thus reinterprets some characters and events, *e.g.* Jeroboam's bid for power[3] and Ahab's character.[4] The LXX is not a uniform translation and is in part interpretative and so 'Midrashic' (Gooding) or 'Targumic' (Kahle). It contains a number of additions ('Miscellanies') not in the MT (1 Ki. 2:35[a–o]; 2:46[a–b]; 12:24[a–z]; 16:28[a–h]) and sometimes changes the order (*e.g.* transposes 1 Ki. 20 and 21) and in its attempt at revision varies the chronology. Gooding judges the LXX to be secondary, and inferior, to the MT and sometimes without sense.[5]

[1] F. M. Cross, 'A New Qumran Biblical Fragment Related to the Original Hebrew Underlying the Septuagint', *BASOR* 132, 1953, pp. 15–26; 'The Oldest Manuscripts from Qumran IV,' *JBL* 74, 1955, pp. 165–172.

[2] D. G. Deboys, 'Recensional Criteria in the Greek Text of II Kings', *JSS* 31, 1986, pp. 135–139 shows up the complexity of the traditon.

[3] D. W. Gooding, 'The Septuagint's Rival Versions of Jeroboam's Rise to Power', *VT* 17, 1967, pp. 173–189.

[4] D. W. Gooding, 'Ahab according to the Septuagint', *ZAW* 76, 1964, pp. 169–179.

[5] D. W. Gooding, *Relics of Ancient Exegesis: A Study of the Miscellanies in 3 Reigns 2*, SOTSM 4 (Cambridge: Cambridge University Press, 1976); 'Temple Specifications: A Dispute in Logical Arrangement between the MT and LXX', *VT* 17, 1967, pp. 143–172; 'The Septuagint's Version of Solomon's Misconduct', *VT* 15, 1965, pp. 325–335.

ANALYSIS

V. THE HISTORY OF JUDAH TO THE FALL OF JERUSALEM (2 Ki. 18:1 – 25:30)
  - A. Hezekiah of Judah (18:1 – 20:21)
    - i. His early years (18:1–12)
    - ii. Opposing Sennacherib's threats to Jerusalem (18:13 – 19:37)
      - a. Sennacherib's campaign in Judah (18:13–16)
      - b. Sennacherib threatens Jerusalem (18:17–37)
      - c. Jerusalem's deliverance foretold (19:1–36)
      - d. The death of Sennacherib (19:37)
    - iii. Other incidents in Hezekiah's reign (20:1–21)
      - a. Hezekiah's illness (20:1–11)
      - b. Envoys from Merodach-baladan (20:12–19)
      - c. Concluding formulae (20:20–21)
  - B. History of reigns (21:1–26)
    - i. Manasseh of Judah (21:1–18)
      - a. Summary of reign (21:1–9)
      - b. God's word to Manasseh (21:10–15)
      - c. Further events and concluding formulae to reign (21:16–18)
    - ii. Amon of Judah (21:19–26)
  - C. Josiah's reign and reformation (22:1 – 23:30)
    - i. Summary of reign (22:1–3b)
    - ii. Temple repairs and the finding of the law book (22:3b–20)
      - a. The temple repairs (22:3b–7)
      - b. The discovery of the law book (22:8–10)
      - c. The enquiry (22:11–14)
      - d. The prophecy of Huldah (22:14–20)
    - iii. Josiah renews the covenant (23:1–3)
    - iv. The purification of national worship (23:4–20)
    - v. The Passover celebrated (23:21–23)
    - vi. Further reforms and deferred judgment (23:24–27)
    - vii. The closing formula (23:28–30)
  - D. The last days of Judah (23:31 – 25:30)
    - i. Jehoahaz of Judah (23:31–35)
    - ii. Jehoiakim of Judah (23:36 – 24:7)
    - iii. Jehoiachin of Judah (24:8–17)
    - iv. Zedekiah of Judah (24:18–20)
    - v. The fall of Jerusalem (24:20 – 25:21)
      - a. The fall of the city (25:1–7)

COMMENTARY

I. THE LAST DAYS OF DAVID AND SOLOMON'S ACCESSION (1 Ki. 1:1 – 2:46)

This court history, commonly called 'Succession Narrative', continues the account of David's reign from 2 Samuel 9–20. The style is vivid, portraying an intimate knowledge by persons involved (possibly Nathan).

It records the history of the struggle for the succession (1:1–53), accentuated by David's physical decline. His failure to name who should follow on the throne was a weakness, especially at a time when it was not clear whether the common ancient Near-Eastern practice of succession by the first-born (or by the 'charismatic' divine selection used in the appointment of Saul and David himself) was to apply. His indecision was aggravated by his failure to discipline his family (v. 6). The Adonijah incident (vv. 1–27) and the reference to Abishag (v. 3, *cf.* 2:13–35) are essential elements in the history of Solomon's reign (2:10 – 11:43) which now begins.

A. David's old age (1:1–4)

He was *old and well advanced in years*, now aged about seventy (4:11; 2 Sa. 5:4–5). The Heb. 'coming in of days' implies the passage of time (against AV 'stricken in years'). The king was now bedridden. The word *covers* ('clothes', AV, NRSV, REB) is used of cloths such as those which covered the tabernacle (Nu. 4:6; 1 Sa. 19:13). *Servants* covers any subordinate from slaves and domestic servants and officers to state officials (2 Ki. 5:6; 25:8) and courtiers. Their normal form of address to royalty is 'the king, my/our lord'.

2–3. The use of a youth to restore vital warmth was an ancient medical practice (Galen, *Method. Medic.* viii.7; Josephus, *Ant.* viii.19.3). Since a young girl of marriageable age (*virgin*, 'maiden', RSV) was employed, the emphasis here is on the absence of sexual relations (v. 4). While this reference is taken by some to denote a virility test to check whether a co-regent was required,[1] there is no sure evidence that disability of itself disqualified a king from reigning (*cf.* Azariah, 2 Ki. 15:5).

Abishag was employed to *lie beside* the king so that he might *keep warm* (*cf.* RSV 'lie in your bosom'). She was to *attend the king* (Heb. 'stand before him') *and take care of him*, or, RSV, 'wait upon the king, and be his nurse' (RSV, REB, *sōkeneṭ* is 'to be of service', Is. 22:15). Her relationship with David is disputed, it being claimed that David accepted her as queen,[2] though she was later considered to have the status of a concubine (1 Ki. 2:22). She was not dismissed when Bathsheba and Nathan were present (vv. 15, 22–23). Adonijah (vv. 17, 21–22) coveted her as a wife, as Abner had wanted Saul's concubine (2 Sa. 3:7) and Absalom those of David (2 Sa. 16:21–22) to legitimize his claim to the throne. The concubine (*pilegeš*) was not a kept mistress but a wife of secondary rank. *Shunem*, modern Sōlem, lay eleven kilometres south-east of Nazareth and five kilometres north of Jezreel in Issachar territory (1 Sa. 28:4), and was visited by Elisha (2 Ki. 4:8). There is no need to identify Abishag with the Shulammite of Song of Solomon 6:13.

B. Adonijah bids for the throne (1:5–10)

Adonijah, aged about thirty-five, was the fourth but eldest surviving son of David, after the deaths of Chileab, Amnon and Absalom (2 Sa. 3:2–4; 13:28; 18:15). He *put himself forward* (v. 5; RSV 'exalted himself'; REB 'was boasting'; Heb. pluperf. 'had been exalting') on the grounds of primogeniture. The insertion of his mother's name, according to the historian's practice in the Judean succession (see Introduction, p. 47), could be regarded as additional support for his claim.

5. *I will be king* signals a public claim to the throne, despite

---

[1] J. Gray, p. 77, based on C. H. Gordon, *Ugaritic Textbook* (Rome: Pontifical Institute, 1965), No. 127, pp. 35–38; *cf.* A. R. Johnson, *The Vitality of the Individual in the thought of Ancient Israel* (Cardiff: University of Wales Press, 1964).

[2] M. J. Mulder, 'Versuch zur Deutung von *sokenet* in 1 Kö.1.2, 4', *VT* 22, 1972, pp. 43–54.

David's known preference for Solomon (v. 10). To win support he establishes for himself a prestigious chariot escort and team (if singular, as JB), as had Absalom (2 Sa. 15:1). In effect this was a personal military force designed to anticipate Solomon's claim by a *coup d'état*. (Out)runners were part of a close royal bodyguard (14:27; 1 Sa. 22:17).

6. *His father had never interfered with him* or 'crossed him' (NASB) is more descriptive than 'displeased him' (RSV), for this comment by the author (*cf.* vv. 8, 10) betrays David's weakness in his unwillingness to cause his children any physical or mental discomfort (Heb. *'ṣb*, 'be angry with, cause emotional upset'; M. Heb. 'to stretch a child into shape'). Such lack of discipline with Amnon (2 Sa. 13:21) and Absalom (2 Sa. 18:5) had previously led to unrest in the family and nation. The Old Testament has examples of other godly men who failed by not correcting their family (*e.g.* Eli, 1 Sa. 2:12–17). On this see Proverbs 22:6; and the obligation placed on Abraham (Gn. 18:19). *Very handsome*: physical beauty, as prowess, was a popular qualification for leadership, as it had been with his father (1 Sa. 16:12), his brother Absalom (2 Sa. 14:25) and King Saul (1 Sa. 9:2).

7–8. Adonijah was supported (Heb. *'zr 'ḥr*, 'lent a helping hand' morally or in person) by *Joab*, son of David's half-sister (2 Sa. 2:18), commander of the militia and rival of Benaiah, the commander of David's bodyguard and the professional army. Joab may have sought revenge for David's preference of Amasa over him (2 Sa. 19:13). *Abiathar*, one of David's consultants (1 Sa. 22:20), may have been jealous of Zadok the High Priest, who was from Jerusalem and so possibly of the old Jebusite line (2 Sa. 8:17),[1] and who now took precedence over him. Adonijah appears to have conferred or negotiated with these two (Heb. 'his words were with') before bringing in the officials of Judah.

9. The feast at which the animals were *sacrificed* may have been given to obtain formal backing (as Absalom had in 2 Sa. 15:7–12) rather than to celebrate a symbolic investiture. The place chosen, *near En Rogel* ('Spring of the fuller', modern Bir Ayub, Job's well, in the Kidron Valley south-east of Jerusalem), was the meeting-place between Benjamin and Judah (Jos. 15:7; 18:16), within easy reach of south Judah, from

---

[1] J. A. Soggin, 'Der Offiziell Geförderte Synkretismus in Israel wahrend des 10 Jahrhunderts', *ZAW* 78, 1966, pp. 179–204.

which most of Adonijah's support came. By holding the feast here he probably hoped to avoid the attentions of David's bodyguard. Some find symbolic significance in the *Stone of Zoheleth* (RSV 'Serpent's stone'), possibly the Serpent's Well of Nehemiah 2:13. This is sometimes identified with Ez-Zahweikeh near Silwan or the slippery surface leading up the Mount of Olives.[1]

10. The omission of Zadok's name, as well the absence of Nathan, Benaiah and Solomon, is significant. The laws of hospitality would prevent the host taking action against them if he were present. The mention of Solomon as *his brother* also serves to introduce the following narrative and to create an awareness of his claim to the throne.

C. Counter-action by Nathan and Bathsheba (1:11–27)

The narrative is vivid and, in traditional Hebrew style, involves repetitions (*e.g.* vv. 19, 25 and 13, 17, 30). Nathan the prophet may have felt responsible for continuing David's promised dynasty and as concerned as Samuel had been as a 'king-maker'. His plot with Bathsheba (vv. 11–14) would agree with her desire to be an influential queen mother (*cf.* 2:19; 15:13; 2 Ki. 10:13) and with his wish that a co-regent and successor be nominated (v. 27). The action follows the usual course of an appeal to the king, and is not necessarily a formal lawsuit, with address (vv. 17–18), presentation of case (vv. 17–19), request for decision (vv. 20–21), confirmation by witness (vv. 22–27) and decision on oath (vv. 29–30).[2]

11–12. Adonijah's action was taken as formally claiming the throne (v. 25; 2:15). Though not yet crowned or adopted as crown-prince he 'acts as ruler'. A usurper would be expected to eliminate all rivals with their families (15:29; 2 Ki. 10:11; 11:1).

13. David's supposed oath (*cf.* vv. 17, 28–30) may not have been fabricated and is implied in his favouring Solomon (2 Sa. 7). Solomon, as Bathsheba's second son, was the 'replacement' for her deceased child (*cf.* 2 Sa. 11:2–5; 12:15–18, 24).

15. Abishag's presence as a witness could be a reason for Solomon not giving her later to Adonijah (2:22).

[1] *Cf.* G. R. Driver, 'Hebrew Notes', *ZAW* 52, 1934, p. 51, 'The Rolling Stone'.
[2] V. Sasson, 'An Unrecognised Juridical Term in the Yavneh-Yam Lawsuit and in an Unnoticed Biblical Parallel', *BASOR* 232, 1978, pp. 57–62.

17–20. *Your* (maid) *servant* (*'āmâ*) is here part of the formal mode of address, though the term is also used of a 'concubine' (Ex. 21:7; 23:12). The claim that David had sworn by the Divine Name would remind him that such an oath was inviolable (*cf.* v. 29; Ex. 20:7; Lv. 19:12; Jdg. 11:30, 35). In order to bring pressure on David she appeals to his continuing popularity and his right to nominate a successor.

21. *Laid to rest with his fathers* ('sleeps with', RSV, AV) denotes more than 'dies', being used of a peaceful death and burial, which is also marked by 'gathered to your fathers/family/ancestors' (as in Ugar., Akkad.).[1] To sleep or be *laid to rest with his fathers* was to be buried in the family vault, though for David, who had initiated a new dynasty, a place of burial was yet to be defined (2:10). If Solomon was not chosen Nathan and Bathsheba would be *treated as criminals* (RSV 'offenders') for plotting and so would be put to death (*cf.* v. 12).

22. On Nathan's arrival Bathsheba withdraws (*cf.* v. 28). He either assumes or presumes that David must have approved and authorized Adonijah's action without informing him. He makes no mention directly of any oath promising the throne to Solomon (vv. 13, 17), but stresses the support which Adonijah is receiving from *the commanders of the army* (v. 25, Heb. plural; *cf.* LXX(L) singular, hence RSV supplies 'Joab the commander'; NEB 'commander-in-chief'). This may reflect Nathan's return to his former outspokenness (*cf.* 2 Sa. 12).

25. *Long live* the *King* (AV 'God save the king') was a public statement of acclamation and the climax of a coronation ceremony (as also in Babylon, *cf.* v. 34; and for Jehu and Jehoash, see 2 Ki. 9:13; 11:12). It also reaffirms loyalty to him (*cf.* v. 31).

D. David confirms Solomon as his successor (1:28–40)

Acceding to the pressure from Nathan and Bathsheba, David designates Solomon as his co-regent (*cf.* vv. 43–44, 47–48) to act as full regent during his sickness (vv. 46, 53). Such a practice was already common throughout Mesopotamia and Egypt.

29. The formal oath *As surely as the LORD* (Yahweh) *lives* is based on David's personal experience of divine deliverance

[1] W. L. Moran, 'New Evidence at Mari on the History of Prophecy', *Biblica* 50, 1969, p. 42.

(Heb. 'redeemed me', *cf.* 2 Sa. 4:9) and God's prior promise (see on v. 13).

32–33. David wisely takes prompt action which would render any continuing claim by Adonijah an act of rebellion. He knew the necessity of public support in a time of crisis. His wise orders included the use of his royal mount. Kings customarily rode on horses or mules as a status symbol (*cf.* 2 Sa. 13:29; Est. 6:8–9 and at Mari). A she-*mule* (Heb. *pirdâ*) was chosen to carry Solomon along the steep track to Gihon (*cf.* vv. 25, 33, *down*). Governors rode on white she-asses (Jdg. 5:10; 10:4), and the Messiah doing so would be interpreted as his coming as king and ruler (Zc. 9:9; Mt. 21:5). *Gihon*, in the Kidron valley east of Zion (modern Ain Umm ed-Daraj, identified with the 'mother of the step' or Miriam Spring), was perhaps chosen to counter Adonijah's meeting-place a kilometre off at En Rogel. There is no support for the view that any initial cleansing was part of the accession ritual for this first coronation of a king in Jerusalem.

34. Anointing was an essential part of the public act of consecration (1 Sa. 9:16) and was done by the high priest (the verb here and in v. 39 is singular) when direct, dynastic succession occurred (*cf.* 2 Ki. 11:12). Nathan was involved in authorizing the act. Prophets anointed those who were chosen by God as king in a new initiative and were not in the line of direct succession, such as Saul (1 Sa. 9:16), David (1 Sa. 16:13) and Jehu (2 Ki. 9:3). The blowing of the *trumpet* (*šôpār*) signalled a new reign (v. 39; 2 Ki. 11:14; 2 Sa. 15:10).

35. Solomon is designated a *ruler* (*nāgîd*), a title given to the charismatic leaders Saul (1 Sa. 9:16; 10:1) and David (2 Sa. 7:8). Here the term may merely mean, as it frequently does, one in a prominent position in government, military or religious affairs. It is not a term necessarily used of tribal militia leaders, or of a crown-prince[1] or 'prince' (as REB; *cf.* its use of the Messiah, Dn. 9:25).

36. Benaiah pledges the army's loyalty with *Amen!* ('confirmed'), as did Hittite soldiers when they swore their oath. Here it is a legal witness and endorsement of a statement (Dt. 27:15–26). There is no need to amend *declare* ('say') to 'do so' (as Gray) or 'become law' (*ya'ᵃmēn*, as LXX(L)). *Greater than ... David* is not just a pious wish for extended territory and power

---

[1] E. Lipiński, 'Le récit de 1 Rois xii.1–19 à la lumière de l'ancien usage de l'hébreu et de nouveaux textes de Mari', *VT* 24, 1974, pp. 447–449.

(*cf.* v. 47); it was fulfilled in Christ's rule, which is greater than Solomon's (Mt. 12:47).

38. *The Kerethites and the Pelethites* were a Philistinian element in David's independent bodyguard (2 Sa. 8:18). This included Cretans and men of minority groups, unless *Pelethites* is a form of *pᵉlištî* (Palestinians).[1]

39–40. *The horn of oil* (with definite article) was that kept in the tent temporarily housing the ark in Jerusalem (2 Sa. 6:17; 7:2). Anointing denoted consecration, not a specific covenant-relationship. *All the people* represents the democratic element participating in all Hebrew coronations rather than any formal assembly (see on 2 Ki. 23:1–3). The noisy celebrations included *playing flutes* or 'pipes' (AV, RSV), though others follow some MSS (LXX, Syr., Targ.) to read 'dancing with dances'. *The ground shook* or 'was split' (NRSV, REB) uses the terminology of reverberation associated with earthquakes known in this area (*cf.* Is. 6:4; 29:6; Zc. 14:5).

E. Adonijah's uprising fails (1:41–53)

Solomon's accession (vv. 35, 44) ended opposition, for if that continued it would be civil war and rebellion.

41. *Heard . . . as they were finishing their feast* could be 'heard and put an end to eating'. Joab, a military man, was alert to the trumpet, which was easily audible in Gihon,[2] and to the *noise* (like buzzing bees, *hômâ*; 'uproar', NRSV, REB) in the 'citadel' (*qiryâ*), rather than *city*.

42. *Jonathan* was the trusted messenger of David when Absalom rebelled (2 Sa. 15:36) and had remained in the city. He was a *worthy man* (*cf.* v. 52), *i.e.* 'honourable' (REB), a person of strength (*'îš ḥayil*) – mental, physical and in wealth.

43–48. In good narrative style this section repeats the instructions of verses 33–35a, 38–40. Jonathan's message was clear. The news was *not at all* good. 'Far from it' (NEB, REB; Heb. *'ăbāl*, 'No, but', is a strong adversative). The 'sound' or *noise* heard is explained as the popular reaction to Solomon's accession. The whole court administration (*royal officials*) had gathered to *congratulate* (Heb. 'bless') the king on accepting the dynastic principle of succession. David now had *a successor,*

[1] *POTT*, p. 56; Montgomery, p. 86.
[2] B. Cobbey Crisler, 'The Acoustics and Crowd Capacity of Natural Theatres in Palestine', *BA* 39, 1976, pp. 139–140.

'given today one to sit'; the Gk./Syr. adds 'of my seed', hence 'one of my offspring' (RSV).

49–53. Solomon's response. Since none dared to oppose an anointed ruler, Adonijah expected swift retaliation and sought asylum in the traditional way by clinging to the *horns of the altar* (v. 50, *cf.* Ex. 21:12–14; Nu. 35:6). The place of refuge is not stated but was probably in the tabernacle at Jerusalem (as LXX(L)) rather than at Gibeon. Horned altars have been found at Megiddo, Gezer, Beersheba and Dan.[1] The horns (Ex. 27:2) were used for tying the sacrificial victim. To grasp them was to claim the protection of God until the case was judged. This prevented excessive blood-revenge (Ex. 21:13). In the Middle Ages a church was called 'a sanctuary'.

Solomon exercised his new royal powers as co-regent, was acknowledged by Adonijah as *king* (v. 51), and issued a conditional pardon, swearing 'first (of all)' (RSV; *cf.* NIV *today*; REB 'here and now'; Heb. 'like the day') before witnesses and granting amnesty so long as Adonijah behaved honourably as a *worthy man* (v. 52); a 'man of worth' (NEB) means more than just 'like a gentleman' but one who did no 'evil'. Otherwise he would be put to death judicially (so *with the sword, cf.* 2:24–25). The order *Go to your home* (v. 53, 'house' RSV, REB) was not house-arrest, retirement from public life or banishment (as for Absalom in 2 Sa. 14:24) but an indication of agreement or reconciliation that was not total (otherwise 'in peace' would have been added, 2 Ki. 5:19).[2]

F. David's charge to Solomon (2:1–9)

By God-given requirement a ruler had to pass on his responsibilities to his successor (Dt. 17:18–20). Such final directives marked a transfer of leadership, as by Moses (Dt. 31:1–8), Joshua (Jos. 23:1–16) and Samuel (1 Sa. 12:1–25). David's political will or testament could well have been spoken (and written?) over an extended period (*cf.* 1 Ch. 28–29). Though David's charge includes personal encouragement (v. 2) and looks to future benefits for the individual and nation (v. 4),

---

[1] *IBD*, p. 35; A. Biran, 'An Israelite Horned Altar at Dan', *BA* 37, 1974, pp. 2–6, 106–107.
[2] See D. J. Wiseman, '"Is it peace?" – Covenant and Diplomacy', *VT* 32, 1982, pp. 311–326.

this is no artificial 'installation genre'.[1] The whole passage includes a summary of the then known Deuteronomic law on which Solomon's own rule and that of his successors would be judged.

The moral problem of removing rivals, even by judicial means, was not new; *cf.* David and the Gibeonites (2 Sa. 21). In failing to take action earlier, David was adopting temporary expedience which left unresolved the basic need to execute vengeance (vv. 32–33) and punish broken agreements (vv. 41–46), which were then obligations laid on a king.

Some argue that this is a later editorial way of exonerating Solomon from blame in taking part in a personal vendetta, by transferring the responsibility to David. Even if David and his house were treated as the historian's ideal, others see this as the writer's way of explaining how the promise of God's unending love and a succession 'for ever' (2 Sa. 7:15–16) was now limited by the failure of his sons to be faithful to God (*cf.* 1 Ki. 2:4; 11:11). It could equally be interpreted as David's concern to pass on the dynasty clear of blood-guilt and curse. The examples chosen then show justice, which hitherto had been neglected (Joab, vv. 5–6), the need for compassion (Barzillai, v. 7) and the requirement of discipline when a royal order or solemn agreement is disobeyed (Shimei, vv. 8–9).

i. Walking in the LORD's ways (2:1–4). The 'last charge' (NEB) was common practice (2 Ki. 20:1; *cf.* Gn. 49:29; Acts 20:18–35). David was well aware of his mortality and impending death (*go the way of all the earth, i.e.* must die). His words of exhortation were reminiscent of Joshua (1:1–9), perhaps his hero as a military leader, and of the laws, with frequent references to Deuteronomy (*e.g.* 8:6, 10–12). The urge to *be strong* is to be steadfast mentally, physically and spiritually (Dt. 31:7, 23) and to act manfully (*cf.* 1 Cor. 16:13).

The basis of all action will be the keeping of God's law, expressed in service (v. 3, *mišmeret,* what God *requires*; Dt. 11:1, *cf.* Gn. 26:5) undertaken loyally as an obligation. The new king's manner of life is to *walk in* God's *ways* and so conduct himself in obedience to every covenant obligation (REB 'duty', so Dt. 5:33 and *passim*). To do this God's *decrees* (declared 'statutes' RSV) must be upheld (Dt. 6:2, *etc.*) and every one of

[1] As suggested by D. J. McCarthy, 'An Installation Genre?', *JBL* 90, 1971, pp. 31–41.

his *commands, laws* and *requirements* kept and passed on. Only in this way will king and nation *prosper* (Dt. 29:9; *śākal* is to discern, gain insight and then prosper; RSV stresses this). This is no doctrine of believing in order to prosper economically, but a call to act wisely with any attendant benefits. This was to be a special characteristic of Solomon (3:28; Mt. 12:42), as of all godly men. In Israel the king was never the source of law but rather under it, for the covenant law was imposed on king and people alike. God's promise is conditional on whether or not Solomon's successors *watch how they live* (Heb. 'guard their (right) way of life') by 'walking before God in truth' (NIV *faithfully*). 'Walk before God' is the Deuteronomic phrase most commonly found in 1 Kings (3:6; 8:23, 25; 9:4, *etc.*), but the same idea is conveyed by the more common 'walk to and fro before God', *i.e.* conduct your life in the presence of God (Heb. *hiṯhallēḵ*).[1]

ii. Retribution on Joab (2:5–6). The problem of David's 'legacy of blood' can only be resolved by determining responsibility. If Joab shed innocent *blood* in peacetime as if it were war (*i.e.* 'blood of war', v. 5; *cf.* Dt. 19:1–13; 21:1–9), then it was not justifiable homicide (*cf.* 2 Sa. 2:18–23). He may well have acted out of treachery, involved in a family feud resulting from his murder of Abner (2 Sa. 3:19–30), rather than in self-defence. He murdered Amasa out of jealousy rather than in vengeance for delay or disloyalty to David (2 Sa. 20:8–10). Thus the MT (and NIV) makes Joab guilty (*his waist . . . his feet*). Others, less probably, assign the guilt to David (after LXX(L)); the Old Latin reading was 'my waist . . . my feet' (RSV, NEB, JB, REB, NRSV; see above).

6. *Wisdom* is discernment and ability in judgment (3:9), based on a wide knowledge of the world (4:29–34) as well as common sense in choosing the right time for action (as here). To *go down to the grave* (Heb. Sheol, 'underworld') in old age (*grey head*) was the preferred ideal. *In peace* is not just 'unscathed' (as Gray) but in covenant accord with God and man (see on 2 Ki. 5:19; 22:20, *cf.* Gn. 15:15). The Hebrews, like their neighbours, had no clear or comfortable view of the

[1] On the legal aspects of this phrase as indicating the act of exercising justice under God see D. J. Wiseman, *Essays on the Patriarchal Narratives* (Leicester: IVP, 1980), p. 147, n. 31 and *Nebuchadrezzar and Babylon* (Oxford: British Academy, 1985), pp. 21–24.

place of death (Sheol), thought to be entered through the dark and dusty underworld of the grave. David was wrong in passing on responsibility to Solomon to execute the judgment he himself should have ordered at the time. This was to cause his son and successors much trouble and feuding. The Hebrew law makes it clear that while the judgment for a parent's wrong actions may well fall upon the children (Dt. 5:9), offspring should not be put to death for it (Dt. 24:16).

iii. Kindness to Barzillai (2:7). In acting judicially there is always a place for kindness. Barzillai had supplied David when he was in exile (2 Sa. 17:27–29), and that, as all hospitality, should be repaid. *Show kindness* (NIV; JB 'treat kindly'; NEB 'show constant friendship with') denotes loyal deeds done to keep covenant requirements (hence RSV 'deal loyally with'). Barzillai's family (including his son Kimham, 2 Sa. 19:37) had acted as any neighbour should and had *stood by* David (NIV; AV 'they came (near) to me'). To *eat at* the king's *table* was the equivalent of having a pension, the beneficiary receiving a regular royal allowance of food and clothing, with a house and land to support him and his family (*cf.* 2 Sa. 9:7; 1 Ki. 18:19; 2 Ki. 25:29–30).[1]

iv. Retribution on Shimei (2:8–9). Shimei, whose ancestor Gera is named (Gn. 46:21; *cf.* Jdg. 3:15) and whose home town was Bahurim, north of Bethany, had uttered 'grievous curses' (AV; NIV *bitter*) against the LORD's anointed king. This was a capital offence (Ex. 22:28; 1 Ki. 21:10), but David on oath had failed to remove the curse which still threatened. So Solomon was firmly directed to find Shimei 'not guiltless' (AV, RSV; *cf.* NIV *innocent*). Heb. *nqh* means to 'exempt from punishment' (*cf.* REB 'not go unpunished') or 'free from oath'. To *bring down . . . in blood* is a direct incitement to impose the death penalty (vv. 34–36).

G. David is succeeded by Solomon (2:10–12)

The end of David's reign is marked by the formulaic details used by the historian to describe the end of each king, *i.e.* burial, length and place of reign and succession (see

---

[1] D. J. Wiseman, *Nebuchadrezzar and Babylon*, pp. 32–33.

Introduction). *Forty years* may be a general expression for the equivalent of a generation (*cf.* 2 Sa. 5:4–5). On *rested with his fathers* see 1:21. David's tomb in Zion (Ophel) was known in Peter's day (Acts 2:29), but its precise location is uncertain. NEB (following a few MSS) makes verse 11 introduce 12ff., but editorial practice weighs against this, as the statement of the length of reign at various capitals (*cf.* 16:23) was part of the closing formula.

H. Solomon exacts retribution (2:13–46)

Solomon's removal of opponents who conspired against him is taken to be the necessary and customary establishment of the Davidic kingdom (v. 12, *cf.* v. 46). It marks the end of David's reign (vv. 1–9) and the beginning of that of Solomon. The reprisals are presented as a legal process which required a king to punish rebels (1:52), murderers, political assassins and those who broke solemnly sworn agreements. The proper outcome was foreseen by David, who had left his son to use his own discretion (vv. 6, 9) in making the judicial decisions. Discretion and compassion were also to be exercised (vv. 7, 26–27). Solomon's action may not necessarily be taken as wise, for it led to divisions which lasted throughout the Davidic dynasty.

i. Adonijah (2:13–25). Adonijah's reprieve had depended on his doing no evil, *i.e.* rebellion (1:52). His request for Abishag was interpreted as making a claim to the throne by Solomon (v. 22), despite his (possibly sincere) acceptance that he had been 'passed over' (NEB) and that 'the kingdom had turned about' (RSV), *i.e. things* had *changed* in favour of his brother, and that the LORD was the author of it (v. 15).

It is difficult to judge whether Bathsheba's action as intermediary was a plot or due to sympathy for her own son (vv. 20–21). Her position as queen mother was respected (v. 19, *the king stood up*) and powerful. A *throne* (seat) at the right hand of the king was a place of honour (Ps. 110:1; Heb. 1:3; 10:12; 1 Pet. 3:22).

22. The fear that Adonijah might be claiming the throne again on the basis of primogeniture (1:5), with priestly and army support and requesting a known royal concubine or wife to legitimize this (see on 1:2–3, 15, *cf.* 2 Sa. 3:6–7; 16:20–22), swayed Solomon.

23. Solomon's decision to impose the death penalty is pronounced with a solemn oath in the name of God (Yahweh). It involved his own death ('God do so to me', *i.e.* kill me) and that of others if he failed to make it a matter of life and death. *God deal with me . . .* (NIV) brings out the sense well (NEB 'so help me God'). The oath claimed divine sanction for the judgment and the promise that the dynasty was securely his (v. 24, Heb.; *cf.* NRSV, RSV), for 'He has made me a house' by the birth of a son, Rehoboam (*cf.* 11:43; 14:22), just as God had promised David (v. 4; 1 Ch. 22:9–10).

ii. Abiathar the Priest (2:26–27). Abiathar had to be dealt with for his support of Adonijah (1:7; 2:22). The ground for clemency was his association with the Levites and David (2 Sa. 15:24, 29; *cf.* 1 Sa. 22:20–23). This rules against the theory that this is editorial comment disapproving the priestly practices (such as the use of the ephod), which is not stated here, but rather it is taken by the historian as the fulfilment of prophecy against Eli's successors (1 Sa. 2:31–33). The distinction between Levitical priests and the Zadokites (by some taken as Jebusite in origin) was of long pre-exilic standing (see also on 2 Ki. 23:8–9).[1] From now until 171 BC (2 Macc. 4:24) the Zadokite family held sway as high priests. Abiathar was confined to Anathoth (Anata), now identified with Deir es-Sid about six kilometres north-north-east of Jerusalem, as against Ras al Harrubeh,[2] where priests lived when not doing service in Jerusalem (Jos. 21:1–3, 18; Je. 1:1).

iii. Joab (2:28–35). Joab had *conspired with* (RSV 'supported') Adonijah (*cf.* 1:7) and knew what to expect. The right of asylum in the sanctuary applied only to those involved in accidental death, not intentional homicide (Ex. 21:13–14), and LXX interestingly adds a question of Solomon to Joab, asking why he had fled there. Punishment for murder is essential (Dt. 5:17), and Solomon realizes that responsibility for the death rested on Joab himself ('on his head') and not on David and his house (vv. 31–33). This precludes the interpretation that the historian is trying to whitewash Solomon by putting the blame back on David. Joab had murdered two

[1] J. G. McConville, 'Priests and Levites in Ezekiel', *TynB* 34, 1983, pp. 4–5.
[2] M. Biran, 'On the identification of Anathoth', *Eretz-Israel* 18, 1985, pp. 209–214.

men (v. 33; 2 Sa. 3:27; 20:9–10). Thus his death was to be a divine retribution through judicial punishment. 'Repaying blood' was an act of God not involving a blood-feud,[1] so 'the guilt of their blood shall recoil upon Joab' (NEB, *cf.* Gn. 9:6; Ps. 79:10) and not on David's house, even though David's men were to be the instrument of effecting Joab's death.

34. *Cf.* verse 31. To be left unburied was a dishonour and a shame on the victim and his family (1 Ki. 13:22; Je. 16:6), and uncovered violent bloodshed was thought to cry out for vengeance (Gn. 4:10–11). Even criminals were buried (Dt. 21:23), as was Joab in his own property (NIV, Heb. 'house') and Samuel (1 Sa. 25:1). This was common practice, here probably in or near the tomb of his father near Bethlehem (2 Sa. 2:32) at 'the edge of the desert wilderness' (NEB) or 'out in the country' (REB).

iv. Shimei (2:36–46). To complete David's will Solomon had finally to eliminate Shimei, a member of the Benjaminite tribe and related to Saul, who had cursed king David. David had temporarily spared him (2 Sa. 16:5–16) but asked for judgment to be passed by Solomon (vv. 8–9). Solomon restricted Shimei to Jerusalem to cut him off from his estates in Bahurim (on the east slopes of Mount Scopus) and so prevent him plotting with fellow-Benjaminites against the throne. This was done by an agreement on oath by Shimei (*good* implies a formal agreement, *cf.* vv. 42–43). Solomon waited until Shimei broke this covenant by going to Philistia to retrieve his runaway slaves. The mutual return of fugitives was commonly allowed in interstate treaties (as in Alalakh text No. 3 and Ugarit),[2] and some special clause to that effect could have been made when David had been in exile with Achish (1 Sa. 27:2–7). Maacah is a common name, so this Achish may be a successor with the same name as his grandfather. But pressing circumstances should not have made Shimei forget his obligations. The historian again implies that the victim brought judgment from God upon

[1] R. Yaron, 'A Ramesside Parallel', *VT* Supp, 1958, pp. 432–433.
[2] W. F. Albright, 'New Canaanite Historical and Mythological Data', *BASOR* 63, 1936, p. 24; F. C. Fensham, 'The Treaty between Solomon and Hiram and the Alalakh Tablets', *JBL* 79, 1960, pp. 59–60; D. J. Wiseman, *The Alalakh Tablets* (London: British Institute of Archaeology at Ankara, 1953), No. 3, p. 31.

himself and that Solomon was administering the law wisely.

46. The statement reaffirming the establishment of Solomon's kingdom after three years of rule is a link with that ending David's reign (v. 12). Since no kingdom is ever successfully established apart from observance of God's law (1 Sa. 13:13), this verse is a fitting introduction to Solomon's reign.

II. THE REIGN OF SOLOMON (1 Ki. 3:1 – 11:43)

The emphasis throughout is on Solomon's God-given wisdom (3:1–15) and his use of the gift to show that he was God's man (3:16–28). Such wisdom included ability in administration in affairs economic (4:1–19), social and military (4:20–28) as well as in learning and in culture (4:29–34). It enhanced his international standing (4:34) and was the basis for the preparation (5:13–18) and execution of work on the temple (6:1 – 9:9). The historian records Solomon's other activities (9:10–28) and describes the splendours of his kingdom, which are internationally acknowledged by the Queen of Sheba (10:1–13) and listed in detail (10:14–29). The characteristics of Solomon's wisdom and glory were not selected just to continue the picture of an ideal king by showing him in a favourable light. Throughout, and in the epilogue on his reign (11:1–13, 33), the history comments on its deficiencies in theological terms. A similar appraisal will be used to judge successive rulers against the reigns of David and Solomon. The sources for these episodes could well be the Acts (*annals*) of Solomon (11:41–42), which were court reports, records of legal cases and administrative state and temple archives of a kind known to have been kept by all contemporary kingdoms.

A. Solomon's wisdom (3:1 – 4:34)

The situation at the outset of Solomon's rule is briefly covered under three headings: (a) political, (b) economic (v. 2) and (c) religious (v. 3). The outworking will be shown later by the historian, who emphasizes the part played by wisdom (see Additional Note). Such wisdom is the hallmark of a just king, and his God-inspired reign will be authenticated by the acquisition (vv. 1–15) and exercise of it (vv. 16–17).

i. Wisdom given and displayed (3:1–28)

***a. A foreword to the reign (3:1–3).* 1.** Solomon 'became the son-in-law' (*ḥātān*)[1] of the Egyptian king. David might have initiated this diplomatic alliance, the first of several 'dynastic marriages' Solomon was to make to increase his power (see on ch. 11). Such arranged marriages were a common confirmation of international treaties, but this one was the beginning of Solomon's spiritual downfall. It illustrates the dangers of action based on political expediency alone, and it was also contrary to the law, since it meant the acquisition of foreign gods (*cf.* Dt. 31:16; 1 Ki. 11:1–6).

If this anticipates 1 Kings 9:16–17; 14:25 the pharaoh could have been Shishak (XXI Dynasty). More likely it was Siamūn (978–959)[2] or his successor Psusennes II (959–945). By this time marriage between an Egyptian king's daughter and a foreigner is known. Solomon was already the husband of an Ammonitess and had a son (14:24; *cf.* 11:42–43).

The capital ('City of David') now occupied the hill of Zion (Ophel) and expanded northwards only when Solomon *finished building* his palace (7:1–2), the temple (6:38) and the city wall (9:15).

2. The *Name* identifies the person(ality), presence and fame. For the Name of the LORD see on 5:3.

3. Solomon is judged by standards set out in the law (Dt. 6:5), *e.g.* his *love for the LORD* (referring to loyalty to the covenant)[3] and his manner of life. Historically he followed his father, but like him he failed (*cf.* 15:5). *Except* introduces the continued use of high places (see Additional Note). This practice will be taken by the historian to condemn subsequent reigns.

Additional Note on high places

High places (Heb. *bāmāh*, usually plural *bāmôṯ*); not necessarily connected with Ugar. *bmt, cf.* Akkad. *bamtu,* 'open country'.

[1] T. C. Mitchell, *VT* 19, 1969, p. 93; *TDOT* V, pp. 270–277.

[2] K. A. Kitchen, *The Third Intermediate Period in Egypt (100–600 B.C.)* (London: Aris & Phillips, 1972), pp. 273–274, 280–283.

[3] W. J. Moran, 'The Ancient Near Eastern Background of the Love of God in Deuteronomy', *CBQ* 25, 1963, pp. 77–87; D. J. Wiseman, *The Vassal-Treaties of Esarhaddon* (London: British School of Archaeology in Iraq, 1958), pp. 49–50, lines 266–268.

These were local cult or sacred places, often in the form of a flat rock-hewn platform with an altar or place of sacrifice. Sometimes they were located on a height (*cf.* Nu. 22:41; 1 Sa. 9:13), as those found at Megiddo and Arad, while others were on low ground within towns (2 Ki. 17:29, Jerusalem, Hazor, Dan) or even in a valley (Je. 7:31). The term appears to have been used for different types of local shrines used for various purposes. While some may have originally been Canaanite shrines taken over after the Israelite conquest and used as places for sacrifice and festivals (1 Sa. 9; 10:5), others seem to have been used for the worship of Yahweh (2 Ch. 33:17). The tabernacle and true altar were located at first at the 'Great High Place' at Gibeon (1 Ki. 3; 2 Ch. 1).

Most high places were primarily rustic or small 'gate'-shrines (Tirzah and Dan) furnished with idols (2 Ch. 33:19), Asherah-poles, standing stones, or altars dedicated to pagan deities (11:7). Some may have held 'tent' shrines in the old patriarchal tradition (2 Ki. 21:3), or been furnished with small buildings or houses (sometimes interpreted as 'temples') for keeping sacred vessels, thus serving a more public function. Any association with a ritual which might include human sacrifice is not well attested (but *cf.* Je. 19:5; 32:35).

These places posed a threat to the pure worship of Yahweh, and after the building of the central temple in Jerusalem most references to them are pejorative, for they represented conflicting loyalty and competing allegiance. Israelites were expressly forbidden to use such places in their worship of God (Dt. 7:5; 12:3), who might, however, sanction the erection and use of special altars there (Ex. 20:24; Dt. 12:6–14). Beginning with Solomon's reign, the toleration of high places led to syncretistic worship and apostasy. So the 'high place' became synonymous with an abomination, and its use or abuse is noted by the historian and marked out as condemning a sinful king (*e.g.* 2 Ki. 17:7–18; 23:4–25).[1] High places were set up by other kings: *e.g.* Mesha' of Moab 'built a high place for the God Chemosh in Qarhoh' (Moabite stone, line 3).[2]

---

[1] Provan (pp. 62–66) argues unconvincingly that the judgment formulae show toleration of the high places and yet that in Jeroboam's sin and Baal worship the high place was 'correct in content but illegitimate in terms of where it was practised'.

[2] *IBD*, pp. 1016–1017.

b. The gift of wisdom (3:4–15). **4.** *Gibeon* (El-Jīb, ten kilometres north-west of Jerusalem) as *the most important high place* or 'chief shrine' (REB) was the site of the tabernacle and altar after the sack of Shiloh (1 Ch. 21:29; 2 Ch. 1:2–6). Some would identify it with Saul's capital (which was not at Tell el-Fūl) or with Mizpah of Benjamin. It was a former Levite sanctuary (Jos. 18:25; 21:7). *A thousand* can be used as a generalization ('very many', Dt. 1:11; 2 Ch. 1:6). Nevertheless it indicates that Solomon provided the offerings and did not himself act as a priest in sacrificing them (*cf.* 8:62–63; 2 Sa. 6:14; 24:25).

5. The result of a night vision. Hebrew does not differentiate between dream, vision or epiphany. Revelation from God through dreams is well attested among the Hebrews (Gn. 26:24; 28:10–17; Jdg. 7:13; 1 Sa. 3; 28:6; Dn. 2:4; 7:1) and in the New Testament (Mt. 1:20; 2:13, 22), as in surrounding nations. In Egypt (the 'royal novel')[1] and Babylonia such visions authenticate a reign and form part of the divine call to the new ruler. They are here not necessarily evidence of foreign influence.[2]

God's request, 'Ask whatever you want', and promise, 'I will give you' (v. 5), are always to stimulate faith (Mt. 21:22; Mk. 6:22; Jn. 14:13–14; Jas. 1:6). Promises of a plentiful answer or victory are also given in coronation rituals (*cf.* Pss. 2:8; 20:4–5).[3]

i. Solomon's prayer (3:6–9). This has four elements:

(i) It acknowledges God's past action. *Kindness* (NIV) is too weak a rendering of Heb. *ḥeseḏ* – 'steadfast love' or 'loving-kindness'. Faithfulness, righteousness and uprightness are the required response to God's covenant, in which he pledges himself to a similar relationship.

(ii) It asks for the continuance of God's favour. The language is that of Deuteronomy (7:6, 9, 12; 9:5). The response is shown by divinely given wisdom (see Additional Note) and *discernment* (*bînâ*, vv. 9, 11–12), reminiscent of the Messianic passages of Isaiah (11:2) which were fulfilled in Christ (1 Cor. 1:30).

[1] *Cf. ANET*, p. 449.
[2] C. H. W. Brekelmans, 'Solomon at Gibeon', in *Von Kanaan bis Kerala, AOAT* 211, 1982, pp. 53–59.
[3] A. K. Grayson, *Babylonian Historical-Literary Texts* (Toronto: University of Toronto Press, 1975), p. 85, lines 4–7.

(iii) It expresses humility. *I am only a little child* (v. 7) shows this (*cf.* Je. 1:6; Mt. 18:4) and confesses lack of experience. Heb. and AV 'how to go out and come in' means to possess leadership qualities or to manage business (Nu. 27:17; Dt. 31:2; Ps. 121:8), hence *carry out my duties*. A prayer we all need to make.

(iv) It asks for the ability to carry out his duties. The people were 'a heavy people', *i.e.* an onerous responsibility (v. 8). As promised to Abraham (Gn. 22:17–18), they were now numerous, *too numerous to count*.

9. The attitude of heart or mind which listens to and obeys God is the foundation of all true wisdom (Pr. 9:10). This results in 'a heart with a skill to listen' (NEB; Heb. 'a hearing heart'; NIV *a discerning heart*) able to distinguish right and wrong and to decide and *govern* (AV 'judge'). The *heart* (Heb. *lēḇ*) includes mind and will and is not the seat of the emotions, for in Hebrew thought compassion emanates from the 'bowels' (see v. 26).

Additional Note on wisdom

Solomon is portrayed as the ideal 'wise' king who demonstrated 'wisdom' (*ḥokmâ*) in its many aspects. Wisdom covers all human experience. It includes 'understanding' (*bînâ*), 'insight' (*tᵉḇûnâ*) and 'intelligence'. Rightly used, it brings success and prosperity (*śākal*). These synonyms of wisdom, with 'knowledge' (*yādāh*), are qualities required in leadership, as shown by David (1 Sa. 18:14) and the Messiah (Je. 23:5; 1 Cor. 1:24). True wisdom is the creative gift of God, of whom it is an attribute (Jb. 12:13; Pr. 3:19).

Wisdom is the right understanding of reality and is the basis of moral and ethical life (Jb. 11:6; Pr. 2:6). It is expressed in the conduct of life in the 'fear (reverence, awe) of the LORD', which is its chief origin and aim (Jb. 28:28; Pr. 1:7, *etc.*). It arises from an attitude of heart or mind (1 Ki. 3:7, 12) and is expressed also in prudence in secular affairs. Wisdom marks technical skills and craftsmanship (Ex. 25:3; 31:3, 6). It is also demonstrated by ability in judgment between right and wrong (1 Ki. 3; 4:28) and its application in good administration (1 Ki. 10:4, 24; *cf.* Joseph: Ps. 105:16–22; Acts 7:10).

Wisdom has to be taught and passed on (Dt. 34:9) and is the main subject of Solomon's collection in the Book of Proverbs.

Solomon, like the academic 'wise men' of contemporary Mesopotamian and Egyptian courts, learned scribal skills and those genres of literature (so-called 'Wisdom Literature') which taught life and nature, ethical and aesthetic values and general behaviour (1 Ki. 4:32). These included serious discussions ('The Righteous Sufferer') and didactic works of all kinds. Among these, scribal reference texts listing natural and philosophical subjects can be compared, in literary form, with the biblical books of Job, Psalms, Proverbs, Ecclesiastes and the Song of Solomon.[1] In the Old Testament wisdom is personified (Pr. 9:1–6) and the knowledge of God in relation to it is stressed (Pr. 2:6; 9:10).

ii. The LORD answers (3:10–15). **11.** *Long life* ('Many days for yourself'), *wealth* (AV 'riches'), victory over enemies ('soul of enemies') and *honour* (v. 13, outward splendour) are typical marks of a great king (*cf.* Pr. 3:16; 21:21 and ancient Near Eastern texts). Such requests are not wrong in themselves. *Long life* (v. 14) may be a reward for keeping God's way (Ex. 20:12; Ps. 91:16). Extension of days may sometimes be given for us to carry out God's plan for us (*cf.* Hezekiah, 2 Ki. 20:5–6). *Wealth* too may be a mark of God's blessing (Ps. 112:3), the result of wisdom (Pr. 14:24), the reward of humility (Pr. 22:4) and of hard work (Pr. 10:4; 14:23), befitting a king (1 Ki. 10:23). The danger of possessions is a wrong attitude to and use of them (Pr. 28:20; Je. 9:23–24; 1 Cor. 1:29–30). The LORD often adds what has not been asked for (Mt. 6:33; Lk. 12:31). Solomon is still remembered for what God gave (wisdom) and added (wealth and glory) beyond his imagining (*cf.* Eph. 3:20). His was no long life by our standards (he died when about sixty years old, 11:42), for he failed to fulfil the divine requirement of verse 14.

15. Solomon passed on the revelation. He acknowledged the new close relationship between himself, the worshipper, and God by offering *fellowship offerings* (NEB 'shared-offerings'; RSV, AV 'peace offerings'; Lv. 7:15–17) rendered

---

[1] W. G. Lambert, *Babylonian Wisdom Literature* (Oxford: Clarendon Press, 1960); E. I. Gordon, 'A New Look at the Wisdom of Sumer and Akkad', *Bi.Or.* 17, 1960, pp. 122–152; Egyptian wisdom (*s3r.t*) is similarly expressed in 'truth' (*ma'at*, 'intelligence, justice'); J. A. Wilson, *The Culture of Ancient Egypt* (Chicago: University of Chicago Press, 1951), p. 48; for bibliography see *TWOT*, p. 284 and translations of Didactic and Wisdom Literature in *ANET*, pp. 405–440.

out of thankfulness on the completion of a work or for a restored relationship (*cf.* Lv. 7:11–17). That Solomon *stood before* (*i.e.* served/worshipped at) the covenant-ark may represent his customary habit before the ark was installed in the new temple (8:1–9). Solomon made his a public testimony of his relationship as king with God as well as that of a king with his people and confirmed it (as in coronation rites) through a *feast* (*e.g.* 'bread and wine').

c. An example of Solomon's God-given wisdom (3:16–28).

Ancient Mesopotamian kings kept records of exceptional legal decisions which were presented to their deity as a report that they had acted wisely as 'a just king'.[1] The detailed written arguments in such cases have survived and Israel appears to have followed a similar practice. The evidence of both parties is presented as orally given (vv. 16–22) and the king sums up (v. 23).

Solomon's wisdom lay in his use of his God-given discerning mind. He saw that the threat of death to the child would reveal the true mother's feelings in an urgent appeal against it (vv. 24–26). He pronounces his decision in brief form ('he responded [to the evidence] and made a declaration'; *cf.* NIV *gave his ruling*, v. 27).

This incident is cited here as an example of Solomon's judicial wisdom. Though it is a type with worldwide parallels, the circumstantial evidence given means that it is not 'late and legendary'.[2] The oppressed had direct access to the king, a privilege exercised especially in matters of inheritance (2 Ki. 8:3). A royal decision was taken to be the equivalent of the divine word and was so accepted (Pr. 16:10). When witnesses differed, sacral methods for guidance (Urim and Thummim) were now no longer used (*cf.* 1 Sa. 28:6). Some take this as part of an argument that Solomon was more concerned with administration than was David, who was preoccupied with war (5:17–19).

---

[1] *E.g.* the Laws of Hammurapi. D. J. Wiseman, 'Law and Order in OT Times', *Vox Evangelica* 8, 1973, pp. 9–10.
[2] *Cf.* R. B. Y. Scott, 'Solomon and the Beginnings of Wisdom in Israel', *VT*Supp 3, 1955, pp. 262–279, takes it as a post-Hezekiah literary phenomenon, but *cf.* the contemporary Egyptian 'royal protocol'.

16. *Prostitutes*, Heb. *zônôṯ*, could equally refer to inn-keepers (so Targum; *cf.* Rahab, Jos. 2:1).[1]

26. *Filled with compassion* (Heb. 'her bowels grew hot', *cf.* AV). In popular Hebrew psychology the 'bowels' (liver), as compared with our 'heart', were thought to be the seat of the emotions (so Heb., Gn. 43:20; Jb. 30:27; Gk. 'spleen', Phil. 1:8; 2:1; 1 Jn. 3:17).

28. The judgment (*mišpāṭ*; NIV *verdict*) is cited as the basis of *awe* at the king's supernatural wisdom, which had a spiritual quality (*cf.* 1 Cor. 1:17, 24–25; Eph. 1:17) that should be the mark of every godly leader (Acts 6:3).

ii. Solomon's wisdom in administration (4:1–34). Solomon's wisdom is now shown to encompass his administration of state affairs, including his choice of cabinet members (4:1–6) and district governors (vv. 7–19) and his reordering of business to control palace and temple supplies, taxes and labour (vv. 20–28). The historian then summarizes the exceptional quality and breadth of the royal wisdom, which embraced international culture and learning (vv. 29–34). See the Additional Note on wisdom (p. 85).

a. Solomon's high officials (4:1–6). For such lists *cf.* 1 Chronicles 18:15–17; 2 Samuel 8:15–18; 20:23–36. Every king made personal appointments to his court and army command. Solomon shows continuity with the policy of David by employing Benaiah son of Jehoiada and Adoniram son of Abda and by the inclusion of his sons-in-law (Ben-Abinadab, v. 11, Ahimaaz, v. 15), nephews (Azariah and Zabud) and close supporters. The grandson of Zadok continued that priestly family influence. Though the emphasis may be on his concern for a united kingdom ('all Israel'), as it was under David (2 Sa. 8:15), Solomon's inclusion of an official in charge of new districts which broke across traditional tribal areas and of one person in charge of forced labour led to a reorganization which sowed the seed for the rupture between the Northern Kingdom and Judah which was to follow.

2. *Chief officials* (RSV 'high officials', REB 'officials', Heb. *śārîm*) is preferable to AV 'princes', for this now designated the top-grade court officials (as Egypt. *śr.w*).[2] *Azariah* was grandson of

[1] D. J. Wiseman, 'Rahab of Jericho', *TynB* 14, 1964, pp. 8–11.
[2] T. N. D. Mettinger, *Solomonic State Officials* (Lund: Gleerup, 1971).

Zadok and son of Ahimaaz (1 Ch. 6:9; 2 Sa. 15:29, 36). *Elihoreph* may be an indication that those of foreign birth (Canaanites?) were included (*cf.* Hurrian personal name E(h)liarip). NEB 'in charge of the calendar' is based on changing the text to 'over the (autumn) year' (*'al-haḥôrep̄*). But the Hebrews, unlike the Assyrian eponyms (*limmu*), never named the new year in this way with the names of officials. Moreover, the beginning of the new year in the autumn is probably unattested (see note on 2 Ki. 25:8).

3. 'Scribe' (*spr*) or *secretary* (NIV) was a professional title ranging from humble writer to Secretary of State. Here the existence of two officials may mean that one covered foreign and one home affairs or, as illustrated in Assyria,[1] that they used different methods or languages when keeping records. NEB 'adjutant-general' emphasizes their principal administrative role based on keeping lists (*spr*). *Jehoshaphat*, who had served under David (2 Sa. 8:16; 20:24), continued as *recorder* (*mazkîr*). As such he was more a chief of protocol[2] than a 'remembrancer' or recorder of the past. His status was almost that of a Secretary of State (NEB).

4. *Zadok and Abiathar* may be the persons of the same names as in 2 Samuel 8:17; 20:28 and not, as some argue, just taken from David's list there.

5. *Nathan* is a common name, but could be that of the son of David (2 Sa. 5:14–15) rather than the prophet (1:11). The office of superintendent of the district officers (vv. 8–19) or 'regional governors' (NEB) was introduced by Solomon to aid his reforms. The 'King's Friend' or *personal adviser to the king* (like our Privy Counsellor) was an office last held by Hushai (2 Sa. 15:37; 16:16). The position is also referred to in Amarna (Canaanite) texts.

6. *Ahishar* was *in charge of the palace* (Heb. 'he who is over the house'), *i.e.* he was 'controller of the (royal) household' and estates (NEB). In time this office increases in prestige to that of prime minister (1 Ki. 16:9; 18:3; 2 Ki. 10:5; 15:5; 18:18–37).[3] Some Gk. MSS add 'Eliab, son of Joab over the army'. *Adoniram* may be the same as David's appointee to the same office (2 Sa.

[1] *IBD*, p. 412.
[2] R. J. Williams, 'A people come out of Egypt', *VT*Supp 28, 1975, p. 235.
[3] This official title appears on the tomb inscription of Shebna (Is. 36:3, 22; *IBD*, p. 1431) and on the seal of Gedaliah from Lachish (2 Ki. 25:22; *IBD*, p. 545).

20:24), who even survived to Rehoboam's time (1 Ki. 12:18, but there read 'Adoram'?). For the part played by *forced labour* (Heb. *mas*,[1] as Alalakh *masu*) in focusing opposition to the regime see 1 Kings 5:13–18; 9:15–22.

b. Solomon's administrative districts (4:7–19). The new sub-divisions helped to centralize control of taxation and the levy for labour-service. The system appears to have been a Solomonic development and not dependent on Egyptian influence.[2] Solomon tried to preserve tribal regions as far as possible (I, II, X, XI), to incorporate adjacent recently occupied old Canaanite areas (II, IV, V) and to make adjustments to bring foreign elements into the kingdom (VI, VII, IX, XII). See the map opposite. The plan was not directed to exploit the roughly equal economic potential of each area, nor deliberately to undermine the independence of tribal families, especially of the 'house of Joseph'. The new system developed from earlier practice and was basically to remain unchanged till the end of the divided kingdoms. The geographical presentation is roughly in the order of the centre (I – V), Transjordan (VI – VII), the north (VIII – X) and the south (XI – XII).[3]

Variations and abbreviations in the personal names have been taken as marking a broken right-hand edge on the original text, or that those given only their father's name (*Ben* = 'son of') held hereditary office.[4] Such administrative lists are attested from earlier times at Mari and elsewhere. The brief geographical details may have been intended not to define precise boundaries but to indicate prominent tribal names or places associated with each tax-district.

8. I. *Ben-Hur*. The hill-country of Ephraim included part of Manasseh to the plain of Jezreel.

---

[1] *Cf.* the seal 'of Pela'yahu who is in charge of forced labour' (N. Avigad, 'The Chief of the Corvée', *IEJ* 30, 1980, pp. 170–173); pl. 18, D–6 (reading *lpl'yhw 'šr 'l hms*; the reverse associates Pel'ayah with one Mattiyah(u), *lpl'yh w mttyhw*).

[2] D. B. Redford, 'Studies in relations between Palestine and Egypt', in J. W. Wevers and D. B. Redford (eds.), *Studies on the Ancient Palestinian World* (Toronto: University of Toronto Press, 1972), pp. 141–156, who argues that Solomon's taxation system was not Egyptian but local in origin.

[3] Mettinger, *op. cit.*, pp. 120–121; *cf.* N. Na'aman, *Borders and Districts in Biblical Historiography* (Jerusalem: Simor, 1986), pp. 167–201.

[4] Mettinger, *ibid.*

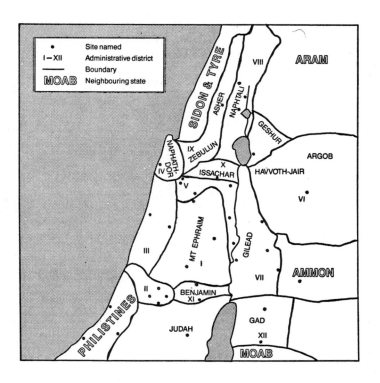

Solomon's Administrative Districts

9. II. *Ben-Deker.* East Shephelah, south-east Ephraim, former Dan territory (Jdg. 1:35). This was marked to the east by *Makaz*, unknown unless identified with Khirbet el-Mikezim, seventeen kilometres north-west of Beth-Shemesh. *Shaalbim* (modern Selbît) to the north in the Ayalon valley (*cf.* Jos. 19:42; Jdg. 1:35). *Beth Shemesh* (Tell er-Rumeilah) to the south, twenty-four kilometres west of Jerusalem. Elon, to the west, might be either 'Ayalon' or 'as far as' (LXX).

10. III. *Ben-Hesed* had the area of the coast to below the port of Dor (Sharon) and part of Manasseh. *Arubboth* (modern 'Arrabeh) on the coastal plain or south of the valley of Dothan. *Socoh* (Khirbet Suweikeh) is named in Egyptian records. The *land of Hepher* might cover the territory of the daughters of Zelophahad (Nu. 26:32–33; Jos. 12:17), Wadi Tirzah to Samaria, rather than be identified with Tell Ifshar in the Sharon plain.

11. IV. *Ben-Abinadab* was Solomon's first cousin and son-in-law (1 Sa. 16:8; 17:13). The area covered was from below Dor to Carmel. *Naphoth* could be descriptive of the 'heights' (*nûp*) or 'wooded country' of Sharon (LXX, Jos. 12:18).[1]

12. V. *Baana*, brother of Jehoshaphat (v. 3) had the southern Jezreel plain, Issachar territory and the west Jordan valley. Included were the Canaanite towns of Taanach (Tell Ta'annak) and Megiddo (Tell el-Mutesellim),[2] where the south palace has been identified as used by Baana. His area also ran south from *Beth-Shan* (Beisan), down the river Jordan west bank to Abel-Meholah (Tell Abū-Ṣûṣ), to near *Zarethan* (Tell Umm Hamad; 1 Ki. 7:46) by the Wadi Far'ah. *Jokmeam* (Tell el-Mazâr) was a Levitical city in east Ephraim (1 Ch. 6:68).

13. VI. *Ben-Geber.* Transjordan, around *Ramoth Gilead* (Tell Rāmît), possibly founded by Solomon. This area was fertile and occupied by *settlements* (NIV; MT *ḥawwôt*; 'tent-villages', NEB) as well as fortified towns formerly ruled by Og king of Bashan (Dt. 3:4). Some take verse 19 as a note supplementing this district, which with VII covered as far as Amman and Moab.

14. VII. Includes south Gilead and Gad tribal lands. *Mahanaim* (Tell ed-Dhehab, north of the River Jabbok) was the

---

[1] M. Ben-Dor, 'נפה – A Geographical Term of possible "Sea People" Origin', *Tel-Aviv* 3, 1976, pp. 70–73.

[2] G. I. Davies, *Megiddo* (Cambridge: Lutterworth, 1986); Y. Yadin, 'Megiddo of the kings of Israel', *BA* 33, 1970, p. 95.

capital under Ishbaal (2 Sa. 2:8) and Absalom (2 Sa. 17:24).

15. VIII. *Ahimaaz* covered Naphtali and Upper Galilee as far as Hazor. He was a son of Zadok (2 Sa. 15:27).

16. IX. *I.e.* the land of *Asher* between Naphtali and the Mediterranean, including west Galilee (thus fulfilling Gn. 49:13). *Hushai* was possibly the same as David's friend (2 Sa. 15:37). *In Aloth* (RSV 'Bealoth', Jos. 15:24) could mean 'Ascents' (*ma'alôt*) or it could be a byname for Zebulun.[1]

17. X. *Issachar* territory (Jos. 19:17–23) ran from the central Jezreel plain to the River Jordan.

18. XI. *Benjamin* lands lay north of Jerusalem and west of Jordan, comprising the southern central Ephraim highlands. *Shimei* is perhaps already named in 1:8.

19. XII. *Geber* is perhaps differentiated from Ben-Geber (v. 13) by *son of Uri.* The zone covered Transjordan south of district VI and part of Gilead. Some follow LXX (2 Sa. 24:5) and read 'Gad' for 'Gilead' (so *New Bible Atlas*, IVP, 1985, p. 43). This was traditionally the land of Sihon (*cf.* Dt. 4:46) and of Og of Bashan (Dt. 3:8–17). The absence of reference to Judah in this list could be explained by 'there was *only one* official in the home-land' (*i.e.* Judah, RSV) – that is, these twelve districts were additional to Judah, which remained unchanged, some say untaxed. Others take this to refer to Azariah (v. 5) – 'in addition one governor over all the governors in the land' (NEB, Josephus). Others follow RSV and take Judah as district XII (see map on p. 91).

c. Provisions for the court (4:20–28). The LXX omits some verses.

20. The social and economic welfare of the state is emphasized (as also in vv. 27–28). *Numerous as the sand on the seashore* stands for 'measureless'.[2] To eat, drink and rejoice (AV 'make merry', Heb. 'be glad') denotes harmonious contentment between the various groups.[3]

21. This verse begins a new chapter in the MT (where 5:1–14 = EVV 4:21–34, so also JB). The kingdom stretched from *the River* (Euphrates) . . . *as far as the border of Egypt* ('frontier', REB;

---

[1] Y. Aharoni, *The Land of the Bible* (London: Burns & Oates, 1979), pp. 89, 315.

[2] Gn. 22:17; 32:12; Ps. 78:27; Is. 10:22; Je. 33:22; *cf.* Heb. 11:12; Rev. 20:8.

[3] *Cf.* 8:65–66 and similar phrases in the Assyrian stela of Ashurnaṣirapli II, *c.* 869 BC.

Wadi el-Arīsh, 8:65); see the promise to Abraham in Genesis 13:14–17. Indeed parts were soon to be lost through rebellion to Edom (1 Ki. 11:14–21) and Damascus (1 Ki. 11:23–25).[1] David had controlled the Aramaeans (2 Sa. 8:3–8; 10:16, 19), Hamath (2 Sa. 8:9) and Philistia (2 Sa. 8:1), and Solomon was to be in league with Phoenicia (1 Ki. 5:24). *Tribute (minhâ)* includes 'presents, gifts' and may not represent regular dues.

There are parallels in Egyptian and Babylonian texts to the arrangement of daily allocations in verses 22–27 (Heb. 5:2–8).[2] It is not possible to calculate the numbers of persons involved, for proportions could vary with the status of recipients, so that estimates have ranged between 12,000 and 35,000.

22–23. The *cōr* (NEB 'kor') is a 'measure' (RSV) of capacity. Like the homer, it equalled six bushels (220 litres), *i.e.* 185 bushels of *fine flour* (*sōleṭ*, a luxury) and 375 bushels of *meal*, a husked barley (*qāmaḥ*). Most oxen were *stall-fed*, 'fattened' (JB) in stalls, but some were pasture-fed (JB 'free-grazing'). The *deer* (AV 'harts', NEB 'stags') and other animals were table luxuries, as were *choice fowl*, variously identified as geese, guinea-fowl, hens or 'fattened cuckoos' (JB).

24. This is no mere repeat of verse 21, for Transeuphrates (*west of the River*) translates the Eber nāri region as seen from Babylon (Ezr. 4:10–11) and is defined by *Tiphsah* (Gk. Thapsacus, modern Dibseh) or 'the ford' crossing the Euphrates; *i.e.* the north-east boundary of Solomon's kingdom, just as Gaza marked its south-west (*contra* AV 'Azzah').

25. *Dan to Beersheba* marks the traditional limits of Palestine (12:29–30, *cf.* Jdg. 20:1). The unique phrase *had peace on all sides* (v. 24) then denotes that Solomon controlled by agreement 'all who passed through' (*'abārîm*) from round about (*missabîb*, Heb. v. 4), not just 'peace on all his frontiers' (JB). The emphasis on transfers from one kingdom to another is found in his international trading (*cf.* 10:28–29). To live *in safety*, in reliance on God (LXX *elpizŏ*, 'hope'), echoes Deuteronomy 12:10. God alone can provide this (Ps. 4:8; Pr. 1:33; Dt. 33:12, 28).

The contentment marked by *each man under his own vine and fig-tree (cf.* 2 Ki. 18:31; the full expression occurs only here in

---

[1] A. Malamat, 'Aspects of the Foreign Policies of David and Solomon', *JNES* 22, 1963, pp. 3ff.
[2] See *IBD*, p. 516; *NBD*[2], p. 386 (sub 'Food').

Kings) echoes Deuteronomy 8:8, Micah 4:4. Could this symbol enhance the significance of John 1:48?

26. *Four thousand stalls* (*'urôt̲*), REB 'stables', follows LXX, 2 Chronicles 9:25 (Heb., RSV, REB, 'forty') in keeping with the needs of 1,400 chariots (10:26) using a pair of horses each plus reserves. However, the word has been more fittingly taken to be a 'team-yoke'.[1] In 853 Ahab supplied two thousand chariots from the Northern Kingdom. *Twelve thousand horses* (*paraš*): the Heb. word can stand for either 'horse' or 'horse and rider'.[2]

27–28. *Supplied provisions* (*klkl*, *cf.* Akkad. *kakkaltu*) as used here (*cf.* Heb. *kûl*, 'to contain', Is. 6:11; 20:17) and by Jeremiah (Je. 6:11, *etc.*) denotes uninterrupted supplies, and 'they lacked nothing' (AV) may better indicate that when 'anyone who approached' (*haqqārēb̲*) the king's table asked for hospitality 'they were not excluded for any reason' (*'dr*, of Akkad. *adāru* used of 'eclipsed'). The *other horses* (Heb. *rekeš*) were not 'dromedaries' (AV) or 'swift horses' (RSV) but those 'bound' and trained by running alongside others either in chariot-teams or as spares (*cf.* 'draught-horses', JB).

d. Solomon's wisdom (4:29–34; Heb., 5:9–14). The definition of wisdom is taken beyond legal and administrative skill and insight to encompass unlimited *breadth of understanding* (v. 29, AV 'largeness of heart', RSV 'largeness of mind'), compared with the school wisdom of *the East* (v. 30, Mesopotamia, Gn. 2:8) rather than Arabia, which was considered the south[3] (Je. 49:28). This was the source of collected wisdom in books of proverbs, riddles, folk-tales, acrostics, songs, dialogues and instructions passed on through the educational system.[4] Egyptian school texts covered many of these aspects of wisdom also. Solomon's wisdom was greater than that of Egypt (*cf.* Gn.

---

[1] K. Deller, *Or.* 27, 1958, pp. 312–313; S. Parpola, 'Collations and other Remarks', *JSS* 23, 1976, p. 172.

[2] D. R. Ap-Thomas, 'All the King's Horses?', in J. I. Durham and J. R. Porter (eds.), *Proclamation and Presence* (Atlanta: John Knox Press, 1970), pp. 135–151.

[3] D. J. Wiseman, 'Light from the East', *Bulletin of the Middle Eastern Cultural Center in Japan*, V: Near Eastern Studies dedicated to H.I.H. Prince Mikasa Takahito Mikasa on the Occasion of his Seventy-fifth Birthday, 1991, pp. 469–471.

[4] See also D. J. Wiseman, 'Israel's Literary neighbours in the thirteenth century B.C.', *Journal of Northwest Semitic Languages*, V, 1977, pp. 77–91.

41:8; Ex. 7:11; Acts 7:22): 'it was because his wisdom sur-passed rather than by-passed theirs that they flocked to hear him'[1] (*cf*. Jn. 7:46) and it became proverbial (Mt. 12:42). He was the wisest until Jesus (Lk. 11:31). The wise men named belonged to no single school or court and may only later have been associated with special gifts such as singing (1 Ch. 2:6–7; 6:31–33, *cf*. headings of Pss. 88–89).[2] The names are probably not Hebrew or Canaanite in origin, nor need they be legendary figures. Later Jewish tradition equates Ethan with Abraham, Heman with Moses, Calcol ('the supplier', *cf*. v. 27) with Joseph and Darda (with difficulty) with the generation (*dōr*) of the wilderness.

32. *Proverbs* were collected in books; these *māšāl* include parables, similes, metaphors and proverb-riddles, all common in the ancient Near East from the third millennium onwards. Extensive writings from Mesopotamia and Egypt attest a simi-lar tradition to that exercised by Solomon. The biblical Book of Proverbs is said to contain 582 of Solomon's proverbs. *Songs* were catalogued by their initial line in antiquity. For Solomon and love songs see the Song of Solomon.[3]

33. The listing of flora and fauna was done in Babylonian texts[4] and reference was made to them in proverbs (*cf*. Pr. 6:6–8; 26:2–3, 11; 28:1, 15) and fables (Jdg. 9:8). The compil-ation of such lists were standard school exercises.

While this account reflects Solomon's education as a wise man comparable with those of other contemporary states of his day in literary and scientific attainment, it was no mere rhetoric. The creation of zoological and botanical gardens in the capital city was an achievement boasted by many kings. Their purpose was not only for pleasure but also for practical purposes and the provision of support for palace and temple. Adad-shuma-uṣur (*c*. 1200 BC) did this at Babylon where later Nebuchadnezzar was to construct his famous 'Hanging Gar-dens' *c*. 600 BC. Other examples of walled royal gardens were already attested at Nineveh, where those made by Tiglath-pileser I (*c*. 1100 BC) were kept by Ashurbanipal (600 BC),

[1] Derek Kidner, *Wisdom to Live By* (Leicester: IVP, 1985), p. 15 (= *The Wisdom of Proverbs, Job and Ecclesiastes* (Downers Grove: IVP, 1985), p. 15).

[2] W. F. Albright, *Archaeology and the Religion of Israel* (Baltimore: Johns Hopkins Press, 1943), p. 127; R. De Vaux, *Ancient Israel: Its Life and Institutions* (London: Darton, Longman & Todd, 1961), p. 392 ('choristers').

[3] G. Lloyd Carr, *The Song of Solomon, TOTC* (Leicester: IVP, 1984).

[4] *E.g.* the Babylonian lexical series HAR.ra = *hubullu*; uru.an.na. *etc*.

while at Calah (Nimrud) Ashur-naṣir-apli II (860 BC) laid out a garden with at least eighty-five named species.

Thus Solomon could well have created parks and gardens (as Ec. 2:5); their beauty and fragrances are reflected in the Song of Songs (*e.g.* 1:14; 2:3; 6:2, *etc.*). According to Jewish tradition (Josephus, *Ant.* viii.7.3) Solomon also had gardens nine kilometres south of Jerusalem, outside Bethlehem at Etan (2 Ch. 11:6, Etam, as LXX Ps. 74:15, modern Etham, Khirbet el Hoh), which abounded with parks and streams. In the time of Zedekiah the King's Garden was watered by sluices from Siloam (2 Ki. 25:4; Neh. 3:15).[1]

The *cedar of Lebanon* was the tallest tree with the greatest spread (*cf.* 5:6; Ps. 80:10) and the Syrian *hyssop* (*'ezōḇ*) was the smallest, stunted from its usual height (50–70 cm.) by growing in a wall. NEB translates 'marjoram'.

34. Oriental wisdom was presented both orally and in writing. It was transmitted between courts by travelling sages. LXX adds 'and he received gifts', as was customary (see 10:1–6).

B. Solomon's building activities (5:1 – 9:9)

The historian concentrates on Solomon's unique work in building the temple (chapter 6) by negotiation for supplies of wood and skills not available within Israel (5:1–18). The construction of the Royal Palace and Judgment Hall (7:1–12) is followed by the furnishing of the new buildings (7:13–51), the bringing in of the ark (8:1–21) and the dedication of the work (8:22–66). The account of the second appearance of God (9:1–9) ends like an epilogue, with the reiteration of terms for the blessing of the dynasty, just as had the prologue when the work was begun (3:4–14).

The construction and upkeep of large buildings for religious and public administration was the responsibility of all ancient Near Eastern monarchs.[2] This was not done just as a tradition and to mark the introduction of a new reign, nor was it done to mark the legitimacy of the king or as a

---

[1] D. J. Wiseman, 'Mesopotamian Gardens', *Anatolian Studies* 33, 1983, pp. 137–144; 'A New Stela of Ashurnasirpal II', *Iraq* 14, 1952, pp. 24–44; Y. Shiloh, 'City of David Excavations 1978', *BA* 42, 1979, p. 168.

[2] *E.g. ANET*, pp. 268, 270; S. N. Kramer, *The Sumerians* (Chicago: University of Chicago Press, 1983), pp. 137–140, and above, Introduction, p. 42, n. 3.

propaganda gesture to condition non-urban people to the centralization of power.[1] The building of a prominent temple in the capital city certainly served as a symbol which primarily stood to honour the national deity, who thus lived among his people as the ultimate authority and demonstrated the unity of the nation. Solomon was doing something unique and new for Israel. God (Yahweh) was present to preside over all his people. His claim that the plans were revealed and given by God is paralleled in the accounts of other kings, like Gudea in Sumer (c. 2050 BC), who had a dream summoning him to rule and giving him detailed plans for his temple building.[2] In his case, too, divine wisdom is said to play a part.

There is little evidence for the theory that the temple was a reconstruction of an earlier Jebusite sacred site and only later attributed to Solomon. The building was to use the best of contemporary craftsmanship and be adapted to emphasize the distinctive view of God as invisible and locatable, yet everywhere. The Jerusalem temple also served to centralize worship and thus, in theory, led to the diminished importance of the high places (*e.g.* Gibeon as the tabernacle site). This coincided with a national plan for the unity of all groups.

The whole building programme ends with details of international trade (9:10–28) given with examples of Solomon's wisdom (10:1–13) and splendour (10:14–29) that highlight his international fame.

There is much speculation as to the original source of this material. It is to be expected that Solomon's scribes kept written plans, accounts, lists and other records in keeping with contemporarily attested practice. The whole is a historically feasible and unified narrative.

i. Organization of materials and workforce (5:1–18; Heb., 5:15–32).

a. The alliance with Hiram of Tyre (5:1–12). Israel lacked timber of sufficient size and quantity, stone and the skilled workmen to undertake the building project on a grand scale. The opportunity to get these came when Hiram, who had earlier supplied David with them (2 Sa. 5:11), sent Solomon

---

[1] *Contra* K. W. Whitelam, 'The Symbols of Power: Aspects of Royal Propaganda in the United Monarchy', *BA* 49, 1986, pp. 166–173.
[2] *ANET*, pp. 268–269; *IBD*, p. 103.

the customary exchange of greetings on his succession.

1. *Hiram* ruled *Tyre c.* 969–936 BC (and possibly as co-regent with his father Abi-Baal from *c.* 980 BC). He was on *friendly terms* with David (translates Heb. *'ohēḇ,* 'love' as used of a close covenant relationship, *e.g.* Dt. 6:5; Mt. 22:37).[1] A trade treaty gave Tyre access to inland trade across Israel to Judah, the Red Sea and Transjordan.[2]

The next section (vv. 2–6) is typical diplomatic correspondence naming the addressee (v. 2), giving reference to previous contacts (vv. 3, 5) and making the opening gambit for a specific economic agreement (v. 6). 2 Chronicles 2 gives additional details. David had himself planned to build the temple but was unable to carry this out because of the unstable conditions resulting from war (2 Sa. 7:1–16) and his family's inexperience (1 Ch. 22:2–5). This does not conflict with the statement that his failure to do the work was because he was a warrior and had shed blood (1 Ch. 28:3). David himself recognized that it would not be feasible before his death and the final victory (v. 5, 2 Sa. 7:12–13). Many a contemporary king who had been to war built temples. Now was God's chosen time (v. 4). To put *enemies under* the *feet* (v. 3, LXX/Kethib 'his (the LORD's) feet'; Qerē 'my feet', *i.e.* Solomon) was the symbolic act marking conquest ('made them subject to him', REB; Jos. 10:24; Ps. 8:6; *cf.* Rom. 16:20; 1 Cor. 15:25, 27; Eph. 1:22). In contemporary art enemies were often depicted as a footstool (as Ps. 110:1).[3]

4. *Rest on every side* (RSV 'peace', *cf.* 4:24) fulfilled God's promise to his people (Ex. 33:14; Dt. 12:10; *cf.* Heb. 4:1–11). This was literally true only at the beginning of Solomon's reign. There was *no adversary* (MT *śāṭān*). Satan was later personalized (*cf.* 11:14, 23, 25; 1 Ch. 21; Jb. 1:6). There was no *disaster,* better 'evil happening', as AV; GNB 'no danger of attack' is too precise.

5. The *temple* here interprets 'house' (*bêt*) as both place of worship and royal house. Temples were often called after the name of the principal deity, but here the Name refers to the person of God and his self-revelation, presence and ownership (Ex. 20:24; Dt. 12:5). *For* is literally 'with reference to' the name of the LORD God (Yahweh or Yhwh). The temple imagery is later

[1] W. L. Moran, 'The Ancient Near Eastern Background to the Love of God in Deuteronomy', *CBQ,* 25, 1963, pp. 77–87.
[2] F. C. Fensham, 'The Treaty between the Israelites and Tyrians', *VT*Supp 17, 1969, pp. 71–87.
[3] *E.g. ANEP,* 417; *IBD,* p. 519.

1 KINGS 5:6–12

taken to apply to the believer (1 Cor. 3:16–17; 6:19; Eph. 2:21).

6. *So* (Heb. 'and then', RSV) introduces the message or main subject-matter in a letter.[1] *Cedars of Lebanon* (*Cedrus libani* Loud.) grow to a height of about thirty metres above an altitude of 1,500 metres and were commonly taken by Egyptian, Assyrian or Babylonian kings to span large temple ceilings. With the cypress (Eastern Savin, *Juniperus excelsa*) and *pine* (v. 10, NEB; the Cilician fir, *Abies cilicica*), timber abounded in the Lebanon/Taurus hills. Hiram agreed to supply and *float them in rafts* (v. 9) to a destination on the Mediterranean coast chosen by Solomon. This was Joppa (2 Ch. 2:16) or nearby Tell Qasileh at the mouth of the River Yarkon.

9. The *rafts* (*dob^{e}rôt* and *rapsōdôt*, 2 Ch. 2:16) occur only here and may imply logs roped back to back (*dbr*) until they were 'broken up' or separated for transport overland. An Assyrian letter *c.* 740 BC refers to the Sidonians (v. 6) in connection with this timber trade.[2]

In return for these supplies, Solomon had to provide food for all Hiram's dependent officials (vv. 10–12). The historian enlarges on the effect of Hiram's reply. The annual payment amounted to a quarter less than the total Solomon himself received for his own court, but in different commodities (4:22–23).

11. *Wheat* covers all types of grain and *pressed olive oil* (Heb. 'beaten oil') finely crushed by pestle and mortar ('pounded olives', REB), as opposed to the rougher residue of the stone mill. The amount of 'pure oil' (so JB, AV) was perhaps *twenty cors* (so MT, RSV) rather than *twenty thousand baths* (a measure), *i.e.* 115,000 gallons, given in 2 Chronicles 2:10 (and LXX). It is not necessary to think that Solomon made a bad bargain in return for the supplies he received. The payment would, however, have helped to impoverish his kingdom in its later years.

12. All this was incorporated in a formal *treaty* (covenant, *b^{e}rît*) between the two kings. Other specific first-millennium economic treaties are known (*e.g.* Assyria and Mati'el of Syria).

[1] *Cf.* 2 Ch. 2:3–10; P. S. Alexander, 'Remarks on Aramaic Epistolography in the Persian Period', *JSS* 23, 1978, pp. 155–170.
[2] H. W. F. Saggs, 'The Nimrud Letters, 1952–Part II', *Iraq* 17, 1955, pp. 126–128.

b. An added note on the use of Israel's labour force (5:13–18).

13. The levy or forced labour is well attested in Syria and Palestine at this time.[1] Forced slave-labour (*mas 'ōḇēḏ*) totalling 150,000 was mainly drawn from the non-Israelite ('Canaanite') population, since a Hebrew was forbidden to enslave his fellow (1 Ki. 9:21; Lv. 25:39). The *thirty thousand* employed away from home for four months a year were temporary conscripts from the Israelites (*all Israel*) themselves.

14. *Adoniram*, cf. 4:6. *In shifts* (*ḥᵃlîp̄ôṯ*; AV 'by courses') may be derived from Heb. *ḥālap̄*, 'to change', or Akkad. *hitlupu*, 'pass in and out'.

15–16. The figures and categories are general, *e.g.* 'carriers of burden' (*nōśē' sabbāl*, as RSV; 'hauliers' REB). The quarrymen worked in places not stated *in the hills* (MT, omitted by NEB, REB), probably outside Israel. The *thirty-three hundred foremen* described as 'chief officials' (RSV; NRSV 'supervisors'; *cf.* 4:1, 7) may be their representatives, *i.e.* a ratio of one to fifty; some MSS, 2 Ch. 2:2 read 'thirty-six hundred'. With the addition of five hundred and fifty supervisors (9:23; *cf.* 2 Ch. 2:18, totalling 3,850), it may be that only the eleven northern tribes were involved (note multiples of eleven). There are few grounds to show that the numbers are exaggerated or composed to enhance Solomon's reputation.

17–18. *The large blocks of quality stone* (*cf.* 'high-grade', 7:11) or 'massive blocks' (NEB) were 'extracted' (*removed*) and dressed (*gāzîṯ*) possibly as the margin-drafted masonry attested in the border-dressed foundation stones found in this period.[2] The highly technical work of shaping wood and stone (*psl*, rather than just *prepared*) involved men from Israel, Sidon and Gebal together (7:13). *Gebal* (JB 'Gebalites'), *i.e.* Gubla, Byblos, is read by some as 'bordered with grooves' (*yagbilîm*, AV 'stone squarers'), but this requires emendation of the text.

ii. Building the temple (6:1–38). *Cf.* 2 Chronicles 3:1–14; Josephus, *Ant.* vii.3.1–3. The exterior (vv. 2–14), interior (vv. 15–30), entrance (vv. 31–35) and courtyard (v. 36) are

---

[1] T. N. D. Mettinger, *Solomonic State Officials* (Lund: Gleerup, 1971), pp. 134–136; I. Mendelsohn, 'State Slavery in Ancient Palestine', *BASOR* 85, 1942, pp. 14–17; A. F. Rainey, 'Compulsory Labour Gangs in Ancient Israel', *IEJ* 20, 1970, pp. 191–202.
[2] *E.g. IBD*, p. 106.

described in insufficient detail for any sure reconstruction to be made. Some aspects (site, orientation, foundations) are omitted, and there are differences between this and the later free account of 2 Chronicles (3–4) and Ezekiel (41–42)[1] which could be explained by subsequent changes. The LXX variants may not all be equally significant[2] and some comments are added by the historian (vv. 11–13). The details of materials, measurements and decoration might presume an archival report, or they might be drawn from the memory of an observer or from oral instruction given to craftsmen.[3]

The temple was sited on the threshing-floor of Araunah bought by David (2 Sa. 24:24), rather than above a Jebusite original sanctuary. The area is now marked by the Dome of the Rock (Haram ash-Sharīf) in Jerusalem. The plan basically follows that of the tabernacle, but at double the size (Ex. 26:15–25; 36:34), and consists of (i) Entrance Hall (Vestibule or Portico, *'ûlām*), (ii) Sanctuary (Holy Place, main hall, nave, *hêkāl*) and (iii) Inner Shrine (Holy of Holies = Most Holy Place, *dᵉḇîr*). See the plan opposite.

As no architectural remains survived the sack in 587/6 BC, the plan has been compared with many earlier temples, notably those from Tell Tainat, Alalakh, Ebla and Ras Shamra in Syria and Megiddo, Hazor, Shechem and Arad in Palestine. Since craftsmen from the coastal Levant and from these areas were involved, similarities would not be unexpected. Solomon appears to have modified the current contemporary design of a 'longroom temple', included a special Holy of Holies at the back and added surrounding structures.[4]

The special and sacred character of the temple was most marked by its name, elevation (visibility) and isolation (holiness, apartness). It was not just a 'royal chapel', though built within the citadel and palace complex, for it was used as the national focus for the worship of Israel's God Yahweh. Its purpose was to house the ark (v. 19). Though it was 'God's house', it was smaller than the buildings around it and yet with adequate space in its surrounding courtyards for mass

[1] *E.g.* J. B. Taylor, *Ezekiel*, TOTC (London: Tyndale Press, 1969), pp. 254–256.

[2] D. W. Gooding, 'Temple Specifications: A Dispute in Logical Arrangement between the MT and LXX', *VT* 17, 1967, pp. 143–172.

[3] Noth, *op. cit.*, pp. 102–106.

[4] C. J. Davey, 'Temples of the Levant and the Buildings of Solomon', *TynB* 31, 1980, pp. 107–146.

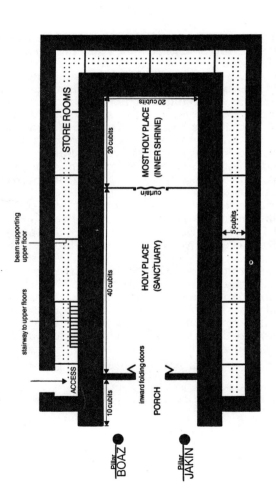

Plan of the First Temple

congregational worship. A suggested reconstruction is given on p. 107.[1]

a. The date of foundation (6:1). This is given in relation to a national event, as was done by Babylonian and Assyrian kings. These give precise details of work at sacred sites carried out by their predecessors; thus Nebuchadnezzar I of Babylon (1150 BC) refers to King Gulkishar 696 years earlier and Sennacherib of Assyria (688/7 BC) tells of the recovery of statues of the gods of Ekallate stolen by Marduk-nadin-ahhe 418 years earlier.[2] Other building inscriptions state the number of years since a temple was founded or last repaired. For example, Shalmaneser I of Assyria (*c.* 1245 BC) repaired a temple at Assur 580 years after Shamshi-Adad I (*c.* 1820 BC) had last done so, Tukulti-Ninurta repaired a temple there which had been founded 720 years earlier by Ilu-shuma, and Tiglath-pileser III (*c.* 740 BC) restored another temple which had itself been repaired both by Shamshi-Adad I and, he says, 641 years later by Ashur-dan I.[3]

The figure *four hundred and eightieth year* could be a generalization to indicate the passing of twelve generations (each of forty years, Dt. 1:3) and so be the mid-point of the historian's overview from the Exodus to the Exile. The LXX tradition ('440 years') has been taken similarly as the eleven generations from Aaron to Zadok. With this may be compared the chronological framework in Matthew 1:7. Others take this literally to indicate the date of the Exodus (*c.* 1446 BC),[4] while others take the view that the 'coming out of Egypt' could refer to a later event. Solomon's *fourth year* has been placed by comparative dating (Hiram, the foundation of Carthage, *etc.*) between 957/6 and 968/7 BC.[5] *Ziv* is explained as *the second*

[1] Reproduced from *IBD*, p. 1527. *Cf. NBD* (1962 edn.), p. 1243; Fig. 204.
[2] J. A. Brinkman, *A Political History of Post-Kassite Babylonia 1158–722 B.C.* (Rome: Pontifical Bible Institute, 1968), pp. 83–84.
[3] S. Lackenbacher, *Le Roi Bâtisseur* (Paris: Éditions Recherche sur les civilisations, 1982), pp. 15–19, 180.
[4] J. J. Bimson, *Redating the Exodus and Conquest* (Sheffield: JSOT Press, 1978), argues again for a fifteenth-century BC date.
[5] *Cf.* Josephus, *Contra Apionem* I.18.116–117; M. B. Rowton, 'The Date of the Founding of Solomon's Temple', *BASOR* 119, 1950, pp. 20–22; H. Y. Katzenstein, 'Is there any Synchronism between the Reigns of Hiram and Solomon?', *JNES* 24, 1965, pp. 116–117; J. Liver, 'The Chronology of Tyre at the Beginning of the First Millennium BC', *IEJ* 3, 1953, pp. 113–120; H. Y. Katzenstein, *The History of Tyre* (Jerusalem: Schocken Institute, 1973).

month (April/May = Lyyar in the Babylonian calendar), as local calendars (*cf. Bul*, v. 38) were no longer used after the second millennium BC (there are similar changes at Mari, Alalakh and Ras Shamra).

b. The structure (6:2–10). The temple is called 'the house' (*bêṯ, byṯ*) throughout the narrative, or 'temple of the LORD' (Yahweh, 6:1), as in a later ostracon from Arad (*byt (l)yhwh*).[1] The interior measurement is thirty metres long by ten metres wide by fifteen metres high, according to the large or royal cubit (*c.* 50 cm.).[2] The Portico entrance was open and equalled the width of the temple and *projected (rōḥaḇ) ten cubits* (RSV 'ten cubits deep') in front of the *main hall (hêḵāl)*. The latter is a loan word, Babylonian *ekallu*, used of any very large structure, palace or temple, or part of it such as a wing (*cf.* v. 17).

4. The three technical terms usually translated *windows* have yet to be understood (MT *ḥallônē šᵉqupîm ᵃṭumîm*). This could describe the form of *narrow clerestory windows* placed high up in both side walls (*cf.* RSV), like 'embrasures' (NEB, REB) in a mediaeval castle, wider on the inside, narrowing to a slit on the outside.[3] But such openings are not yet archaeologically attested for this time. Heb. *ḥallônē* has been taken as a typical Syrian-Assyrian architectural feature of an elaborate portico in front of a main building (*bît hilāni*) with side rooms, columns (*cf.* Assyr. *ṭimmu*), threshold with lintel and doorposts (Assyr. *askuppatu*), windows and a balcony.[4] Our author may have had such a construction in mind here.

5–6. The side-rooms were a *structure, i.e.* on a platform. They were probably curved inside like flying buttresses (Heb. *ṣᵉlā'ôṯ*, 'ribs'; Akkad. *ṣillu*, 'arch', hence NEB 'arcades') to give access. This may explain how they were ranged against the wall with floor space between the outer wall and the 'rib' increasing at each upper level. The joists rested on offset ledges or 'rebatements' (REB; vv. 9–10, *miḡrā'ôṯ*, 'diminishings')

---

[1] *IBD*, p. 1531 (sixth century BC).

[2] The royal cubit measure averages Heb. 51.82 cm.; Bab. 50.3 cm.; Egypt. 52.45 cm.; *cf.* NIV fn.

[3] *Cf.* Ezk. 40:16; Syr. 'oblique and narrow', not 'opening and closing' (*contra BA* 4, 1941, p. 26). J. Ouellette, *"atummîm" in 1 Kings xii:4', Bulletin of the Institute of Jewish Studies*, 2, 1974, pp. 99–102, takes it as an upper storey.

[4] J. Börker-Klähn, 'Der bît hilāni des Assur-Tempels', *ZA* 70, 1981, pp. 29–59, 258–273; the *hilāni* is also described as having a 'nose' or 'openings' (*appāte*) and 'folding doors' (*bît muterrēti*).

all around the outside wall of the main temple, thus avoiding making holes in the sanctuary wall (v. 7). The total floor space of this storage area – 3,060 cubits, used for 'treasury' offerings paid in kind – was twice that of the worship area within the temple itself.[1] A possible reconstruction is given in the diagram on p. 108.[2]

7. As an iron tool was thought to violate a holy structure, the dressing of the stone would have to be done at the *quarry* (*cf.* Ex. 20:25).

8. The way in to the side store-rooms, used for storing equipment, offerings and possibly priestly vestments and utensils, was through an opening at the south or 'right hand corner' (JB, Heb. *ketep*) into the ground floor ('lowest' so NIV, RSV). The MT 'middle' implies that the stairway (*lûllîm*, LXX, Vulg., Targ.) led up to this and then to the upper floors (*cf.* JB, Syr. 'trap doors'). 'Spiral staircase' (NEB) is influenced by a supposed architectural feature once thought to have been found in an Alalakh temple.

9–10. The whole completed temple is roofed and now clad inside with cedar (and possibly pine or cypress, see on vv. 8, 14–16). The woodwork included flat deck (*spn*) floors and a roof with rows (*sᵉdērôt*) of *beams* rising to a summit with planks forming a vault (Heb. *gēbîm*).

c. A reminder of God's promise (6:11–13).

These verses are not in LXX. The historian reminds the reader of the spiritual conditions on which the presence of God will dwell with his people (Lv. 26:11–12). If there is to be a continuing house (the term includes the ruling house or dynasty, 2 Sa. 7:12–16) the covenant must be kept. The promise is that God will never *abandon* or forsake his own (Dt. 31:6, 8; Jos. 1:5; 1 Sa. 12:28; Heb. 13:5). These are apt words, perhaps brought by a prophet or dreams (1 Ki. 3:5; 9:2–9) at a crucial point in the project.

d. The interior woodwork (6:14–18).

The technical terms are not yet fully understood and the repetitive and explanatory phrases could well be the historian's comment when the temple has been destroyed. The *planks* of *pine* (v. 15, NRSV

---

[1] K. A. Kitchen, 'Two Notes on the subsidiary rooms of Solomon's Temple', *EI* 20, 1989, pp. 107–112.

[2] *Cf.* G. E. Wright, 'Solomon's Temple Resurrected', *BA* 4, 1941, p. 26.

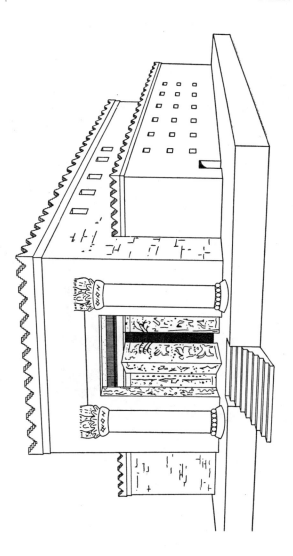

Solomon's Temple (Steven's reconstruction)

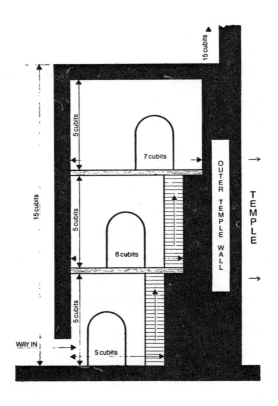

Temple Store Rooms (side elevation)

'cedar', see 5:6) may have formed an arched (*ṣal'ôṭ*) or vaulted roof (*ceiling* follows LXX reading *qôrôṭ* rather than MT *qîrôṭ*, 'walls'), see also on verse 10.

16. The *inner sanctuary* ('shrine', REB) is defined here as *the Most Holy Place* ('innermost part', REB),[1] 'partitioned' (NEB) or screened off from the main hall (*hêḵāl*). The word for the inner shrine (*dᵉḇîr*) is used only in the description of the temple building[2] and may relate to the 'back' part (Heb., II *dāḇār*, 'turn the back'; Akkad. *dabāru*) rather than to 'oracle' (Heb., I *dāḇār*, 'to speak', as AV, RSV).

18. A summary of the woodwork done is not in LXX or related to verses 19–22, which describe the gold-plating. The designs of wild fruits (*gourds*, *Citrullus colocynthis*, *cf*. 1 Ki. 7:24; 2 Ki. 4:39–40) and rosettes (JB, *cf*. NIV *open flowers*, LXX 'lilies') were not necessarily symbols of fertility but were common decorative motifs found in wide use at this time.

e. The inner sanctuary (6:19–28). This was designed just to house the ark of the covenant – the box or chest in which the tablets of God's covenant requirements (the law) were kept (Ex. 25:16; Dt. 10:1–5). The temple was to be the guardian of, and witness to, the law. In common with the ancient Near Eastern principles of religious architecture, the holiest place was to be a perfect cube.[3] The difference in height between the inner shrine and the main hall could be accounted for by a lower ceiling (with a chamber above, 2 Ch. 3:9),[4] by the roof sloping to the rear,[5] or by steps up to a raised platform.

20. The use of *pure* or the best 'red' *gold* (*cf*. NEB) – a symbol of past glory, splendour and purity (*cf*. Rev. 21:18–21) – follows the precedent of the tabernacle. Its extensive use here is corroborated by other ancient structures, with gold covering even the floors (v. 30), and this is no exaggeration.[6]

---

[1] *I.e.* the superlative 'Holy of Holies'.

[2] 1 and 2 Kings, 2 Ch. 3–5 and Ps. 28:2.

[3] D. J. Wiseman, *Nebuchadrezzar and Babylon* (Oxford: British Academy, 1985), pp. 71–73; also the dimensions of Ezekiel's altar (43:16) and the temple-towers (ziqqurrats); 'A Babylonian Architect?', *Anatolian Studies* 22, 1972, p. 143.

[4] M. Noth, *Könige*, 1968, p. 121; Th. A. Busink, *Der Tempel von Jerusalem von Salomo bis Herodes* (Leiden: E. J. Brill, 1970), p. 209.

[5] Davey, *op. cit.*, p. 109.

[6] A. R. Millard, 'Solomon in all his Glory', *Vox Evangelica* 12, 1981, pp. 5–18; K. A. Kitchen, *The Bible in its World: The Bible and Archaeology Today* (Exeter: Paternoster Press, 1977), p. 103.

21. The *gold chains* (*rattîqôt* occurs only here) were probably those on which the curtain (or veil) was hung or drawn (*cf.* 2 Ch. 3:14; Mt. 27:51; Heb. 6:19). These *extended* (Heb. 'cause to pass over'), and this is interpreted by NEB as 'draw a veil with golden chains'.

22. The altar here is that for incense (7:48; Heb. 9:3–4).

23–28. *The cherubim.* This may refer to winged sphinxes of Syro-Phoenician style, or to protective figures with specific non-human features (Akkad. *kuribu*) guarding the entrances to palace and temple doorways, with their feet ready to drive off evil, or to figures making a gesture of adoration (Assyr. *karibu*). Others consider them the supporting figures on which God was invisibly enthroned (Is. 37:16; Ps. 80:1). This would be similar to the winged figures on the arms of the royal throne (*cf.* the Megiddo or Nimrud ivories).[1] They may be distinct from the spread-winged figures, *each ten cubits high*, whose wings covered the lid or 'mercy seat' (AV, Ex. 25:17–22; 30:6) and spanned the whole width of the inner sanctuary. Their location is unclear, whether at either side of the ark (8:6–7) or at the rear wall facing the curtain (2 Ch. 3:10–13). Indeed, they may represent the protective and overshadowing wings of God all around.

f. The carvings and the doors (6:29–38). Items of design additional to those in verse 18 are listed. Cherubim, palm tree (palmette?) and rosette are found on gold-covered boxes and decorations of Syrian design (the Nimrud ivories). If symbolic, they could represent the Garden of God (Eden) to which entry was now possible again only through the atonement.

29. The *inner and outer rooms* (NIV, RSV) renders the Heb. 'from the outside to the inside' (AV 'within and without').

31–35. The doors were of *olive wood* (NEB 'wild olive'; Heb. *ªṣê-šemen*). Repetition of details such as the carving are common in ancient lists and should not be discarded as glosses. The doors had *four-sided jambs* or 'the lintel and the doorposts formed a pentagon' (RSV) or may refer to the space covered by the doors to the inner sanctuary, *i.e.* 'a fifth part' (AV) of the total width (four cubits equals about two metres),[2] just as the doors

---

[1] These figures are illustrated in *ANEP*, nos. 128, 332; *IBD*, pp. 974, 1560; *cf.* M. E. L. Mallowan, *Nimrud and Its Remains*, II (London: Collins, 1966), pl. IX, pp. 442, 465.

[2] *I.e.* the main wider entrance was 5 cubits (= *c.* 7½in; 2.5m.); A. R. Millard, 'The Doorways of Solomon's Temple', *EI* 20, 1989, pp. 135–139.

to the main hall covered a quarter of its width. The larger
doors had folding panels rather than shaped lintels. These
turned in stone carved *sockets* (*geˡlîlîm*; Akkad. *galālu*, 'each leaf
having two swivel-pins', REB). Over all the thin gold foil was
spread evenly (*yāšar*, *cf.* RSV, not as NIV *hammered evenly*).

36. The *inner courtyard* implies the existence of a larger
outer one (8:64; 2 Ch. 4:9, *cf.* 'upper courtyard', Je. 36:10).
The construction technique, placing a course of wood between layers of stone, is attested in several excavated buildings
in Syria and may also have served as a protection against
earthquake damage.[1]

37–38. The temple took seven and a half years to complete
in all *its details* and *specifications*. This was said 'with reference
to all matters (*dbr*) and all its agreed plan' (*mišpaṭ*, so Heb.). On
Bul as the eighth month of the old calendar, see verse 1.
Solomon throughout used the best available skills and
materials in his work for his God. This attests his devotion at
the time and should be the attitude of all true worshippers (*cf.*
v. 7: Mt. 2:11; 2 Cor. 8:1–5; 9:6–15).

iii. Building his palace (7:1–12). Since the temple is the
main focus of the historian's account, less space is devoted to
the complex of royal secular buildings for administrative and
judicial purposes. All these were within a large courtyard to
which general reference is made (vv. 9–12). This section is not
in 2 Chronicles and is placed elsewhere by LXX and Josephus
(*Ant.* viii.5.2). Yet the work on these buildings took almost
twice as long as the smaller temple construction, perhaps
undertaken concurrently, in seven years (vv. 6–38), giving a
total of twenty years.

2. The Pillared Hall (called the *Palace of the Forest of Lebanon*)
was used as an audience chamber or throne hall, and at
forty-six metres by twenty-three metres by thirteen and a half
metres was larger than the temple. It also served as a state
treasury, displaying selected precious objects received as
tribute (*cf.* 10:16–17). It was not essentially an armoury which,
in the ancient Near East, occupied separate guarded quarters.

The building was named after the *four rows of cedar columns*
which made it appear forest-like. Two rows may have been
against the walls (*cf.* LXX reads 'three rows') and two down the

[1] *IBD*, p. 102; H. C. Thomson, 'A Row of Cedar Beams', *PEQ* 92, 1960,
pp. 57–63.

centre, allowing for the broad doorways. The roof rested 'upon the forty-five pillars, fifteen in each row' (RSV) and could have served as the support for the floor of an upper room. This is more likely than that the trimmed beams ($k^e r$-$u\underline{t}\hat{o}\underline{t}$ 'sawn things') were an architectural feature (*e.g.* JB 'capitals').

4-5. *The windows* ($meh^e z\bar{a}h$, 'places of seeing' occurs only here, *cf.* 6:4) seem to have been set in *steps of three* (AV 'three ranks'), probably above each other, *i.e.* they 'corresponded with each other at three levels' (NEB). The precise form of the windows is not obvious (*cf.* 6:4), but these and all openings were said to have *rectangular frames* (*cf.* NRSV 'four-sided', REB 'square') and are found only *in the front part*, *i.e.* the main hall.

6. The pillared *portico* or porch ('*ulām*, *cf.* 6:3) may have served as a waiting-room for those seeking audience, with its front being characterized by *an overhanging roof* (RSV 'canopy', REB 'cornice', Heb. '$\bar{a}\underline{b}$, *cf.* Ezk. 41:25-26; AV 'thick beam'), a distinctive architectural term which some take as a projecting roof or protuberance ('nose', '$a\underline{p}$). A window or balcony could be part of this feature (*cf.* 2 Ki. 9:30, 32).

7. The *throne hall* is explained as *the Hall of Justice*, the place where the king governed ($\check{s}p\underline{t}$). It was possibly part of the large 'Forest of Lebanon' building, since no dimensions are given. The throne is described in 10:18-20. The hall was clad with *cedar from floor to ceiling* (NIV follows Vulg., Syr.), the latter being also a *floor* (MT) forming the ceiling of the main hall (RSV 'floors to rafters', *cf.* NRSV 'floor to floor', requires a change of text, $q\bar{o}r\hat{o}\underline{t}$). The picture given may be of the cedar planking running 'from one floor to another', *i.e.* right through the throne hall to the pillared hall behind. The royal appartments were off a further courtyard to the rear (as RSV).

8. The historian, having concentrated on the temple, simply notes the similarity of design. The queen's quarters (and harem?) were not necessarily of separate or Egyptian design.

9. The courtyard was of stone and wood construction (see on 6:36) and more than one courtyard is implied. The major buildings include stone *trimmed with a saw*, such as limestone which hardens after exposure to the air. Examples of stones of four to five metres in length from the Herodian period have been exposed in Jerusalem. This whole account serves to emphasize the splendour of these capital buildings.

iv. The temple furnishings (7:13–51). *Cf.* 2 Kings 25:13–17; 2 Chronicles 4:11–18. The technical terms are not precisely known and hamper interpretation. It is made clear that non-Israelite skills were used in the decoration of God's house. This was considered as another expression of practically-inspired wisdom shown in 'understanding and knowledge' comparable with that used in the construction of the tabernacle (tent) shrine (*cf.* Ex. 31:3–5). Separate basic information is given on the bronze pillars (vv. 15–22), the basin 'Bronze Sea' (vv. 23–26), the mobile stands (vv. 27–37) and basins and lavers (vv. 38–39) as well as items not elsewhere described (vv. 40–45). A note is added on the place where the work was done (vv. 46–47) and lists given from different sources of the gold-work (vv. 48–51). Correlation with other lists indicates the originality of these details.

a. Huram of Tyre (7:13–14). Architects are sometimes named in ancient building texts. Huram (the Huram[-abi], *cf.* vv. 40–45; 2 Ch. 2:13) may have been given reference to his mother and connection with Israel to bring this into a 'nationalistic' picture. The link with the Napthali/Dan border (as 2 Ch. 2:14) could have been through his mother's first marriage.

b. The Jakin and Boaz pillars (7:15–22). The two *bronze pillars* (*cf.* vv. 41–42) may have been hollow (RSV, LXX gives a width of four fingers = 7.5 cm.). The measurements, 8.1 m. high and 5.4 m. circumference (1.9 m. diameter) agree with Jeremiah 52:21 and may include the original capitals (vv. 16–20; *cf.* vv. 41–42).

17. The *interwoven chains* were of 'filigree work' (JB), 'nets of checker work' (NRSV), or 'bands or ornamental network' (REB) and were draped *seven* to each capital (MT *šiḇ'â*, read 'nets', *śᵉbāḵîm*, by RSV).

18. Some MSS read 'pomegranates' (*rimmônîm*), others 'pillars' (*'ammûḏîm*), set in two strings of a hundred (Je. 52:23) above the globular or *bowl shaped* projection (RSV, Heb. *beṭen*, 'belly'). An ivory pomegranate with the inscription 'belonging to the House of YHWY', perhaps the head of a staff used in the temple at this time, has survived.[1]

19–21. The top of the pillar had the working of a *lily* (Heb. *šûšan* or Egypt. *ssn*, 'lotus flower') possibly taken as a symbol of life.

The location of the pillars is debated. They could have been free-standing, as in a number of Phoenician and other examples.[2] They may have supported the projecting roof. The pillars to the right (south) and left were respectively named Jakin and Boaz (v. 21) but their purpose and significance is yet unknown. They seem too tall to be refillable cressets or light standards symbolic of the pillar of fire and cloud demonstrating God's presence. Other suggestions include one that here we have comments by the craftsmen that 'it is firm' or (*yākîn*) 'solid' and 'it is strong' (lit. 'with strength', *bᵉʿōz*). This seems unlikely, as are parallels within mythology and standing stones (fertility symbols). Some take the names as the first word of statements that *'He* (God) *will establish* the throne of David and his kingdom for ever' and *'in the strength* of the LORD shall the king rejoice', denoting the position of the Davidic dynasty.

c. 'The Bronze Sea' (7:23–26). This huge basin or reservoir was one of the great Hebrew technical works, corresponding in modern metallurgy to the casting of the largest church bell. It was viewed as a large expanse and volume of water (Heb. *yām*, 'sea' is only used figuratively here, v. 23) and corresponded with the bronze basin in the tabernacle (Ex. 30:17–21). It was used by priests for cleansing their hands and feet and perhaps also to supply water to the standing basins for the rinsing of offerings (2 Ch. 4:10).

23. The size is given as five metres in diameter and two and a half metres in height and a *handbreadth* (v. 26, a sixth of a cubit = 7.5 cm.) thick. The capacity was about ten thousand gallons (*two thousand baths* is a measure, *cf.* the post-exilic 'three

[1] N. Avigad, 'The inscribed Pomegranate from the "House of the Lord"', *BA* 53, 1990, pp. 158–166; *Israel Museum Journal* 8, 1989, pp. 7–13; *cf. BAR* 16, 1990, pp. 48–51 (Tell Nami). For further discussion see now 'The Pomegranate Scepter Head – From the Temple of the Lord or from a Temple of Asherah', *BAR* 18, 1992, pp. 42–45.

[2] From Hazor, Kamid el-Loz, Arad and Kition. See *IBD*, pp. 726–727; 2 Ch. 15–17 implies that they were free-standing 'in front of' the temple.

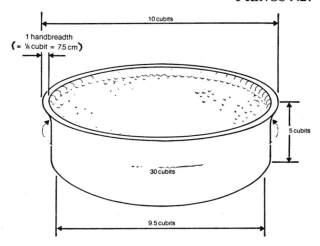

The Bronze Sea

thousand', 2 Ch. 4:5).[1] Its form has been reconstructed with the circumference given generally as *thirty cubits*.[2]

The heavy basin stood on twelve bronze oxen, with flattened hindquarters, set in groups of three facing outwards. There is no need to look for symbolic interpretation of a common architectural feature, whether representing the twelve tribes or, unlikely at this early date, the signs of the zodiac. For the technique of casting see verses 46–47.

d. The mobile stands (7:27–39). Ten identical stands (REB 'trolleys') to hold water basins, filled from the Bronze Sea, were four cubits square (2 m.) and *three high* (1.5 m.). Rare Hebrew terms are used in the description, and the detail of the cast metal structures is obscure. A circular framework supported the basin; and the struts and panels (vv. 28–29), 'bevelled' (RSV) rather than *hammered work* (NIV), were engraved with *wreaths* and chains, possibly the familiar Levantine guilloche or spiral patterns (as NEB) and other designs

[1] The *bath* is attested archaeologically as varying locally between 18 and 45 litres.

[2] A. Zuidhof, 'King Solomon's "Molten Sea" and (π)', *BA* 45, 1982, pp. 179–184.

set *in every available space* (v. 36), which may meant that they were spaced out rather than placed 'wherever there was a blank space' (NEB).

32. The wheel structure was elaborately made (vv. 30, 32) with axle-trees (rather than just *axles*) fixed to the stand as 'hand-shaped' sockets (Heb. *yāḏôṯ*, 'hands'; *cf.* NEB 'wheelforks').

39. The location of the Sea and stands shows that they were treated as heavy permanent fixtures, perhaps due to their weight when full of water.

e. Summary of bronze work (7:40–47). This is carefully listed and may come from Hiram or temple records. The detail differs only slightly in passages in which it is repeated (vv. 15–39; *cf.* 2 Ch. 4:11–18; 2 Ki. 25:13–17; Je. 52:21–23).

45. The *pots* were large cauldrons used for cooking the offering meat for the fellowship offerings (Lv. 7:15, 17); the *shovels* were for handling the ash and the *sprinkling bowls* (REB 'tossing-bowls') for ritual use with blood or water (Ex. 27:3). The gold examples may have been employed only on special occasions, the bronze ones being for everyday use.

46–47. The manufacture of all these articles by the *cire perdue* or lost wax process was done east of Jordan between *Succoth* (Deir 'Allah, north of the River Jabbok) and *Zarethan* (Tell es-Sa'idiyeh, west of Succoth, Jos. 3:16), where excavation shows much copper slag and the clay is suitable for digging moulds (*cf.* 'in the foundry', NEB) and there was ample water nearby. The firing of large wax shaped cores and filling them with the molten metal was a technique long employed in Egypt and Mesopotamia but required great skill to effect. That their weight was not counted is a common oriental way of emphasizing the large scale and value of the work which was such that it was later worth transporting to Babylon (Je. 52:17).

f. The list of gold articles (7:48–51). This includes the gold (incense-) *altar* (*cf.* 6:22), the ten tables for the *bread of the Presence* (AV 'Shewbread') and other items not mentioned elsewhere (for the main bronze altar see 2 Ki. 16:14).

49–50. The candelabra were arranged down the length of the main sanctuary to give light on these tables (Ex. 25:31–40). Golden door fittings, such as the *sockets* (AV 'hinges') are mentioned in Assyrian texts. The ladles (NIV *dishes*, but *kappôt* are tongs, lit. 'palms of the hands') were long-handled spoons in the form of cupped hands of which examples in metal, wood and ivory have been found in excavations.

51. Solomon added to his own gifts to the temple (1 Ch. 29:3) from the spoils of war already dedicated by David to God (2 Sa. 8:10–12). This resulted directly from the Hebrew concept of 'holy war' whereby a share of any spoils was dedicated as 'the LORD's part' (*e.g.* Nu. 31:25–47).

v. The dedication of the temple (8:1 – 9:9). The centre of 1 Kings' record of Solomon's reign is the building and dedication of the great temple in Jerusalem, into which the ark was carried to mark continuity with the Tent of Meeting which was the previous symbol of the divine presence (vv. 1–13). The ceremony was marked with prayer (vv. 14–61) and sacrifice, as well as a fellowship meal in which all the people participated (vv. 62–66). In this way the Covenant of God (lodged in the ark) was linked both with the temple as a precursor of the synagogue and church and with David's dynasty.

Reference to the books of the law, especially Deuteronomy and Exodus, abound but there is no direct reference to the destruction of the temple or to the exile in 587 BC which would make this account a post-exilic redaction.

a. The introduction of the ark (8:1–13). *Cf.* 2 Chronicles 5:2 – 6:11 and Josephus, *Ant.* viii.4, LXX is shorter.

1. To unite the nation a solemn assembly (*qhl* – hence the traditional association of Solomon with Qoheleth (Ecclesiastes)) was called to witness (v. 3) and mark their agreement to the new location of the national shrine. David had moved the ark from Obed-Edom's house to newly captured Jerusalem (2 Sa. 6:1–12; 15:24–29) and now it moved on from Zion on the south hill of Jerusalem to the 'citadel' (JB, 'city', *cf.* 2:10) to the new city extension to the north. The whole city would from now on be referred to as *Zion* (2 Ki. 19:31; Ps. 9:11).

2. The date is given as September/October (*Ethanim* by the old local calendar, *i.e.* Bab. Tishri) and the *festival* would be the Feast of Tabernacles (Ingathering or harvest; Dt. 16:13–15) which normally lasted a week (15th – 21st day). As an additional week's festival was added (see on v. 65), some conclude that this must have been one year after the completion of the building (6:38, the eighth month, *i.e.* Bul).

3–4. The *Tent of Meeting* (AV 'tabernacle'; NEB 'Tent of the Presence'; Ex. 33:7–11) was brought in from Gibeon (3:4; 1 Sa. 7:1; 2 Ch. 5:4–5) and would remind the people of the festival 'booths' and Exodus tents (Lv. 23:42) at the pilgrim festival time. The *priests* carried the ark and probably the *Levites* (from the country cities) the Tent, apart from furnishings, for the former alone would enter the inner sanctuary. The theory that the historian gives prominence to the role of the Levites here is disputed.[1]

5. *Sacrificing* (the subject is indeterminate and the verb indicates repetition or intensity) does not necessarily mean that individuals did the slaughtering themselves. Possibly sacrifices were made at each stopping-place following David's action (2 Sa. 6:13). For the *assembly of Israel* (RSV 'congregation') is more than just the priests (see Nu. 14:35; 16:11). The lack of accounting does not mean this was an exaggeration (*cf.* vv. 63–64; 7:47).

6–8. The positioning between the cherubim (*cf.* 6:23–28; Ex. 25:15, 20) meant that the ends of *the poles* of the ark were visible only from just outside the inner sanctuary (*Most Holy Place*, v. 8), either because the drawn curtain was hung inset from the opening or, less likely, because the poles pressed against the curtain as placed east-west. *There today, i.e.* before the ark and the covenant tablets were lost in the destruction of 587 BC. The absence of reference to Aaron's rod and the urn of manna (*cf.* Nu. 17:10; Ex. 16:33; Heb. 9:4), originally lying alongside the ark (*cf.* Ex. 25:16; 40:20), could be explained by their earlier removal with other items 'laid up' with the ark (1 Sa. 6:3–5).[2]

9. *Horeb* was another name for Sinai or a specific place within it (*cf.* Dt. 1:2). For the covenant made there see Exodus 20; Deuteronomy 4:13.

10–13. The *glory of the LORD* always marks his presence just as at Sinai (Ex. 24:15–17) and later in the tabernacle when the cloud (Heb. *ʿārāpel*; Ex. 20:21; Dt. 4:11), a thick cloud whether of darkness or light, signifies that God was now possessing his

---

[1] J. G. McConville, 'Priests and Levites in Ezekiel', *TynB* 34, 1983, pp. 4–9, argues that the Deut. use of terminology shows that 'Levites' is used in a general way, of the 'priestly' tribe.
[2] J. Boyd, 'What was in the Ark?', *EQ* 11, 1939, pp. 165–168.

house. It was not present all the time (Is. 6:3–4; *cf.* the trans-figuration of Jesus, Mk. 9:7; 2 Pet. 1:17). The poetic frag-ment of verse 13 has been taken by some to come from the book of the Song (*šîr*), a possible reference to 'The Book of Jashar' (*yāšār*, Jos. 10:13; 2 Sa. 1:18) and the RSV, NEB and Gk. add 'The LORD who has set the sun in the heavens' after *the dark cloud* (v. 12, RSV 'thick darkness') which shrouds God (Ex. 24:15; Dt. 4:11; Ps. 18:10–11) had *filled the temple of the LORD*. This is no evidence for sun worship, as some suggest.

13. The *magnificent temple* (RSV 'exalted house', AV 'settled house'; *bêt zᵉbul*) attempts to translate a difficult word, taken either as 'royal (princely) house' (Ugar. *zbl*), 'lofty abode' or, by change of text, as 'sitting enthroned' (*lᵉšibtᵉkā*). In Hebrew thought there is no incompatibility between divine omni-presence and a local dwelling-place on earth where he made himself known (Is. 8:18; Ps. 76:2).

b. Solomon's declaration (8:14–21). This begins with verse 12, but launches into a review of acts of God in the nation's history in choosing a people, a place (Zion) and a person (through David's line, *cf.* Pss. 68; 89; 132). Facing the assembly, the king stands to greet them (*blessed, brk*, a gesture that does not apply only to a priest; for *praise*, v. 15, RSV reads 'blessed'). God's promise to David came through Nathan (2 Sa. 7:5–16).

16. *My Name* denotes the LORD himself (5:5). David had planned it but been told that Solomon would be the builder (5:5; 2 Sa. 7:13). The family line is associated with the temple.

c. Solomon's prayer of dedication (8:22–61). This prayer was made not only for himself but for the royal family and the nation that it would remember the true significance of the temple as showing God's presence even amid national calamity.

i. The approach to God (8:22–31). **22.** *He stood before* is used of being 'in attendance on' (10:8), the place was on a plat-form near the bronze altar in the outer court used for mass worship (*cf.* 2 Ch. 6:12–42). Standing is not as common an Old Testament attitude for prayer as is kneeling (*cf.* v. 54) and the spreading out of both hands (v. 38, Ex. 9:29; Is.

1:15). Prayers of dedication were commonly made at the opening of temples and palaces (*e.g.* Esarhaddon in Babylon).[1]

Effective prayer is based on three facts about God:

(i) His incomparability (Ex. 15:11; Dt. 4:39; Ps. 86:8–10).

(ii) His trustworthiness to fulfil his covenant, never failing to keep his word (v. 24; Dt. 7:9), or to show his covenant love (*ḥeseḏ, cf.* 3:6). For the promise of verse 25, *cf.* 2 Samuel 7:5–16. The answer to prayer depends also on the obedience of the person who prays (v. 25, *cf.* 9:4–9; 2 Ch. 7:14, 17).

(iii) His transcendence (vv. 27–30). God is both up there and down here. Where he is (his Name, Dt. 12:5), there is the answer (*cf.* Mt. 18:19–20), and God's temple will not limit or localize his activity.[2]

28. Three different words for prayer are used here:

(i) *Prayer* (*tᵉpillâ*): intercession and praise (vv. 29–30, 33, 35, 38, 42, 44–45, 48–49).

(ii) *Plea for mercy* (*tᵉḥinnâ*): earnest prayer for help (vv. 45, 52), 'entreaty' (JB; REB v. 52), 'supplication' (AV, REB).

(iii) *Cry* (*rinnâ*): ringing cry of joy or sorrow, petition (vv. 28, 52).

ii. 'The sevenfold petition' (8:32–53). Within each of the seven parts of the prayer is a sevenfold reference or key phrase relating to the temple's place as God's 'house of prayer' (Is. 56:7; Lk. 19:46) and to the answer needed. This should be so in our homes also. *Towards this place, cf.* verses 29–30, 33, 35, 38, 42, 45, 48; and as did Daniel (Dn. 6:10). *Hear ... and forgive* (vv. 30, 34, 36, 39) / *judge* (v. 32) / *restore* (v. 34) / *teach* (v. 36) / *act* (v. 39) / *do what he asks* (v. 43) / *uphold their cause* (vv. 45, 49). The format of the seven requests is that used in case law, *i.e. when a man* (RSV 'should a man ...'); *if* / when *a man ..., cf.* the Laws of Hammurapi, which assumes that he has or will so act. These show seven common instances in which people would turn to God:

31–32. I. When a man wrongs a neighbour: When this was

[1] M. Weinfeld, *Deuteronomy and the Deuteronomic School* (Oxford: Oxford University Press, 1972), pp. 33ff., 248ff.

[2] This has been taken as a typical 'argument from the minor to the major', perhaps used also in 1 Ki. 8:27; 2 Ki. 10:4. It represents a hermeneutical principle also used by later rabbis to expand and elaborate on biblical teaching (L. Jacobs, 'The qal va-ḥomer argument in the Old Testament', *BSOAS* 35, 1972, pp. 221–227).

alleged to have happened he had to submit to an oath to show his innocence. Before the altar in the outer court he would swear an oath (v. 64) to prove innocence (*cf.* Ex. 22:7–12) and God as judge would declare him innocent (MT 'righteous') or guilty (*cf.* Dt. 25:1). Whatever the means of discerning the truth, following the use of the high priests' Urim and Thummim to provide the answer (Ex. 28:29–30), which now may have been displaced by a legal judgment, this is ratified in the temple's sacred precincts. A guilty person finds that this is self-judgment (Heb. 'bring his way [of life] *on his own head*'). So Romans 6:23.

33–34. II. When the nation is defeated: Such disaster is taken to be the result of sin against God by disobeying or departing from his covenant (Jos. 7:11–12). The only way of restoration is to repent (*turn back* to God), *confess* (RSV 'acknowledge') and pray. *Bring them back to the land* does not itself imply that they were in long exile (see on verse 46 below).

35–36. III. Disaster following drought: When the blessing of rain was held back, as periodically, this was to be taken as a sign of sin against God (Dt. 11:13–14; 28:23–24). The purpose of divine punishment is to 'make humble' (*cf. afflicted*) and to educate (*teach* or direct *the right way to live*; MT, REB 'The good way which they are to follow') – that is, according to God's covenant plan (Dt. 6:18; 1 Sa. 12:23).

37–40. IV. Other natural disasters: Famine (Dt. 32:24; Lv. 26:19–20) and plague (Dt. 28:21–22; 32:24; Lv. 26:25) are taken to be another sign of divine displeasure even though the fault of ruler or people. As verse 37 shows, there were many 'natural' causes: (a) The *blight* (*šiddāpôn*) due to the scorching east wind (Dt. 28:22; Hag. 2:17). This is usually taken as a plant disease called 'paleness' or 'the green disease'. The word is also used of jaundice.[1] (b) The *mildew* (*yērāqôn*) caused by rain too abundant or at the wrong time. These are also taken to be 'blight either black or red' (REB). (c) Attacks by flying insects on growing crops, *e.g. locusts* ('*arbeh*). (d) Crawling insects such as the 'caterpillar' (RSV; *ḥāsîl, cf.* NIV *grasshoppers*, so Dt. 28:38, 42). Some take this as another stage in the life-cycle of the locust (see commentaries on Joel 1:4).[2] Manmade curses include famine due to siege (Dt. 28:52) *in any of*

[1] F. Rosner, *Medicine in the Bible and the Talmud* (Ktav: Sanhedrin Press, 1977), p. 70.

[2] *Cf.* D. A. Hubbard, *Joel and Amos*, TOTC (Leicester: IVP, 1989), pp. 42–43.

their cities (LXX; MT 'in the land, in the gates' may denote 'in country or in town'). For *disaster* harsh and prolonged see also Deuteronomy 28:59–61; 32:23–25 and for *disease* severe and lingering see Deuteronomy 28:22.

The reference to an individual (v. 38, *any of your people*) and conscience (*affliction of his own heart*, NEB 'remorse') need not be a later addition. God alone knows the *heart* (v. 39, *cf.* Je. 17:10). One aim of punishment is reverent loving submission following forgiveness (Ps. 130:4).

41–43. V. The need of non-Jews: The foreigner (*nākrî*, as opposed to the resident alien, *gēr*) is the subject of the next prayer. Many non-Jews would be attracted to the LORD through his widely known mighty deeds and fame (*Name*). They were to be allowed to worship (Nu. 15:14) and acknowledge God's saving power (*outstretched arm* is not an attitude of prayer). Many would hear and respond (see on 9:9; 10:1, *cf.* Jos. 2:9–11). The LORD's house was to be a 'house of prayer for all nations' (*cf.* Is. 56:7; Mk. 11:17).

44–45. VI. Success in war: Military action might be taken with divine sanction ('holy war') in punishing evil-doers (Dt. 20; 26:10; Lv. 26:7; 2 Sa. 5:19, 24). Even in this God must be constantly in mind so that God will *uphold their* (righteous) *cause* (MT 'do their [right] judgment', *mišpaṭ*).

46–51. VII. Defeat in war: This too may be attributed to sin and God's consequent anger (*cf.* Dt. 4:21). From the ninth century BC, if not earlier, exile was known to the Israelites as common among ancient Near Eastern peoples, and to *take captive* (*šābāh*), which is here used with a play on the word *repent* (*šûb*), does not necessarily imply a reference to the later exile in Babylon (so *far away or near*). Return of captives is mentioned in early Babylonian texts, *cf.* the Laws of Hammurapi § 27, *c.* 1730 BC. Prayer always demands action by the suppliants to rethink the situation (Heb. AV 'bethink themselves'), *repent* (change of heart), *plead* (as v. 28), and confess their sin.

Verse 47 has different words for *sin*(ner) (*ḥāṭā'*, 'miss the mark'), *done wrong* ('*āwā*, 'acted perversely', RSV, a deliberate action) and *acted wickedly* (*rāšā'*, doing what is against the accepted, right way). In verse 50 *offences* (*pēša'*) denotes rebellion against God and his law.

Toward the land . . . city. This practice (v. 48) could have begun before the Babylon exile (*cf.* Dn. 6:10; Jon. 2:4). *Uphold their cause* (v. 49, NEB 'grant them justice', *cf.* v. 59) does not specifically imply the grant of freedom but *cf.* verse 51. *Show them mercy* (v. 50), better 'grant them compassion' (MT, AV, RSV) in the presence of those who took them away.

52–54. The prayer ends with reference to the Sinai Covenant (Ex. 19:5; Dt. 7:6) as it began with the Davidic Covenant (vv. 23–30). *You singled them out* (*hiḇᵉḏîl*), separated them (RSV, AV), a verb used of the veil dividing the Most Holy Place from the sanctuary (Ex. 26:33). There is no direct allusion here to the so-called 'Holiness Code' (*qdš*).

iii. The concluding act (8:54–61). The 'Blessing of Solomon' is not strictly a blessing but a prayer for the continuing close relationship between God and his people. If taken as a blessing, this is not always an act exclusive to priests (v. 14, *cf.* Nu. 6:23). True prayer rests on God's promise *never* to *leave* or *forsake us* (v. 57, so Dt. 31:6–8; Ps. 94:14; Heb. 13:5). God does not do what men are prone to (*cf.* Dt. 32:15, 'not forsake' is taken as 'heal'). For God leaving his people because they abandon him see 2 Kings 21:14–15; Psalm 27:9; Jeremiah 2:13; 5:7, *etc.*

58. To keep us close God turns *our hearts to him* (Ps. 119:36) to enable us to keep his covenant (Dt. 30:6; Ps. 51:10; Phil. 2:13), *i.e. to walk in all his ways.*

59–61. Reference to Solomon's own prayer is not unusual (*cf.* v. 57). Prayer for *each day's need* (RSV 'as each day requires'), as in the Lord's prayer (Mt. 6:11). The purpose of God's choice of his people (v. 60) is *that all peoples of the earth may know that* he alone *is God* (*cf.* Dt. 4:35; Is. 45:5). For this to happen they must be *fully committed* (*šālem 'im, cf.* REB 'in perfect loyalty'), *i.e.* in covenant relation (peace) with the LORD.

d. Solomon's feast (8:62–66). This inaugurates the temple as the place of sacrifice. That all *offered a sacrifice* means that they brought their offerings (12:27). *Dedicated: ḥānak* is literally to 'begin, inaugurate, initiate'; of a child, Pr. 22:6; or a home, Dt. 20:5. Later the Feast of Hannukah commemorated the rededication of the temple in 164 BC. The large number of sacrifices is given in general terms, but details of similar acts at the opening of new buildings at Nimrud,[1] Ashur and

[1] D. J. Wiseman, 'A New Stela of Aššur-naṣir-pal II', *Iraq* 14, 1952, p. 32, l. 149; 869 BC with 69, 574 participants in 869 BC.

Nineveh[1] also tell of many sacrifices and participants. The *fellowship offering* (AV, RSV 'peace offerings', *šᵉlāmîm*; cf. JB 'communion sacrifice offerings', REB 'shared offerings', others 'thank offerings') was shared by God, priests and worshippers. Some argue that this offering was the last offered and listed, hence 'concluding sacrifice', and see in Ephesians 2:14 Christ's final sacrifice for humankind (cf. Heb. 9:27; 10:12–14).

64. The number of offerings required greater space (and altars), so the whole courtyard was consecrated (*qdš*) and used. The *bronze altar* is now introduced (cf. 9:25). The other offerings were part of the regular daily sacrifice.

65. *At that time.* See Introduction, p. 57 (iv). From *Lebo-Hamath* in the Beqaʻ valley on the north boundary (*i.e.* Assyr. *Laba'u*; modern Labweh), mentioned in eighteenth-century BC Egyptian execration texts. For Solomon's dominions see 4:21. The south boundary was the *Wadi of Egypt* (Assyr. *Nahal-Muṣri*, modern Wadi al-'Arish).[2]

66. *They blessed the king, i.e.* thanked him (*brk*). Misunderstanding this, the LXX makes Solomon give a final blessing of dismissal. As in the Assyrian examples, the crowds left 'happy in heart' (JB, MT *ṭôḇ lēḇ*, 'goodness of heart' ranges from *joyfulness* and contentment to pleasure at the covenant relationship being celebrated). All the people recognized the good that Solomon had done as the LORD's action.

e. The LORD appears to Solomon again (9:1–9). Cf. 2 Chronicles 7:11–12. An empty temple would be meaningless. Solomon is told again that the continued presence of God with his people will depend on obedience to his requirements and trust in his promises. The promises made to David and reaffirmed to his son at *Gibeon* (3:4–15) refers back to Solomon's *prayer and plea* (v. 3, 8:25–30). The LORD God answers the 'dedication' of the temple to him by Solomon (8:63–64) by the statement *I have consecrated this temple* (v. 3, *qdš*). Only God can make a person or place holy. He *put his Name* and reputation *there* (cf. 8:10–13). That God's Name 'will be fixed on it' (v. 3, NEB) answers 8:29.

---

[1] D. D. Luckenbill, *The Annals of Sennacherib* (Chicago: Chicago University Press, 1924), p. 116 ('Palace without a Rival', viii.65–76, 'countless sacrifices' at the dedication).

[2] D. J. Wiseman, 'Two Historical Inscriptions from Nimrud', *Iraq* 13, 1951, pp. 23–24.

4. The reference to what *David did* (15:5, 11) will be a yardstick judging future kings in a dynasty which will be named by David, not Solomon. The rest of Kings will be preoccupied with the blessing which follows obedience and the curses enacted after any failure to obey. The reference point will be to God's revealed word and the language is that of Deuteronomy.

Walk before me is to conduct oneself (live) in the presence of God and his law. This is timely advice because Solomon, now in his twenty-fourth regnal year, is pressed by his own desires (vv. 1, 19, *ḥāpēṣ*, 'what he took pleasure in, ambition'; *cf.* 2 Ch. 7:11, 'all he had in mind to do') which led to wealth and fame and then to self-reliance. The latter can be the enemy of *integrity of heart* (v. 4, 3:6, *tām lēḇāḇ*), 'completeness' in the sense of being in accord with truth, not perfectionism. *Uprightness* includes honesty. There are qualities which must distinguish God's covenant-keeping people.

6–7. *If you . . .* The glory and continuance of the temple and dynasty are conditional. This is a warning, not a threat. The plural is used here as ruler and people are involved equally in maintaining the distinctive tenets of Israel's faith (*cf.* Rom. 9:4).

The fate of the temple will be the opposite to that prayed for (*cf.* 8:43). The *byword* (*māšāl*, 'proverb') and *object of ridicule* (*šᵉnînâ*, RSV 'byword', NRSV 'taunt', REB 'object-lesson') are used of taunt-songs. For this fate see Deuteronomy 28:37; Jeremiah 24:9. These terms, with *appalled* and 'scoff' (NEB 'gasp', Heb. 'hiss'), are expressions of the utmost surprise and horror (*cf.* Je. 18:16).

8. *This temple*, far from being *imposing* (*cf.* AV 'high', *ʿelyôn*, 'the lofty one'), will become a 'heap of ruins' (NEB, RSV by reading *ʿiyyîm* unnecessarily).

9. *The LORD brought disaster* (Heb. 'evil', *cf.* Is. 45:7). That this was foretold emphasizes that it is, in effect, self-judgment. AV, RSV make this a question.

C. Solomon's other activities (9:10 – 11:43)

Cf. 2 Chronicles 1:14–17; 8:1–9. Solomon's work outside Jerusalem required additional resources. These he now sought by (i) a further agreement with Hiram (vv. 10–14), (ii) the extended use of forced labour (vv. 15–25), and (iii) the profits from maritime expeditions (vv. 26–28). In carrying out the work (vv. 15–19), Solomon seems to have run into debt after the earlier commercial contract (5:1–11) expired with the completion of the temple and royal palaces.

i. A summary (9:10–28).

a. A further agreement with Hiram (9:10–14). **11.** To pay for the *gold* (*cf.* v. 14; no gold is mentioned in the earlier transaction) Solomon mortgaged *twenty* 'settlements' (rather than *towns*, for *'îrîm* is used of any group of habitations from a hamlet to a metropolis). As with eighteenth-century BC contracts from Alalakh in Syria, the 'exchange' of villages was used to adjust a border, here that to the north-west with Phoenicia.[1] The border villages may have been fortified for defence purposes and seem to have been redeemed later (2 Ch. 8:2), perhaps following successful trade (v. 14) or tribute brought from Sheba (*cf.* 10:10).

13. *Brother* is used diplomatically to mean 'ally'. Some equate *Cabul* with the new border at modern Kābûl, recently excavated thirteen kilometres south-east of Acco (*cf.* Josephus, *Ant.* viii.5.3). Others see it as a play on words meaning 'as nothing' or 'defective'. It could simply mean 'border-land' (*cf.* Heb. *yᵉbûl*).

14. This is a massive quantity of *gold*, about four tons (Phoenician *talent* of 60 minas, *i.e.* 3,000 shekels or 75 lb.).

b. The use of forced labour (9:15–23). *Cf.* 2 Chronicles 8:3–16; LXX varies. This is marked as from a separate *account* (or 'record', REB, *dᵉḇar*, 'matter'). Lists of royal building projects are common among ancient Near Eastern texts. For the supporting terraces see on verse 24.

15. Solomon fortified strategic cities to guard the main approaches to his kingdom. The list runs north to south. All show archaeological evidence of identical construction work of the Solomonic period, casemate-type walls and similar 'six-roomed' gate towers.[2] *Hazor* (Tell el-Qedah), eight kilometres

---

[1] D. J. Wiseman, *The Alalakh Tablets* (London: British Institute of Archaeology at Ankara, 1953), Nos. 76–80.

[2] The excavator Yadin (*BA* 33, 1970, p. 67) said, 'There is no example in the history of archaeology where a passage helped so much in identifying and dating structures in several of the most important (ruin-)tells in the Holy-Land as has 1 Kings 9:15.'

south-west of Lake Huleh (now almost drained dry), control-led the road from the north; *Megiddo* (Tell el-Mutesellim, see on 4:12) the road from Phoenicia and through the Carmel range.

16. *Gezer* (Tel Jezer, south-east of Ramleh) guarded the south-west approaches from Philistia. There is no need to read 'Gerar' here. Verses 16–17 are added to show how the Israelites had taken over the city from the Canaanite vassals of the Philistines (*cf.* vv. 20–21; Jos. 10:33; Jdg. 1:29).[1] For the *Pharaoh* see on 3:1. *Wedding gift (šilluḥîm)*, a present on send-ing away the bride, is better than 'dowry' (RSV).

17. *Lower Beth Horon*, eighteen kilometres north-west of Jerusalem (modern Beit 'Ur et-Taḥta), commands the road through the Ayalon Valley to the west. *Baalath*, south-west of Beth-Horon in Dan (Jos. 19:44). *Tadmor* (MT $Q^e r\bar{e}$) is read as Tamar (LXX, RSV, $K^e \underline{t}\hat{\imath}\underline{b}$) and identified with 'Ain Husb, south of the Dead Sea. This is *in the desert* ('wilderness', NEB)[2] but the change might be unnecessary if there was a Tadmor in the south, as distinct from the famous caravan city (= Palmyra, 240 kilometres north-east of Damascus).

19. This is a general statement about military garrison facili-ties at *store cities* ('places for putting things', see Ex. 1:11). At a number of places (Megiddo, Lachish, *etc.*) long pillared store-rooms have been found. Solomon may well have built a sum-mer palace or other frontier defences *in Lebanon* (not in LXX).

20–23. There is no reason to believe that the system of forced labour differs from that employed in 5:13–16, where two forms were used: (i) The short-term, but unpopular, conscription of Israelite (Hebrew) citizens. No Israelites could be used as true *slaves*. (ii) Non-Israelites are referred to by their tribes, though with the Canaanites (*cf.* v. 16) and Gir-gashites omitted from the traditional seven groups here (*cf.* Ex. 3:8; Dt. 7:1; 20:17). *Captains (šālîš)* were originally the armour-bearer or 'third-man' in the chariot, though they by now had become an aide-de-camp (NEB 'lieutenant'), *cf.* 2 Kings 7:2. For the *government officials* see on 4:5. The number *550* is again a multiple of eleven (possibly representative of the tribes less Judah); see 5:16.

Verses 24–28 provide additional data, possibly from later in the reign.

[1] A. R. Millard, in *POTT*, pp. 64–65.
[2] Y. Aharoni, 'Tamar and the Road to Elath', *IEJ* 13, 1963, pp. 30–42.

c. Further construction (9:24). This verse continues the reference back to 3:1–4. The *supporting terraces* or Millo (Heb., *i.e.* 'Fill') may have been a construction either forming the extension of the stepped terrace and city wall on the east flank of the palace, or a fill bridging the depression between Zion and Ophel (*cf.* v. 15; 2 Sa. 5:9; 1 Ki. 11:27; 2 Ki. 12:20). However, the use of the word *ml'* elsewhere may indicate a platform or terrace inside the encircling acropolis walls, perhaps as an aid to defence.[1]

d. Temple worship and sacrifice (9:25). The three annual festivals were Passover, Pentecost and Tabernacles (as Ex. 23:14–17; Dt. 16). The annual ritual and the central national position of the temple were by now established. Solomon provided, but did not make, the sacrifices himself (see on 8:63–64). The *burnt offerings* were totally burned (NEB 'whole-offering'), while the *fellowship offerings* were shared (see on 8:63). *Burned incense*: the difficult Heb. *'a šer* (LXX omits) is commonly taken to mean 'his fire-offering' (*'iššô*, NEB 'making smoke-offerings'). *Fulfilled* (*šillam*) *the temple obligations* probably is better taken to mean 'completed the (temple) arrangements' rather than 'finished the house' (RSV), 'paid his vows' (NEB), or 'kept the temple in good repair' (JB), both of which would be expected anyway.

e. Solomon's sea-trade (9:26–28). To be read with 10:11–12; 2 Chronicles 8:17–18 for the full picture. The *fleet* of *ships* (*'°nî*, AV 'navy') was built and manned by experienced Phoenician shipwrights, as was Sennacherib's Assyrian fleet operating in the Persian Gulf. The home-port of *Ezion Geber* is now identified with Guzarat al Far'un and the nearby facilities for storage discovered by N. Glueck at Tell el-Kheleifeh, Gulf of Aqabah. It was always a strategic site controlling also the caravan routes from Arabia. It was rebuilt by Jehoram in 848 BC and Azariah (c. 780 BC; 22:48). *Elath* (near modern Elat; *cf.* Eloth, 2 Ki. 16:6; Dt. 2:8) is also on the Gulf of Aqabah (*yām sôp*, 'sea of Land's End', Je. 49:21) and is to be distinguished from the Red (or Reed) Sea (*yām sûp*) of the Exodus (13:18).

28. *Ophir* was a source of gold (Jb. 28:16; Is. 13:12), a trade

[1] R. C. Steiner, 'New Light on the Biblical Millo from Hatran Inscriptions', *BASOR* 276, 1989, p. 19; *cf.* K. Kenyon, *Digging up Jerusalem* (London: Benn, 1974), p. 100.

attested by the Tell Qasileh ostracon inscription.[1] Its location is probably South Arabia, for excavations at Madh ad-Dhahab between Saba (Yemen) and Hawîlan agree with the Genesis 10:29 description (*cf.* Ps. 72:15). Others have suggested Oman, Somalia, Baluchistan, India (Supara, north of Bombay) or even Zimbabwe, mainly on the assumption that a two- to three-year voyage implies a long distance (see 10:22). The gold *brought back* (*lāqaḥ*) implies exchange for goods traded.

ii. The Queen of Sheba's visit (10:1–13). *Cf.* 2 Chronicles 9:1–12; Josephus, *Ant.* viii.6.5–6. The history now includes an example of both Solomon's wisdom and wealth as it was viewed internationally. Both were the fulfilment of the divine promise of 3:13. The detail is sufficient for this to be no mere legend marked by exaggeration and can in a measure be paralleled in contemporary ancient texts. The visit was no 'wisdom contest' between rulers of great powers, for such is unattested at this time, but is based on a trade mission, since Solomon now controlled the 'Red Sea' and the caravan routes from east Arabia through Ezion Geber.

The Assyrians record encounters with queens ruling Sheba (Saba) in southwest Arabia (modern Yemen) down to the eighth century and thereafter with its priest-kings. This continuation of the account of the wisdom of Solomon is clearly related to his divinely given abilities and 'with reference' to (Heb.) *the name of the LORD* (v. 1), *i.e.* the temple (8:20). His wisdom is also expressed as the mastery of all learning and wit as well as military and civilian administration, in common with all ancient Near Eastern views of wisdom and prosperity (see Additional Note on wisdom, p. 85).

1. The *queen* is unnamed, it not being customary to do so other than by place of origin. The *hard* ('enigmatic', REB) *questions* (*ḥîdôt*) were not just 'riddles', as in Judges 14:12, but included difficult diplomatic and ethical questions. According to Josephus, Hiram had made similar approaches. The test was not an academic exercise but to see if he would be a trustworthy business partner and a reliable ally capable of giving help.

Later Jewish tradition interpreted *she came to . . . him* (*bô' 'el*) as implying sexual relations in a love affair ('all she had on her

---

[1] *I.e.* 'gold from Ophir for Beth Horon, 30 shekels' on a Hebrew ostracon inscribed *zhb 'pr lbyt hrn š≡*. See illustrations in *IBD*, p. 1120.

heart', v. 2; and 'all she desired', v. 13) which resulted in the birth of Nebuchadnezzar (Rashi) or Menelik I, founder of Ethiopia, but since the parentage of both these rulers is known, that is legendary.[1]

2. It was customary for a visitor to bring a gift to a royal audience. The quantities involved here could well imply a trade mission, *cf.* vv. 10, 13. The *caravan* (*ḥayil*) denotes a company of men (better RSV 'retinue', as NIV at v. 13). *Camels* were used as burden bearers in Arabia from the early third millennium onwards (*cf.* Gn. 12:16) and carried *spices* (*bᵉśāmîm*, 'sweet smelling things'). Such luxuries would have included balsam (Song 5:1) and frankincense traded through her territory.[2]

4. Solomon's display of his own wealth and trust in riches will be condemned, as it can lead to trust in things other than God alone (*cf.* Pr. 11:28). The historian includes it as a by-product of wisdom, but later rejects it when vanity is involved (as in Hezekiah's display to Babylonian visitors, 2 Ki. 20:13). On the connection between wisdom and wealth see pp. 85, 131ff.

5. The scale of sumptuous entertainment (*the food*), and the *seating* (*môšab*) which would be according to rank (NEB 'courtiers sitting around him'), as well as the accommodation for his officials may be in mind. The *attending servants* (*mᵉšārᵉtîm*) 'in their livery' (NEB) were not waiters but officials, nor were the *cupbearers* part of the drinking service but officers of high rank (as the *rab shakeh* of 2 Ki. 18:19).[3] The *burnt offerings* (*'ōlātô*) would have been numerically impressive (*cf.* 8:62; 9:25), though some think the reference may be the 'ascent' (NIV mg., AV *'ālâ*, 'to go up'), or the stairway leading up to the temple (REB, 2 Ch. 9:4). This walkway might later have been that known as 'Solomon's Colonnade' (Jn. 10:23; Acts 3:11).

The queen is 'left breathless' (MT, *cf.* NIV *overwhelmed*), and acknowledges (vv. 6–7) Solomon's *achievements*, wisdom (Mt. 12:42) and *wealth* (*ṭôb*, 'good'; others interpret this as 'prosperity', AV, RSV, NEB reading *ṭûb*).

8. Her statement acknowledges both Solomon's spiritual inheritance and his God. The phrase *How happy* (*'ašrē*) is not a

---

[1] For an excellent survey of these traditions see E. Ullendorff, *Ethiopia and the Bible* (London: British Academy, 1968), pp. 131–145.

[2] F. N. Hepper, 'Arabian and African Frankincense Trees', *JEA* 55, 1969, pp. 66–72.

[3] A. Malamat, 'Philological Note', *BA* 46, 1983, p. 171.

beatitude but an exclamation. Some read 'wives' (RSV, NEB) on the surprising assumption that a queen would not say *your men*, which is a general term used of citizens or household alike, and the fact that his officials are mentioned separately (*cf*. 1:9; Dt. 32:26).

9–10. The queen seems to have been told much about Solomon: his selection for the throne (3:7; 8:20), Israel's concept of kingship and the need under God to maintain *justice and righteousness* as the expression of God's *eternal love* and care for his people Israel. This includes the exercise of law and order (*cf*. 3:28; 4:24–25). *Praise be to the LORD* implies recognition of Israel's national God and need not necessarily be an expression of personal faith. A parting gift was usually given by the host (as v. 13) but the large donation of *gold* (v. 10) implies the conclusion of a commercial or even vassal treaty.

11–12. Hiram's participation in trade is inserted here in parenthesis to illustrate another successful joint agreement (*cf*. 9:26–28). The luxuries included *almug-wood* (*cf*. Ugar. *'lmg*; Akkad. *elammaku*) rather than 'algum', also available from Lebanon (2 Ch. 2:7–8). This may be red sandalwood[1] or Red Saunders imported from India and Ceylon and used to make musical instruments.[2] *Harps and lyres* attest early temple music and psalms, as already known from Ras Shamra (1300 BC) and Mesopotamia (2300 BC).[3]

13. The trade was confirmed by granting all requests 'according to the resources (lit. 'hand') of king Solomon'.

iii. Solomon's wealth (10:14–29). *Cf*. 2 Chronicles 9:13–24. Solomon's splendour became proverbial (Mt. 6:29), as did his wisdom (Mt. 12:42). Those who would consider his income of *666 talents* (*c*. 21.6 tons) *of gold* exaggeration should compare this with amounts registered in ancient Egypt about this time, 'where gold is like dust in the land' and Osorkon I in his first four years (*c*. 924–920 BC) accumulated eighteen tons of gold, to which some of the loot taken by his father Shishak from

---

[1] W. E. Clark, 'The Sandalwood and Peacocks of Ophir', *AJSL* 36, 1920, p. 103.

[2] M. Zohary, *Plants of the Bible* (Cambridge: Cambridge University Press, 1982), p. 125.

[3] Bît Rimki, *Sounds from Silence* (University of Berkeley, California, 1977), with recording; A. D. Kilmer, 'The Cult song with music from Ancient Ugarit', *Revue d'Assyriologie* 68, 1974, pp. 69–82; I. H. Jones, 'Musical Instruments in the Bible', *The Bible Translator* 37, 1986, pp. 101–143; 38, 1987, pp. 129–143.

Jerusalem should be added (*cf.* 14:25–27). Similar large-scale acquisition and use of gold in temple buildings is attested from Mesopotamia.[1]

14. Large amounts were easily accumulated both by *yearly* receipts of tribute (RSV 'in one year') and by income from transit and other taxes.

15. *Revenues* follows LXX (reading *mēʿonšē* for MT *mēʾanšē*, 'men'). They came from 'tolls levied by the customs officers, and profits on foreign trade and tribute' (NEB) or from the *merchants* (*tārîm*), agents who arranged the return of goods, and *traders* (*sᵉḥar*) – perhaps Solomon's own sales force who went around trading.[2] *Cf.* 'travelling salesmen and wholesale dealers' (Delitzsch). The *Arabian kings* were probably local sheiks dealing with Solomon. For the district or regional *governors* see 4:7–19.

16–17. Ceremonial shields. The *large shields* (*ṣinnāh*) protected the whole person and *small* round *shields* covered with beaten gold (*šāḥûṭ*) as a thick foil weighed up to nine kilogrammes (assuming that the unstated measure of 'shekels' was omitted, as in the earlier Alalakh tablets from Syria). These shields may have been carried on ceremonial occasions (*cf.* 14:28). David's treasures had been rededicated in the new temple (7:51), but these were added to the palace treasury, where they were looted by Shishak and replaced by Rehoboam with bronze substitutes (14:26–27).

18–20. The royal throne. Its use is implied in 7:7. As was common in fine furniture, ivory was inlaid and covered with *fine gold* (or 'Gold from Uphaz', Dn. 10:5) affixed by bitumen. The throne set on top of steps was an architectural convention used also in the later Babylonian six-staged tower with a temple on top of a zigurrat and in altars (Ezk. 43:13–17). There is no sure evidence that this had cosmic significance. Archaeological illustrations deny the theory that for the customary *rounded top* (*ʿāgol*) this should be read *ʿēgel*, 'a calf' or as 'a footstool' (*cf.* 2 Ch. 9:18). Examples of lion-sphinxes beside the throne and lions couchant leading up to it are found in Egypt, Palestine and Syria.[3] The rearward curving back is paralleled in Egypt but the whole appears to be a

[1] A. R. Millard, 'Solomon's Gold', *Vox Evangelica* 12, 1981, pp. 13–17.
[2] On *šḥr* see *TWOT*, p. 1484; W. F. Albright, 'Abram the Hebrew: A New Archaeological Interpretation', *BASOR* 163, 1961, pp. 36–54; 164, p. 28.
[3] *E.g.* on the Megiddo ivory plaque, see *ANEP*, p. 111 (No. 332).

unique local creation. The steps at the side and front with the pairs of lions focused attention on the king.[1]

21. The devaluation of a currency (silver) due to abundance of a once rarer commodity (gold) is found elsewhere (*e.g.* Ashurbanipal of Assyria).

22. The *trading ships* (*cf.* 9:26–28) were 'ships of Tarshish' (MT), once thought to refer to Phoenician trade with Tartessus in Portugal *c.* 800 BC. This idea, like that of the 'refinery fleet' (from *rss*, 'to refine') and the supposed refineries at Ezion Geber (9:26), is now questioned. The term is used of a large ocean-going vessel.[2] *Once every three years*, a parallel concept to 'three day journey', means departure in one year, a year for business acquisitions and then, after trading along the coasts of Arabia, India or Africa, from which luxuries were brought, return in a third year. *Ivory* (*šēn*, 'tooth' in v. 18) was available in Syria, and this rare word here (*šenhabbîm*, 'elephant's teeth') may denote ivory tusks and ebony (*šēn wᵉhobnîm*, Ezk. 27:15). Foreign words (*qōpîm*) are used for *apes* (Egypt. *g3f*, Akkad. *uqupu*) and *baboons* (NEB 'monkeys', *tukkîyîm*), which some interpret as 'peacocks'.[3]

23. Solomon's commercial ventures (see vv. 26–29) are not incredible.

26. For the *twelve thousand horses* see on 4:26. *Horses* can also be read as 'horsemen' and *chariots* (*rekeb̠*, collective) as 'charioteers' (NIV mg.).[4] As did the Assyrians, Solomon dispersed his mobile forces between the capital and outlying, strategically placed, military bases (*e.g.* Megiddo, Gezer, Hazor).

27. For the effect of inflation due to excessive amounts of precious metal available see on verse 21. The comparison here is with the abundant Sycamore-fig trees (*Ficus Sycomorus*) of the coastal (Shephelah) plain, useful for wood but bearing poor fruit.[5]

28–29. Solomon's trading gains may have been due to the

[1] M. Metzger, *Königsthron und Gottesthron* (AOAT 15), 1985, pp. 298–308; *cf.* *BSOAS* 50, 1987, p. 127 (review by K. A. Kitchen).

[2] S. B. Hoenig, 'Tarshish', *JQR* 69, 1979, pp. 181–182.

[3] On the identification with Dravidian *tokei* which was dismissed by W. E. Clark, 'The Sandalwood and Peacocks of Ophir', *AJSL* 36, 1920, pp. 106–119.

[4] Y. Yadin, *The Art of Warfare in Bible Lands in the Light of Archaeological Discovery* (London: Weidenfeld & Nicholson, 1963), p. 286.

[5] M. Zohary, *Plants of the Bible* (Cambridge: Cambridge University Press, 1982), p. 68.

ability to control imports of chariots from *Egypt* (possibly of expensive ceremonial models, see the price, v. 29) and horses from *Kue* (JB, 'Cilicia') for re-export to allies in the north-west (Hatti- (Hittite) land) and north-east (Aram). The common suggestion that Egypt (*miṣrāyîm*) should be read as Muṣru (*cf.* 2 Ki. 7:6), an uncertain location in north-west Assyria, does not give any easier interpretation.[1]

iv. Splendour outmatched by failure (11:1–43). At the beginning of his reign Solomon had been promised and given wisdom, which he successfully employed in the accumulation of wealth and displayed in a massive building programme, rearmament and government. However, the continuance of his ruling house was dependent not on this outward show but on his inner spiritual state. Thus the account of his reign ends with his decline and with the seeds of evident unrest which were to lead to the break-up of the united kingdom. The theological evaluation of this is found here in the description of his personal failure to keep the law forbidding inter-marriage with non-believing wives (vv. 1–13), and in part attributed to his weakening internal unity in the face of external adversaries (vv. 14–24). All this culminated in the rebellion of Jeroboam, inspired by foreign foes (vv. 14–25) and fuelled by internal dissent (vv. 26–40). The account is interspersed with theological comment to show that these events were divinely allowed as self-judgment brought upon Solomon for the sin of law-breaking, despite warnings (Dt. 7:1–4; Ex. 34:11–16).

a. Solomon's wives (11:1–8). Large harems were not unknown. David had fifteen wives (1 Ch. 3:1–9), some of whom Solomon inherited; Jeroboam had eighteen wives and sixty concubines (2 Ch. 11:21) and other contemporary kings had more than Solomon. The large number resulted from political alliances, sealed by marriage, with neighbouring states: Moab, Ammon and Edom to the east; Sidon, through the treaty with Hiram (5:1), and Syria ('Hittites' and Arameans, 10:22) to the north. LXX adds 'Aramaeans' here, since David had such a wife (2 Sa. 3:3). These are cited as examples; *besides* (v. 1) could be 'for example' or 'as well as'

[1] Y. Ikeda, *Studies in the Period of David and Solomon* (Tokyo: Yamakawa-Shuppanstra, 1982), pp. 215–218.

(Heb. *w^e'et*). The reader would be aware that though poly-
gamy was allowed (Dt. 21:15) it was rarely practised. To *inter-
marry* (v. 2) with foreigners was strictly forbidden (Dt. 7:1–4).
This was due to the danger of being led astray and spiritually
turned *after other gods* (v. 4, and the example in Nu. 25:1–15).
Strong sexual desire would be aroused ('followed after') despite Solomon's prayer (8:23); loyalties would be divided (v. 6)
and the king would not be in perfect wholehearted relationship with God, *i.e.* 'at peace with' (Heb. *šālēm*) him.

3. *Seven hundred wives* (RSV, REB 'princesses') may be a significant round number (*cf.* three thousand wives and concubines
in one royal Egyptian household).

5–6. David is henceforward taken as the standard by which
a king will be evaluated as 'doing the right' (v. 12; 3:14; 9:4;
14:8; 15:3). Similarly Solomon is the first to be classified in
that he *did evil in the eyes of the LORD* by personally following
other gods.

Solomon was misled by marriage agreements allowing the
re-introduction of Canaanite values. The false (no-)gods
included *Ashtoreth* (Canaanite Attarat, Babylonian Ishtar, Gk.
Astarte), the goddess of love and fertility, attested by figurines
found at many ancient sites. She was worshipped especially at
Tyre and Sidon and the vocalization of her name is thought to
be influenced by *bōšet* ('shame'). Milcom, national god of
Ammon, represents either a title, 'the king', or a synonym for
Molech (v. 7), a deity like the Syrian Reshef ('flame'), associated
with initiation of children who 'pass through fire'.[1] Whether
this involved actual human sacrifice is uncertain.[2] Such
worship is dismissed contemptuously as *detestable* because the
practices involved were degrading (AV 'abomination', NEB
'loathsome', LXX 'idol-god'). To do this is deliberately to do *evil*
in the sight of the LORD – a key phrase in the judgment of
leaders throughout this history (see Introduction, p. 49). It

[1] *Cf.* 2 Ki. 16:3; 21:6; 23:10; Lv. 20:2–5; Je. 32:35.
[2] A. R. W. Green, *The Role of Human Sacrifice in the Ancient Near East* (Missoula: Scholars Press, 1975), pp. 176ff.; M. Weinfeld, 'The Worship of Molech
and the Queen of Heaven', *UF* 4, 1972, pp. 113–154; G. C. Heider, *The Cult of
Molek: a Reassessment* (Sheffield: JSOT Press, 1985), argues that it always
denotes a deity (originally associated with Jerusalem); *cf. JAOS* 107, 1987, pp.
727–731. J. Day, *Molech: a god of human sacrifice in the Old Testament* (Cambridge:
Cambridge University Press, 1989), pp. 13–16, takes Molech as always a deity
and involving human sacrifice and not merely cultic dedication.

vitiates any attempt to *follow* the LORD *completely* (RSV 'wholly'; AV 'fully' accords best with Heb. *millē'*) as required by Deuteronomy 13:3.

7. On the use of hill shrines see on 3:2. Chemosh (Kamus) and the high place dedicated to him are mentioned in his Moabite Stone (l. 4).

8. The move away to syncretistic worship (polytheism) is stressed by the iterative forms of repeated action, *burned incense* ('made smoke') and offered sacrifices (repeatedly) to these gods.

b. Divine judgment foretold (11:9–13). The Old Testament history is open about the failures of its great men (one sign of veracity) and gives clear warnings of the consequences of disobedience to God. The divine requirements have been made fully known both in writing and oral teaching (the law, *e.g.* Ex. 20:1–17; 34:28), and reiterated by prophets and other means such as theophanies (v. 9). Failure to obey God ('walk in my ways') justly results in God's anger.

His consequent judgment is (a) prophetic, *Since this is your attitude* (heart, NRSV 'mind'), *I will* . . .; (b) thorough, *tear the kingdom away* (emphatic); (c) follows warnings (vv. 12–15; 1 Sa. 15:28); (d) deferred in mercy, *Not . . . during your lifetime* (v. 12, *cf.* 2 Ki. 20:19); and (e) mitigated for the sake of the godly David, who had unswervingly kept the covenant (2 Sa. 7:11–16, *cf.* Abraham, Gn. 18:19). Note that *one tribe* will survive (v. 13, *cf.* 2 Ki. 17:18), Judah now being merged with Benjamin. Solomon's failure does not annul the divine promise to maintain the surviving remnant. The fate of the Davidic dynasty, Jerusalem and the temple are always closely linked.

c. Political causes of the break-up of the united kingdom (11:14–40). Once again opposition may be the fruit of earlier action:

i. Hadad and Edom (11:14–22). God's judgment may be progressive. The disintegration of Solomon's kingdom began early in his reign. Edomite opposition was first roused by their defeat and massacre (2 Sa. 8:13–14). Joab seems to have stayed there *to bury the dead* (v. 15), interpreted as 'to search out the caves' (Gray), *i.e.* he had ruled on as governor of Edom for a time.[1] This mutual mistrust between Edom and Judah was to persist to the time of Herod of Idumea.

14. The *LORD raised up . . . an adversary (śāṭān)*. The permissive and personified character of Satan was later used as a personal proper name for the opposer of God and his people (*cf.* 1 Ch. 21:1; Jb. 1:6–12). *Hadad*, the god of storms (Baal), the Syrian (H)ad(a)du, was used also in royal names[2] in Syria and in Edom (v. 23, 1 Ch. 1:30, 46).

17–18. As a young teenager (*na'ar qāṭān*) Hadad fled to Egypt. The route, first south through *Midian*, where Moses had fled from Egypt, then north of Aqabah through the Wadi Feiran in Sinai, is uncertain.[3] He was treated as a royal hostage, being given a home and land to support him (see on 2 Ki. 25:28–30).

19. The queen's position (Heb. 'queen mother') may be emphasized by giving her the title *Tahpenes* (Egypt. *t.hmt.nsw*, 'wife of the king'), both she and the king not being named.

21–22. *Let me go!* echoes Exodus 9:1. This event took place early in Solomon's reign and Egypt appears not to have interfered deliberately in his affairs.

ii. Rezon of Damascus (11:23–25). Political changes are attributed to God's action (v. 23). Solomon's kingdom was further whittled away by the takeover of Zobah, south of Hamath, by Rezon. This may have followed David's victory there (2 Sa. 8:3–8), which enabled a rival dynasty to take over Aram (*cf.* 15:18). Hezion could be his personal name and Rezon a title. The name E(h)li-Ada is Syrian.

24. The tactic of joining with a 'marauding' (RSV) *band of rebels* ('captain of freebooters', REB) was similar to that used by David (1 Sa. 22:1–2). They *took control* (MT 'they became rulers'); there is no need to follow NEB 'he became king'. The result was hostility to Israel ('he alienated'; Heb. 'loathed' Israel).

iii. Jeroboam, son of Nebat (11:26–28, 40). The greatest threat came from within. The life and action of this usurper was to

---

[1] Y. Aharoni, *The Land of the Bible: A Historical Geography* (London: Burns & Oates, ²1979), pp. 223, 307, also thinks that Hadad led Edom in the break from Solomon (11:25).

[2] N. Avigad, 'Seals of Exiles', *IEJ* 15, 1965, pp. 222–232; J. R. Bartlett, 'An Adversary against Solomon, Hadad the Edomite', *ZAW* 88, 1976, pp. 205–226.

[3] N. Glueck, 'The First Campaign at Tell el-Kheleifeh (Ezion-Geber)', *BASOR* 71, 1938, p. 7 (Nu. 12:16; 13:3).

become symbolic of 'sin against God and his people'[1] and subsequent kings were warned of, or described as, 'walking in the ways of Jeroboam' (15:34; 16:2, 19, 26; 22:52).

26. The naming of his mother may be to bring the entry into line with all future kings of Judah (see Introduction, p. 47). The Ephraimites would have been threatened by the expansion of Jerusalem. *Zeredah* is Banat-Bar near *'Ain Seridah*, north-west of Bethel.[2]

28. Jeroboam is described as *a man of standing*, 'very able' and 'very industrious' (RSV), 'of great energy' (NEB) or 'great ability' (REB), especially in overseeing the reconstruction of the Millo in Jerusalem (see on 9:24). The northern tribes (Joseph) were used as porters (*sēbel*) rather than as forced labour (*mas*), unless the former was a local dialect word for the latter.

iv. Ahijah's prophecy (11:29–39). It was important for a claimant to the throne to have prophetic backing. This came from someone recently appointed (with *a new cloak?*) and opposed to sweated labour. For symbolism in prophecy see 2 Kings 2:20; 1 Samuel 6:7 and frequently in Jeremiah.

30. The action is explained here of the tearing away, just as the act of cutting off the hem of a royal garment denoted rebellion, see verse 11 (*cf.* 1 Sa. 15:27; 24:4–6). In practice this meant a clear break between the ten northern tribes (vv. 31:32) and the Judah (Simeon)-Benjamin group (see later). The 'Deuteronomic' language is that of a legal charge (v. 33).

The promise is conditional (vv. 34–36). Solomon was to be the *ruler* (*nāśî'*, elsewhere 'prince') only during *all the days of his life* (v. 34). This title does not necessarily imply a lesser status than king, but was used of elected leadership.[3]

36. The *lamp* was a symbol of:

(i) Continuing life. To put out a lamp (*nîr*, a rare form for *nēr*) or a brazier meant the end of the family line.[4]

(ii) Continuous succession (*cf.* 2 Sa. 14:7). There is no need to equate this with 'dominion' (Akkad. *nīr*, 'yoke').

(iii) And, elsewhere, divine guidance (see on 15:4). For

---

[1] 12:31; 13:33–34; 14:16; 15:30.
[2] M. Kochavi, 'The Identification of Zeredah, Home of Jeroboam, son of Nebat, King of Israel', *EI* 20, 1989, pp. 198–201.
[3] Gn. 14:24; 15:18–21; D. J. Wiseman, *Essays on the Patriarchal Narratives* (Leicester: IVP, 1980), p. 145.
[4] *CAD* B 73, *cf.* Jb. 18:5–6; 21:17; Pr. 20:20.

God's word is always 'a lamp to our feet' (Ps. 119:105; 2 Sa. 22:29; Pr. 6:20, 22). But to forsake God's law is to condemn oneself to walk in darkness. See also on 1 Kings 15:4.

38. 'There could have been two God-fearing kingdoms if Jeroboam had kept his word. That he did not do so was the sin of Jeroboam son of Nebat.'[1] The promise that Davidic territory will be restricted but *not for ever* indicates a pre-exilic date, and continues the promise of restoration and of the Messiah (*cf.* Je. 30:9). More detail of this abortive rebellion (v. 40) is given in the LXX after 12:24. Shishak is the first Egyptian Pharaoh (*king*) to be mentioned by name in the Bible (see 14:25–26).

d. The closing formula (11:41–43). This is the first use of this formula in its expanded form to end a reign (see Introduction, pp. 50–52). *Forty years* can be used to denote a generation (*cf.* 2:11). Solomon died *c.* 932 BC, aged about sixty. On burial see 2:10–11. His successor is introduced in 14:21. 'In spite of its glory Solomon's political kingship has sealed the doom of the Kingdom' (H. J. Blair).

III. THE HISTORY OF THE DIVIDED KINGDOM
(1 Ki. 12:1 – 2 Ki. 10:36)

The historian relates the break-up of Solomon's kingdom by narrating the events from the point of view of someone closely informed. No direct account of the actual division is given but its causes are indicated. There was no principle of hereditary or dynastic succession yet in operation, so that each ruler is characterized by the method of his election and succession. His reign is subsequently evaluated in spiritual terms. The hostility between the northern tribes and Judah in the south, with but temporary respite, made it necessary to recount the doings of the north and south alternately. Some scholars argue that the accounts of these regions are composed from competing sources (*e.g.* 12:12–14) which sought to explain such matters as Rehoboam's inaction from an Israelite (or even Shechemite) or Judean (Jerusalem) viewpoint. The

---

[1] S. Talmon, 'Kingship and the Ideology of the State', in A. Malamat (ed.), *The Age of the Monarchies: Culture and Society* (Jerusalem: Massada Press, 1979). *WHJP* V, pp. 13–15.

comments may well reflect the historian's discussion of his sources.[1]

A. The division of the kingdom (12:1 – 14:20)

i. Rehoboam (12:1–24). *Cf.* 2 Chronicles 10:1 – 11:4; Josephus, *Ant.* viii.8.1–3.

a. Rehoboam's action (12:1–5). After taking, or being called to, the throne of Judah in Jerusalem or Hebron, Rehoboam sought endorsement by the northern tribes, who were already restive under Solomon's harsh rule. He chose Shechem (Tell Balaṭa, near modern Nablus) as a religious centre associated with the patriarchs (Gn. 12:6; 33:18–20) and with the divine covenant which all the tribes reaffirmed through Joshua (Jos. 24). *All* the representatives of the tribes of *Israel* over whom David had been elected king (2 Sa. 5:3) were present. The timing of Jeroboam's intervention is not clear. He may have returned after hearing of the assembly while he 'remained' in Egypt (MT *wayyēšeb*, so AV, NIV mg.) and did not arrive until after Rehoboam's rejection of the elders' advice (so LXX, *cf.* v. 20). Others imply that Jeroboam had already 'returned' (RSV reading *wayyāšob*; *cf.* 2 Ch. 10:2) from Egypt. Not for the first time Egypt sought to exploit division in Palestine.

b. Right and wrong advice (12:6–15). The demand to alleviate taxation, forced labour and military call-up was reasonable, for they had been an increasing burden under Solomon.

7. *If . . . you will be a servant . . . they will always be your servants.* Authority and power exercised in service elicits loyalty. Jesus as Messiah the servant supremely illustrates this (Mk. 10:43–45; Rom. 12:1). If Rehoboam had responded by showing a right understanding of authority, which aims to serve people and make them willing to serve together, the outcome could

---

[1] Similarly LXXA adds additional information after 12:24 *a–z* (D. W. Gooding, 'The Septuagint's Rival Versions of Jeroboam's Rise to Power', *VT* 17, 1967, pp. 173–189); 'Problems of Text and Midrash in the Third Book of Reigns', *Textus* VII, 1969, pp. 11–13, in which the character of Jeroboam is blackened as the ringleader of the rebels (24*n*). He is denounced, when his son died, for his idolatry even before he ascended the throne (24*g–n*). LXX has a contradictory interpretation at 1 Ki. 12:24 to fit in with its general scheme for the reinterpretation of the whole book.

have been far different and the break-up of that unity which should characterize God's people might never have happened. His indecision shows him unaware that immediate action (*today*) often influences life for 'all the days' (Heb. *always*). Was Rehoboam's concern for his own position? The elders' request was for 'good words' or favourable terms, *i.e.* for leniency, not independence.

8. The position of the *elders* (NIV, NEB rather than 'old men', RSV) was long distinctive and respected in Israel (Ex. 12:21). There is no certainty that the *young men* represented a specific group forming part of a recognized bicameral legislature as proposed by Malamat,[1] or were 'newcomers' as opposed to 'veterans' (DeVries).

Rehoboam, now aged forty-one (14:21), identified more readily with the younger group, who quoted a popular proverb (v. 10). Their uncompromising answer (vv. 10–11) seems to have swayed Rehoboam to favour increased state-imposed burdens: he would *scourge* them with *scorpions* (vv. 11, 14) – a (nail)-barbed scourge as opposed to the common 'whip' (NEB 'lash'). Though these human elements and possibly personality clashes leading to the breakdown are clear, the historian interprets them as divinely overruled to bring about the will and judgment of God as prophesied by Ahijah (v. 15, *cf.* 11:11–12).

This aspect of the interpretation of history is consistent within the whole book and with the rest of Scripture (see Introduction, pp. 23–24). There is no need to view this episode as a polemic to teach respect for elders and the wisdom of following the advice of the old (as does the Talmud), though it well shows the folly of neglecting it.

c. Israel breaks away (12:16–20). As so often, rigid stupidity by one party forces the other to make an impulsive decision. The answer by all Israel (whether taken as the Israelites in general or their representatives) is in the form of a solemn declaration. The strong statement ('We have no share in David', rather than *What share do we have . . .?*, v. 16) and the idiomatic form of dismissal (*To your tents, cf.* 2 Sa. 20:1) both imply a total rejection of any possible reconciliation. Tents may not literally be involved. Malamat argues with some

[1] A. Malamat, 'Kingship and Council in Israel and Sumer. A Parallel', *JNES* 22, 1963, pp. 247–253, with possible ancient Near Eastern parallels.

reason that this was not an outright statement of rebellion so much as the answer given to the Shechem assembly for the demand for leniency, not independence (DeVries, p. 158).

Rehoboam's indecision and ambivalence is shown in that he takes varied measures to recover the situation. He first tries diplomacy (v. 18), then resorts to force (vv. 21–24).

18. *Adoniram* (Heb. Adoram, *cf.* 4:6; 5:14) was a poor choice, for he was renowned for strictly applying forced labour (*mas 'ōbēd*), whereas Jeroboam represented lesser levy duties (*sēbel*). Perhaps a bargain between two kinds of state service was envisaged.

19. *This day* marks the date of the source of the comment, which must have been before the fall of Samaria (722 BC). *Rebellion (pāša')* is used elsewhere of sin against God (Is. 1:18; Hos. 8:1).

20. For Jeroboam's return see above on verse 2. His rise to power may have owed much to Egyptian backing.[1]

d. Rehoboam's plan for war averted (12:21–24). 21. *A hundred and eighty thousand* skilled warriors (LXX 120,000) implies a real strike for unification. DeVries takes this as symbolic ($12 \times 10 \times 100$). Such methods always fail to settle family feuds. In averting war the prophet does not support the new king, but ensures that God's word is heard and obeyed in the new situation. The threat of invasion by the Egyptian Shishak (14:25–26) may have helped Rehoboam to desist.

22. *Man of God*: see Additional Note.

24. The LXX here adds extra details sympathetic to Jeroboam. Hostilities between Jeroboam and Rehoboam restarted, according to 14:30.

Additional Note on the man of God

This expression is synonymous with 'the prophet' (*cf.* 13:1, 18) and is so used in Kings thirty-seven times, predominantly of the prophets Elijah and Elisha (twenty-eight times). Shemaiah as a 'man of God' prophesied in Jeroboam's reign (2 Ch. 11:1–4), and his words were recorded as those of the

[1] *Cf.* M. Aberbach and L. Smolan, 'Jeroboam's Rise to Power', *JBL* 88, 1969, pp. 69–72; A. W. Klein, 'Jeroboam's Rise to Power', *JBL* 89, 1970, pp. 217–218; 'Once More: "Jeroboam's Rise to Power"', *JBL* 92, 1973, pp. 582–584.

prophet (2 Ch. 12:5–8, 15). 'Man of God' is used of named persons: Moses (Dt. 33:1; Jos. 14:6; Ezr. 3:2; Ps. 90 (title); 1 Ch. 23:14; 2 Ch. 30:16) and once of David (2 Ch. 8:14). The only other named man of God is Igdaliah (Je. 35:4). It is used of unnamed messengers who brought God's word to Samson's parents (Jdg. 13:6, 8), to Eli (1 Sa. 2:27), to Jeroboam (1 Ki. 13:1–31) and to Amaziah (2 Ch. 25:7, 9). The common characteristic is that the men spoke authoritatively ('This is the word of the LORD . . .') and were known as those whose words came true (*e.g.* 1 Ki. 17:24). These are the marks of a true prophet (Dt. 18:22, *cf.* Dt. 13:2). Paul's use of the term 'man of God' of Timothy (1 Tim. 6:11; 2 Tim. 3:17) could reflect this Old Testament usage.

ii. Jeroboam (12:25 – 14:20).

a. Jeroboam's sin (12:25–33). **25.** Jeroboam first rebuilt Shechem (see 12:1), where excavations show the wall and two gates strengthened in his reign. It became the first capital of the Northern Kingdom. Other sites were added to gain security on the borders and to lessen the need for the tribes to depend on Jerusalem. *Peniel* (NIV mg. Penuel; Tell ed-Dhahab esh-Sherqîyeh) in Gilead, Transjordan (Gn. 32:31, Peniel) would guard against Aramaean and Amorite incursion and serve as a reserve site, in the face of Shishak's pressure from the west. Tirzah was later added as another capital (15:33). Such details could have been preserved in the newly commenced 'book of the annals of the kings of Israel' (14:19).

26–28. Jeroboam's sin of making a rival capital was compounded by his disbelief in God's promise to him made through Ahijah (11:38). His decision was deliberate, after *seeking advice* (v. 28) or 'after giving thought to the matter' (NEB, *cf.* NRSV 'took counsel'), and defensive. The two bullcalves represented fertility symbols to which the power of God was attributed, despite their ineffectual nature as idols having been shown already by Aaron (Ex. 32:4–8). Some think the *golden calves* were pedestals on which the invisible god stood (*cf.* the Assyrian practice of showing bulls on which deities stood). The aim was to divert worship by the Israelites far from Jerusalem and to mark the borders of the new kingdom. Jeroboam himself may not have initially intended any anti-Yahwehism.

29. *Bethel* (modern Beitin) on the southern Ephraim border in Benjamin territory lay on the pilgrim road nineteen kilometres north of Jerusalem. It had long been a sacred place of worship (Gn. 28:11–19) and became a royal sanctuary (Ho. 10:5, NIV mg.; 8:4–6).

30. *Dan* (Tell el Qaḍi) by the source of the River Jordan (near Mount Hermon) was made to serve the north for reasons of convenience and expediency. 'All the people went to the other, as far as Dan' (MT) perhaps indicates that they did this in procession (so JB). Excavation shows a sacred enclosure and a high place built at Dan in the time of Jeroboam I.[1]

31–33. The sin of Jeroboam and his 'way of life' to which the historian often refers (15:30, 34 and twenty other times in the Books of Kings; *cf.* Ho., Am.) is clearly described as:

(i) Breaking up the unity of God's people, both physically (vv. 25–26) and spiritually (vv. 26–27).

(ii) Creating man-made idols to be worshipped as national gods (vv. 28–30).

(iii) Increasing the role of Israelite sanctuaries. On the *high places* see on 3:3. For building up shrines *cf.* 1 Kings 13:32; 2 Kings 17:29, and for detestable practices *cf.* Deuteronomy 18:9–13.

(iv) Diverting worship from the LORD and his house in Jerusalem where his presence was attested and declared.

(v) Possibly taking on himself the role of priest (vv. 32–33; *cf.* 2 Ch. 26:16–21).

(vi) Introducing non-levitical priests taken from 'every class of the people' (v. 31, NEB) against Deuteronomy 18:1–8. This action led to the evacuation of true priests (2 Ch. 11:13–14) and the introduction of priests from Canaanite shrines in the country (1 Ki. 13:33–34).

(vii) Reorganizing the religious calendar and festivals (vv. 32–33). The Feast of Tabernacles was put a month early (*cf.* Lv. 23:24) to forestall that at Jerusalem. There is no sure evidence that this was to link it with the common New Year Festival (Gray) at which a new king was inaugurated. It may have been a new institution and not simply to adjust the calendar to the solar year (DeVries). Nor is it likely that

---

[1] M. Biran, 'Dan' in M. Avi-Yonah (ed.), *Encyclopaedia of Archeological Excavations in the Holy Land*, Vol. I (Oxford: Oxford University Press, 1977), p. 320.

Jerusalem itself made the change of timing.[1]

Each of these actions defied and broke God-given requirements in the law and implied that civil matters were considered more important than religious principle and practice.
Such expediency directly forfeited God's promise (11:38) and
brought upon the sinner punishment that was self-inflicted
yet divinely allowed.

b. Jeroboam and the prophets (13:1 – 14:18). Increased
prophetic activity is attested at special times of tension among
God's people (*e.g.* Elijah – Elisha, the birth of Christ, the early
days of the church, *etc.*). It aims to heighten awareness of
God's word and the inevitable consequences of rejecting it. An
unrepentant Jeroboam (*cf.* 13:33–34) hears from a man of
God from Judah (13:1–10), a prophet from Bethel (13:11–32)
and Ahijah the prophet, who reiterates a former warning
(14:1–18). These episodes are commonly interpreted as a
clash between the true prophet ('man of God') from Judah
and the false prophet (and cult) at Bethel.[2] Others see here
'the first extensive case of Midrash in the historical books'
(Montgomery), that is, a homiletic commentary on Scripture
using allegory and legendary illustrations. Yet it cannot be
denied that we have here a unified story from which spiritual
lessons may be learned in every generation. It shows that
despite an unjustified claim to have the word of God, even a
false prophet can be used (vv. 18–19; *cf.* Balaam, Nu. 22–23)
to pronounce punishment on an evil and upon a disobedient
man of God (vv. 20–32). Others find here a prophetic conflict
in which the voice of Judah is unheeded by the north and the
faithful oppose a disobedient prophet. Since the only Judean
witness to these events was killed (v. 24), the story may have
been preserved at Bethel.

The miraculous elements – the broken altar (v. 5), Jeroboam's recovery in answer to prayer (v. 6) and the lion not
touching the body or donkey (vv. 24–25) – are significant at a
time of new beginnings. Many take the story as a 'prophetic
legend' (Long), assuming that these elements are not necessarily factual and that the story has been expanded by a later

[1] On the sin of Jeroboam see also E. Danelius, 'The Sin of Jeroboam Ben-
Nebat', *JQR* 58, 1967, p. 98.
[2] J. L. Crenshaw, *Prophetic Conflict; Its effect on Israelite Religion* (*BZATW* 124,
1971).

historian or historians. Thus they account for the reference to Josiah (vv. 2–3), to an event which occurred in his time (v. 5) and for the mention of Samaria (v. 32). But the story is an acknowledged unity (Noth) and could well have been added after the list of Jeroboam's sins (12:31–33) to illustrate the historian's main argument that judgment will inevitably befall those who defy God's word.

i. The man of God from Bethel (13:1–10). **1.** The *man of God* (see Additional Note on 12:22) is named Yadon by Josephus (*Ant.* viii.9.1; *cf.* Iddo, 2 Ch. 13:22). Jeroboam may have been standing by the altar as Solomon had done during a temple inauguration ceremony (1 Ki. 8:62–64).

3. The *sign* (*môpēṭ*) marks an event to be surely accomplished in the light of a fulfilment both immediate (v. 5) and subsequent (2 Ki. 23:15–16). The sacrifice and altar were both immediately shown to be invalidated. The means is not given; perhaps the altar was *split apart* (*cf.* RSV 'torn down') by an earthquake or by cold water poured on the hot *ashes* (*dešen, i.e.* the fat-soaked ashes normally removed ceremonially to a clean place, Lv. 6:10–11).

4–6. Jeroboam's sickness. The outstretched hand indicating his denouncer suffered a muscular spasm or nervous rigidity at the shock of identifying his victim as a prophet. The sudden malady has been attributed to a hemiphlegia, to a sudden blocking of the main artery, or the result of a cerebral haemorrhage or embolism of which the clot dispersed.[1] The shrivelled hand (Heb. *ybš*, 'dried up') would be taken as a sign of divine disfavour (Zc. 11:17), just as the healing was a sign that the man of God was an authentic messenger. A prophet was also known for his role as intercessor (Am. 7:2; 1 Sa. 7:8). This is not 'another legendary element'.

7–10. If the man of God were to make an agreement or show fellowship ('eat bread', vv. 7, 18) with the king, that would have been tantamount to a withdrawal of judgment. The king's motive could have been 'to link himself in fellowship with him as a form of insurance' (Robinson, p. 161; *cf.* Noth, p. 298), and so to seek for the prophet's endorsement

[1] D. J. Wiseman, 'Medicine in the Old Testament World', in B. Palmer (ed.), *Medicine and the Bible* (Exeter: Paternoster Press, 1986), p. 28; *cf.* F. Rosner (Rosen), *Medicine in the Bible and the Talmud* (Ktav: Sanhedrin Press, 1977), p. 6.

of his new royal position. The ban on the return route might serve to avoid further contact with a cursed place and people.

ii. The old prophet from Bethel (13:11–32). This story represents the northern resistance to God's pronounced judgment. The man made no claim to a direct word from the LORD (which came via an angel or messenger, v. 18) and was lying (v. 18), contradicting the true word of God (v. 9). Yet at the same time he was used to rebuke the man of God (also a prophet, v. 18) for his disobedience.

14. The *oak* (*'ēlâ*, NEB 'terebinth') need not be the same tree (*'allôn*) as the one beneath which Rachel's nurse Deborah was buried (Gn. 35:8).

20. A *table* was normally the mark of a wealthy home (see *IBD*, p. 671 for illustration). *The word of the LORD came.* This distinguishes true prophecy from false prophecy, which arises from the imagination (Je. 23:16).

21. The reason for the coming punishment is, as usually, clearly given and makes sense. This need not be dismissed as a later comment but is a real word given to the old (lapsed?) prophet.

22. For a body to lie unburied was a curse, hence the emphasis on detail of the place of burial. It was a disgrace to be buried away from the family among strangers (*cf.* 1:21).

23. *Had brought him back*, rather 'whom he (the prophet) had brought back' (RSV). The prophet felt responsible for his guest and this may be an attempt to salve his conscience.

24–25. Lions were attested in Palestine until at least the thirteenth century AD. It would be taken as a sign of the man of God's status that the lion neither further mauled his body nor touched the donkey.

30. The family tomb at Bethel was still recognized three hundred years later (2 Ki. 23:17). The Bethel prophet may have wished for kudos in being associated with an attested man of God, or wanted to mark the unity of the prophets of Israel and Judah (Jones, Wurthwein). For the existence of Samaria as a known location before the city was named after it, see 1 Kings 16:24.

iii. The sin of Jeroboam (13:33–34). This is emphasized by recording his 'evil manner of life' (*cf.* 12:30–33) as continuing despite the significant episodes and warnings (*after this*). 'Such conduct made the House of Jeroboam a sinful House' (JB; 'sin' is here 'sin-offering', *ḥaṭṭā't*). This may be an Old Testament example of the commission of a mortal sin despite warning (*cf.* 1 Jn. 5:16). Jeroboam's family did not survive the death of his son (15:29), though the memory of his sinful life was never forgotten.

iv. Ahijah's prophecy concerning Jeroboam (14:1–18). Since the whole history depends on the evaluation of the Northern Kingdom of Israel as a failure, the narrative continues with a further prophecy about the end of Jeroboam's house. The emphasis shows how his promised position is forfeited due to apostasy. There is no need to dismiss these as merely prophetic legends. The text in language and comment shows them to be consistent with the viewpoint from which the whole history is written. The original detail could have come from prophetic records, whether kept at Shiloh (Jones) or elsewhere (v. 19, *cf.* 1 Ch. 29:2; 2 Ch. 13:22).

1. *Abijah* ('my (divine) father is Yah(weh)') may have been Jeroboam's firstborn, for his name implies that his father acknowledged the LORD God of Israel at that time. No details of his sickness are given (vv. 1, 5, 12, 17), so it is speculation to say that his death was 'caused by God'. A son's death was often viewed as the result of a parent's sin (*cf.* 2. Sa. 12:14; Jn. 9:2), and this would be a further confirmation of God's word through Ahijah. Jeroboam may have thought that the prophet would show favour to him as he had earlier (11:29–39; 12:15). Prophets were commonly consulted on health matters (2 Ki. 1:2; 4:22, 40; 5:3).

2. The wife's disguise may have been motivated by the hope of receiving an unbiased interview and of allaying any encouragement to rebel if it were known that the health of the heir was at risk. But disguise is always considered wrong and ineffective, as with Saul (1 Sa. 28:8), Ahab (1 Ki. 22:30) or Josiah (2 Ch. 35:22, *cf.* 1 Ki. 10:38). *Shiloh* (modern Khirbet Seilun), once destroyed by the Philistines *c.* 1050 BC, was now reoccupied.

3. Normally high dignitaries would take a substantial gift (*cf.* 2 Ki. 5:5, 15; 8:8), but the ordinary person brought only a small 'audience-gift'.[1] The present chosen here was of food,

[1] *Cf.* 1 Sa. 9:7–8 and, for the audience *nāmurtu*-gift, *VT* 32, 1982, p. 315.

since its acceptance would signify favour, but its constituents, other than bread and honey or syrup (a delicacy), are uncertain. *Cakes* (AV 'cracknels'; NEB 'raisins' follows a LXX interpretation): it has been suggested that this word (*niqqudîm*) may relate to a speckled sheep (*nqd*, Gn. 30:32) and possibly be sheep's milk (or cheese) or be a play on words such as 'to be gravely ill, cause concern' (Akkad. *naqādu*).

4. The prophet's 'eyes were dim' (*qāmû*), fixed (REB, *cf.* Gn. 48:10), or set (as Eli, 1 Sa. 4:15), *i.e.* 'his sight was failing' is better than *his sight was gone.* He had inspired second sight, surprisingly greeting the person coming to 'enquire of the LORD' (*cf.* 1 Ki. 1:16; 22:8; 2 Ki. 22:18) with her identity and the purpose of her visit. This further authenticated his message as from God.

6–8. The *bad news* (*qāšâ*) would remind the hearer of something 'hard to hear' and so the burdensome yoke of 12:11. The prophet reminds Jeroboam (i) of God's gracious provision in that he had risen from humble origins (v. 7)[1] to be appointed by God as a *leader* (*nāgîd*, 'ruler', *cf.* 1:35) and princely governor (*nāśî'*, 11:34);[2] (ii) that he was the subject of a clear but conditional promise of power; (iii) but that he had failed to keep to the example of David (v. 8, *cf.* 11:31–33).

9. Jeroboam's evil is couched in no mere 'Deuteronomistic stock phrases'; he was compared with all preceding rulers (as well as 'judges', *i.e.* 'governors') including Saul, as Omri was later (16:25). In his case his introduction of *other gods* (*cf.* 12:28–30) had now treated God with disdain (*thrust me behind your back*, 'turned your back on me', REB) and so provoked God to active opposition to sin.

10–11. This so-called 'judgment oracle' is couched in the language of popular 'scurrilous ditties' (DeVries).[3] The rhythmic *slave or free* (Heb. *'āzûr we'āzûḇ*) denotes 'everyone', as does 'great and small' elsewhere.[4] To lie unburied was a curse (Dt. 28:26), as later happened to Baasha (1 Ki. 16:4) and Jezebel (1

---

[1] 12:24, LXX says his mother had been a harlot.

[2] D. J. Wiseman, *Essays on the Patriarchal Narratives* (Leicester: IVP, 1980), pp. 144–145.

[3] *E.g.* 'every male' (v. 10); Heb. lit. 'he who urinates against the wall', as AV, 1 Ki. 16:11; 21:21; 2 Ki. 9:8) may be chosen to go with 'dung'.

[4] Some introduce limiting interpretations, *e.g.* 'whether under the protection of the family or not' (NEB, REB); 'unborn or born' (J. Lewy, 'Lexicographical Notes', *HUCA* 12/13, 1937/8, pp. 99–101, Akkad. *Izbu* series); 'married or single' (Slotki).

Ki. 21:24). Dogs were the scavengers in town as birds of prey were in the open country (Robinson).

12–13. *Boy* (*yeled̠*) can be used of varying ages, as is the English 'lad'. His death could also be seen as an act of mercy to spare him the dishonour and disaster which was to follow Jeroboam's reign. While nothing is said of *anything good* (*t̠ôb̠*) done by Abijah, this term is used of covenant-keeping.[1] Traditionally he is said as crown-prince to have removed the guards set to prevent the faithful going up to Jerusalem where he himself participated in festivals (Talmud M. K. 28b). Thus he was the only member of his family given burial.

The following section (vv. 14–16) is not just 'an appendix to the original threat' (Jones) but the reasoned statement of the means for carrying it out. A new family line will initiate the end (Baasha, 15:27 – 16:7) and exile complete it. The swaying reed is a common metaphor for the instability of public opinion, soon to be experienced in the frequent rise and fall of ever-changing ruling families (*cf*. Mt. 11:7; Lk. 7:24).

15. *Uproot* (*nt̠š*) or 'abandoned' (NEB), used of God's activity and exile, is predicted for any covenant breaker.[2] This was to be fulfilled with the fall of the Northern Kingdom in 722 BC when Israelites were taken east *beyond the River* (Euphrates) into Assyria (2 Ki. 17:23). The *Asherah* wooden poles (Heb. is plural; hence AV 'grove') were set up by the altar as a symbol or representation of the Canaanite mother-goddess of fertility, the consort of Baal (15:13; 18:19) with whom they were thus associated (Jdg. 3:7; 2 Ki. 23:4). The Hebrews were told to cut such images down (Ex. 34:13) or to burn them (Dt. 12:3).

c. The concluding formula to Jeroboam's reign (14:19–20).

This customary end to the account of a reign usually gives (i) other aspects not given in the history; (ii) sources of information; (iii) length of reign; (iv) death and burial; (v) succession (see Introduction, pp. 46ff). In the light of this the emphasis here is interesting. It records the continuing *wars* with Judah (see on 15:6; 2 Ch. 13:2–20). By comparison with Jeroboam's great sin his other doings were not noteworthy. Since there had been no introductory statement, his initiation having been

---

[1] M. Fox, 'Tôb as Covenant Terminology', *BASOR* 209, 1973, pp. 41 ff.; *TDOT* 5, 1986, pp. 308.

[2] Dt. 29:25–28; *cf*. D. J. Wiseman, *The Vassal-Treaties of Esarhaddon* (London: British School of Archaeology in Iraq, 1958), p. 52 (iv. 295).

subsumed in the events leading to the break-away of Israel (12:3, 15–33), the length of reign is added here. The *twenty-two years* span the reigns of Rehoboam and Abijah and part of that of Asa of Judah. Note the absence of burial data (see on 1:21). *Nadab*, see 15:25–26, and for the name *cf.* Nadabiah ('Yah[weh] has given generously') in Lachish Letter III.

B. The history of individual reigns (14:21 – 16:20)

i. Rehoboam of Judah (14:21–31).

a. Summary of reign (14:21–24). **21.** The formal history of Judah resumes from 11:43. From now on *Judah* is used as the name of the Southern Kingdom with Israel for the Northern Kingdom. No synchronistic detail is appropriate as Jeroboam was never acknowledged as the rightful contemporary king of Israel. Other details of his reign and family are given in 2 Chronicles 11–12. *Seventeen years* = 930–913 BC. Jerusalem's title as *the city the LORD had chosen . . . in which to put his Name* is characteristic of Deuteronomy (12:57–26) and 1 Kings (8:16, 44; 11:13; *cf.* 9:3; 2 Ch. 12:13; Ps. 132:13). The mother's name is only given for rulers of Judah (see Introduction, p. 47). *Naamah* was a daughter of Solomon through treaty-marriage with an Ammonitess (11:1); a LXX supplementary text makes her a daughter of Hanun son of Nahash (*cf.* 2 Sa. 10:2).

22. *Judah*, here the people stand for Rehoboam (though Gk. here and 2 Ch. 12:14 makes Rehoboam the subject) – 'like king like people'. For the theological evaluation of his reign see Introduction, p. 47. He began well under the influence of priests loyal to the LORD (Yahweh) who had been driven out of the north, but he later turned away from them by allowing local cult centres to develop (12:24; 2 Ch. 11:17; 12:1). The historian is not afraid to castigate the favoured house of David.

23. The pagan developments included *high places* (see on 3:3) and *sacred stones* (NEB 'sacred pillars'). The Heb. *maṣṣēbôṯ* (plural) denotes standing stones representing a deity, some with divine symbols carved upon them (2 Ki. 3:2). These were erected alongside altars, a practice long forbidden when associated with 'other gods' (Ex. 23:24; Dt. 16:21–22) but not when put up in memory of God himself (Gn. 28:18; 31:45; Ex. 24:4). The reference to *every high hill* and *every spreading* *tree* may stem from the idea that these were associated with local deities and the natural symbols of fertility on them (*cf.* Dt. 12:2; Ho. 4:13; Je. 2:20).

24. *Male shrine-prostitutes* attempts to translate 'those set apart as holy' (Heb. *qᵉdēšîm*, plural), which is used of both sexes and taken to be a reference back to Canaanite ritual prostitution. Such *detestable practices* (AV 'abominations') indicate what should be the true believer's attitude to these and similar activities which are forbidden (Dt. 23:17–18).

b. Shishak's invasion (14:25–28). See map opposite. This is the only reference to a political event in Rehoboam's reign which was taken as a sign of divine punishment and led to a temporary reformation (2 Ch. 12:2–12). Sheshonq I (Shishak) had founded the Egyptian (Libyan) Dynasty XXII (945–924 BC) and his raid into Palestine in this year (925 BC) is well attested on the Amon temple reliefs at Thebes (Karnak).[1] From the one hundred and fifty place-names recorded there, his aim seems to have been to reassert Egyptian control over the main trade routes throughout Palestine and the Negeb. His force of 12,200 chariots and sixty divisions (60,000) of cavalry swept through the fortified areas of Judah exacting tribute, including a major payment from the temple treasury, made in a vain attempt to save Jerusalem itself (v. 26, 2 Ch. 12). As the Egyptians raided Israelite territory and set up a stele in Megiddo it may be that another aim was to maintain a hold over Jeroboam. It is significant that the Egyptians did not claim the capture of Jerusalem and a year later Shishak was dead. For a reconstruction of the route taken in this campaign and the defences against further attacks from the south-west set up by Rehoboam (2 Ch. 11:5–12) see map opposite.[2] These defence posts were to serve succeeding generations well.

26. The substitution of bronze for Solomon's gold shields (v. 27, *cf.* 10:16–17) shows the economic decline of Judah at this time. Yet the temple panoply and ritual was maintained.

27–28. The royal body*guard* ('escort', REB) as originally developed for David's sons (*rāṣîm*, runners; 1:5; 2 Sa. 15:1–2) was used with caution, if the emphasis on the return of their

[1] K. A. Kitchen, *The Third Intermediate Period in Egypt (1100–600 B.C.)* (London: Aris & Phillips, 1972), pp. 293–300, 432–447, 575.
[2] Y. Aharoni, *The Land of the Bible: A Historical Geography* (London: Burns & Oates, ²1979), pp. 323–325.

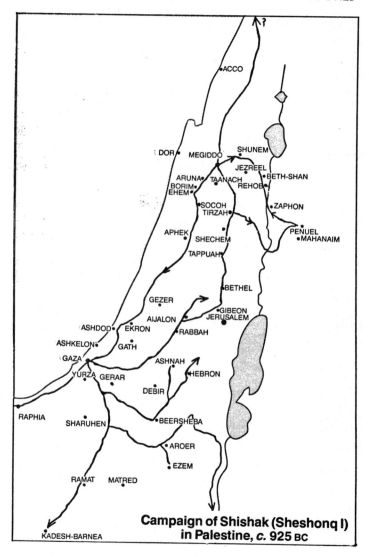

ACCO

DOR•   MEGIDDO•   SHUNEM

JEZREEL•
ARUNA•   TAANACH•   •BETH-SHAN
BORIM•   REHOB•
EHEM•
    •SOCOH   •ZAPHON
    TIRZAH•

APHEK•   SHECHEM•   PENUEL•
                        •MAHANAIM
        TAPPUAH•

                •BETHEL

    GEZER•
        AIJALON•   •GIBEON
ASHDOD•   EKRON•   JERUSALEM•
ASHKELON•   RABBAH•
    GATH•
GAZA•
YURZA•   GERAR•   ASHNAH•
            •HEBRON
        DEBIR•

RAPHIA•
    SHARUHEN•   •BEERSHEBA

            •AROER

            •EZEM

RAMAT•   MATRED•

        Campaign of Shishak (Sheshonq I)
KADESH-BARNEA   **in Palestine,** *c.* **925** BC

ceremonial arms to an inner *guardroom* is significant (Heb. *tā'*; Akkad. *ta'û*).

c. The concluding formula for Rehoboam's reign (14:29– 31). This is the first use of this abbreviated formula for a king of Judah (but *cf.* 11:41–43) and the first reference to post-Davidic Judean sources available to the historian (see Introduction, pp. 40–41). The latter would include details of the *continual warfare* (v. 30) between Judah and Israel, whether this was a 'state of hostility' or frequent border skirmishes. For the place of burial in the *City of David* see Introduction, p. 51 and on 2:10. The name of the king's mother is normally given in the formal introduction to the reign (see v. 21) and the LXX omits it here. *Abijah*. This rendering of the name follows 2 Chronicles 12:16 and some Heb. MSS, but most read here Abijam. The name is probably a variant of Abiyam (so MT, RSV, NAS; *cf.* 2 Ch. 12:15; Josephus and LXX(L) read *Abiou*).

ii. Abijah of Judah (15:1–8). Abijah ('My father is Yah- [weh]') continued the war with his contemporary Jeroboam of Israel. He is here censured for his religious corruption and divided loyalty to the LORD God yet, for David's sake and in response to his faith, he was allowed a spectacular victory over the encircling Israelites whom he had challenged, for being even more apostate than he (2 Ch. 13:3–20). His position and power was increased in Jerusalem (v. 4), and by the annex- ation of Bethel, Jeshanah and Ephraim (Ophrah) and their environs in the hill-country, he pushed the boundary north- wards. This is an instance of God blessing the unworthy for the sake of the worthy.

1. The accession formulae from this reign onwards make cross-references between Judah and Israel. It is not clear whether this was to correlate the sources for the reader or to emphasize the essential unity which should have marked both peoples.

2. *Maacah*'s father was Abishalom, which was understood to be a rendering of Absalom (2 Ch. 11:20–23; Josephus, *Ant.* viii.10.1), but this is not necessarily so. She was the grand- daughter of Uriel of Gibeah (2 Ch. 13:2) who, if he had married Tamar, Absalom's daughter, would have made her Absalom's granddaughter (so NEB).

3. The historian is interested in commenting on the

character of kings. That *his heart was not fully devoted* to God (*šālēm*, 'wholly at one with'; AV 'perfect', REB 'faithful', NRSV 'true to', *cf.* 11:4) means that he was double-minded and so unstable (Jas. 1:8). It is only when a ruler is in the right relationship with God that the promise of succession can be fulfilled.

4. The *lamp* (Heb. *nîr* only here and Pr. 21:4) symbolized this (see on 11:34–36). God himself had been the guiding light and life of David's leadership (2 Sa. 22:29) through his word (Ps. 119:105) and commandment (Pr. 6:23) which was quenched by his death (11:36; 2 Sa. 21:17). Solomon was blessed *for David's sake*, a recurrent thought in this book.[1]

5. For *Uriah the Hittite* see 2 Samuel 11.

iii. Asa of Judah (15:9–24). *Cf.* 2 Chronicles 14:1–15.

a. Summary of reign (15:9–15). Asa continued his father's policy, though of that the historian had not commented in detail (15:6–7) as he does here, stressing that he had done what *was right in the eyes of the LORD* (vv. 11–15) and yet, as with the few of whom this is said, there are exceptions to a perfect stewardship (v. 14a). He used a time of peace to begin religious reforms and to oust abuses and pagan trends. By God's help he defeated an Egyptian threat. Alas, despite his lifelong commitment (v. 14) and the encouragement given by Azariah's prophetic words (2 Ch. 15:1–7), he moved away into distrust by renewing an alliance with the Aramaeans of Damascus. This single step would eventually lead to the downfall of Israel and Judah.

9–10. As Abiyah's son (vv. 2, 10) he may have been a minor forced by his father's brief reign of only one full year to allow his '(grand)mother' to exercise undue influence. He curtailed this and her religious apostasy by deposing her later in his own long reign (v. 13).

11. Note how 'doing the right' is shown in specific acts (vv. 12–13) and yet is a general statement.

12. The expulsion of male prostitutes associated with Canaanite and pagan practices may well have been an unpopular move.

13. Only here is the *Asherah* (see on 14:15) described as a

---

[1] 1 Ki. 11:12, 13, 32, 34; 2 Ki. 8:19; 19:34; 20:6; Ps. 122:8–9; *for the sake of* (Heb. *lᵉma'an*, 'on account of'; lit. 'in response to').

'sculpture in the round' (*gillūlîm*, v. 12, *idols*) which should cause the beholder to 'shudder' (*mip̄leṣeṯ*), a term used elsewhere of an earthquake (*cf.* Ps. 55:5; Is. 21:4), at the *repulsive* (RSV 'abominable') image. The Asherah pole also was *repulsive* and 'obscene' (NEB; Vulg. a phallic symbol; RSV, 'abomination') in the eyes of the true worshipper of God and was associated with the worship of the Canaanite mother-goddess. The *Kidron Valley* east of Jerusalem was then the city's main rubbish dump.

15. The things dedicated in the temple could have included the shields made by Rehoboam as well as spoils of war.

b. The renewed war with Israel (15:16–22). This was a reaction to Israel's blockade of the north route from Jerusalem (*cf.* 9:17). They had penetrated as far south as Ramah (Er-Ram, nine kilometres north of Jerusalem). Asa counted on his existing treaty-relations (of which Kings gives no detail) and possibly the queen mother's Aramaean origin to invoke help from Ben(Bar)-Hadad I of Damascus. It is noteworthy that the Chronicler rebukes Asa for trusting in this treaty relationship rather than the LORD and for his suppression of those who opposed his policy (2 Ch. 16:7–10). This is not mentioned here, as the stress is on the good and right Asa did as David's successor. *Tabrimmon* (v. 18) means 'good is Rimmon', the Thunderer-god, a title of Baal. The payment (v. 19) was more substantial than an audience-gift, it was *silver and gold* – silver being more valuable than gold at this time (*cf.* 10:21). It succeeded in getting the Aramaeans to attack the frontier of Israel north of Galilee (Kinnereth) and Naphtali to the east. This resulted in the interruption of the main trade route to Tyre and Sidon, the loss of Israel's last possessions in north Gilead and her withdrawal from the territory recently taken in the south (v. 21) in order to meet the new threat.

18. *Hezion* may be the name of the founder of the dynasty, while Rezon was his title. *Aram* (NIV, NEB) denotes the city-state centred on Damascus and is to be preferred to 'Syria' (AV, RSV), a geographical designation not used till many centuries later.

20–21. *Ijon* and *Dan* (Tell el Qāḍi) lay by the headwaters of the River Jordan. Hazor is not named and there is no sure archaeological evidence for a supposed sack of the city about this time. *Tirzah* was to be the capital of Israel (v. 33) until it was displaced by Samaria (16:23–24).

22. The usual total call-up (*mas*, not *mas 'obēḏ*) was required by the urgent need to re-establish a new frontier post at *Geba* to defend the land regained in Benjamite territory thirteen kilometres north of Jerusalem just east of Ramah. This place is not to be confused with Jeba' near Beersheba (2 Ki. 23:8). The massive defences unearthed at *Mizpah* (Tell en-Nasbeh) show that these were now reorientated northwards and strengthened against a chariot attack. The use of stones and timber in buildings of this period is already attested in the temple courtyard walls (6:36; *cf. IBD*, p. 102).

c. The concluding formula for Asa's reign (15:23–24). The closing statement of Asa's reign includes the unusual note on his poor physical condition which 2 Chronicles 16:12 associates with his reliance on physicians rather than the LORD. The Old Testament usually commends the use of medical practitioners and prayer. The ailment is specifically stated to be in *his feet* ('*eṭ*, v. 23) and is commonly interpreted as gout (podogra), described by the Babylonian Talmud as 'like a needle in the raw flesh'. But gout was uncommon in Palestine and ancient Egypt and it is more likely, in view of Asa's age, the severity of the disease and death within two years, to have been a peripheral obstructive vascular disease with ensuing gangrene.[1] Some interpret 'feet' as used euphemistically here for sexual organs (*cf.* 'he covered his feet', AV Jdg. 3:24) and find a reference to a venereal disease such as tertiary syphilis. But this has not yet been identified in the Old Testament period.

24. The Chronicler (2 Ch. 16–14) may refer not to the cremation of Asa but to a huge fire in honour of his house by way of celebration or of fumigation at his burial (as here v. 24).

iv. Nadab of Israel (15:25–32). The history reverts to the kings of Israel who were contemporaries of Asa. The end of

[1] A. de Vries and A. Weisberger, 'King Asa's Presumed Gout', *The New York State Journal of Medicine*, Feb. 1975, pp. 452–455; rather than dropsy: D. J. Wiseman in B. Palmer (ed.) *Medicine and the Bible* (Exeter: Paternoster Press, 1986), pp. 33–34. 2 Ch. 16:12 may indicate that the disease spread upwards ('*aḏ lᵉma' 'alāh*; RSV, NIV 'severe').

the house of Jeroboam is foretold by the coup under Baasha. These sources include local records of the rebellion (vv. 27–28) and prophetic history (vv. 29–30).

25–26. This summary of the reign gives Nadab two years, covering part of his accession year and part of his first full regnal year, so in fact it may have covered less (vv. 24, 33).

27. *Baasha* is here given his family name and place of origin (Issachar in south-west Galilee) to distinguish his father Ahijah from the person of the same name in Shiloh (v. 29). Israel was strong enough to attack Philistia to the south-west (*cf.* 16:15). *Gibbethon* (Tell Mal'aṭ) lay five kilometres west of Gezer near the border where Israel, Philistia and Judah met.

28–30. Baasha's reign is introduced here to explain Nadab's death at his hand, which is interpreted as fulfilment of Ahijah's prophecy (14:10–16). That involved the extermination of Jeroboam's house. The justification for killing *anyone that breathed* in the regime now terminated seems terrible, but was a common practice of the time. David was expected to do this of Saul's house, but refrained. The purpose was initially to avoid any focus for reprisals or a blood feud after a coup (*cf.* 16:11; 2 Ki. 10:1–7; 11:1). It may here be related to the thoroughness of divine punishment (Dt. 9:14; 25:19) to prevent the deliberate spread of sin (v. 30). The command to the Israelites entering the land was for total destruction of those who opposed God (Dt. 7:2). Here that is taken as applying to fellow Hebrews who opposed God, and this required special prophetic sanction (v. 29). The contamination of sin must be prevented.

v. Baasha of Israel (15:33 – 16:7). Baasha, by taking power through the assassination of Nadab, led to the end of the originally God-appointed house of Jeroboam, and for this he was cursed, as it was prophesied (16:3, 7, *cf.* 15:29). The basic details of his long reign are given in 15:33–34; 16:5–6. These serve as an introduction to the history of the house of Omri (Omrides), and the historian stresses the theological appraisal of his rule by citing the prophecy of the obscure prophet Jehu, whose writings may well have been included in his source, 'The book of the kings of Israel' (*cf.* 2 Ch. 19:2; 20:34).

33. Excavations in *Tirzah* (Tell el-Fara') show that reconstruction at the high point there began in the ninth century BC.

16:2–4. This prophecy by Jehu is not necessarily modelled on the earlier one (15:30), since similar messages were often directed against the same sins (Jeroboam, 14:7–11; and Saul, 1 Sa. 15:17–19). The language is declamatory and necessarily formal and includes common curses (v. 4, *cf.* 21:24; 2 Ki. 9:10, 36).

God raises to leadership from the dust, as he sometimes does the poor (1 Sa. 2:8; Ps. 113:7, *cf.* Ps. 40:2). Israel did not always follow the principle of the dynastic monarchy. It has been suggested that to be *leader* (v. 2, AV 'prince'; *nāgîd*, 'prominent position') relates to the tribal hierarchy. The word is used of various military, government and religious functions, but here reflected the status given by God to David (1 Sa. 25:30) and Jeroboam (1 Ki. 14:7) and later Hezekiah (2 Ki. 20:5). It is taken by some to refer to a divine (charismatic) appointment.

vi. Elah of Israel (16:8–14). Apart from the usual introductory (v. 8) and concluding formulae (v. 14), only the assassination of Elah is recorded (vv. 9–11). It is interpreted, by comparison with an earlier similar event (v. 12, *cf.* v. 7), as divine judgment on the evil done by the Baasha family, which required their elimination as it had the house of Jeroboam. Such godlessness (v. 13) means that there can be no stability in the succession, and this is the more so since the earlier dynastic principle established for Judah is lacking.

8. Elah's reign lasted less than two full years (*cf.* 15:25).

9. *Zimri* (possibly an Aramaean name, *cf.* Zimri-Lim of Mari) was a royal 'servant' (AV, RSV) and thus the *official* who commanded half the chariots, a division prompted by strategic not tactical reasons. Half the force was based at Megiddo, the other near Tirzah ready for action against Judah.[1] Hence Zimri's location enabled him to consort with the principal administrative officer of state, Arza (Heb. 'He who was over the house [palace]'). The AV 'steward', NEB 'controller of the household', are inadequate descriptions, hence some consider this office that of 'the prime minister'. He acted when the main military forces were at Gibbethon (v. 15), and Elah was not with the army, probably because the operation was left to his commander-in-chief (v. 16), rather than because he was careless or fearful.

[1] Y. Yadin, *The Art of Warfare in Biblical Lands* (London: Weidenfeld & Nicholson, 1963), p. 301.

11. The total extinction of the family (*cf.* 15:25) was planned so as to leave neither male nor 'kinsfolk' (AV), that is, male relatives (as NIV) who would have the moral obligation to act in blood revenge (*gō'ēlîm*).[1] The addition of his *friend* may reflect the role likely to be taken by royal advisors (*e.g.* 'friend of the king', see 2 Sa. 15:37; 16:16).

12–13. Emphasis is placed on the prophecy fulfilled by Zimri, even if he did so unwittingly (*cf.* vv. 1–4). *Sins* are recorded in terms applied to Jeroboam's deliberate paganism with its *worthless idols* (AV 'vanities'), a description used of any gods other than Yahweh (1 Ki. 12:28; 14:9; 2 Ki. 17:15; Dt. 32:21).

vii. Zimri of Israel (16:15–20). This section is included in the history in that Zimri was an official monarch even though the facts available, apart from the introduction (v. 15) and concluding formulae (v. 20), are only those of his murder of Asa (v. 16), his own suicide (v. 18) and a rebellion he had instigated (v. 20). This one action is sufficient for a theological evaluation to be made (v. 19).

15. The siege of *Gibbethon* lasted intermittently for twenty-four years (15:27). The general term 'the people' (Heb. *hā'ām*) would include 'the army' (so NIV, Noth) as in 20:15; *cf.* 1 Samuel 14:25 where *the entire army* translates 'all the people of the land'.

16. *Omri*, possibly a non-Israelite name. That his father's name is omitted simply means that he was not of the royal line and that he was of humble or landless origin. He was, however, the military superior of Zimri (v. 9).

18–19. The *citadel* ('keep', NEB) was a part of the royal palace complex (*cf.* 2 Ki. 15:25) sealed off (*'armôn*) from the public quarters. Either the besiegers (collectively) or Omri (so Jewish commentators, to whom suicide was abhorrent) set the place afire. It could well have been suicide, as in the case of the last Assyrian king in Nineveh. This act, with his murder of Elah as well as his general manner of life shown in his brief reign, would be sufficient grounds for the summary condemnation of a life which was so characteristic of Jeroboam's evil religious policy.

20. His *rebellion* (*qišrô*, AV 'treason', NEB better 'conspiracy')

---

[1] On this see Jos. 20:3, 5; 2 Sa. 14:11; Dt. 19:6–12.

implies that verses 9–10 were only a summary of a longer account. Zimri hereafter was taken as a major example of a perfidious regicide (2 Ki. 9:31).

Civil war (vv. 21–22) followed Zimri's death. *Tibni* received sufficient popular support to oppose *Omri* despite the latter's acceptance by the army. Tibni must have held out against Omri for three to four years (*cf*. vv. 15, 29) and have been counted as an official ruler of Israel, since the latter did not become king until three years after the death of Zimri. The text does not say that Tibni was ever actually made king. There is no evidence that this was a clash between popular democracy and a formally established dynasty,[1] nor that the record of Tibni's 'death' refers to his being divested of the royal authority rather than to his physical demise.[2]

C. The house of Omri (16:21 – 22:40)

i. Omri of Israel (16:21–28). The mere seven verses given to this sixth king of Israel who founded a new dynasty (the Omrides) which lasted three generations (*c.* 885–874 BC) emphasizes the historian's selective viewpoint. He has nothing good to say of him and his successors, though their reigns occupy a third of his total narrative (1 Ki. 16 – 2 Ki. 12) and that includes the emphasis on the struggle between the kingdom of God and its prophet-champions Elijah and Elisha against the rule of evil. Apart from the usual regnal details (vv. 23, 27), only the foundation of the new capital at Samaria (vv. 23–24) and the historian's appraisal of Omri's reign as evil (vv. 25–26) are given.

23. No details are given of the struggle before Omri could commence his sole reign as king of Israel. The twelve years in Tirzah includes the time of civil war with Tibni.

24. Excavations at Samaria, modern Sebastiyeh eleven kilometres north-west of Shechem (Nablus) (Heb. *šomᵉrôn*, Assyr. *samerina*), show that Omri was the first builder on the one-hundred-metre-high hill. This site was a good choice, for it was to withstand several sieges (*cf*. 20:1–21; 2 Ki. 6:24–25; 18:9–10). Omri's plan could have been to gain (a) a personal possession he could bequeath; (b) an independent Canaanite

---

[1] J. A. Soggin, 'Old Testament and Oriental Studies', *Bi.Or.* 29, 1975, pp. 50–55.
[2] J. M. Miller, 'So Tibni died (1 Kings xvi.22)', *VT* 18, 1968, pp. 392–394.

centre (*cf.* 16:32, Baal worship); (c) a communications centre west of the hill ridge and so more open to trade with Tyre and Sidon than Tirzah, which faced east; and (d) an independent new capital for the Northern Kingdom as David had at Jerusalem to rally his supporters in the south.

25–26. 'He outdid all his predecessors in wickedness' (NEB). Apart from a passing reference to his other achievements (v. 27), described as the mighty (warlike) acts (RSV) 'he shewed' (AV), his major contributions to the history of Israel as one of its most distinguished rulers are outside the purpose of this history. These include the unification of the Northern Kingdom, peace with Judah, effective control over north Moab where 'he humbled . . . and occupied the land of Medaba' and built fortresses at Ataroth and Yahez according to the Moabite (Mesha') inscription of *c.* 830 BC (*IDB*, pp. 1016–1017). Omri's dynasty lasted more than forty years. His strong government and administration earned recognition by the Assyrians, who for the next one and a half centuries still referred to Israel as 'the house/dynasty of Omri' (*bīt ʾHumri*).

ii. Ahab of Israel (16:29–34). The usual pattern of the resumé of the reign of Ahab is followed by reference to its chronological setting (v. 29) and an evaluation of the increasing evil of the family (vv. 30–32) as progressively worse than that done by Omri. For Ahab treated the sins of his predecessors as *trivial* ('a light thing') and by his marriage to a zealous foreigner introduced the worship of *Baal* officially alongside that of the LORD God (Yahweh). An unusual note on an incident at Jericho, shown as fulfilment of prophecy (v. 34), is followed by events in the lives of those anti-Baal champions, Elijah and Elisha, encouraging worship and service of the true God (17:1 – 22:38). After this the concluding data for Ahab's reign are given in 22:39–40.

29. *Ahab*, the seventh king of Israel to rule alongside the stable regime of Asa in Judah, had a unique non-Israelite name, possibly 'my brother is Abba (the Father god)'. He was called by his contemporary, the Assyrian king Shalmaneser III (859–824 BC), *Ahabbu (māt)sirʾilaia*, 'Ahab the Israelite' (Kurkh stela ii. 90).

31. *Ethbaal* (*Ittobaʿal* = 'Baal is alive') was king of Tyre and Phoenicia (*the Sidonians*) who had murdered his predecessor and, according to Josephus (*Ant.* viii.12.1 – 13.1; *Contra Apion* i.18), was a priest of the gods Astarte and Melquart. He ruled there for thirty-two years. His granddaughter Dido founded Carthage. His daughter Jezebel probably married Ahab early in Omri's reign to mark the political and economic 'treaty' between the states. This attempt to serve two masters, Baal (= lord, master, husband) and Yahweh, was to lead to the downfall of the Northern Kingdom. The alliance reflected a situation when Tyre and Sidon had ceased to send tribute to the Assyrian Ashur-nāsir-apli II and so now acted independently and were desirable commercial allies.[1]

33. On Asherah poles see on 14:15.

34. *In Ahab's time* introduces contemporary data. Jericho (Tell es-Sulṭan, about two kilometres north-west of the modern city) lay within the south-east border of Israel (Aharoni, p. 322). Excavation shows no trace as yet of Iron Age ninth- to eighth-century BC occupation, though it may have been slenderly reoccupied (2 Sa. 10:5). This rebuilding by (A)hiel, perhaps against a threat from Moab (2 Ki. 3:5), would have been subject to Ahab's overriding permission. This violation of the divine curse against Jericho (Jos. 6:26) is to be taken as another example of Ahab's sin. Hiel paid the penalty 'at the cost of' (Heb. 'with'; AV 'in') his sons. Their deaths as foretold do not necessarily imply foundation sacrifice of the children, a very rare phenomenon (*cf.* 2 Ki. 16:3). But, whatever the cause, they were interpreted as an example of the fulfilment of prophecy.

iii. Elijah and the prophets against Ahab (17:1 – 22:40).

The rest of 1 Kings is taken up with reign of Ahab and his successors, with emphasis on confrontation by the outspoken prophets Elijah and Elisha against their sinfulness and resistance to God's word. For these Elijah stories generally see Introduction, pp. 44–46. The interest in 'miracles' here must be compared with their special occurrence at other times of national crisis such as the period of the Exodus and, for the church, the period of Christ's birth, death and resurrection and the subsequent birth of the church.

a. God keeps Elijah safe (17:1–16).

Note how the LORD intervenes to provide food and comfort for his messenger to

[1] B. Oded, 'The Phoenician Cities and the Assyrian Empire in the Time of Tiglath-pileser III', *ZDPV* 90, 1974, pp. 38–49.

enable him to continue his work. For this he uses humans (v. 15), nature (birds, v. 6) and messengers or angels (19:4–8). God similarly intervened for his people at creation (Gn. 1:29–30; 9:3), in their desert wanderings (Ex. 16:31–35) and for Jesus Christ himself (Mt. 4:11). Here such provision is not explained in detail but is taken as miraculous, as was the feeding of the five thousand (Jn. 6:10–14, 30–31).

i. The first miracle of provision (17:1–6). **1.** *Elijah* ('My God is Yah[weh]') bore a name which signifies his message (*cf.* 1 Ki. 18:39). He was a prophet (so LXX adds here) and man of prayer (18:36; Jas. 5:17–18). His birthplace *Tishbe* is stated to be *in Gilead* (v. 1, north Transjordan) to distinguish it from Tishbi in Naphtali (Tobit 1:2). This reading requires no change of consonants (*cf.* MT *tōšāḇê*; 'of the inhabitants', AV). Since Byzantine times Tishbe has been identified with Mar Elias, thirteen kilometres north of Jabbok. The strong oath *as the LORD . . . lives* (RSV 'by the life of God (Yahweh)') is common, and binding on the person on whom it is made on the pain of death if he disobeys. Elijah is conscious of his status with God 'whose servant I am' (RSV; Heb. 'before whom I stand' implies a close confidential official position). The prediction of the cessation of life-bringing rain and dew implies sin among the people (8:35; Dt. 11:17; 28:23; *cf.* Lv. 26:18–19). The Palestinian dew and rainfall pattern was consistent. The 'former rains' fell between late October and early January and the 'latter rains' between April and early May (*NBDR*, pp. 869, 1010). Menander records this severe drought as lasting a full year during the reign of Ittobal of Tyre (*cf.* 16:31). Certainly it spread to Phoenicia (17:7) and would have lasted longer on the desert fringes.

The power and control of the living God in contrast with the ineffectiveness of Baal the Canaanite god of rain is the theme (*cf.* Am. 4:6–11). Elijah's confidence was to be tested over three-and-a-half years as he prayed that there would be no rain (Lk. 4:25; Jas. 5:17). This challenge by the 'troubler of Israel' to Ahab, who knew of Elijah's earnest prayer life (18:42–45), followed fruitless attempts to get Ahab to forsake his idolatrous ways.

2. *The word of the LORD came to . . .* stamps the authority of God on the subsequent action. This is no mere formula or introduction to an addition to a kernel story in verses 5–6 (*cf.*

v. 8). Elijah was not trying to avoid serving God, nor to escape his universal presence (Ps. 139:7–10), when he fled to the Wadi Kerith which 'overlooked' (Heb. *'al p^ené*) rather than lay *east of the Jordan* (NIV, RSV, NAS, *cf.* AV 'before'). Elijah was hiding in an area not easily accessible to Ahab through his family and allies, as he did later at Zarephath (v. 9; 18:10). The area might be that of the Wadi Qelt west of Jericho. There is no need to look for a site outside Ahab's jurisdiction east of Jordan (as does Eusebius, *Onomasticon* 174).

4–6. Our obedience is an essential aspect of God's protecting grace. The means God uses may be varied. Some object to the reading *ravens* (*'ōr^e bîm*), which, even if it could be proven to be the modern name for the black arabs (*^a rābîm* – same consonants) east of Jordan, is taken by others as an 'unnecessary rationalisation'.[1] The bringing of 'meat' would be a luxury and the provision of food and meat morning *and* evening should remind the reader of God's unfailing provision (Ex. 16:8, 12).

ii. The widow of Zarephath (17:7–16). The following two incidents or miracles emphasize God's unceasing provision based on what others first gave to the prophet (vv. 7–16). God tests before prayer is answered (vv. 17–24). Such a supply is taken to be the fulfilment of God's promise (v. 9, *cf.* vv. 14, 15), just as the ravens had been (v. 4, *cf.* v. 6). So the woman realized that Elijah (*a man of God*, vv. 18, 24) was extraordinary and learned the blessings of sharing hospitality.

9–14. *Zarephath* (modern Sarafand, thirteen kilometres south of Sidon) lay in the Phoenician territory controlled by Ahab's father-in-law. Elijah was visiting enemy territory and showing the power of God in an area where Baal was worshipped, though ineffective through drought. He illustrates how a prophet can be accepted outside his own country (Lk. 4:25–26). Elijah challenges a seemingly poor woman to help as she gathered mere stubble or *sticks* ('twigs', *qšš*) to respond to a stranger's request. But he was sent by God. His request for 'a bit of food' (v. 11) evoked the reply that she had no ready food, for a *cake of bread* (v. 13) needed baking on charcoal and she had 'nothing baked' (RSV, rather than *bread* or 'sustance', NEB). Similarly she had only a handful of 'barley-flour' (Heb.

[1] M. Seale, 'The Black Arabs of the Jordan Valley', *Exp.T* 68, 1956–1957, p. 28, *cf.* Wenham, p. 121.

'meal') in a large pottery jar (*cf.* 18:33; Jdg. 7:16) and very little oil in a small portable flask (*ṣappaḥaṯ*, NEB; RSV 'cruse', NIV, NRSV *jug*) to prepare something to eat.

This and the following incident are compared with the similar action of Elisha in providing oil and raising a child to life (2 Ki. 4). Because the latter is more detailed many find it to be the origin of both accounts (so Jones, Gray). However, details differ and there is no certainty that similar miracles were not performed more than once, as also by Christ and the early apostles, and this one may have been selected to show that Elisha had the same powers as his master.

b. The raising of the widow's son (17:17–24). The boy was certainly dead according to the mother (v. 18), the prophet (v. 20) and observers of the time interval before treatment. This first example in the Bible of revival from death cannot be explained away as contactual magic nor as the prophet's life-force transmitted by the mouth-to-mouth method of resuscitation.[1] At that time death was considered as indicated when breathing finally stopped, and it is difficult to consider death here as just physical weakness, and new life (*ḥāyāh*, v. 22) without any previous death (as do Gray and Johnson). The act of revival leads to a remarkable statement of faith by the most intimate witness (v. 24, *cf.* Ex. 18:11).

18. *What do you have against me?* or 'Why did you interfere?' (*cf.* NEB) interprets the Heb. 'What is it to you . . . ?' (*cf.* Jn. 2:4). She believed, as often in Old Testament thought, that death and sickness must be punishment for some hidden sin now brought 'to the light' (NEB, Ps. 19:13; Jn. 9:1). *Man of God* means more than a very distinguished person. See Additional Note on p. 142. It is applied to a divine messenger (Jdg. 13:6, *cf.* v. 9) as well as to prophets like Moses (Dt. 33:1; Jos. 14:6), Samuel (1 Sa. 9:6) and rulers like David (2 Ch. 8:14; Neh. 12:24) who spoke with divine authority. It should be the description of any devoted servant of the LORD (1 Tim. 6:11; 2 Tim. 3:17) whose faith is demonstrated by works (so v. 24).

20. Nothing much is gained by interpreting *I am staying with* (Heb. *miṯgōrēr*), *i.e.* receiving hospitality from, as 'for whom I am causing trouble' (a rare biform of Heb. *gārâ*).

21–22. *He stretched himself* is the unique Heb. 'measured

[1] F. Rosner (Rosen), *Medicine in the Bible and the Talmud* (Ktav: Sanhedrin Press, 1977), p. 216; D. J. Wiseman, in B. Palmer, *op. cit.*, p. 42.

himself'. The rendering 'breathed deeply upon' (NEB) derives from a LXX paraphrase influenced by 2 Kings 4:34. *Life (nepeš, cf.* 'soul', AV, RSV) is of itself no basis for any doctrine of the survival of the soul after death.

c. Confrontation and vindication (18:1–46).

i. Elijah and Obadiah (18:1–16). Elijah challenges Ahab prophetically through Obadiah (vv. 1–19), and Baalism through the demonstration that 'the LORD Yahweh is the (true) God' (vv. 20–40). Prophecy and prayer are fulfilled in the acceptance of the burnt offering and the end of drought (vv. 41–46). This most dramatic story marks the turning point when the worship of the LORD is almost wiped out by the opposition. A single prophet challenges the whole state to return to God.

Arguments against the unity of this episode include Ahab's initial absence from the Carmel scene and the lack of any clash between him and Elijah, the alternating allusions to drought and rain, and some repetitive sections. Against this it can be shown that Elijah's opposition to Ahab is basic to the whole and both the introduction (vv. 1–20) and the conclusion (vv. 41–46) show affinity, and throughout Yahweh controls affairs. The whole chapter is an editorial unity incorporating very early traditions.[1]

1. *The third year* can represent literally three years (Lk. 4:25; Jas. 5:17) and include the time spent at Zarephath and Carmel (Keil). This is better than taking it symbolically as a full seven-year drought cut short, or as indicating part of one year, a second, and part of a third (*cf.* 15:2).

3. *Obadiah* ('servant of Yah[weh]') was a high royal official (Heb. 'who was over [*in charge of*] the house/palace', see on 4:6). He 'revered the LORD greatly' (NRSV), *i.e.* was a devout believer.

4–5. Ahab's response to the famine contrasts with David's repentance (2 Sa. 21:1). His priority need was fodder for his military forces, including the horses to draw the two thousand chariots he was to contribute to the allies fighting Assyria (Shalmaneser III, Kurkh Stele ii. 29 ff.). The prophets hidden 'fifty in a cave' (Heb.) imply the existence of many groups (fifty equals a company or military formation, as indicated by

[1] Long, p. 137; and this despite his analysing the text into 89 literary sub-units.

1 Samuel 10:5; *cf.* 1 Ki. 13:11 ff.) raised up in opposition to Baalism (v. 13). There are more than two thousand caves in the limestone Carmel range dating from palaeolithic times and later.

7. Elijah's person and position were recognized, probably because he was well known at court rather than because of his dress (the hairy mantle and leather belt, 2 Ki. 1:8; *cf.* John the Baptist, Mt. 3:4).

8–9. This is a challenge to side publicly with Elijah rather than be a secret supporter (vv. 4, 13).

12. Elijah's freedom from capture was due to God's preserving hand more than mere elusiveness or the use of abnormal powers of *the Spirit of the LORD.*

15. This first occurrence in Kings of 'the Lord of Hosts', which also occurs in other prophetic utterances (19:10; 2 Ki. 3:14; 19:31), denotes more than the heavenly hosts (Yahweh Sabaoth) or all subordinate gods or the armies of Israel (1 Sa. 17:45). It includes the idea of God as the God of order and hence refers to his irresistible royal majesty and power (NIV, *the LORD God Almighty*).[1]

ii. The Carmel contest (18:17–46). Mount Carmel (six hundred metres high, south of modern Haifa) may have been chosen as it lay on the border of Israel and Phoenician territory and possibly as a high place venerated by both parties. (It may be the 'holy headland' (*rs qdš*) in Thutmose III's Palestinian List.)

17. Elijah was accused of being the *troubler of Israel* ('*āḵar* is 'taboo, cast out from (social) intercourse') because he was thought to have brought the drought (*cf.* 17:1), and incurred the wrath of Baals (v. 18, plural). This was a crime against the state worthy of death (like that of Achan, Jos. 6:18; 7:25; and Jonathan in 1 Sa. 14:24–29).

18. Elijah's reply is that Israel's trouble is not the dearth of rain but lack of faithfulness to God's covenant. Note the reference to the *commandments* (LXX omits).

19. 'All Israel' probably here denotes the nation's representatives (Robinson) rather than *people from all over Israel.* Prophecy was not unique to Israel and is attested in earlier

[1] J. P. Ross, 'Jahweh *ṣᵉḇā'ôṯ* in Samuel and Psalms', *VT* 17, 1967, pp. 76–92.

Syria and Mesopotamia (especially Mari, *c*. 1700 BC;[1] Wen-Amun at Byblos, *c*. 1100 BC; Zakir of Hamath, *c*. 800 BC). For the *prophets of Asherah* (Astarte, the wife of Baal) see 16:31, and for the numbers compare verse 4.

21. The challenge 'How long will you go on limping (*waver*) between two opinions?' (*s*ᵉ*'ippîm*) can be interpreted also as hobbling between two forks (denoting tree branches or cross-roads or even crutches). This is the English idiom to 'sit on the fence' (so NEB). The clear choice is between acknowledgment of the LORD (Yahweh) or Baal. Syncretistic worship of both at the same time is impossible. Elijah alone was standing out publicly here (v. 22), though the LORD had indeed other true witnesses.[2]

23–26. Altars. Either two separate adjacent altars, one to Baal (whether Baal of Carmel, Melqart or Shamem cannot be known), or just one to the LORD (Yahweh) which was repaired (v. 30). Elijah allowed choice of altars and bullocks to be sacrificed to avoid risk of any accusation of fraud. The people agreed (v. 24). The test was to be God-sent fire. The people believed Baal to represent the sun-god also and in their epics thought he rode the thunderclouds and sent lightning (as did the Hebrews the LORD, Pss. 18:14; 104:3–4). Elijah's action as a priest offering sacrifice is not unusual. The Baalites 'danced wildly' round the altar (the same word as in the challenge, v. 21; Heb. *psḥ* denotes a circumambulation of the altar, *cf*. 'Baal of the Dance') as an act of devotion similar to that undertaken by pilgrims round the Ka'ba at Mecca. This was no rain-making ceremony.

27–29. Elijah's taunt is that Baal was acting in a merely human manner. He uses terms known to the people from the Ugaritic Baal myths. Was the god musing on the action to take (*deep in thought*)? Had he gone aside to answer the call of nature (so Targum; NEB 'engaged'; NIV, after LXX, *busy*) or had he left on a journey with Phoenician merchants? Was Baal asleep as Yahweh was not (Ps. 121:3–4)? The practice of self-inflicted wounds to arouse a deity's pity or response is attested in Ugarit when men 'bathed in their own blood like an ecstatic prophet'.[3]

---

[1] A. Malamat, 'A Forerunner of Biblical Prophecy: The Mari Documents', in P. D. Miller *et al.* (eds.), *Ancient Israelite Religion: Essays in Honor of Frank Moore Cross* (Philadelphia: Fortress Press, 1987), pp. 33–52.

[2] *Cf*. v. 4, 19:10, 14; 20:13, 28, 35; 22:6–8.

[3] See J. J. M. Roberts, 'A New Parallel to 2 Kings 18:28–29', *JBL* 89, 1970, pp. 76–77.

In mourning this was forbidden to the Hebrews (Lv. 19:28; Dt. 14:1). Baal's priests acted like ecstatic prophets (v. 29, NIV, *frantic prophesying*; better RSV 'ranted and raved'). This rare form of the verb (Heb. *hiṯnabbēʾ*) is used of mad actions (*cf.* 2 Ki. 9:11; Je. 29:26). The fact that there is no response indicates Baal's impotence (Je. 10:5).

30. Elijah's actions (vv. 30–39) underscored the significance of the test.

31. The repaired altar – the twelve stones represented the true Israel (as at Gilgal, Jos. 4:2–5) and the twelve tribes restored to united worship.

32a. The named altar as well as the fire upon the altar, as in Solomon's temple, were witnesses to the covenant. There can be no question of trickery, such as the use of naptha instead of water, or mirrors for ignition as suggested by some scholars. The opposition was observant and close (v. 30). Lightning was not necessarily the sole cause of the intense heat (v. 38).

32b–34. The trench size can be interpreted as holding fifteen litres or extending three hundred square metres. It was hardly a magic circle or for holding seed to sprout with water in imitative magic! (So Gray.) A rain-making ritual or sympathetic magic would be out of place. In pouring the water Elijah was just 'loading the dice against himself' (Rowley) as a guarantee against fraud.

36–39. The simple prayer (*cf.* v. 24) contrasts with the long Baalistic ravings. He asks not just for a miraculous demonstration that Yahweh is God but for the conversion of Israel. He reminds God of his previous interventions, using 'Jacob' for Israel possibly as a term of rebuke for the latter's apostasy. On 'fire from heaven' (v. 38) as demonstrating God's power and judgment, see 2 Kings 1:10, 12; Job 1:16. The people's acknowledgment (v. 39) is itself an answer to prayer (*cf.* vv. 21, 24).

40. The slaughter of the Baal prophets was not an act of wanton cruelty but the necessary retribution, ordered by Elijah as the 'new Moses' on behalf of God, against false prophets as decreed in Deuteronomy (13:5, 13–18; 17:2–5) following the action of Moses and Phineas (Nu. 25:1–13). Christians view idolatry as no less sinful, but see total judgment as reserved for the final Day (1 Cor. 6:9; Rev. 20:11–15; 21:8; 22:19). The *Kishon* is the Nahr el-Muqatta' below Carmel. Those who seized the false prophets might include men freed from caves nearby (v. 4) or the people who saw the falsehood of their worship.

42. Ahab is urged to be satisfied now that the drought is coming to an end, and this act between Ahab and Elijah need bear no sense of renewed fellowship. Elijah *ran ahead of* 'the king' (v. 46) to get to Jezreel first. This does not denote an act of homage such as in 1 Samuel 8:11. Elijah's posture with *his face between his knees* marked humility, mourning and prayer. It was too general to be taken as imitation of an incipient rain-cloud (as Ap-Thomas).

46. Elijah was able to run twenty-seven kilometres to Ahab's summer palace at Jezreel (modern Tell Jezreel) due to the 'hand' (RSV; NIV *power of the LORD*) which may not necessarily be so much supernatural power here (but *cf.* v. 12; 19:3; 2 Ki. 2:16) as due to a strong motivation. Alternatively, *all the way* (*cf.* RSV) to the 'entering in' *to Jezreel* might mean he went to the point where the road turns off to Jezreel.

d. Elijah encouraged (19:1–18).

i. Elijah flees to Horeb (19:1–8). Faced with threats to kill him, continued opposition from the royal house and apostasy by Israel, Elijah flees to Horeb. The Bible typically exposes the weakness of a man of God, for Elijah exhibited symptoms of manic depression, wishing for death, together with loss of appetite, an inability to manage and with excessive self-pity. He was unmoved by visitors, even by a visit from God and visions, but was restored when given a new and demanding task to fulfil. It is not certain whether the historian here intended to recount events in chronological sequence.

1–3. This account may cover a long period in which reversal after the Carmel victory took place. Jezebel was undaunted by the demonstration of God's exclusive power, and she was not the first religious persecutor in history (*cf.* Ikhnaton of Egypt against Amun's followers). The queen sends a messenger, because she is afraid to confront Elijah in person, with a strong curse, *may the gods deal with me* (v. 2); meaning either Baal Shemayim or all the Baals.[1] Some sources (LXX(L)) add

---

[1] Ugarit texts (RS 20.24; RS 1929 No. 17) list the pantheon, including eight Baals defined as 'the Baals of the hills' (*špn*) and as Baal (H)adad I-VII (J. Nougayrol, 'Textes Suméro-Accadiens des Archives et Bibliothéques privées d'Ugarit', *Ugaritica* V, 1968, pp. 44–45).

'As surely as you are Elijah ('My God is Yah') and I am Jezebel ('Where is the Baal?')'. Elijah goes to the most southerly city of *Judah,* a designation which must therefore pre-date 722 BC, after which there was no longer an Israel to set over against Judah. Elijah *was afraid* follows LXX and Syr., while MT (NIV mg.) 'saw' has the same consonants but different vowels – and could therefore be equally valid. The historian deliberately selects events which parallel Moses who also left his servants (Ex. 24:2ff.; 33:11), as did Abraham (Gn. 22:5), so that he could face God alone. So must all of us who would reconsider God's call and our mission.

4. To ask God to *Take my life* will always get a sure reply. But God will take his servant to himself in his own time and manner (2 Ki. 2:11). It is not up to us to ask for death but for life.

5. Meanwhile the extraordinary provision would remind Elijah of what God had done at Cherith and Zarephath (17:2–16). The (specific) *angel* or messenger (*maleʾāḵ*) is here an abbreviation for the angel of the LORD (v. 7; *cf.* Gn. 16:7). The white broom tree (v. 4, Heb. *rōṯem; Retama raetam Forssk. Webb*) is common near Sinai and northwards. It grows to a height of about three metres.

8. *Horeb* (= Sinai), whether located at Jebel Musa (south Sinai), Qudairat or further north,[1] was thought of as the mountain of God (Ex. 3:1), and as a place of pilgrimage under Moses (Dt. 1:2, 6, 19). It lay about four hundred kilometres south of Beersheba. The *forty days and forty nights* marks a long time and identifies Elijah as a second Moses (Ex. 24:18; 34:28; Dt. 9:8–10), just as it did Christ (Mt. 4:2).

ii. The LORD appears to Elijah (19:9–18). **9.** The theophany is introduced by *the word of the LORD came*, a constant and dominant aspect of the inspiration of Elijah's works. *The cave* (as Heb.) may well have been the specific 'clift of the rock' where God appeared to Moses (AV, Ex. 33:22) rather than the 'cave-region' generally.

The question *'What are you doing here?'* is ever God's call to the individual to reassess his or her position (*cf.* Gn. 3:9). It contains an implied rebuke, and yet evokes confession of our fears and feelings.

[1] G. I. Davies, *The Way of the Wilderness* SOTSM (Cambridge: Cambridge University Press, 1979), pp. 63–69.

10. The reasons for Elijah's depression include sadness at Israel's apostasy (*cf.* 18:18), desecration of sacred places and martyrdom of the LORD's prophets (*cf.* 18:13) despite Elijah being *zealous*. This word (AV 'jealous', 'ardent', Heb. *qānā'* meaning 'to be enthusiastically and exclusively devoted') is used both of God (Ex. 20:5) and of man in his disruptive passions (envy, jealousy, 2 Ki. 10:16). Elijah's complaint is that he is alone and *they* (the numerous *Israelites*, not just Ahab, 18:13, and Jezebel, 19:1) are *trying to kill me*. This will be answered by God's renewed call and commission (vv. 15–18). The repetition of the question (vv. 13–14), if not the well-known ancient Semitic narrative device for emphasis, could be to give Elijah a further chance to show what he had learned from the previous experience.

11–14. The upheaval of nature in powerful winds, earthquakes, floods or storms is associated with God's action in revelation and judgment. It is reminiscent of the covenant at Sinai and the commissioning of Moses and the people (Ex. 19:9, 16; 34:6; Dt. 5:23–26). Each were well-known signs of judgment on sin (Ps. 18:7, 12; Is. 13:13; 29:6) but did not themselves convey the whole message. God does not always speak so clearly through these manifestations as he does through his individual word to his prophet. The 'still small voice' (AV) was *a gentle whisper* (*cf.* Heb. 'a thin [fine] subdued sound'), rather than 'a low murmuring sound' (NEB); 'stillness' is not incompatible with the words for 'sound, voice' ('a sound of sheer silence', NRSV) and the word 'thin' (*dāqqâ*). The soft voice of God speaking to the conscience, illuminating the mind and stirring resolve in individual and nation may follow and is often preferable to the loud roaring and thunder of cosmic events at Sinai and Carmel. Elijah realized that he, like Moses, could not look at God and live (Ex. 33:20–22, *cf.* Gn. 32:30), so he covered his face.

15–18. A new task for the dispirited prophet. The LORD's command (*said*) involved a return to the scene of action. The *Desert of Damascus* (referred to in Qumran texts) was not so much another place of refuge, but like Galilee in Jesus' life, a springboard for the next tasks which for Elijah related to the threat to Israel from Aram. Finding Hazael could involve Elijah, as it did his contemporary Jonah, in travel to lands outside Israel. Jehu, the successor to Ahab, would bring about subservience to Assyria and this eventually led to the destruction of Israel. Nevertheless Elijah, and Elisha ('God saves') as his successor (2 Ki. 8:7–15), would be involved in implementing the divine will. *Anoint* (Heb. *māšaḥ*) denotes the designation or authorization of a regal or priestly successor (*cf.* Jesus [Joshua] followed John the Baptist). Only here is the term used of a prophet appointing a successor (*cf.* Is. 61:1). Such anointing ceremonies could partly be in private (as in ancient Near Eastern coronation ceremonies), and partly in public as here.

Abel Meholah (v. 16), the scene of Gideon's victory (Jdg. 7:22), lay in the Jordan Valley sixteen kilometres south of Beth-Shan, so Elijah would have to go north via Elisha's home. Despite the coming holocaust a remnant will be left (v. 18). *Seven thousand* may be symbolic of a perfectly complete and not insignificant number. For *kissed* idols see Hosea 13:2.

e. The call of Elisha (19:19–21). Such detail could have been recorded by the Elisha group of prophets. The name Elisha ('God is salvation') appears also on a seal from Amman of the seventh century.[1] Elijah fulfils his task of appointing his successor (v. 16) in order that he in turn may complete the other tasks allotted him. So always in God's planning (as with Christ and his apostles).

Elisha comes from a prosperous background (Jones) where twelve teams of oxen were used for ploughing. Elisha himself drove the last pair with the others 'ahead of' (Heb. *lᵉpānâw*) him. In an act of investiture denoting authority rather than contactual magic, Elijah throws his outer garment – possibly a distinctive hairy skin or *cloak* (LXX 'sheepskin', *cf.* 2 Ki. 1:8; Mt. 3:4; Heb. 11:37) – over him. There is no sure evidence that this act was a symbol of adoption as a son or that it represented transfer of the power of its owner (2 Ki. 2:8). That theory rests only on the reference to the hem of the garment (1 Sa. 24:4–11) which, when cut off, denoted the breaking of allegiance.

20–21. *What have I done to* (prevent) *you?* (*cf.* NEB) could mean,

---

[1] Ammonite seals reading a name of Elisha (*'lyš'*) have been published, by P. Bordreuil, 'Trois sceaux nord-ouest sémitiques inédits', *Semitica* 24, 1974, pp. 30–34; A. Lemaire, 'Nouveaux sceaux nord-ouest sémitiques', *Semitica* 33, 1983, pp. 20–21, pl. II no. 6 (*'z' bn 'lyš'*); and from Ur, C. L. Woolley, *Ur Excavations IX* (London: British Museum, 1962), pl. 30, U.16805; *cf.* K. Galling, 'Ein hebraisches Siegel aus der babylonischen Diaspora', *ZDPV* 51, 1928, pp. 234–236, Taf.17C 'Saul son of Elisha' (*š'l bn 'lyš*), both of the neo-Babylonian period.

'Go back, but remember what I have done to you.' It might be a rebuke at any delay in following (Mt. 8:21; *cf.* Lk. 5:11, 28). Burning the wooden yokes, rather than boiling the yoke of oxen (as RSV!), marked a break with his past life. The farewell feast celebrated his new role in becoming the aide (NIV *attendant*; AV 'servant') to Elijah.

f. Ahab's wars (20:1–34). The history turns from that of Elijah to recount two wars in the campaign between Aram and Israel at Samaria (20:1–21) and Aphek (vv. 22–34). Both accounts underline that this was the final opportunity for Ahab to show whether he would obey God's word through his prophet, and both stress the danger of punishment and reverse if the LORD's command was not carried out to the full. These narratives prepare for the death of Ahab and the abandonment of a rebellious Israel. Commentators disagree on the historical reconstruction of these events but unite in the supposition that this chapter must draw on a variety of sources, including the records of the prophets (the Elisha circle?) and possibly the official account of the acts of Ahab.

This was a crucial period in Israel's history. Aram turned south, perhaps in an attempt to gain new trade routes, since the north had been cut off by the wars of the Assyrian Ashur-naṣir-apli II (883–859 BC) and his successor Shalmaneser III (859–829 BC). Some think the wars recorded here took place early in Ahab's reign, to allow time for the mellowing of Israel's relation with Aram when Ahab contributed to the coalition which faced Assyria at the battle of Qarqar in 853 BC (Bright). Yeivin argues that the first war was early but the second followed after Qarqar, but this is unlikely in view of 22:1. The aggression of Ben-Hadad II (Hadadezer, Assyr. Adad-'idri) may have aimed to secure his southern flank while he faced the Assyrian drive to the Mediterranean *c.* 888–885 BC. There is no need to view the prophetic allusions as secondary, for their interpretation of events is consistent with that of the Deuteronomic historian throughout. The picture of the Omride dynasty is consistent and Ahab is condemned for his failure to follow God's word.

i. The battle for Samaria (20:1–21). This is an example of God's self-disclosure and long-suffering towards Ahab (vv. 13–14).

1–4. The *thirty-two* kings would include minor tribal chiefs and compares with Ben-Hadad II's ten allies named with Ahab at Qarqar in 853 BC and ten in the Zakir stela.[1] Ben-Hadad is likely to be a dynastic throne-name ('son of the god Hadad'). For Ben-Hadad I see 15:18–19. His claim that Ahab was a vassal is shown by Ahab addressing him as 'my lord the king', which follows common ancient Near Eastern terminology, so the attack could imply that Ahab had rebelled against him. Similarly *'all I have are yours'* (v. 4) were normally the words used by a subordinate and were employed by Ahab formally to avoid the plundering of his capital.

5–6. The Aramean reply is more specific and was a statement designed to instigate war rather than to imply discontent with a merely verbal submission. *To search your palaces and houses* implies handing over the whole city (*cf.* REB 'ransack').

7–8. To consult *all the elders . . . and the people* is to call a consultative assembly without which a king should not take major action such as war (*cf.* 1 Ki. 12).

10–12. War was formally initiated by a solemn oath taken in the name of the nation's gods and, as here, in oral and written statement to the opponent (*cf.* 1 Sa. 17:43–44). The threat was the total obliteration of Samaria by an enemy numerous enough to remove all the rubble. *One who puts on armour . . .* – a four-word proverb to indicate that preparing for war was one thing and winning it another – the equivalent of 'Don't count your chickens before they are hatched.' NEB 'The lame must not think himself a match for the nimble' is a paraphrase of the LXX(L). Proverbs are quoted in diplomatic exchanges (see also 1 Sa. 17:43, Mari Amarna Letter 61 and Assyrian letters).[2]

---

[1] Shalmaneser III of Assyria cites 'Ahab the Israelite' with Irhuleni of Hamath, Adunu-Ba'al of Shizana, Matinu-Ba'al of Arvad, Gundibu' of Arabia, Ba'asa of Ammon and men of Cilicia, Muṣru, Uqanata, Usantu among his opponents (*ANET*, pp. 278–279). In another inscription Zakir, king of Hamath, says that Benhadad (Bar-Hadad) son of Hazael king of Aram united a group of ten kings including Bargush, the kings of Cilicia, 'Umq, Gurgum, Sam'al, Milid to besiege him in Hatarikka (the stela of Zakir from Apish, *ANET*, p. 655).

[2] *Cf.* also the proverbs cited in 1 Sa. 17:43, 'Am I a dog that you come at me with sticks?'; 1 Sa. 10:12; 19:24, 'Is Saul among the prophets?'; Je. 31:29. Similar proverbs are found in diplomatic correspondence from Mari, Syria (*Archives royales de Mari* I, 1:5), Amarna, Egypt, 'When ants are struck they do not take it passively but bite the hands that strike them' (Letter 61, *ANET*, p. 426) and Assyria (L. Waterman, *Royal Correspondence of the Assyrian Empire* (Ann Arbor: University of Michigan Press, 1930–1936), Assyrian & Babylonian Letters Nos. 37, 403:4–7; 13–15; 595, r. 3–6; 652 r. 9–13).

13–20a. The sure promise of victory which would ensure that it would be recognized as Yahweh's (*you will know that I am the LORD*, vv. 13, 28) is said to belong to the 'holy war' tradition. The plan had elements of surprise in the timing (*noon*, vv. 12, 16), approach and tactics using a select group of 232 young (unmarried?) commanders (Heb. *neʿārîm*). Also the use of men in the initial attack selected by the *provincial* or 'district-officers' (NEB) responsible for both fiscal and military affairs, was unusual. They appeared to engage in individual combat (*cf.* David and Goliath) on the initiation of Ahab himself (v. 14). They may well have been mistaken initially for a delegation seeking terms of peace (v. 18, for *šālôm* in this sense see 2 Ki. 9:17–19).

'Mustered' (RSV, REB), 'called up' (NEB) are to be preferred to *summoned* and *assembled* (v. 15), for the Heb. (*pāqaḏ*) means 'to review to see who is missing'. The *7,000* would be only a representative group (LXX 'men of substance') and less than a full army (= 10,000), to show that the LORD does not rely on numbers (*cf.* Jdg. 7:2). For this number see 19:18. They seem to have been held in reserve or moved behind the main Syrian force (v. 19), the main clash being by the 232-strong vanguard.

20b–21. Ben-Hadad's escape was 'on a horse with horsemen' (Heb., RSV). The Hebrew for horseman (*pārāš*) can also mean chariot-horse. There was a spare horse with each chariot and this may have helped his escape. The main Israelite force overpowered (MT, NIV *struck down*; RSV 'captured') the remainder, showing that horses were used for the pursuit.

22. At times of success God warns of undue self-confidence. Practical steps must be taken ahead of time against an expected counter-attack.

ii. The battle for Aphek (20:22–34). The second campaign is directed specifically at Israel and her God rather than at her luxurious capital. The prophet had a word on military strategy. The 'turn of the year' is the spring not the autumn, though military campaigns could take place throughout the year except at the height of the rainy seasons.

The Arameans believed that Yahweh, like their own gods, was limited geographically and viewed him as they did any other god (*gods*; but LXX interprets 'a mountain God is the

God of Israel'). For the nations viewing Samaria as having many gods see on 2 Kings 17:7. They thought that the previous action in hilly terrain precluded the use of chariots, so now they chose to fight in the plain with a change of commanders (v. 24) which, though not immediately successful, was to prove so later at Qarqar. The commanders chosen were the experienced provincial officers (Assyr. *pahāt*) rather than lower rank *officers* (NIV, NEB) or 'commanders' (RSV, *cf.* NRSV 'servants', REB 'ministers') who would themselves raise the replacement troops. The place of battle was either Aphek east of Lake Galilee (El Fiq, modern En Ger) on the route from Damascus to Israel near the junction of the Yarmuk and Jordan rivers, or the Afek in the Esdraelon Valley near Endor. If the former, serious entry into Israel was prevented.

29. The seven day delay by the Aram forces may have been to await a favourable omen. The casualties at *a hundred thousand* may be symbolic of a massive number, for the total Aramean army group at Qarqar was 62,900. However, the 'thousand' (*'elep*) might be revocalized without change of consonants to 'officer' (*'allûp*).[1] One hundred casualties a day in ancient warfare was heavy. Similarly the 27,000 killed in Aphek would include everyone in the city when the walls fell. This would remind the Israelites of the victory at Jericho (Jos. 6), otherwise the number might represent twenty-seven officers killed.

Ben-Hadad is treated well (vv. 30–34).

30. The king may have first sought refuge in an *inner room* or sanctuary ('room within a room', *cf.* 1 Ki. 22:25; 2 Ki. 9:2), rather than underground (Josephus, *Ant.* viii.14.3) or moving from room to room (Gray).

31–33. Was the reputation of the Israelites really more merciful? The word used of them (*ḥesed*) is a characteristic of God's loyal covenantal love ('loving-kindness', AV 'mercy'). At least it was worth a try, and the royal party emerged clothed in goatshair (sackcloth) as a sign of mourning and a rope around the head as a symbol of submission, not a sign of a porter

---

[1] R. E. D. Clark, 'The Large Numbers of the OT', *Journal of the Transactions of the Victoria Institute* 87, 1955, pp. 82 ff.; J. W. Wenham, 'Large Numbers in the Old Testament', *TynB* 18, 1967, pp. 19–53; A. R. Millard, 'Large numbers in Assyrian Royal Inscriptions' in M. Cogan and I. Eph'al, *Ah, Assyria, Scripta Hierosolymitana* 33 (1991), pp. 213–222 which shows the balanced use of round numbers and estimates alongside accurate accounting.

(*šanda*) or of supplication (Josephus) but rather that they were ready to be led off as prisoners. The pleas to be spared was taken up by the men 'watching for an omen' (RSV) who took the reference by Ahab to Ben-Hadad as *brother* (v. 33, that is ally, equal or treaty partner) as a hopeful sign confirmed by the prisoner being taken up into the royal chariot (v. 33). This is a more reasonable interpretation than rearranging the MT to 'caught it up at once' (NEB) or 'was quick to take it as definite' (Gray). The Heb. (*ḥlṭ*) occurs only here, hence uncertainty over its meaning.

34. Ahab imposes an agreement (*bᵉrît*) with two requirements prior to granting freedom. This he confirmed later by a formal treaty. The first stipulation was the return of (border?) villages taken in the days of Omri. The Old Testament gives no reference to that seizure, but the account of Omri's reign is brief (see 16:23–28) and deliberately omits his major deeds (*cf.* Moabite Stone). Alternatively they could have been those places lost to Baasha (15:20; 16:3). This is preferable to relating this to a later recovery by Joash of towns lost to Jehoahaz (Gray).

The establishment of *market areas* or protected (trade) zones (Heb. *ḥuṣôt*) was common practice to stimulate inter-state trade and finance by merchant groups.[1] Yet in all this neither the LORD God, his prophet nor his people were consulted.

g. A prophet rebukes Ahab (20:35–43). An acted parable is used to lead Ahab to realize his inconsistency and guilt in going against God's express will and postponing judgment on Ben-Hadad. This was to cost Israel dearly in death and destruction (*cf.* 2 Ki. 10:32) and lead to the final fall of the Northern Kingdom. The literary device of the story to bring conviction of error can be compared with Samuel's condemnation of Saul (1 Sa. 15:14–30), and Nathan of David (2 Sa. 12:1–13). It is the responsibility of a prophet to direct one who errs to the right interpretation of events and so lead to self-judgment. Here we are reminded that not even a king is above the law but is subject to divine justice (v. 42).

Those who doubt the historical reliability of this narrative appeal to what they regard as its similarity to the lion incident

[1] M. Elat, 'Trade and Commerce', *WHJP* V, pp. 184–186; M. Elat in E. Lipiński (ed.), *State and Temple Economy in the Ancient Near East* II (Louvain: Editions Peeters, 1979), p. 543.

(13:20–25). This story and its interpretation are, however, essential to the portrayal of the character of Ahab and to contrast with his attitude in the Naboth episode (ch. 21).

35. *One of the sons of the prophets* is interpreted by Josephus (*Ant.* viii.14.5) as Micaiah. *Sons* denotes a class or membership of a group (rather than an organized guild) under a director ('father'). This is the first reference to these special bands of prophets (2 Ki. 2:3–7, 15; 4:1, 38; 5:22; 6:1; 9:1) who appear during the critical period of the Omride dynasty but are otherwise not well attested.

37–40. To attract the king's attention the man disguised himself as a wounded soldier with a 'bandage' (NEB) or *head band* over his eyes (vv. 38–41). The term ($^{a}p\bar{e}r$) occurs only here and may be a general head covering (Assyr. *apāru*, Cohen). The prophet may have borne a distinguishing mark on his forehead or chest (vv. 38, 41). The principle that a captor is responsible for the life of a captive is important. The potential fine of a *talent* (3,000 shekels, 34 kilos) of silver, which is a hundred times the cost of a slave, is not fictitious but typical of the prohibitive legal penalties in cases of breach of contract at this time.

42. The concept of the LORD *determining* that a man should *die* (Heb. 'the man of my ban', *cf.* NIV mg.) is difficult for many in our modern society to accept. The total extermination or ban (*ḥērem*) was a divine requirement for complete destruction of anything designated alien to God and his people (Dt. 7:2; 20:16; *cf.* Is. 34:5). It is often classed as a 'holy war' concept, but all ancient wars were considered such (*cf.* the ban at Mari[1]). The practice may derive from the fear of contagion, and God's action cannot be condemned and Ahab's condoned when the latter caused far greater suffering. Failure to exact this punishment would bring curse and punishment on the offender (Jones).

h. Naboth's vineyard (21:1–29). Scholars disagree as to the sources for this chapter which nevertheless reads as an integrated unity. They consider the original story (vv. 1–16) to have been supplemented from the Elijah records (vv. 17–21, 27–28) and the historian's comments added (vv. 22–27). The Greek versions place this incident between chapters 19 and

[1] A. Malamat, *Mari and the Early Israelite Experience* (London: British Academy, 1989), pp. 70–75.

20. The prophecies of this chapter (*e.g.* 21:19–24) are logically fulfilled in the next chapter (22:38; *cf.* 2 Ki. 9:36).

Elijah is shown to step in dramatically to denounce Ahab the king for acting above the law. His sin is exposed and judgment by God pronounced to bring an end to the whole dynasty (vv. 21–22). Following repentance, this was deferred for a while (vv. 27–29). Ahab's clemency, publicly shown to the Arameans, is now contrasted with his despotic behaviour to one of his own citizens.

i. The clash between king and commoner (21:1–6). Though Ahab may have acted lawfully and in a straightforward manner when he offered to buy (vv. 2, 3, 6 *sell* rather than AV 'give') or exchange Naboth's vineyard, a practice commonly attested in Syria (Alalakh and Ugarit texts), the request may have aroused in Naboth memory of Samuel's warnings of the possibility of royal confiscation (1 Sa. 8:14). Ideally the royal power in Israel was limited to protect human rights (Dt. 17:14–20; 1 Sa. 10:25).

Naboth's strong rejection in Yahweh's name (v. 4) has been taken to be that the loss of the ancestral inheritance (vv. 3–4) would make Naboth a royal dependent. There is no sure evidence that the Israelite and Canaanite conception of real estate differed, or that in Israel such inheritances were inalienable since the land belonged to God and was allocated to a king or family as his tenants (Lv. 25:23–28; Nu. 26:52–56). To dispose of land was not a grave crime (Whitelam, *contra* Andersen). Certainly in the ancient east a transfer of many types of land was always subject to royal sanction, legal proceedings and strict control. Appropriation (vv. 15, 16, 18, Heb. *yrš*) by the crown of land lacking a present tenant was not unknown (*cf.* 2 Ki. 8:3). A tablet from Syria records the forfeiture of possession by the palace when a man had been found guilty of treachery and put to death.[1]

2. Royal gardens were always located close to the royal palace and water, and furnished with 'green growth', trees and shrubs for colour and shade[2] (so *yārāq*, rather than *vegetable garden*, NEB 'vineyard', or AV 'garden of herbs').

3. *The LORD forbid.* This introduces a strong oath in religious

[1] D. J. Wiseman, *The Alalakh Tablets* (London: British Institute of Archaeology at Ankara, 1953) No. 17; *ANET*, p. 546.

[2] D. J. Wiseman, 'Mesopotamian Gardens', *Anatolian Studies* 33, 1983, p. 139.

terms using God's name (*cf.* 1 Sa. 24), which should always be used with great caution (*cf.* Ex. 20:7). Andersen's theory that Jezebel reinterpreted this to be a permissive statement that Naboth had finally made the land-grant is most unlikely, as is his view that to dispossess a man from his family estate was blasphemy.[1]

4. The reaction of Ahab shows his real character. *Sulking* (NIV, Vulg.; 'sullen', NRSV, REB) implies that the full Heb. phrase was 'turned his face (to the wall)' (2 Ki. 20:2).

ii. Jezebel's plot (21:7–14). As an unscrupulous double-dealer she enforced her own Phoenician concept of despotic kingship by turning the public legal proceedings to her own ends. She involved Ahab by the use of his seal on directives to the local magistrates (v. 8). The use of the king's royal dynastic, administrative or even personal seal to gain his authority would require Ahab's collusion. Jezebel's own inscribed seal has been found.[2] The *letters* (plural) to the elders and nobles (RSV; NEB 'notables') who were sanctioned by the king to act as subordinate judges – among whom Naboth 'sat' (in council), rather than *lived* or 'dwelt' (RSV) as a trusted person – did not summon a court.

9. To *proclaim a day of fasting* lay in the power of the king (2 Ch. 20:3–4; Je. 36:9). The purpose, whether to do with the great drought or a local or national crisis, is not defined here. The catastrophe which occasioned it would be thought to have been sent by God. Any person who had been the cause of such divine judgment had to be identified and punished, as had been Achan (Jos. 7:16–26) and Jonathan (1 Sa. 14:40–45). The royal instructions (vv. 9–10) were followed by confirmation that they were carried out (vv. 11–13, LXX curtails this). Jezebel carefully follows the Deuteronomic law by having two witnesses in a case involving a capital offence (Dt. 17:6; 19:15; Nu. 35:30) and by demanding the prescribed death sentence for blasphemy (Dt. 13:10; 17:5).

10, 13a. The charge was stated to be that Naboth *had cursed both God and the king*. This arose from Jezebel's deliberate falsification of Naboth's refusal in saying 'I will surely not give you the vineyard' (v. 6).

[1] F. I. Andersen, 'The Socio-Juridical background of the Naboth Incident', *JBL* 85, 1966, pp. 46–57.
[2] N. Avigad, 'The Seal of Jezebel', *IEJ* 14, 1964, pp. 174–176.

The false witnesses were 'sons of Belial' (AV), Heb. meaning either 'without worth' or 'wicked men' (Dt. 13:13), so NIV *scoundrels* (also Pr. 6:12, *cf.* REB 'unprincipled rogues'), RSV 'base fellows' or 'those who do not get up', *i.e.* 'ne'er do wells' who could easily be persuaded to give false witness (*cf.* Mt. 26:60). Belial is later used of Satan as the personification of lawlessness and wickedness (2 Cor. 6:15). The Heb. word 'blessed' is here taken to be a euphemism for *cursed* (as in Jb. 1:11; 2:5, 9; Ps. 10:3) to avoid anyone reading or hearing an impious expression. NEB mg. 'cursing' assumes this (*cf.* Heb. 'blessed', lit. 'bidding farewell to') to be a greeting at departure implying that Naboth was saying farewell to God and king (Robinson). This is unlikely, though several Hebrew expressions encompass their opposite meaning (by polarity).

12. It may well be that Jezebel set a trap for Naboth who was set (as instructed, v. 9) *in a prominent place* (RSV 'on high'; Heb. 'at the head of the people'), rather than 'in front of' (with Andersen). If this were a selection or identification procedure, Naboth was chosen as the cause of the trouble when the false witnesses accused him of the capital offence of cursing God and king (Ex. 22:28). The local court, under royal duress, agreed.

13b–14. The death penalty was effected *outside the city* on rubbish ground, to avoid further pollution (Nu. 15:36, *cf.* Acts 7:58; Heb. 13:12).

iii. Elijah prophesies the death of Ahab's house (21:17–24). Again Elijah moves in swift answer to God's direction (v. 17). The order is precise.

18. *Go down* is typical of the exact detail recorded, for Jezreel (115 metres above sea level) lay well below Samaria (412 metres). 'Who (is) in Samaria?' (AV, REB) is too limited, for Ahab at that time was in Jezreel (v. 17), hence NIV, NRSV *who rules in Samaria.* Elijah confronts Ahab at the very scene of his crime. His purpose in coming might be thought to be to reclaim the land himself for its rightful owner, to clear the dead man's name and represent God as the avenger of blood (hence his designation here as *my enemy*, v. 20). For when there is injustice and oppression the only restraint on a despot's conduct may be an appeal to the justice of God who always does what is right.

19–20. The fulfilment of prophecy is sometimes by stages.

Here it was partially fulfilled by the dead body of Ahab being exposed at Samaria (22:38) and then, due to the deferment promised by God (v. 29), when the body of his son Joram was left on Naboth's ground (2 Ki. 9:25–26). Elijah pronounces the final verdict on the guilty party in a prophetic judgment. Ahab had broken two commands of the Decalogue, the prohibition of murder (Dt. 5:17, 'you shall not murder') and covetousness ('or your neighbour's ... land', Dt. 5:21). That Ahab had 'given himself over' (Heb. v. 20, *cf.* NIV *sold yourself*, LXX and Versions add 'to no purpose') to *do evil* shows that he had made a deliberate choice. The result would be the inevitable 'evil' (v. 21, AV, *cf.* NIV *disaster*) of total retributive destruction brought by God (so Is. 45:7).

21–22. Elijah speaks for God in the first person when giving the divine word. This is unusual and is no warrant for similar modern practices. There is, however, no need to take this as part of the historian's comment aligning the fate of the Omride dynasty with that of its two previous houses of Jeroboam and Baasha, though this is a recurrent theme (*cf.* 14:10–11; 2 Ki. 22:16). The comment in verses 25–26 certainly makes Ahab to be the worst of all twenty kings of Israel.

23. The fate of Jezebel is given in 2 Kings 9:36. Her end was particularly marked by lack of burial, which was a major disgrace. Sources vary over the place meant by the circular outer *wall of Jezreel* (RSV 'rampart'; MT *ḥēl*). Some MSS read here 'plot of ground' (*ḥlq*), as in 2 Kings 9:10.

iv. Ahab's repentance (21:27–29). This section explains why the fulfilment of the prophecy concerning Ahab's end was delayed after what seems to have been a genuine repentance with Ahab exhibiting the typical behaviour of one in mourning (v. 27), showing contrition and meekness (v. 29, *humbled himself*, RSV 'dejectedly'; he went about (= behaved) gently, Heb. *'aṭ*). Temporary deferment of punishment may result from repentance, as it did for Hezekiah (2 Ki. 20:1, 6, 11) and Nineveh (Jon. 3:10).

i. Ahab's final war against Aram (22:1–38). *Cf.* 2 Chronicles 18. This third campaign continues from 20:34 and fulfils Elisha's prophecy that there would be three victories over Aram (2 Ki. 13:14–19). Interpreters differ as to whether this was before or after the battle of Qarqar on the River Crontes

in the summer of 853 BC, when Ahab is named by the
Assyrians as a strong element in the Syrian coalition which
checked their march westwards. There is no support for those
who seek to disassociate the prophetic traditions from the
political and battle records, for the narrative is inseparable.
Nor is there unity among those who argue here for a con-
flation of two accounts of different battles at Ramoth Gilead
under Jehoahaz and Ahaziah, or that the Jehoshaphat
material has been introduced to stress the superior theological
standpoint of Judah (Miller, Jones). The three years of peace
(v. 1) may have been that of the preparation for Qarqar which
required Ahab to protect Israel's southern flank. To do this he
took the opportunity of a treaty with Jehoshaphat, his son-in-
law, to enforce the terms imposed on Ben-Hadad at the treaty
of Aphek (20:34), following which Ramoth Gilead belonged to
Israel (v. 3) but had not been returned.

i. Ahab consults the prophets (22:1–7). **2–4.** The king of Israel is
unnamed but must be Ahab, as in verse 20. For details of his
reception of Jehoshaphat see 2 Chronicles 18:1–2; 2 Kings
8:18. *Ramoth Gilead* was a border city between Aram and
Israel, modern Tell ar-Ramith (Glueck) rather than Ḥuṣn-
'Ajlūn, south-east of Irbid (Gray). It was lost to the Syrians
later by Jehu (2 Ki. 10:32–33). This was now a purely Aram-
Israel conflict (Oded) and the question *Will you go with me to
fight?* (v. 4) implies no subordination of Judah to Israel. Nor is
it a request to join a coalition with northern city-states as some
surmise. The reply *I am as you are . . . my horses as your horses* are
common terms of a parity agreement – here to a joint military
command later to be condemned by the prophet when Judah
went back on her previous alliance between Asa and Aram (*cf.*
15:17–23).

5–6. It was customary to *seek the counsel of* ('consult', JB; Heb.
dāraš) the national deity for his word before a major war. This
was necessary if it was to be made a 'holy war'. Jehoshaphat's
clear stance as a non-Baal worshipper was to seek Yahweh's
word as opposed to his partner seeking omen support from
his own deities for his own action (*cf.* 2 Sa. 2:1; 2 Ki. 3:11).
The importance of seeking God's will before any future act is
stressed. The *four hundred* 'nationalistic prophets' were perhaps centred on Bethel (12:28–29). Their numbers are no
exaggeration (1 Ki. 18:19). They were uncritically loyal to the

king of Israel and their unity must have aroused suspicion since they aimed to please the king rather than proclaim the truth (Am. 7:10–13). The ground of their verdict that the LORD would give victory would be the success of earlier campaigns (20:13, 28).

ii. Micaiah prophesies against Ahab (22:7–28). Here again the historian emphasizes the Judean perspective. There was a clash between Judah and Israel over the nature of true prophecy (*cf.* Je. 27; 29). Micaiah ('Who is like Yah[weh]?' – a common name) was God's man for this occasion (Elijah will reappear later). Some identify him with the prophet who had previously foretold disaster to Ahab (20:42; *cf.* 22:18). The true prophet speaks only what the LORD says (v. 14), which may be woe, as here; while the false prophet, like any omen diviner today, aims only to please the enquirer (v. 18, *cf.* 18:17; 21:20).

Ahab sends for Micaiah (22:7–12). **9.** It would not be inappropriate to send a high official to fetch the prophet (AV 'officer'; Heb. *sārîs* is the Assyrian *ša rēš(i) šarri*, who is not necessarily a 'eunuch' as JB).

10. The kings were clothed *in their royal robes* (LXX 'in full panoply') which may well not mean 'in shining armour' (NEB; 'in uniform' (Gray)) but in their state robes as it was a formal occasion (*sitting on their thrones*) in a public place. *The threshing-floor*, 'open space' (AV) 'at the entrance' (NEB) to the city gate was used for major crowded assembles. For another open-air court see 1 Sa. 14:2; 22:6.

11. *Zedekiah* used symbols to reinforce his group's message, choosing the *horns* as representing power to drive back Aram (as Joseph in Dt. 33:17). Similar use of enacted or illustrated prophecies was a feature of Jeremiah (19:1, 10–12, a pot; 28:10–11, a yoke; *cf.* Ezekiel 4, a drawing of a city under siege), and vividly emphasized the message.

Micaiah's warning (22:13–18). For Ahab to consult the prophet twice was common practice when seeking assurance (as at Mari and in seeking omens before a battle). When Micaiah merely repeated the false prophecy it could have been out of irony or to test Ahab's sincerity. This is no later insertion to bring out the contrast between the true and the false which is clear from the whole incident.

16. Ahab desired an authoritative statement on oath *in the* *name of the* LORD, whereupon Micaiah foretells Ahab's death and the break-up of the army, using a narrated vision (v. 17). Note that he also took the opportunity to 'refrain' (*cf.* v. 15) or plead for a peace-treaty (rather than read 'unmolested', JB).

17. *Sheep without a shepherd* depicts a lack of leadership which can only result in division and ruin (Nu. 27:16–17; Zec. 13:7; Mt. 9:36; 26:31).

A second vision (22:19–28). This was more direct and condemnatory than the first. It involved a view into the secret place of the Most High (as in Is. 6:1; Rev. 4:2). The true prophet will not only recount God's word itself (v. 14) but what he has seen for himself. The 'host of heaven' are not astral deities or a heavenly court such as is reflected in Ugaritic myths, but God's servants doing his bidding.

22–23. Many are concerned that the use of *a lying spirit* (the spirit of v. 21 sent to *entice*, NIV, NRSV; *cf.* JB 'trick' or 'deceive', *cf.* Je. 20:7) is contrary to God's moral nature. There is no evidence to equate it here with Satan the opposer of God's will and father of all lies, or with a general spirit of revelation (DeVries). It is rather a personified spirit of prophecy (Zc. 13:2; 1 Jn. 4:6), for even the false prophets may be governed by supernatural spiritual forces rather than merely human reason. It represents the power of a lie in the mouth of someone opposed to the truth and speaking for his own ends (Je. 14:14; 23:16, 26; Ezk. 13:2–3, 17). Such a use of a lying spirit in the person of Satan is consistent with Scripture (Jb. 1:6–12; Jn. 8:44). The LORD in truth decrees not only good but evil (v. 23, *disaster*; Is. 45:7). The prediction of Ahab's end had already been made by Elijah, and this use of false prophecy would emphasize that God controls everything including the final judgment on unbelief. God had given Ahab up (*cf.* Rom. 1:24–28) yet still was giving an opportunity for him to use his freewill and repent. Ahab's delusion can but lead on to his further backsliding and destruction and so reproves him (Je. 2:19).

24. 'Strike the cheek' (RSV), better than *slap in the face* or jaw (JB), as this is a long used and recognized legal and symbolic act in making a public challenge to speak the truth (as with Jesus Christ in Jn. 18:22). The inquiry *Which way did the Spirit of* (NIV mg.) or *from the LORD go?* may question either Micaiah's prophetic source or imply that anyone can make up lies (*cf.* 2 Ch. 18:23). The Hebrew text is difficult and LXX and

Chronicles are possibly an interpretation ('What kind of spirit . . .?').

25–28. The outcome will prove that Micaiah was right. It is a common human reaction to try to silence the word of God when it decrees judgment, and Micaiah, like Jeremiah (36:26; 38:2–6), was not the first or last to be so imprisoned. The city governor and 'Prince Joash' (JB), an otherwise unknown son of Ahab, were made responsible for the prophet's harsh custody. There is no contemporary evidence for the use of *king's son* to denote merely a minor official (v. 26, NEB mg. 'deputy'; *cf.* Je. 36:26; 38:6 where custody on behalf of the palace is also involved). 'Until I return in peace' (MT) may well be with a victory pact concluded rather than just *safely* (NEB, NIV). Micaiah's reply is attested by historical events. Some assume *Mark my words, all you people!* (not in Ch., LXX) to be an attempt to identify Micah (1:1) with Micaiah. It is appropriate for the prophet as the prisoner to make this challenge to look for the confirmation of his prophecy which was to come about very soon when Ahab failed to return safely (v. 35).

iii. The battle at Ramoth Gilead (22:29–38). The account follows logically and there is no need to assume that similarities with J(eh)oram in 2 Kings (8:28–29; 9:14–16) means that the latter record has influenced this one. There are marked differences in that Jehoahaz's death is not recounted and Jehoram's blood is not licked by dogs (*cf.* v. 38). It is not certain that by disguising himself (*hiṯḥappēś*) Ahab was seeking to direct attention away from himself and so avoid his predicted fate, or that he was acting out of superstition in order to draw evil away from himself. Malamat suggests that the word may mean donning a helmet to render himself unrecognizable[1] rather than 'royal uniform' (JB) (though some Gk. MSS read wear *my* robes).

31. The *thirty-two* need not be a scribal addition from 20:1, because 2 Chronicles 18:30 omits. The number could emphasize that Ahab had foolishly spared these men earlier (20:1, 16, 24).

32. Concentration on the enemy commander to disrupt the unity of one's opponents is an old tactic which Ahab bravely sought to negate by staying visible on the battle field till the

[1] A. Malamat, 'Josiah's Bid for Armageddon', *Journal of the Ancient Near Eastern Society of Columbia University* 5, 1973, p. 278 n. 35.

evening (v. 35). Jehoshaphat *cried out*, when surrounded, to establish his identity or to summon aid. 2 Chronicles 18:31 interprets it as a prayer to be answered by God who 'helped him' by drawing the chariot-commanders away from him. Jehoshaphat was to be rebuked for his part in this battle (2 Ch. 19:2).

34. It took a bow-shot *at random* (AV 'at a venture' gives the force of the Heb. 'in his simplicity', *i.e.* without particular aim) to bring down the prophesied target (NRSV 'unknowingly'). Armour made up of linked small metal plate segments from this period has been found at Lachish and at Nuzi and Nimrud in Iraq, the shot appears to have struck between the chain mail (Heb. *dᵉḇāqîm*) and the breastplate. The *chariot driver*, for there appears to have been no third man with a defensive shield as in some Assyrian chariots of this period (2 Ki. 7:2), turned sharply (Heb. 'turn your hand').

37–38. *So the King died* is taken by some (LXX 'the king is dead!') as part of the ringing cry (v. 36). The detail of verse 37 fulfils Elijah's prophecy (21:19). The pool in Samaria could be the one 10 m. × 5 m. excavated in the courtyard of the palace (see plan, *IBD*, p. 1377) and where *they washed the chariot* (v. 38) and the dogs licked the blood while the prostitutes washed there (so the Heb. order). There is no need to take this as 'added by an overzealous editor' (Robinson) or 'a clumsy attempt of a pious editor to ensure that no detail of the original prophecy went unfulfilled' (Jones) especially as it was only a partial fulfilment (see 21:19). If taken as a note of *where the prostitutes bathed* then this might be to identify the pool as in another place. Attempts to clarify this by reading that the women washed in the royal blood for fertility purposes, or that they washed his armour (Gk.) or weapons (NIV mg.) require a change in MT.

j. Closing notice of Ahab's reign (22:39–40). This follows on from the introduction given in 16:29–34. Ahab *built* (v. 39, could be 'rebuilt' or 'fortified') a new palace and made extensive changes in Level II at Samaria as well as at Megiddo (Level IVb-Va) where he built storehouses formerly designated 'Solomon's stables'. He was also responsible for doubling the size of Hazor. All this, with the revival of Jericho (16:34), betokens a period of high prosperity.

The 'house of ivory' (MT; AV, NEB 'ivory house') was not one palace *inlaid with ivory* but, as elsewhere at this time (Nimrud, Arslan Tash) noteworthy for its precious objects, furniture and fittings inlaid with ivories carved in Phoenician, Egyptian and local style motifs. This was a mark of great opulence, but there are no known instances of ivory panelling of whole rooms or exteriors.

That *Ahab rested with his fathers* (v. 40) is not an error by the historian, though it is normally used of those who met a peaceful death. The phrase is used of all kings of Israel other than those who died by assassination.

D. Further history of reigns (1 Ki. 22:41 – 2 Ki. 10:36).

i. Jehoshaphat of Judah (1 Ki. 22:41–50). The historian here returns to his usual form of introductory and synchronistic formulae (vv. 41–42); an appraisal of the reign – here one of those rare estimates of the king doing the right (vv. 43–45) – is based on the king's reforms (see Additional Note). Since details of his reign have been included separately (vv. 1–26; 2 Ch. 17–20; *cf.* Josephus, *Ant.* ix.1–3) they are not repeated here. The historian emphasizes Jehoshaphat's positive action without eliminating reference to his failures. The concluding formula (vv. 45–50) is a long and frank addition (vv. 46–49).

41. The reference may be to the beginning of his sole reign (869 BC), his full reign dating from the thirty-ninth year of Asa (*cf.* 16:29) who reigned forty-one years (15:10). Jehoshaphat may have been influenced by his father's works since he too had not removed high places (15:11–14).

44. The alliance (*at peace*) with Ahab had been sealed by the gift of his daughter Athaliah to Jehoshaphat's son (2 Ch. 18:1). *The king of Israel* could refer to Ahab or Ahaziah or Joram, but the phrase may highlight the fact that Jehoshaphat was the first since Rehoboam to negotiate peace with Israel.

45–46. 'How he warred' (RSV; NIV *military exploits*) against Edom and Ammon and the judicial and military reforms of Jehoshaphat are given in 2 Chronicles 17–19. He continued the work of Asa (15:12) to remove *male* (cult) *prostitutes* (see on 14:24).

47. *Edom,* lost to Solomon (11:14–25), must have been regained and, placed under a commissioner subject to Judah and thus open to the exploitation of Ezion Geber (Tell Kheleifeh), a port on the Red Sea refortified at this time with a thick wall and triple gate similar to that of Megiddo (level IVA). In the Negeb other forts were now built (2 Ch. 17:12) and Beersheba refortified with a new wall (Level III).

48. The *ships of Tarshish* (AV, NIV mg., 'merchantmen' NEB, *fleet of trading-ships* NIV) were ocean-going traders sailing as far as Ophir, see on 9:28. That they were 'broken up' (MT, AV) does not necessarily imply that they were *wrecked* (NIV). They were constructed to implement a trade-pact with Ahaziah who had access to Phoenician skills but, according to a prophecy of Eliezar, they were never used (*cf.* 2 Ch. 20:35–37).

50. For *Jehoram* see 2 Kings 8:16–24; 2 Chronicles 21. Edom may have had a hand in denying the use of Ezion Geber as a port (*POTT*, p. 236).

ii. Ahaziah of Israel (1 Ki. 22:51 – 2 Ki. 1:18). *Cf.* 2 Chronicles 22:1–9; Josephus, *Ant.* ix. 2. Ahaziah's reign of *two years* represents one year in Jehoshaphat's *seventeenth year* = 854/3 BC and part of one year during which his successor parallelled the 18th year of Jehoshaphat (2 Ki. 3:1). The LXX 'twenty-fourth year' is adjusting to 2 Kings 1:17.

a. Summary of reign (1 Ki. 22:51–53). The introductory summary traces the son of Ahab's evil as emulating all his predecessors (*cf.* 16:30–33). For the worship of Baal as provoking God's anger see 12: 28–33; 16:13, 26.

Additional Note on Jehoshaphat's reforms

The historian concentrates on Jehoshaphat's political relations with his northern neighbours and makes only a formal note of one aspect of his reforms as an example of his doing the right (v. 43a). This was his removal of male prostitutes, referring the reader to the official Judean annals for further details (v. 45). At the beginning of his reign Jehoshaphat began a religious revival with a teaching mission to bring the people back to the LORD (2 Ch. 19:4). The consequence was a call to root out corruption and reform the judiciary by appointing district or provincial courts centred on the main fortified towns, and possibly in every large settlement. These were able to concern themselves with civil (taxation) and military (levy) affairs (*cf.* Dt. 16:18–20) based on administering the law of the LORD (2 Ch. 19:5–7). It is not clear how far the jurisdiction of the older tribal system and of the elders were affected. However, in Jerusalem the court was reorganized both to act as higher court over all the kingdom and, with priests on it, to include religious sanctions and cases (2 Ch. 19:8–11; *cf.* Dt. 17:8–13).[1]

b. Elijah and Ahaziah (2 Ki. 1:1–8). The historian shows that the clash between Elijah, with his belief in the LORD God (Yahweh) as supreme, and the Israelite monarchy who still relied primarily on other deities, continues. Ahaziah is reproved for consulting a foreign god (vv. 2–8) and his attempt to reverse the judgment pronounced by Yahweh upon him is shown dramatically (vv. 9–17a). The issue is still the same as at Carmel. God demonstrates by fire that he will not share his supremacy with any other. The second book of Kings follows the first without a break (see Introduction, p. 26).

1. Moab rebelled *after Ahab's death*, for according to the Moabite Stone (Mesha' inscription; *ANET*, p. 320) it had been controlled by Israel in Omri's 'days and half the days of his son(s), fifty years'. The rebellion began in Ahaziah's second year (Herrman).

2. The *upper room* with its latticed balustrade or windows (for there was then no glazing) was part of a second storey and not just a 'roof-chamber' (NEB) with projecting balcony, or a pillared *bīt-hilāni* Syrian type building (*cf.* Robinson, Gray).

3–6. *Baal-Zebub*, 'Lord of Flies' (so LXX, *Baal-myian*) is not a proven deliberate change from Baal-Zebul ('the Lord Prince' or possibly 'Lord of the house'; an epithet of Baal or Ugar ('the flame') as *e.g.* Mephi-bosheth for Mephi-Baal). The god-name is unique but it is quoted in Matthew 10:25. *Consult* here means to seek the divine will by means of an oracle (Am. 5:5–6), a divination practice forbidden to God's people (Lv. 19:31). To do this he had to send to Ekron, modern Khirbet el-Muqanna' near 'Aqir, about sixteen kilometres southeast of Jaffa, the northernmost city of Philistia on the Philistine-Judea border. The god may have been renowned for his healing qualities. Such consultation concerning the outcome of any sickness, regardless of cause (Heb. *ḥ°lî*), 'illness' (JB), or *injury* (NIV, v. 2) – was common practice at the time. The result

[1] K. W. Whitelam, *The Just King. Monarchial Judicial Authority in Ancient Israel*, JSOTS 12 (Sheffield: JSOT Press, 1979), pp. 185–206.

as usually given in medical prognostic texts is 'he will live/die' *cf.* verses 6, 16 ('*You will certainly die*').

The swift return of the messengers assured the king that they had not had time to go to Ekron, about seventy-two kilometres from Samaria, and return, hence the question. God intervened yet again through his servant to keep the messengers from their destination, for if Ahaziah had obtained a verdict from Baal-Zebub it might have belittled Yahweh in the popular estimation. God normally spoke directly to Elijah (but *cf.* 1 Ki. 19:5) but here may have sought to show the contrast between his messenger (v. 3, *angel of the LORD*) and those of Ahaziah. For the king of Samaria see 1 Kings 22:37. The sure word Ahaziah sought from Baal-Zebub was given by God himself (v. 4, *cf.* v. 16).

7–8. The description (*kind*, AV 'manner', *cf.* Jdg. 13:12) of the prophet was sufficient for recognition by a king whose father had met Elijah many times. He wore camel or other animal-skin clothing which may have been distinctive of a prophet (Zc. 13:4; Mt. 3:4, *cf.* 1 Ki. 19:19). The Hebrew 'possessor of hair' ('a hairy man', AV, NEB, Gk., Vulg.) is consonant with this and does not apply simply to the common beard. There is no certainty that any protest against those in luxurious garments (Is. 3:18–22; Mt. 11:7–8) is implied.

c. Elijah and the fate of the army captains (2 Ki. 1:9–17a).

Ahaziah is desperate to get a reversal of the prophecy against him and would use massive force if needed. The morality of the act has often been misunderstood as the 'inhumanity of the destruction of the innocent captains and fifties' (Montgomery). It is insufficient to dismiss this as a later addition to verses 2–8, for verse 17b would read abruptly if it followed verse 8 directly. Nor should this be measured solely by New Testament standards, for Jesus rebuked his disciples for wanting a similar demonstration of fire (Lk. 9:54–55) though the circumstances differed. It must be noted that the demand made of Elijah was wrong. A king had no right to ask such allegiance and his actions should always be subordinate to God's word (*cf.* 1 Sa. 10:25). God was protecting his word and his servant. Contradiction of this passage must imply denial of other similar Old Testament judgmental events. Elijah acted not out of private vengeance but for the Name of God and such divine judgment is clear in the New Testament also (Heb.

12:29; Rev. 11:5; 2 Thes. 1:7–9). Some sensitive Christians would like to think that no one will be damned – but that is not biblical.[1] The repetitions with minor variants (vv. 9–10; 11–12; the second with a more formal command) are customary in such narratives.

10. *Fire* links Elijah with Moses again (Lv. 10:2; Nu. 11:3) and should have reminded the king that God had already revealed himself and authenticated Elijah by that means (1 Ki. 18:38–39). It has been suggested that there is a play on the words *'ēš 'elōhîm* ('fire of God', *i.e.* severe fire) and *'îš 'elōhîm* ('man of God'), but this is unnecessary here.

13–15. The third group were spared not because of the plea for mercy but through divine intervention. *Do not be afraid* (v. 15) shows that Elijah's life was in danger. 'The king already knows the will of the God of Israel but is unwilling to heed it' (Robinson) and so brings the judgment on himself.

d. Concluding formula for Ahaziah's reign (2 Ki. 1:17b–18).
The concluding formula differs from the standard format. The evaluation of Ahaziah's reign has already been given (1 Ki. 22:52–53). *Joram*, a shortened form of J(eh)oram, possibly Ahaziah's *brother* (so LXX, Syr.), came to the throne in 852, synchronizing with the second year of Jehoram's co-regency with Jehoshaphat in his eighteenth year in Judah (3:1).

iii. Elijah leaves with his successor appointed (2:1–25).
Elijah's successor had already been designated (1 Ki. 19:19–21), but the dramatic event which marks Elijah's unique departure or accension (vv. 1–18) also introduces the commissioning of his successor who is immediately confirmed as, and by, having similar miraculous powers. These are not the mere emphasis of an expansionist editor but a fitting climax in confirmation of Elisha's commission by God. Two examples given, the healing of the waters (vv. 19–22) and the judgment on mockers (vv. 23–25), can be shown to have a moral, ethical and didactic purpose.

a. A farewell tour (2:1–6).
Elijah took his young student on a farewell visit to the groups of prophets at Bethel (v. 1), Jericho (v. 4) and Gilgal by Jordan (v. 6). His coming

---

[1] *Cf.* Jn. 3:18.

departure was reiterated (vv. 3, 5), as was his assurance that the LORD had sent him on the journey (vv. 2, 4, 6). Elijah wished to face the experience alone unless the command to *stay here* (v. 2) was a test of Elisha's faithfulness which was answered by the threefold refusal of Elisha to leave his master. Peter's eagerness as Christ's disciple (Mk. 14:29) and Christ's threefold order to his disciple may echo this theme (Mt. 26:38–45).

1–2. While the *Gilgal* between Jericho and Jordan (Jos. 4:19–20; modern Khirbet al-Mafjar[1]) is the likely site in view of verse 19, others seek it at Jiljulieh, eleven kilometres north of Bethel, since from it they *went down* to Bethel ('House of God').

3. For the *company* (AV 'sons') *of the prophets* see on 1 Kings 20:35; and for Bethel founded by Jacob (Gn. 28:11–19) see 1 Kings 12:29–33; 13. Elijah's departure is imminent and foretold (vv. 3, 5).

b. The divided waters (2:7–10). Elijah is again linked with Moses who had used the symbol of his office, a staff, to smite the Re(e)d Sea waters in bringing God's people out of Egypt (*cf.* Ex. 14:21–22). So Elijah used his rolled up (now finished with) long cloak to do the same to cross the Jordan (*cf.* Jos. 3–5).

The request for a *double portion* (v. 9, 'share', RSV, NEB, JB), was not that he might excel his master but that he should receive the eldest son's share according to the law (Dt. 21:17). Such a son had the responsibility to carry on the father's name and work. The 'hard thing' (RSV, NIV *difficult thing*) for Elijah was that since God alone can make the gift of his Spirit to anyone (*cf.* Jn. 3:34; 1 Jn. 3:24; 4:13) it was impossible for him to meet Elisha's request. The test would be to see if Elisha had 'the ability to see and comprehend the spiritual world . . . and of a visionary to penetrate the heavens' (Jones, p. 385).

c. Elijah's ascension (2:11–12). Elijah was taken up to heaven in the *whirlwind*, not in the *chariot of fire and horses of fire* which merely 'came between the two of them' (Heb.) and cut him off from human sight. These *chariots* and *horsemen* symbolized strong protection as well as the forces of God's

---

[1] J. Muilenburg, 'The Site of Ancient Gilgal', *BASOR* 140, 1955, pp. 11–33.

spiritual presence which were the true safety of Israel (as also in later Jewish tradition, *cf.* Sirach 48:9). They are not a particularly local or solar mythology nor the means of Elijah's passage to heaven. Elijah *went up to heaven* (v. 11) is qualified also as *taken from* (over) Elisha (vv. 3, 9). Similarly Enoch disappeared, for God had taken him (Gn. 5:24), as he had Moses (Dt. 34:4–6; *cf.* Jude 9).

12. Elisha *saw him no more* means that Elijah had disappeared (so Akkad. phrase 'he stood on his mountain'; *cf.* v. 16). *The chariots and horsemen* (collective) hardly denote God crossing the heavens as other sun-deities are so depicted in ancient reliefs, for this is not immediately evident here from the repeated phrase *of Israel* (*cf.* 2 Ki. 13:14). The latter may be a cryptic way of saying that Elijah was the mighty defender of the true Israel and was worth more to them than all its boasted military defences.

d. Elisha takes over (2:13–25).

i. The striking of the waters (2:13–15). There was need to show that the same Spirit controlling Elijah was Elisha's also. Following an expression of mourning shown by deliberately ripping up his clothes (v. 12b), he dropped the symbol of his prophetic office and used it to repeat Elijah's miracle (v. 14, *cf.* v. 8) in the presence of a host of witnesses (v. 15). The Hebrew, by repeating *he struck the water*, may have been reflected in the LXX addition of 'and the waters were not divided', which led to the question, *Where now is the LORD, the God of Elijah?* NIV reads *now* ('*ēpô*') for the MT '*ap hû*' ('where is he?'). Some Greek versions omit this, as do a number of LXX MSS and RSV, NEB, and take it as temporal, *when he struck*. It may well be that nothing happened the first time, so Elisha struck again.

15. The proof of the spirit of his master in him led Elisha to be acknowledged as leader (*bowed . . . before him*).

ii. The unsuccessful search for Elijah (2:16–18). The search for Elijah by fifty 'strong, active' (*able*, REB 'stalwart') men in the rugged terrain is no mere secondary editorial intrusion. It was important to them to avoid the dishonour of a corpse lying unburied, and the need for confirmation of his final disappearance would be essential to them if not to Elisha, for Elijah had been known to disappear (and reappear) suddenly

(1 Ki. 18:12). *Until ashamed* (v. 17) has been rendered 'beyond measure' (*cf.* its only other occurrences in 8:11; Jdg. 3:25). Others interpret it as 'until he had not the heart to refuse' (REB).

iii. The healing of the waters (2:19–22). Note that this further selected example to show that the miraculous powers of Elijah were also in Elisha was performed not for his own glorification but to help others. The explanation of *the water* as *bad* (JB 'foul'; Heb. 'evil') rather than non-existent (AV 'naught') usually given is that Jericho still experienced the covenant curse (Dt. 28:15–18; Jos. 6:26). It has been suggested that the spring (modern 'Ain es-Sulṭān near ancient Jericho, now called 'Elijah's Spring') led to sterility from its contact with radio-active strata and the sudden clear-up was due to a geological shift,[1] or from some infection.[2] Whether it was the land that was *unproductive* or (as MT, NEB, JB) 'the country suffers miscarriages' is open to question; the Hebrew (*mᵉšak-kelet*) is normally used of persons or livestock, except in Malachi 3:11. The method of cure used may have been symbolic, with a *new bowl* for purity and *salt* representing preservation, pointing to cleansing (despite the nearby Salt [Dead] Sea) and God's faithful covenant (of salt, 2 Ch. 13:5). It was the LORD who *healed* (v. 21) rather than any act of sowing salt as a symbol of the forces of separation from evil (Gray, 'restore to fertility'). Elisha's act was one of showing God's mercy to a community in time of stress.

iv. Elisha mocked (2:23–25). This passage is often cited as a major moral problem in the Old Testament[3] or dismissed as 'in every respect a puerile tale ... There is no serious point in this incident, it does not reflect much to the credit of the prophet ... at the best the memory of some catastrophe which happened to coincide with Elisha's visit to Bethel' (Gray, p. 479). It does, however, show the continuing opposition to a

[1] I. M. Blake, 'Jericho (Ain es-Sultan); Joshua's Curse and Elisha's Miracle – One Possible Explanation', *PEQ* 99, 1967, pp. 86–97.
[2] E. V. Hulse, *Medical History* 15, 1971, pp. 376–386 considered that the water at Jericho may have been infected by *Bulinus truncatus* leading to its abandonment due to parasite infection (schistosomiasis) found in snails; D. Sperber, 'Weak Waters', *ZAW* 82, 1970, pp. 114–116.
[3] J. Wenham, *the Goodness of God* (London: IVP, 1974), pp. 128 f.; R. G. Messner, 'Elisha and the Bears', *Grace Journal* 3, 1962, pp. 12–24.

true prophet in Bethel, the chief centre of pagan calf-worship. The main objection lies in the *curse . . . in the name of the LORD* (v. 24). In the Deuteronomic doctrine of retributive justice (Dt. 7:10) this was a requirement against anyone mocking a prophet, an act which was the equivalent of belittling God himself (Dt. 18:19; Lv. 24:10–16). The word for *jeered* (NIV, REB, JB) occurs in Habakkuk 1:10; *cf.* 'insult' in Jeremiah 20:8. To deride God's representative (*cf.* 2 Ch. 36:16) as God himself (Gal. 6:7) or his city (Ez. 22:5) inevitably incurs judgment.

23. The *youths* (rather than 'little children', AV, or 'small boy', JB, for the Hebrew *nĕ'ārîm* is used of servants or persons in early life of marriageable age, *cf.* Absalom in 2 Sa. 14:21; 18:5) may have challenged Elisha to demonstrate that he was really the equivalent of Elijah by ascending (*Go on up*, 'get along with you', REB) and mocked him as a *baldhead*. Baldness, contrary to popular mythology, is not a sign of inferiority of infertility, for Elisha was still young, as opposed to the hairy Elijah (1:8), though long hair may have been thought a sign of strength (2 Sa. 14:26).[1] He may have suffered from early loss of hair (alopecia). There is no external evidence that a tonsure was then a mark of a prophet. The youths may well represent Bethel as the headquarters of idolatry and the main seat of Baal worship in Israel at this time.

24. *Bears* are attested in the hill ranges until mediaeval times. The *forty-two* may represent an organized mob attacking the prophet rather than signify a number for the ill fated (*cf.* 2 Ki. 10:14; Rev. 11:2; 13:5).

25. The places mentioned here are all associated with Elijah's ministry. Elisha may have moved on to Mount Carmel where the site of Elijah's faith and victory would have made it a continuing place for prophetic testimony (1 Ki. 18:19).

iv. War against Moab (3:1–27). The historian now selects an event which will show that Elisha's word is as powerful and his prophecy as effective as had been another's in similar circumstances (1 Ki. 22). The history of Jehoram is continued from 1:17–18 with the usual introductory formulae (vv. 1–3). The unity of the war narrative (vv. 4–27) has been questioned on grounds of the abrupt appearance (v. 11) and departure of

[1] Gray, p. 480 considers that 'the reference could not have been to natural baldness, since the oriental, particularly a stranger on a journey as distinct from a slave or labourer at work, would not have had his head uncovered'.

Elisha, but in this characteristic also he follows Elijah. The withdrawal (v. 27) following the almost complete victory as promised (vv. 24–25, *cf.* vv. 18–19) is not necessarily evidence of divergent sources but is open to various interpretations. The preponderance of theological terms in the prophet's words is to be expected as is the historian's continued favourable view of the king of Judah in contrast with the king of Israel. The extra-biblical evidence from the Mesha' Inscription (*DOTT*, pp. 196–197) gives a helpful Moabite perspective on these events.

a. Moab revolts (3:1–12). **1–3.** The chronology of the *eighteenth year* would agree with 1:17 if Jehoram of Judah had been co-regent with his father; his *twelve year* reign was *c.* 852–841 BC. The formula for Israelite kings usually states his capital city, so *in Samaria* may do this, though Greek omits it, placing verses 1–3 after 2 Kings 1:18. Jehoram's *evil* is not that of Ahab (1 Ki. 16:30–34) or the queen mother Jezebel (1 Ki. 18:4; 19:1–2; 21:7–15) who lived throughout his reign (9:30). The pillar of Baal (*sacred stone*) was a standing stele (MT *maṣṣēḇâ*), probably a particular example similar to the inscription and relief on Baal images found near altars at Hazor, Zenjirli (Panammu) and in Syria (the Barhadad stele for Baal-Melqart).[1] One such stone remained in the temple (2 Ki. 10:26–27), perhaps reinstated by Jezebel acting as an unhelpful mother (1 Ki. 16:32–33). They were not necessarily connected with fertility symbols (see on 1 Ki. 14:23).

4–5. Mesha' *rebelled* against his subordinate role as vassal in which he would need his skill as a 'sheep-breeder' (*nōqēd*, so NEB) to supply the uncounted mass (*a hundred thousand*) of yearling lambs and rams annually or 'regularly' (NEB, the verb is frequentative) rather than as a one-off tribute. His rebellion after Ahab's death (see on 1:1) united Israel and Judah against him. Joram reactivates the treaty with Judah made between equals, *i.e.* a parity treaty, which is accepted by Jehoshaphat (as in 1 Ki. 22:4) with the added assurance that he would march with him.

8–9. The plan was to avoid the route through Ammon and thus the newly fortified and rebuilt strongholds of Moab by attacking Moab in the rear. Others propose a route into

[1] *ANEP*, nos. 490, 827; *IBD*, p. 153; *cf.* A. Lemaire, 'La stèle araméene de Bar-Hadad', *Orientalia* 53, 1984, pp. 337–349.

Moab from the southeast, both required free access through Judah and Edom whose viceroy (here *melek*, 'king') was Jehoshaphat's vassal. To 'go up' (*attack*, v. 8) to the high plateau of Moab they chose the way through the *Desert of Edom* via the desert from Arad and round the south end of the Dead Sea by the road from Zoar Horonaim to the capital Kir-Haresheth (Is. 15:5; Je. 48:5). After 853 BC Mesha' seems to have taken the opportunity to rebel when he thought Israel was preoccupied with Assyria.

10–12. J(eh)oram may well have consulted his own prophets. But under stress their different characters are shown up. Jehoram despairs while Jehoshaphat looks to God. The lessons of the encounter at Ramoth-Gilead were remembered (1 Ki. 22:7–20) and Jehoshaphat demands assurance from his God. In ancient warfare it was customary to *enquire* ('consult') the divine will (v. 11) by oracle at different stages. Some think Elisha was acting on behalf of Elijah who had previously written to Jehoram (2 Ch. 21:12–15). Certainly here he is portrayed as that aged prophet's servant. The pouring of water to provide running water for ablutions was a menial task. This time the kings go to the prophet rather than summon him to them (*cf.* 1 Ki. 22:9). Jehoshaphat supports Elisha as the true prophet, *i.e.* the one who has and fearlessly tells out God's word (v. 12).

b. Victory over Moab and abundant water promised (3:13–19). Elisha's antagonism to the king of Israel is shown by asking 'What do we have in common?' or *have to do with each other?* (v. 13), though the Heb. ('What is it with reference to me and to you?') could imply that we must each play our part (so Christ at the Cana wedding, Jn. 2:4) rather than implying 'Why do you interfere?'

14. Elisha's words echo those of Elijah (1 Ki. 17:1). To 'have regard for' (RSV, REB) or *respect for* translates an idiomatic expression 'to show favour to' (lit. 'raise the head').

15. The request for *a harpist* (Heb. 'one who plays a stringed instrument'), a minstrel playing a portable small lyre (1 Sa. 16:15), does not mark Elisha out as an inferior type of ecstatic or dervish or as distinct from Elijah. Music was one means of the *hand* (Heb. 'hand, power') *of the LORD* coming upon a person, whether to calm or control (as with Saul in 1 Sa. 16:16, 23).

The prophecy of verses 17–19 required the recipients' hard work to make it effective and unseen powers to bring it about in a miracle of provision. The dried-up river bed (probably the Wadi Ḥesa; River Zered) was to have many trenches (Heb. 'trenches trenches') dug to retain the flash-flood (Arab. *sayl*) which would result from rain falling out of sight on the distant Moabite hills. This form of irrigation is still common in central and southern Arabia.

17. *Cattle*, some read 'army', but this requires the change of one MT consonant. Our difficulties take on a different aspect in the light of God's ability to provide water and change the enemy's outlook.

19. This verse is a promise rather than a command. The cutting down of fruit-bearing trees is banned in Deuteronomy 20:19.

c. The defeat of Moab (3:20–27). **20.** The early *morning* is often a time when God acted in power (*cf.* 2 Ki. 19:35).[1]

21. Those who 'were able to put on armour' (AV) would include even youngsters *who could bear arms* and resist invasions from across the border.

22. The *red – like blood* (Heb. *ᵃdummîm*) is no mere play on the word Edom, for the red stone of the Wadi Ḥesa reflecting on the water could have been interpreted as an ominous sign of bloodshed among the enemy and so have misled the Moabites. The Hebrew allies effected a total destruction (v. 25, *cf.* v. 19) until stopped at the southerly capital of Moab, Kir Hareseth or Kir Moab (Is. 15:1), *i.e.* modern Kerak astride the King's Highway, seventeen kilometres east of the Dead Sea and twenty-four kilometres south of the River Arnon (*cf.* Jer. 48:31, 36).

26. The Hebrew here is difficult. The king of Moab tried to fight the break out *through to* (RSV 'opposite') or against the king of Edom, perhaps choosing the weakest point of those attacking. There is little textual support (Old Latin) for reading Aram (*'rm*) for *Edom* (*'dm*) here, since that distant northerly state is not involved.

27. The human sacrifice of the crown-prince publicly on the

---

[1] To 'rise early' (AV, Heb. *šākam*) is literally to 'put the shoulder to it', *i.e.* take up the burden as when breaking camp. This was significant in the life of leaders like Abraham (Gn. 21:14; 22:3), Jacob (Gn. 28:18), Moses (Ex. 34:4), Joshua (Jos. 3:1; 6:12; 7:16; 8:10), Gideon (Jdg. 7:1), Samuel (1 Sa. 15:12) and David (1 Sa. 17:20).

wall of the capital was a rare practice (Jdg. 11:31, 39) used to appease the national god Chemosh 'who was angry with his land' (Moabite Inscrip. 5) and had showed his displeasure in their calamitous defeat. The subsequent great *fury against Israel* could be taken as the Moabites' angry reaction which caused Israel to return (so Josephus, *Ant.* ix.3.2), the wrath of God turned against the alliance who had provoked such an action or, more likely, Israel's horror and dismay made them withdraw.

v. Stories about Elisha (4:1 – 8:15). Continuing the Elijah group of episodes these stories now recount similar miraculous happenings associated with Elisha. While they show that he was a worthy successor who could act in a similarly effective way as his master, the main purpose is to show his, and thus God's, support for those who fear the LORD. The incidents, apart from those connected with the sons of the prophets, may not be arranged in chronological order. They serve also to indicate the everyday life of the times. Attempts to explain away the miraculous elements as merely pictures of ordinary events have not been successful.

a. The widow's oil (4:1–7). This shows the prophet's moral concern for a serious social problem. The enslavement of defaulting debtors or their families was common throughout the ancient Near East (*cf.* 1 Ki. 2:39–40; Lv. 25:39; Is. 50:1; Neh. 5:5; Laws of Hammurapi §§ 117, 119, 213). To avoid misuse the Hebrew law set a time limit (Ex. 21:2–3, 7).

The Targum names the dead prophet Obadiah (1 Ki. 18:4) who, according to Josephus (*Ant.* ix.4.2), had borrowed money to feed the young prophets.

1. *'Your servant'* was a common polite form of address to any superior (GNB 'sir').

2–3. The 'pot (*'āsûk*) of oil' (AV; NIV *a little*) is a unique word here, possibly for a small anointing flask. Relief often begins with the little we have at hand. Elisha elicits faith and action by questions, encouragement ('not a few') and word. The quantity of oil was only limited by the woman's lack of faith in failing to ask for more *empty jars* (AV 'vessels', *kēlîm*) – a general word for utensils irrespective of type and size.

4. The need for privacy is stressed to show the ability of God to work through his servant at a distance, to mark the personal nature of God's action and to emphasize the power of God. This is no common folkloristic motif of an unfailing vessel (as Gray) but may have been chosen for its resemblance to the deed done by Elijah for the widow in Zarephath (1 Ki. 17:8–14).

5. *She kept pouring*; the piel participle stressing the ongoing action of faith (*cf.* Jn. 2:7).

7. *Pay your debts* (plural as NIV, GNB, NEB mg), *cf.* 'redeem your pledge' (JB), NEB paraphrases 'redeem your boys who are being taken as pledges'. God's giving is often abundant (Mk. 6:43; Eph. 3:30). One lesson implied by the historian here is that God does not fail as the God of the widow and fatherless (Dt. 10:18; Jas. 1:27) as do some earthly rulers.

b. The Shunammite's son (4:8–37). The story of the Shunammite woman and her son's restoration to life became a long-remembered confirmation of Elisha's inherited prophetic and healing powers (*cf.* 8:1–6). It reiterates also the blessings of hospitality and the care of God.

8. *Shunem* (modern Solem) lay about eleven kilometres south of Mount Tabor, eight kilometres from Jezreel and thirty-two kilometres from Carmel (*cf.* v. 25), and so near a route likely to have been used frequently. The *well-to-do woman* (literally 'great' as MT, AV) lays less stress on her importance or standing than on her wealth (GNB 'rich').

9. The recognition of Elisha as *a holy man of God* is unique and implies a special quality (see on 1 Ki. 17:24; 2 Ki. 5:8).

10. The *small room on* the flat *roof*-top was, according to the Hebrew (*ªliyyaṭ qîr*), a permanent rather than temporary shelter (*cf.* 1 Sa. 9:25) furnished for privacy, comfort and immediate use. It implies that it was walled (*qîr*), so RSV 'with walls', AV 'on the wall', though some read 'cool' (*qôr*). The lamp would be an open saucer or bowl-shaped vessels to hold sesame or olive oil, with a pinched open neck spout for the wick (see *IBD*, p. 870).

12–16. The use of a servant as messenger was to make a preliminary sounding out of sight, rather than out of dignity or reverence (*cf.* vv. 15–16). For the prophetic promise of a child, *cf.* Sarai (Gn. 18:10–12) and Manoah (Jdg. 13). The name Gehazi, perhaps the unnamed servant of 2 Kings 4:43, 6:15, may mean 'man of vision' (*BDB*) or 'avaricious' (Gray). The woman, content with her lot (v. 13), but needing a son to maintain the family title to the property, had no need for favours or remission of taxes which Elisha's status could have acquired for her. Her concern was not to be misled or deceived (*cf.* v. 28 *raise my hopes*). No precise time is given, for *about this time next year* (NIV) is a general expression of time.[1] The emphasis is on the fulfilment of prophecy (v. 17).

18–20. The child's illness may not be diagnosable. His death after a few hours is commonly taken as an instance of sunstroke (insolation, *siriasis*) marked by acute headache. That would be rare among children even in the plain of Esdraelon at harvest-time. Cerebral malaria has been suggested, for meningitis seldom kills so quickly.[2]

21. The woman had lost her child but not her faith. Placing him in the prophet's room was an emotional or convenient act. This need not have been done as a reproach, to enclose the child's spirit (Gray), nor does it indicate that he had not really died but only been 'electrocuted', a condition related to acute sunstroke (Mishnah *Niddah* 70b).

23. *New Moon or Sabbath* (Lv. 23:3; Nu. 28:10, 14). This earliest reference to worship and work on the Sabbath implies that journeys and work were then allowed on such days (*cf.* 2 Ki. 11:5–8). Jesus' attitude may reflect earlier Israelite rather than later Pharisaic practice (Mk. 2:23–28; *cf.* Heb. 4 allowing for rest and work by saints in heaven). Keil argues that the pious in Israel went to the prophet's house for worship and teaching since such was absent from the current levitical priest's role. Some take these as 'favourable' days for *the New Moon* was a non-working day or festival (1 Sa. 20:5, 18, 24) to be used for worship (Is. 66:23, *cf.* Col. 2:16).

24. The story has an increasing sense of great urgency: so 'urge on' (v. 24, RSV for NIV *lead on*, Heb. 'drive on' and v. 29); 'Gird up your loins' (AV, RSV); *Tuck your cloak into your belt* (and JB) so as not to delay by stopping for greetings (as in Lk. 10:4) but run unhindered.

27. A prophet needed special divine revelation for specific occasions. Disciples can be an obstacle to the needy reaching the master (Mt. 19:13–14).

---

[1] R. Yaron, 'Ka'eth ḥayyah and Koh leḥay', *VT* 12, 1962, pp. 500–501 followed by J. Barr, *Biblical Words for Time* (London: SCM Press, ²1969), pp. 119–120.

[2] D. J. Wiseman, 'Medicine in the OT World' in B. Palmer (ed.), *Medicine and the Bible* (Exeter: Paternoster Press, 1986), p. 28.

29–31. Gehazi, with the prophet's staff a symbol of authority, as used by Moses to effect a miracle (Ex. 4:1–4; 17:5–6), went ahead to reassure the parents, but there was *no sound or response* (NIV, JB as 1 Ki. 18:29) or 'sign of life' (NEB). The boy was dead.

32–35. The gradual revival of this boy differs from Elijah's method in 1 Kings 17 where there was instant response to the word (as to Christ in Mk. 5:41–42; *cf.* Acts 9:40). This was no mere artificial respiration, and Gehazi was a witness both to the child being dead as well as to his revival which became widely known (8:5). Nor is it overtly a case of communication of power by the extension of the individual.[1] Elisha's faith in God, while not expressed directly here, is shown by his prayer (*cf.* Jas. 5:17–18).

c. Death in the pot (4:38–41). This event shows the power to make the harmful innocuous (*cf.* Lk. 10:19) as well as God's care and provision for his own.

38. *Gilgal.* Here probably the one in Ephraim southwest of Shiloh (*cf.* 2 Ki. 2:1) rather than that near Jericho (Jos. 4:19) or Qalqaliyah (= Baalshalisha, as Gray). The *famine* (MT) was probably that of 8:1. As the prophets were 'sitting before' him (AV) this *meeting* is thought to be a 'school' session (Yeshiva, Ben Sira 51:29). The 'pottage' (AV, RSV) was a 'broth' (NEB) or *stew* (NIV, GNB) – a customary communal dish.

39. The *gourds* (*paqqûʿōt*) or wild cucumbers (LXX *colocynth*) were a strong purgative. Yellow 'bitter apples' (NEB), like small melons, are characteristic of the *citrullus colocyntis*. No reason is given why these commonly recognized plants were unpalatable. The symbolic act of cleansing or healing (as the salt in Jericho's spring, 2:19–22) is not diminished by those who seek to irradicate the poison and the miracle on the assumption that it was a case of counter-imitative magic, that something else was added or that the meal-flour was intended to counter their superstition of ill-omen.

d. Feeding a multitude (4:42–44). This event may not be connected with the foregoing, though it equally shows the LORD's care for his own. The acceptance by Elisha of the first fruits, normally offered to God through priests (as Lv. 23:10)

[1] A. R. Johnson, *Vitality of the Individual in Thought of Ancient Israel* (Cardiff: University of Wales Press, 1949).

and his sharing the gift for the benefit of all, may indicate recognition of him as the LORD's representative. The whole incident is described as fulfilment of predicted prophecy. As a miracle it is to be compared with the later feeding of the five thousand by Jesus (Mt. 14:13–21).

42. *Baal Shalishah* lay twenty-two kilometres north of Lydda in the Sharon plain (*cf.* 1 Sa. 9:4) and is to be identified with Khirbet al-Marjamah in Ephraim.[1] The *first ripe* (fresh ears of) *corn* (*wᵉkarmel bᵉṣiqᵉlōnô*; NEB 'new season's head') may be the delicacy 'roasted ears of corn' (*cf.* Lv. 2:14).

43. *His servant*, the unusual Hebrew word (*mᵉšārᵉtô*) as used of Joshua (Ex. 24:13, 'assistant'), may refer here to Gehazi who was sceptical of the sufficiency of the provision, as were Jesus' disciples (Mt. 14:17; 15:34–39), possibly because they were brought in by one man in a small sack. The figure of a *hundred* may represent a large company in general (*cf.* 1 Ki. 18:4).

e. Naaman healed (5:1–27). Though the main focus after the introduction (vv. 1–7) is on Elisha (vv. 8–14), Naaman (vv. 15–19) and Gehazi (vv. 20–27), the chapter is a unity. It is, moreover, unique among Bible stories in its length and content. In the Elijah-Elisha narratives here alone we have the healing of a leper and the conversion to, and worship of, Yahweh by a non-Israelite. The miracle is given its moral significance. This is an 'apt example of a Biblical narrative in which art and theology are symbiotically related'.[2] The structure includes reversal of roles between servant and master, and the selfless and the selfish, a leper is cleansed and someone punished by leprosy imposed.

1. Na'aman, a name common in Syria (Alalakh and Ras Shamra texts), means 'gracious'. He is pictured as *a great* (*i.e.* important) *man* ('*îš gādôl*) who was *highly regarded* (Heb. 'shown favour') and a man of substance (*gibbôr ḥayil*) *but* a leper. The latter description is no editorial addition, for he evoked deference (v. 16) and was introduced in the royal letter as 'my official'.

2. The King of Aram could be Ben-Hadad III who had made a truce with Israel (8:7).

[1] A. Mazar, 'Three Israelite Sites in the hills of Judah and Ephraim', *BA* 45, 1982, pp. 167–178.
[2] R. L. Cohn, 'Form and Perspective in 2 Kings 5', *VT* 33, 1983, pp. 171–184.

3–4. Captive helps commander. Elisha's role was widely recognized by Israelites as that of prophet (*nābî'*). The girl knew he could remove (*'sp*) the effects of leprosy (*cf.* Nu. 12:10, 14); perhaps this rare word for 'healing' reflects the work of the Mesopotamian ritual-physicians (*ašipu*). Leprosy (*ṣāra'aṭ*) in the Old Testament is used of different 'malignant' (NEB) or infectious skin diseases (*cf.* NIV mg.), which is a more accurate translation. It is marked by a variety of swellings, scabs, white spots (*cf.* v. 27), bright or dark patches or flaking skin. It also describes a mildew on wool, linen or leather, and fungus on walls (Lv. 13–14).[1] Hanson's bacillus disease (leprosy — *Elephantiasis graecorum*) is as yet first identified in Egypt in the second century BC.

5–6. Inter-state letters on medical matters are attested (Mari, Hittite and Assyrian archives),[2] as is the practice of giving gifts on seeking an audience. This one was exceptionally rich, amounting in silver alone to five times what Omri had paid for the site of Samaria (1 Ki. 16:24). The 'changes of raiment' (AV) or *sets of clothing* were rolls of cloth used at this period in Syria as additional payment rather than made-up garments (*cf.* 'festal robes' JB).

The King of Aram assumes that a prophet would be a member of the royal entourage, but Israel took the letter as a provocation to renewed war (v. 7). Elisha's power as a 'man of God' contrasts with the powerlessness of the unnamed 'man of state'. This may well be done to emphasize Elisha's act as a testimony to God's power (v. 8).

9–12. Naaman expected respect ('*to* one like *me*', v. 11) and a public ritual with 'something great' rather than a simple private act. The aim was to teach him humility and faith. A great man may expect *some great thing* (v. 13, NRSV, REB 'something difficult') while God often tests us with small things. The clear rivers in Damascus flowed from the snow-covered Amanus Mountains (Heb. *Qerē* reads Amana for Abana, modern River Barada) or from Mount Hermon, River Barbar (modern 'Awaj).

13–14. The ritual cleansing of a leper (Heb. *rḥṣ*, v. 10) required a sevenfold act (Lv. 14:7–9). Naaman 'plunged' (Heb. *ṭbl*, NIV *dipped*, JB 'immersed himself') in the River Jordan. This signified total obedience to the divine word and so

[1] E. G. Browne, *Leprosy in the Bible* (Christian Medical Fellowship, 1974), p. 5.
[2] D. J. Wiseman in B. Palmer, *op. cit.*, p. 32.

'rebirth'. *Seven times* is a symbolic perfect number and probably has no reference to the cleansing of baptism (1 Pet. 3:21) or to separation from the past, as in Israel's crossing the same river, where the emphasis is on 'standing in' it (Jos. 3:8; 4:9).

15–16. Naaman's attitudes are stressed. When his flesh was *restored* ('turned around', v. 14) so was he (v. 15). This is no evidence that the Syrian cult of Baal-Shamaim in Damascus was already monotheistic, though Naaman's confession may simply acknowledge the LORD God Yahweh as universal. Elisha's refusal to accept a *gift* or 'token of gratitude' (NEB; Heb. *bᵉrākâ*, 'blessing') contrasts with the attitude of false prophets and of Gehazi (vv. 22–23).

17. The loads of *earth* were to prepare the base for a 'sacred place' on which an altar could be erected, and not because the LORD God could only be worshipped on Israelite soil. Naaman's knowledge of God was as yet weak.

18. Elisha does not reprimand him, for his official position required him to attend the king. The Hebrew 'lean on the hand' does not imply physical support but that he was the king's 'right hand man' (*cf.* 2 Ki. 7:2, 17). For *Rimmon* see on 1 Kings 15:18, where reference is also made to the payment of gifts.

19. Naaman's relation with Elisha is couched in diplomatic language. *'Go in peace'* is not simply 'farewell' (as NEB), but an acknowledge that the recipient is in covenant relation with the speaker and his god. Similarly 'is it well?' (v. 21, *hᵃšālôm*) commonly marks the reopening of negotiations (2 Ki. 9:17–19).[1]

20. Gehazi's action broke the relationship when he sought to enrich himself. His attitude was one of avarice (v. 22), deception (vv. 23–25) and derogation of superiors (v. 20, *'this Aramean'*). Moreover he swore deceitfully by the LORD (v. 20, contrast Elisha, v. 16) and covered up for it and so was justly punished (Lv. 19:12; Acts 5:2–3). Naaman was more faithful to his new LORD than Gehazi was to his.

24. The *hill* (Heb. *'ōpel*, AV 'tower') can be taken as the district of Ophel in Jerusalem, but here more likely it is 'the hill' in Samaria (RSV).

26. 'Did I not go with you in spirit' (RSV, NEB, GNB) may

[1] D. J. Wiseman, '"Is it Peace?" – Covenant and Diplomacy', *VT* 32, 1982, pp. 320–324.

indicate both the prophet's concern (AV 'heart') and knowledge.

27. Gehazi's departure *from Elisha's presence* (so MT *mil-l^epānāw*; cf. 6:32; Jon. 1:3; Gn. 41:46) is a word for dismissal from an official audience. That Naaman's leprosy *will cling to* Gehazi and to his *descendants for ever* illustrates the punishment, foretold in Exodus 20:5 and visited on Achan's family (Jos. 7:24–26), as on those who break the commandment prohibiting the making of idols (here the love of money and possessions). In his mercy God sometimes exacts this on the first, or only to the fourth generation. In the days of Jesus Christ the episode of Naaman was well known and cited as a unique case of a non-Israelite leper being cleansed through obedience to God's word through a prophet, at a time when many Jews did not heed the call of the prophet of their day (Lk. 4:27).

f. The floating axe-head (6:1–7). This was a miracle of provision for the needy disciples 'similar to that of the stater in the fish's mouth' (Mt. 17:27, Keil) rather than of personal aggrandisement. The explanation that Elisha probed with a stick at the place indicated to locate and recover it is contradicted by he *threw* the *stick* and *made the iron float* (v. 6). Here also is evidence of the expanding prophetic community.

5. The *iron axe-head* (Heb. 'iron') had been asked for, (MT *šā'ûl*), that is, begged or prayed for, and not necessarily 'borrowed' (as EVV).

g. The Arameans entrapped (6:8–23). The record of miraculous incidents with moral lessons continues, vision contrasts with blindness, spiritual resources with man-made tactics (vv. 15–16), etc. It is a prelude to the dealings of Elisha with the court and his conduct in the Aramean war (6:24 – 7:20). Elisha had close relations with the unnamed king of Israel for whom he provided an efficient intelligence service. His knowledge was probably gained from informants (cf. 2 Ki. 5:3) rather than second sight. Hence the concern over betrayal (v. 11, Heb. '*for* the king of Israel'; NEB emends to 'has betrayed us to').

8. The Aramean plan was for a raid or ambush (MT *tah^anōtî*), *my camp* only here and is of uncertain meaning, possibly 'attack in . . . direction' (NEB).

13. *Dothan* lay strategically at the head of the valley leading to the Jezreel plain, about fourteen kilometres north of Samaria.

16. Divine majority support and protection is always available to God's people at times of testing (*cf.* Ps. 91:11; Acts 7:56; Rom. 8:31).

17–18. A negative and positive view are always possible. The need is for revelation (to *open the eyes* – only used of God's action) to see the superior forces encircling the besiegers. Blindness (MT *sanwērîm*) is sometimes taken as a divine punishment on heathen unbelieving peoples (*gōy*; Gn. 19:11), but Jesus affirms that the cause may not be attributable to sin (Jn. 9:3). Elisha's statement (v. 19) was a *ruse de guerre* (Delitzsch).

21–23. The king acknowledges Elisha's superior authority (*my father*) and call for restraint. Prisoners of war, even under the initial ban (*ḥērem*), were not normally sacrificed or put to death (unless rebel leaders). *Would you kill them?* (NIV, JB) reinforces this, the *not* (v. 22) being a strong asseverative. Others (Montgomery) think that Elisha thought those captured in battle should be slain and those who surrendered be spared (*cf.* the criticism of Ahab in 1 Ki. 20:31–43). NEB interprets verse 22 as 'You may destroy those whom you have taken prisoner with … but as for these …'. The giving of a *feast* (v. 23, Heb. *kārâ*, Akkad. *qirētu*) followed a covenant-agreement and in principle precluded revenge (so Rom. 12:20–21). Clemency often leads to peace.

h. The siege of Samaria (6:24 – 7:20). This section may not relate directly to the preceeding events (so v. 24 'afterwards', *some time later*) or to the great famine (8:1).

i. Famine in the city (6:24–33). **23.** *Ben-Hadad* was a Syrian throne-name for contemporaries of Jehoram Ben-Hadad II) or here Ben-Hadad III.

25. The siege brought the city to such dire straits that even the forbidden ass's head (*cf.* Lv. 11:3) was eaten at exorbitant cost. A third of a litre (one-eighth of a pint; MT *qab*) of carob beans (*ḥarûbîm*; NIV *seed pods*) rather than 'dove's dung' (AV; MT *ḥir°yyônîm*) or 'wild onions' (JB) was sold for fifty-five grammes of silver or more than a month's wages for a labourer (*cf.* Mt. 20:1–16 and the famine rates of Rev. 6:6).

26–29. Individuals could always appeal direct to the king.

His reply implies that he cannot help. MT 'let not the LORD . . .' could be 'No, let the LORD help . . .' (Robinson) or *'If the LORD does not help . . .'* (NIV, NEB).

Cannibalism in time of siege is well attested (*cf.* Dt. 28:55–57; Ezk. 5:10; also at Jerusalem (Josephus, *War* v.13.7; vi.34) and Babylonia).[1]

30–31. The royal mourning, even if secret, was sincere, viewing the siege as punishment for the nation's sins (*cf.* Jon. 3:6). His solemn oath against Elisha (*cf.* 1 Ki. 2:23) presupposes that he attributed Israel's trouble to him (*cf.* 1 Ki. 18:17).

32–33. *This murderer* (Heb. *ben-ham^{e}raṣṣēaḥ*; AV 'son of a murderer') denotes a class-type rather than a reference to Jehoram as son of Ahab. While the king was talking the *messenger* (*male'āḵ*; NIV, RSV) arrived, although reading 'king' (*meleḵ*; NEB, GNB) also makes good sense (*cf.* 7:2). *This disaster,* (calamity or evil) could come from the LORD as part of his sovereign purposes (Jb. 2:10; Is. 45:7).

ii. The siege relieved (7:1–20). **1.** Elisha had made a prophetic utterance (*had said*) that was fulfilled in the successful outcome of the siege (v. 1, *cf.* vv. 18–20) which would lead to the price of basic commodities falling well below the normal price. Such a prophecy was the more effective since no crops could grow in time to restore supplies. The *gate* was the market-place as well as the local court of justice.

2. The *officer* (*cf.* AV 'LORD'; MT *šālîš*) denotes the third man of a chariot-team who acted as armour-bearer, aide-de-camp (NEB 'lieutentant') and so as adjutant to the king (*cf.* 2 Ki. 9:25; 2 Ki. 5:18).[2] The *windows* (NIV *floodgates*) of heaven are figurative (Gn. 7:11; Mal. 3:10).

6. The *sound* or rumour which produced the panic is attributed to divine action. God uses diverse means. At this time the neo-Hittites dominated northern Syria (Hatti-land)[3]

[1] A. L. Oppenheim, '"Siege-documents" from Nippur', *Iraq* 17, 1955, pp. 69–89.

[2] B. A. Mastin, 'Was the *šālîš* the Third Man in the Chariot?', *VT*Supp 30, 1979, pp. 125–154.

[3] H. Hoffner, 'Some Contributions of Hittitology to Old Testament Study', *TynB* 20, 1969, p. 88; *POTT*, p. 213.

and for Egyptians (MT *miṣrayim*) possibly read *Muṣri*-peoples (*muṣrîm*), allies of the Hittites and Aramaeans (as 1 Ki. 10:28). In their headlong flight the Aramaeans even abandoned unharnessed chariot-horses.

9. Moral considerations may prevail due to fear of punishment (MT *'awôn*). The word denotes both the deed and its consequences. A concern not to violate the social norms can be a valid reason for changing behaviour.

10–15. The king suspected a tactic similar to that employed by his ancestors at Ai (Jos. 8:3–28). However, he decided to take the low-risk action of sending *five of the* remaining *horses* (against NEB 'some'), though apparently only two mounted men (v. 14, NEB, MT *rekeḇ sûsîm*); against AV 'chariot horses', or NIV *chariots with their horses*, were sent.

17–20. The test of true prophecy is its fulfilment (Dt. 18:21–22). This section is no mere doublet or dittography, but a moralizing summary to emphasize the historian's view on this episode. God never fails to meet the need of his people when they trust him. Here a meal-measure (7.3 litres) of expensive fine flour could be bought for only twice the cost of common barley, so prolific were the available supplies.

i. The Shunammite regains her land (8:1–6).
This appendix to the Elisha narratives aims to confirm the miracle of the boy restored to life (2 Ki. 4:8–37) and continues on from that story. It shows also the prophet's influence at court was used to help a widow as Elijah had done. The dating of this famine in relation to that at Samaria (4:38; 6:24 – 7:20) is not clear, but any famines were taken to be decreed by God and a warning of God's displeasure on a nation and made necessary a call to repentance (see 1 Ki. 17:1; 18:2; Hg. 1:6, 9–11; 2:16–17; Rev. 6:5–8). The incident may have taken place in the reign of Jehoram and following judicial reforms in the south (Whitelam).

1–2. The prophet had foretold that a famine is decreed and this explains the absence of the widow from Israel. She stayed temporarily (as a resident alien, so Heb. verb *gûr*); thus NIV *stay for a while wherever you can* (*cf.* REB 'find lodging', NRSV 'settle') represents the Hebrew 'sojourn where you sojourn'. There is no reason to think that the *seven years* of famine was an artificial device to agree with the seven year period needed by the law before debts can be cancelled (Dt. 15:1–4). Such long famines are recorded in ancient texts (*cf.* Gn. 41:30).[1]

3. The king was the court of appeal for all matters of land-tenure (*cf.* 1 Ki. 21), so she *went to the king* as the owner of all property taken over during her absence. That she went to 'cry out' (Heb. *ṣʿq*) for her house (v. 5) indicates that this was a legal term of stronger import than *beg* (NIV or 'sought an audience of the king' to beg, NEB, REB; 'appealed', RSV). 'Lodge a claim' (JB) brings out the sense well (as in Akkad. *ragāmu*). The king (v. 4) is not named, and since Gehazi is in the royal presence it may be assumed that this was before his dismissal as Elisha's servant (5:27). If so, the king might be Jehu, for J(eh)oram knew Elisha well (3:13).

6. The *official* (*sārîs*) appointed to look into her case was not a 'eunuch' (JB; see on 1 Ki. 22:9). He had to calculate all the income (usufruct) owing from her fields during her absence ('revenues' NEB, rather than 'produce' RSV). God often uses the authorities to make provision for widows and the fatherless as a charge on the state (Dt. 10:18; 24:19–20; Je. 7:6–7).

j. Elisha and Hazael (8:7–15). The source of the intimate details may be Elisha's disciples. It is certainly distinct from that on the Aramean wars (2 Ki. 6:24 – 7:20). Elisha goes to Damascus, not in imitation of Elijah but to fulfil the God-given task his predecessor had not completed (1 Ki. 19:15). This time a pagan king seeks the God of Israel (*cf.* 2 Ki. 1:1–4).

7. *Ben-Hadad*, probably a throne-name of the king of Damascus (Aram) 844–818 BC, is here the second holder of that title whose personal name was Hadadeser (Assyr. *Adad-ʿidri*). He is mentioned in Assyrian annals during the eighteenth (840 BC) and twenty-first year (837) campaigns of Shalmaneser III, king of Assyria.

9. *Hazael* see Additional Note. The audience gift he sent (*cf.* 1 Sa. 9:7; 1 Ki. 14:3) was such that it may have aimed to bribe an oracle from Yahweh. Since the approach was diplomatic (*your son*, v. 9) and implied politeness rather than subservience (*cf.* 6:21; 1 Sa. 25:8) there is no need to suggest that the *forty camel-loads* was just to impress by numbers, that the camels were only lightly loaded, or that the number conventionally indicates a large number.

---

[1] W. H. Shea, *Famines in the Early History of Egypt and Syro-Palestine* (Ann Arbor: University of Michigan, 1977), pp. 129–235.

Additional Note on Hazael

Hazael (Heb. *ḥᵃzā'ēl*) was a strong king of Aram (*c.* 843– 796/7 BC). He is named in contemporary Assyrian records as *haza'ili mār la mammana*, the 'son of a nobody', *i.e.* his lineage is not recorded, probably as a commoner and not necessarily as a usurper. He seized the throne after the assassination of Ben-Hadad II and was forced to pay a hundred talents of gold and a thousand talents of silver as tribute to Shalmaneser III of Assyria who besieged his capital Damascus (later known in Assyr. as *Bīt-Haza'ili*, 'the House of Hazael'; *cf.* Am. 1:3–4; Black Obelisk 102).

Hazael was the scourge of Israel in the reigns of Joram, Jehu and Jehoahaz, fighting against Shalmaneser again in 837; with Joram at Ramoth Gilead in 843/2 (2 Ki. 8:28) and Jehoahaz (13:22). In old age he was a vassal of Adad-nirari III (*c.* 805/798) who referred to him as *mari'*. This could be a title ('my LORD') or a personal name, abbreviation of Mari'-Hadad, for an inscribed ivory from Arslan Tash (Til Barsip) reads 'lord Hazael' (*mr'n ḥz'l*). His name is also found on an ivory from Nimrud and written on a bead captured by Shalmaneser. A possible representation of him appears on another ivory (*IBD*, p. 612). He was succeeded by his son Bir-Hadad (Ben-Hadad III) who ruled *c.* 796–770 BC (13:24). The Aramaic Zakir stela inscription reads 'Bar-Hadad bar (son of) Hazael, king of Aram'.

10. *You will certainly not recover* or live (NIV mg; MT *lō ḥāyōh ṭiḥᵉyeh*) is what is written (Kethib), but to avoid an embarrassing lie by the man of God many MSS have changed this to *lô*, 'to him', and so read this as 'you will surely live' (Qerē). Most LXX MSS follow this. However, the explanation could be that the reply was truthfully that first, the king would die but not from the illness about which he enquired and secondly he would surely die by the hand of an assassin. The first but not the second message was passed on by Hazael (v. 14). This is more likely than that the first was a general answer with the second a more considered reply (Montgomery), or that it was addressed to Hazael rather than his master (Labuschagne) or must be taken as a mere greeting (Gray).

11. This verse is also not clear, since the subject is not specified. Heb. 'He set his face until he was ashamed' (*cf.* NEB 'the man of God stood there like a man stunned until he could bear it no longer'), assuming that Hazael found the meeting with an ecstatic prophet uncomfortable, takes him to be the subject throughout, while NIV (*He [Elisha] stared at him . . . until Hazael felt ashamed*) allows a change of subject. This may be the best solution.

12–14. Elisha was moved at the outcome of his prophecy. He envisaged the *harm* ('evil', AV) that Hazael would do to Israel (see 10:32–33; 13:3 ff). The dastardly barbarities in war, forbidden by the Hebrew law, were to be long remembered (Am. 1:4). Hazael protests with self-depreciation ('dead dog') that he would not do such things. This traditional phrase occurs in many texts (Lachish ostracon VI; Amarna Letter No. 60, *cf*. 1 Sa. 24:14; 2 Sa. 9:8). The revelation of Hazael's coming status does not necessarily imply that Elisha himself encouraged, legitimized or took part in the *coup d'état*. There is no record of his anointing Hazael (but *cf*. 1 Ki. 19:15) who was not a legitimate successor in that he was not of the dynastic line.

15. The manner of Ben-Hadad's death is disputed. If, as usually presumed, it was Hazael (*he*) who took a 'coverlet' (Heb. *makbēr* occurs only here) it could have been deliberate murder. The article could be either a *thick* matted *cloth* (AV, NIV) or a sieve-like blanket (*cf*. Am. 9:9, RSV) used like a mosquito net which when soaked was either used to suffocate the king or, as Gray thinks, to cover the window or body so that the corpse was not immediately seen.

vi. History of reigns (8:16–29).

a. Jehoram of Judah (8:16–24). Cf. 2 Chronicles 21:1–20. This continues the history of Judah from 1 Kings 22:50.

The usual introductory formulae (vv. 16–17) and concluding date (vv. 23–24; see Introduction, pp. 46ff.) have between them a long evaluation of this king by the historian (vv. 18–19) and an episode in his war with Edom (vv. 20–22). It so happens that the kings of Judah and Israel have the same name at this time. The MSS vary in writing the full Jehoram or abbreviated Joram for both throughout, but for convenience here Jehoram for Judah and Joram for Israel are used. Note also that both are classified as *evil* rulers.

16–17. The *fifth year* of Joram of Israel, and so the first of Jehoram was 848 BC (see v. 25; 1 Ki. 22:42, 51; 2 Ki. 3:1). The length of reign in Jerusalem, *eight years* is given as 'ten' (LXX(L)) or 'forty' (LXX), but the figure here could well denote his sole reign not counting his co-regency with Jehoshaphat from 853. RSV and some MSS of LXX omit 'Jehoshaphat (was) king of Judah'. The omission of Jehoram's mother's name, unexpected for a Judean ruler, might be explained if she were dead before he came to the throne.

18–19. The *evil* of Jehoram's reign is stressed here (contrary to the view that the historian presents an ideal picture of Judah). He was associated with Israel by dynastic marriage to Athaliah, daughter of Ahab, who introduced Baal worship into Jerusalem (v. 27, 11:18) presumably with Jehoram's connivance. Hence *granddaughter* of Omri (v. 26) since the Hebrew for daughter (*bat*) is used of any female descendant as 'son' (*ben*) is of any male offspring. The influence of an evil woman, as of an evil man, can persist. The historian views *evil* in Judah as worse than in Israel, and this forms the backdrop of God's covenant mercy (v. 19). *For the sake of his servant David* (see 1 Ki. 11:12–13, 32, 34; 15:4). The *lamp* was more than a symbol of life and of testimony, it reminded the hearer of the covenant (Ps. 132:17, *cf* 2 Ch. 21:7). See on 1 Kings 11:36. There is no evidence for changing MT 'for his sons', *descendants* (*lᵉbānāw*) to 'before him' (*lᵉpānāw*) as some propose.

20–21. The Edom rebellion does not contradict 1 Kings 22:47 which implies that there was earlier no king, only 'a viceroy' (NEB). *Zair* may be located at Zior northeast of Hebron (Jos. 15:54), though others look for a site in the Arabah. It cannot be Zoar (Gn. 13:10). The Hebrew of verse 21 is difficult and can be interpreted either with *Jehoram and his chariot commanders* as the subject (RSV, NIV, REB) who broke out of an encirclement by night or with the Edomites as the army that defeated Jehoram (NEB mg.). The latter is possible since *fled back home* or 'to their tents'[1] implies a battle ending in defeat.

22. Certainly Edom hereafter 'remained independent of Judah' (REB), and was never again totally under Judean control, though Amaziah later attacked it (14:7) and Elat was built by Azariah (14:22). Hence NIV *Edom . . . in rebellion against*

---

[1] This is not just 'went home' (as Dt. 5:30; Jos. 22:4–8) or a term for dismissal (2 Sa. 20:1; 1 Ki. 12:16). For 'tent' as designating a dwelling in general see D. J. Wiseman, 'They Lived in Tents', in G. A. Tuttle (ed.), *The Bible and Near Eastern Studies: Essays in Honor of William Sanford Lasor* (Grand Rapids: Eerdmans, 1978), pp. 195–200.

Judah. Libnah was a frontier town with Philistia (19:8) at Tell eṣ-Ṣafi in the western foothills of the Shephelah or Tell Burnāṭ south of it.[1] For the connection of this area with the Arabs, and Edom, see 2 Chronicles 21:16–17. Their invasion of Judah and the death of Jehoram's sons and wives, and the sacking of the royal palace are omitted here.

23–24. Similarly the historian makes no reference to Jehoram's death as due to an incurable intestinal disease of the large bowel which led to chronic diarrhoea and a massive rectal prolapse (2 Ch. 21:18–19). Nor does he recount that though buried in the *City of David* it was not in the royal mausoleum with public honours. The Chronicler introduces a letter, based on earlier Elijah phraseology, to administer a severe rebuke on Jehoram for his alliance with Israel (2 Ch. 21:12–15).

b. Ahaziah of Judah (8:25–29). *Cf.* 2 Chronicles 22:1–9, Josephus, *Ant.* ix.5. The form, as usually taken by the historian, is for the introductory formulae (vv. 25–26) and evaluation of his reign (v. 27) to be followed by a summary of the most important event of the reign, the war with Aram (vv. 28–29). The detail of Ahaziah's death and concluding formulae are left to 9:28–29, following the story of his encounter with Jehu.

25–27. The synchronism implies that he ruled for less than one year, though the historian counts parts of a year as a whole. The 'accession year' is here counted as the first regnal year (*cf.* 9:29, *eleventh* year of Jehoram). Athaliah was the *granddaughter* of Omri; see on v. 18. The relation of Jehoram to Ahab's Omri dynasty was *by marriage* (so NIV; JB). The word used (MT *ḥᵃtan*) means 'a family relative' (as Akkad. *hatānu*) and not merely 'son-in-law' (AV, RSV).[2]

28–29. *Cf.* 1 Kings 22:29–28 for Ahab's war at Ramoth Gilead and 2 Kings 9:15–27 for this episode. The text here does not clearly state whether the fact that Ahaziah went with Joram (his uncle) *to battle with Hazael* was a special alliance for this specific purpose, since he may not have been present at the Ramoth Gilead battle but had only visited the king of

[1] Y. Aharoni, *The Land of the Bible* (London: Burns & Oates, 1979), pp. 86, 353, *cf.* p. 392.
[2] T. C. Mitchell, 'The meaning of the noun *ḥtn* in the Old Testament', *VT* 19, 1969, pp. 93–112.

Israel in Jezreel (9:21, 27, 29). 'Ramah' (RSV, MT 'height') may be a shortened form of Ramoth (Gilead), so NIV. He *went down* from Jerusalem.

vii. Jehu's revolution (9:1 – 10:36). Jehu, a military commander (9:5), is endorsed by the prophet Elisha, and the historian, for his zeal in removing Baal worship from Israel and bringing the Omri dynasty, and above all the house of Ahab, to an end. All this is recorded with a constant emphasis on the way these deeds fulfilled the earlier prophecies made by Elijah and Elisha. Thus there are evidently some comments by the writer (rather than editors) which incorporate résumés (9:14–15) or notes (9:29) into the historical detail which would have been available from prophetic or secular sources. The whole also forms a protest against the policy of the Omrides in supporting the dynastic (Canaanite) principle against the charismatic ideal of kingship which the historian hoped Jehu would renew. The motive is to recount the end of the house of Ahab and of Ahab's wife who have been shown to be doubly evil and fatal to God's people. The political background includes the Assyrian pressure on Israel during their incursion into Transjordan and to Carmel (Baal-ra'si) under Shalmaneser III in 841 BC when Jehu submitted to him. Under Tiglath-pileser III (745–727 BC) the Assyrians meanwhile maintained a tight hold over Phoenicia.[1]

a. Jehu anointed king (9:1–13).

i. The anointing commissioned (9:1–3). Elisha sends a member of a prophetic group (*cf.* 1 Ki. 20:35) to fulfil the task of anointing Jehu that Elijah had passed on to him (1 Ki. 19:16). This unnamed young prophet is identified in Jewish tradition (*Seder Olam*) with Jonah (2 Ki. 14:25) and involves a foreign mission. Doubtless Jehu was motivated also by personal ambition and the current disaffection with the regime and its heavy taxation. He was, however, God's agent using the army to end it just as the army had originally brought Omri to power.

Jehu is the only king of the Northern Kingdom (Israel) to

[1] H. W. F. Saggs, 'The Nimrud Letters, 1952 – Relations with the West', *Iraq* 17, 1959, pp. 126–154; M. Cogan, 'Tyre and Tiglath-pileser III', *JCS* 25, 1973, pp. 96–99; B. Oded, 'The Phoenician Cities and the Assyrian Empire in the time of Tiglath-pileser III', *ZPDV* 90, 1974, pp. 38–49.

have been anointed, perhaps to indicate that he should follow in the Davidic tradition, as Saul had been anointed by Samuel (1 Sa. 9:16; 10:1); David by Samuel, to mark the Spirit of God endowing him for the task (1 Sa. 16:12–13); and Solomon by the high priest Zadok and Nathan the prophet (1 Ki. 1:45). Such anointing was symbolic and probably confined to Hebrew practice (see also on 1 Ki. 1:34).[1]

The travelling *flask* used (Heb. *paḳ*) is the same type as used by Samuel (1 Sa. 10:1). Jehu, whose name may mean 'Ya(h-weh) is the (true) one', could have already been sympathetic to the worship of God (Yahweh). According to the Assyrians in 841 BC they referred to him as 'Yaua the son of Omri' (Black Obelisk of Shalmaneser III *Ya-ú-a mār Humri*)[2] thus treating him as the next legitimate ruler in Samaria. Later prophets were to think little of him (Hos. 1:4). The paternal name *Jehoshaphat son of Nimshi* may have been added to avoid confusion with the Judean king Jehoshaphat, son of Asa. The 'brothers' may have been *companions*, 'fellows' (RSV) or simply associated brother-officers (REB). The *inner room* would provide secrecy to leave Jehu to choose his own time to go public.[3] The need to *run* or flee would be because of the uncertainty of the reaction of the army, which would include pro-J(eh)oram elements.

ii. The young prophet's mission accomplished (9:4–10). The messenger was 'a young man, a young man the prophet' (MT) of which one 'young man' (Heb. *na'ar*) is omitted by most EVV (and LXX). It may not mean here 'a very young man', so it is usually taken as describing an assistant of the prophet (so Vulg., *cf.* 2 Ki. 19:6), for the term is used of a wide age range from a youthful helper to the mature Absolam (2 Sa. 14:21; 18:5). He found the officers 'sitting' (so Heb.) *together* (NIV, JB), 'in council' (RSV) is one interpretation. When the anointing had been completed the prophet (some say the later editor) expanded the divine declaration (vv. 7–10, *cf.* v. 3) to define Jehu's mission. Jehu would have known this already (see vv.

---

[1] Z. Ben-Barak, 'The Coronation Ceremony in Ancient Mesopotamia', *Orientalia Lovaniensia Periodica* 11, 1980, pp. 55–67.

[2] For this portrayal of Jehu (rather than his messenger) on the Black Obelisk see illustrations in *IBD*, pp. 742, 1427; *ANEP*, p. 352.

[3] However, Babylonian Coronation ceremonies took place in part in an inner room (*kummu*) and partly in public (temple court).

25–26; 1 Ki. 21:21–24). As well as the termination of Ahab's house it would include the vengeance required by Deuteronomy (*cf.* Dt. 32:43) for the slaying of God's servants. Only here in Kings is emphasis placed on Yahweh as an avenging God, using as he does a human agent as the avenger of blood (*cf.* Gn. 4:24; Rev. 6:10). This concept was strong in the Davidic tradition (2 Sa. 4:8; 22:48; *cf.* Pss. 9:12; 79:10). Jezebel's victims had included Naboth and his sons and many prophets (1 Ki. 18:4; 19:10) of whom Obadiah had saved a hundred only (1 Ki. 18:13). Jehu's work was to be carried out thoroughly, just as had been the case for the whole family of Jereboam (1 Ki. 14:10) and Baasha (1 Ki. 16:3, 11–12).

Kingly power often brings political and religious corruption and so divine judgment with it (*cf.* 1 Sa. 8:6–18; Hos. 13:11). Verse 10 fulfils 1 Kings 14:11; 16:4; 21:23.

iii. The army's reaction (9:11–13). When Jehu emerged his companions asked him 'Is it peace?' (MT) meaning more than *Is everything all right?*, but rather, 'Has he come to make an agreement with (the Akkad. 'ask the peace of') you?' When Jehu evades the question they prompt him to tell all ('It's a *lie*') since they denied that they recognized ('knew') the man and his 'communication' (AV, Heb. *śîḥô*). The main use of this word is of 'meditation' (1 Ki. 18:27; Pss. 104:34; 119:97) or of a type of prayer (Ps. 64:1; Pr. 23:29 'complaint' could be used of mumbling in meditation, *cf.* AV 'babbling').

11. Thus NIV *the sort of things he says* or 'the way his thoughts run' (NEB). These renderings are better than 'empty talk' or 'prattle' (Montgomery), which are sometimes tinged by the associated description of the prophet as *madman*, 'crazy' or the like. It is assumed that this word (*mᵉšuggāʿ*) has to do with ecstatic behaviour. It is not used of lunacy or mental derangement, but of symptoms of a disease (Dt. 28:34) or condition which excluded David from the palace of Achish (1 Sa. 21:13–15) and was distinguishable from true prophetical behaviour (Je. 29:26; Hos. 9:7). The cognate Akkadian (*šegû*) is used of animals and women and may mean to act furiously, *i.e.* the opposite of peacefully.[1] See also on verse 20.

13. The army officers *took their cloaks and* placed, *spread* or 'set' *them under him* to acclaim him as king. The act of

[1] D. J. Wiseman, '"Is it Peace?" – Covenant and Diplomacy', *VT* 32, 1982, p. 321.

spreading out the garment was one of recognition, loyalty and promise of support (*cf.* the people to Christ in Mt. 21:8; Lk. 19:36). The place where they did this is not clear, for the word translated *bare steps* (Heb. *gerem*) occurs only here. If the same as 'bone' it is taken as the steps 'themselves', on the basis of the Hebrew reflexive based on 'my bone', *i.e.* myself. It may well be an architectural term, the landing part-way down the steps (Gray) or a raised supported structure (*cf.* Akkad. *girnû*). The *trumpet* (*šôpār*)-call (as used in the coronation of Solomon, 1 Ki. 1:34; and Joash, 2 Ki. 11:14) was to herald a public proclamation and assembly. It may be noteworthy that they said 'Jehu rules as / is king' rather than the popular acclamation 'Long live the king' which was only made when the full public assent had been made: as for Saul (1 Sa. 10:24), Absalom (2 Sa. 16:16), Solomon (1 Ki. 1:34, 39), Joash (2 Ch. 23:11) and Josiah (2 Ki. 11:12). Negotiations to that end for Jehu still ay ahead.

b. The death of the kings of Israel and Judah (9:14–29). Speedy action was necessary if Joram was not to rally support. The situation is set in an editorial note (vv. 14–15a, set in parenthesis in some EVV). Jehu issues a challenge. 'If you have your life' or 'soul' (MT literally) may be 'If you are on my side' (REB, *cf.* Gray) or better 'If this is your mind' (RSV) or 'wish' (NRSV) *if this is the way you feel* to prevent anyone slipping out of the city (either a survivor, here 'defector') giving the news to Joram. Jehu wished to have an element of surprise, so he rides off to see the convalescent Joram in his summer palace at Jezreel. On the report of a 'mass of' *Jehu's troops approaching* (v. 17; *troops*, Heb. *šip̄ʿâ* is used of 'abundance', Dt. 33:19; Ezk. 26:10) Joram sends out a *horseman* (*rekeḇ*, Akkad. *rakbu*, the term used also for a diplomatic messenger) to ask 'Is it peace?' secretly. When he obeyed Jehu's call to 'turn to going after me' in file and thus indicated a change of allegiance, the kings changed their attitude and sent a second messenger to say 'it is peace' (v. 19, *šālôm*). They observed the manner of Jehu's approach, not that he drove like a madman, 'furiously' (AV) or with abandon, all of which would be expected of a skilled charioteer, but that he drove on aggressively (Heb. *mᵉšuggāʿ*, see on v. 11.; *cf.* Targum 'quickly'; Josephus 'gently, steadily').

Seeing that Jehu would not negotiate with their envoys, the watching kings went out to challenge (MT 'to call out to') Jehu personally with 'Is it peace?' (negotiation). But Jehu rejected any possibility of a covenant-agreement on the grounds that he would not be associated with them so long as Jezebel's pagan influence was allowed to continue (v. 22). The naming of their meeting place as the very place of Ahab and Jezebel's tyranny against Naboth (see on v. 26) is significant. Close association with idolatry ('harlotry') – false worship of false gods – is out for God's people, for he demands an exclusive allegiance. This does not allow place for false practices including *witchcraft*, 'monstrous sorceries' (RSV), or taking omens (Je. 27:9). All these are punishable by death according to the Covenant (Dt. 13; 17:2–7; 18:10–12). There can never be true peace in any relationship without religious agreement.

24–25. God's word that Ahab's house would be destroyed was brought about through the brash actions of his agent Jehu. The experienced warrior deliberately aimed to shoot Joram. A technical archery term is used: 'filled his hand with the bow' (MT; *cf.* Akkad. *qašta mullû*), that is, stretched the bow 'with his full strength' (RSV after Rashi). Sidkar was Jehu's, or, less probably, Ahaziah's third man in the chariot (Heb. *šāliš*, *i.e.* not the driver, or just an *officer*, but the royal aide-de-camp; *cf.* 2 Ki. 7:2). It is possible that Bidkar was driving his own chariot alongside.[1]

26. The act was thus a calculated fulfilment of Elijah's prophecy (1 Ki. 21:18–24).

27–28. Ahaziah's death is recorded to conclude the account here in greater detail than is usual in the concluding formula of a reign and seems to fit in with the longer narrative of his partner's demise. This shows the historian's style is adaptable. Ahaziah appears to have been trying to flee to Judah but had to turn back to Megiddo.

Beth Haggan (v. 27; 'garden house', NIV mg.) could be associated with the royal gardens at Jezreel (1 Ki. 21) but most identify it with En-gannim (Jos. 19:21; 21:29), modern Jenin, eleven kilometres south of Jezreel. The *way up to* or 'ascent of' (RSV), 'up the valley near' (REB) *Gur* would then be the road to modern Gurra near Taanach (Aharoni, p. 169). It could well

---

[1] The reference here is unlikely to be *šāliš*, meaning three horses to a chariot, as has been suggested (*UF* 19, 1987, pp. 355–372), though the practice of having a third (spare) horse running behind a chariot is known elsewhere (D. J. Wiseman, 'The Assyrians', in Sir John Hackett (ed.), *Warfare in the Ancient World* (London: Sidgwick & Jackson, 1989), p. 43).

be that Jehu was going beyond his remit in extending the purge of Ahab's house to Judah, and for this he was later abhorred (Hos. 1:4). Later, however, the elimination of Athaliah was considered a justified extension of the divine punishment (11:16; *cf.* 8:18, 26).

29. This verse is hardly 'a corrected dating' by a late reviser, but co-cordinates the Judean calendar with that of Israel to indicate that he had ruled between eleven and twelve years (*cf.* p. 47).

c. Jezebel killed (9:30–37). This event is specially added to show the complete fulfilment of Elijah's prediction (1 Ki. 21:23) and to demonstrate the outcome of the disastrous influence she had brought on Israel and the evil policies she had pursued.

30. To paint the eyes with stibium (Heb. *pûk*; 'antimony', Arab. *qhl*) was to darken round them to give an enlarged effect. She was not necessarily acting coquettishly and her statement 'Is it peace?' could be a sincere, not sarcastic, question (see on vv. 17–22 above). Her request may have been made in the hope of some agreement. If that is so, the reference to Zimri was not to that short-lived usurper (1 Ki. 16:18–20) which would, to say the least, have been tactless. Her request was just that, and is possibly a play on a rare word for 'hero' (Ugar. *dmr*). To have *looked out of a window* does not necessarily mean that she acted in a shameless fashion as a prostitute. Such scenes shewing cultic figures carved in ivories found at Samaria and at Nimrud may not be applicable here.

32. The Hebrew 'Who is with me, who?' was interpreted as 'Who are you, come down with me' (Gk.) or 'Who is on my side?' (RSV) a general call for support which was answered by a few 'officers' (see on 1 Ki. 22:9, Heb. *sārîs*) not necessarily by eunuchs (EVV) who acted as harem attendants.

33. Following her fall, Jehu trampled her to death under his horses' hooves, after which dogs ate her edible remains.

36–37. After reflection Jehu appears to have determined on burial since it was believed that an unburied corpse and unhallowed memory were an evil omen and a major insult. There is no certainty that the delay in his decision was caused by a conference (*ate and drank*, v. 34) with the community (as Gray).

d. The extermination of the royal families of Israel and Judah and of the Baal worshippers (10:1–36). The history is here concerned to show the zeal of Jehu, acting as the divine agent, to obliterate completely all descendants and relatives of Ahab and Amaziah who might perpetuate evil of any type in opposition to God in both Israel and Judah (vv. 1–14). Jehu also acted to forestall any continuing blood feud and to protect his newly founded dynasty. He also massacred Baal worshippers in Samaria (vv. 15–27). These actions were considered to go beyond Jehu's remit and were severely disapproved of by Hosea (1:4). Many commentators wish to delete references to these horrible events as simply carried out in fulfilment of God's prophetic word (*e.g.* vv. 10, 17) or they apologize for it (vv. 19, 23). Whatever our present view of such action, the elimination of rivals was customary in biblical times in Israel and among her neighbours and conforms to the historian's philosophy.

The apparent discrepancy between verse 20 and Hosea 1:4 which condemns Jehu's action could be explained in a number of ways: (i) though Jehu had carried out the divine directive (9:1–10), he had killed more people than had been called for; (ii) this may show more a desire for personal advancement than obedience to God; (iii) although checking Baal worship, for which he was commended and for which his immediate successors were spared judgment (10:30), his lifestyle showed (iv) that he took no positive steps to reform Israel by acting wholeheartedly according to the law of the LORD (10:29, 31); (v) he implicated others in the affair (v. 6). Thus four generations later judgment fell on his own royal house, just as he himself had brought the dynasty of Omri to an end (Ho. 1:4).[1]

i. The end of Ahab's family (10:1–11). The extant male members (*sons*) of Ahab's family could well number *seventy*. The number could also symbolically represent a dynasty as seventy years does the span from grandfather to grandson. The dynasty of Panammuwa of Sam'al was rubbed out by one man who massacred seventy of his kinsman, according to an eighth

---

[1] L. J. Wood, *Hosea*, Expositor's Bible Commentary 7 (Grand Rapids: Zondervan, 1985), p. 171; D. A. Hubbard, *Hosea* TOTC (Leicester: IVP, 1989), p. 62.

century BC text.[1] Seventy was the number of Jacob's descendants in Egypt (Gn. 46:27), as of Noah who repopulated the earth (Gn. 10), of the elders (Nu. 11:16), and of the total family of Gideon (Jdg. 9:5). The large numbers would certainly cover all those likely to seek reprisals or have any legitimate claim to the throne.[2]

1–2. The *letters* follow the standard literary form of addressee and brief message introduced by *he said* since they were often written by a scribe to be read aloud by or to the recipient. More than one copy might be needed for despatch even to different recipients within the same town of origin. They were sent to (i) the 'city rulers' (RSV) of Jezreel (Vulg. and some Gk. MSS read 'the city'), perhaps those associated with Naboth's trial (*cf.* 1 Ki. 21:8) but more likely the military hierarchy; (ii) to the secular elders, formerly tribal leaders, but now part of the royal administration of justice, and on this occasion (iii) to the palace *guardians* or 'tutors' (NEB) of the royal family. *A fortified city* is here probably Samaria (*cf.* NEB 'cities' against most Heb. MSS).

3–5. The challenge was no bluff, for it called for them to select, nominate and publically support a rival to Jehu. Knowing Jehu's previous actions, 'he who was over the house', *i.e.* the chief *palace administrator* equivalent to prime minister (see on 1 Ki. 4:6) and other officials all of whom were crown-appointees immediately wrote to submit (*we are your servants*, *cf.* Jos. 9:8) and to protest that 'we will not cause/let anyone else to rule'.

6. The second letter may contain deliberate ambiguity, for the word *heads* (MT *rā'šê*) can also mean 'chiefs'. Many versions omit the Hebrew ('the sons [plural] of your lords . . .' so NEB, RSV, NIV) which, if included, would remove any doubt, as the outcome does when the actual heads were brought in (v. 8).

7. The carrying out of the harsh order was the work of the notables or *leading men* (v. 6) who included *the guardians* (v. 5). So Elijah's prophecy that every male in Ahab's family would be cut off was now fulfilled (1 Ki. 21:21).

8. It was contemporary custom throughout the ancient east

---

[1] G. A. Cooke, *A Text-book of North-Semitic Inscriptions* (Oxford: Oxford University Press, 1903), p. 62.

[2] F. C. Fensham, 'The Numeral Seventy in the OT and the Family of Jerubaal, Ahab, Panamuwa and Athirat', *PEQ* 109, 1977, p. 115.

to 'pile-up' (REB) the heads of captured rebels by the main city gate as a public warning against rebellion.[1]

9. Jehu, in a formal assembly (*stood before all the people*), either absolved the people from blame for the holocaust (*you are innocent*, Heb. 'righteous') on the grounds that it was a fore-ordained action or put the onus on them to decide whether his action had their approval ('you are fair judges. If I conspired against my master and killed him, who put all these to death?' NEB), thus they had already implicated themselves.

10–11. This is no mere editorial intrusion but a typical emphasis on the divine sanction for Jehu's deeds and on the fulfilment of repeated prophecies (*cf.* 1 Ki. 21:20–24, 29; 2 Ki. 9:7–10). *No survivor* (*cf.* v. 14; Dt. 3:3; Nu. 21:35; Jb. 18:19). In destroying those outside Ahab's family including all the notables, the *chief men* (*gᵉdōlāw*, 'nobles'), Jehu exceeded the classes whose death had been foretold. To read 'kinsmen' (*gôʾᵃlāw*, Burney, Gray) would require a change of text from *notables* (*cf.* v. 6, *gᵉdôlāw*). That the king's *close friends* (*mᵉyudāʿîm*) were included may be an indication of a link between court practices in Samaria and Canaan (Akkad. *mudû*).[2]

ii. The massacre of Ahaziah's family (10:12–14). It is likely that the Judean princes were returning from Jezreel before the atrocities there and at Samaria were known to them. Their visit could be explained by their relationship with the Omride house through the queen mother (2 Ki. 9:30).

12. *Beth Eked of the Shepherds*, a proper name (as LXX, *cf.* Je. 41:7), has been linked with Beit Qad, five kilometres northeast of Jenin. REB takes it as 'a shepherd's shelter' and the Targum as 'meeting-house' (Arab. *ʿakad*).

14. On *forty-two* see 2 Kings 2:24.

iii. Jehu meets Jehonadab (10:15–17). This information is introduced to explain their later action together (v. 23) though some take it as an artificial note to show that Jehu received support from a strict puritanical sect.

---

[1] A. K. Grayson, *Assyrian Royal Inscriptions* 2 (Wiesbaden: Harrassowitz, 1976), p. 161; *ARAB* I. 213, 215, 219; *cf.* 2 Sa. 4:8.

[2] F. I. Andersen, 'The Socio-Juridical Background of the Naboth Incident', *JBL* 85, 1966, p. 50.

15. The Rechabites originated among the Kenites (1 Ch. 2:55, *cf.* Jdg. 4:11–12) and are generally thought to have harked back to the supposed purity of a nomadic simple lifestyle in the desert which stood for the following of Yahweh better than later urbanism. They abstained from wine. *Jehonadab* was remembered as the leader of this conservative movement (Je. 35:6, 14–16). Some believe the Rechabites were craft workers in metal.[1] Josephus (*Ant.* ix.6.6) makes Jehonadab to be a longstanding friend of Jehu so that their association would not alarm the Baal priests in view of their known standing in the community. In the question 'Is it good with your heart as my heart is with your heart?', the text asks if they are allied in this matter (*Are you in accord with me?*). The act of 'giving ... the hand', *i.e.* shaking hands, is shown on Assyrian reliefs as a sign of agreement by equal parties pledging themselves to each other (*cf.* Ezr. 10:19; Ezk. 17:18).[2]

16. Jehu now had support to show his *zeal for the LORD* in deeds, as Elijah had done (1 Ki. 19:10, 14). This was not fanaticism (as Gray, p. 560) but an overacting eagerness to complete a God-given task. *He had him ride in his chariot* (RSV, NIV singular; MT 'they made him ride.') to show their association in public.

17. A repetition or summary for emphasis (*cf.* 1 Ki. 15:29).

iv. The worshippers of Baal killed (10:18–27). This account tells of a great destruction of the Baal worship, its followers and the temple erected by Ahab and Jezebel (1 Ki. 16:31–32). It was accomplished by trickery (v. 19), *deceptively* (NIV; Heb. '*qb*) and using 'subtilty' (AV) and 'with cunning' (RSV). The same verb occurs in Jacob's name (Gn. 25:26; 27:35–36). As Elijah had summoned all the prophets of Baal (1 Ki. 18:19) so Jehu now calls together all the 'worshippers'. This is a better translation than *ministers*, who would be included (NIV; MT '*bd* means 'to serve, worship, minister'). The call was based on a proclamation of a special feast day, used by Jehu perhaps as a pretext for challenging the religious dignitaries (*summon*) just as he had already the secular rulers (vv. 1–6). There may be an oral play on words between 'worship' (*'ābad*) and 'slaughter' (*'ibbad*), as in verse 19.

[1] R. S. Frick, 'The Rechabites Reconsidered', *JBL* 90, 1971, pp. 279–287.
[2] The Nimrud throne dais. D. Oates, 'The Excavations at Nimrud (Kalhu) (1962)', *Iraq* 25, 1963, pp. 21–22, pl. VII c.

20. The compulsory summons was for a closed or restricted session *in camera* (MT *ʿᵃṣārâ*), so that the building was crammed full (lit. from 'one mouth to the other').

22. The wearing of special (usually white or red) garments adds to the solemnity of the occasion, since they were provided by the *keeper of the wardrobe* (AV 'him that was over the vestry'). The word for robes (*meltāḥâ*) only occurs here and of the clothes put round Jeremiah to lift him from a cistern (38:11).

24. There is some ambiguity here, since *they went in* (RSV after LXX has singular 'he', *i.e.* Jehu) could refer to Jehu and Jehonadab, or to the ministers of Baal, or both. On *your life for his life* see Joshua 2:14, 1 Kings 20:39.

25. The person who made the sacrifice is not stated, it may be indefinite ('one made'), NIV supplies *Jehu*. The text does not say that Jehu acted as sacrificing priest (*cf.* 1 Ki. 8:5). The *guards* were the royal escort or 'outrunners' (*cf.* 1 Ki. 1:5) and *the officers* were the royal adjutants ('third officer', *šālišîm*, see on 2 Ki. 7:2). They seemed to have moved on 'into the city' (*ʿîr*) after throwing the people out. This explanation seems better than taking this word uniquely to be *the inner shrine* (NIV; Gray finds an analogous Ugaritic word *gr*, but this is doubtful) or 'the keep of the temple' (NEB). Others looted the temple, removing the cult-objects which would be easier smashed outside.

26-27. The major pagan ritual objects were sacred pillars (*maṣṣᵉḇ̄ôṭ*) or standing stones (AV 'images'). If it were not the associated poles sacred to Baal's consort Asherah which were burned (so NEB changes the text to 'sacred pole', *cf.* 1 Ki. 14:15) then the stones (without warrant some change to *miz-bēaḥ*, 'place of sacrifice, altar') must have been fragmented by heating, much as happened to the Moabite stone when found in 1868. The fate of the temple is not clear, except that its use was changed to a dumping place (*mōḥār'ôṭ* only occurs here) which on doubtful etymology is taken to be 'a place of dung', *i.e.* a *latrine* (AV 'draught house') or 'privy', an old word for a public lavatory. Some associate the word with 'market-place' (Akkad. *mahīru*).

v. Résumé of Jehu's achievements (10:28–36). The assessment of Jehu's reign underscores the good (the *right*, v. 30) yet without neglecting to give an honest appraisal of his failures

(vv. 29, 31). An explanation is given of the longevity of this new dynasty (102 years), longer than any other in Israel through Jehoahaz, Joash, and Jeroboam to Zechariah. The viewpoint of the later historian is clear in reproving Jehu in that he *was not careful to* 'walk in' (NIV, *keep*) *the law*, that is, he did not conduct his life according to God's principles. 'He seems to have been driven more by a political desire to secure his own position on the throne of the Northern Kingdom than by a desire to serve the LORD. In this he was guilty of using God's judgment on the house of Ahab to satisfy his self interest.'[1] Nonetheless Israel, like any failing believer, was granted unique mercy amid God's rigid principle of retributive justice. God will triumph even through the unconscious efforts of those who do not acknowledge him and only gradually brought his predicted judgment to bear (vv. 31–32).

32–33. Meanwhile the Arameans took advantage of the new political situation in Israel and the cessation of pressure from the Assyrians, engaged elsewhere, to *reduce* or 'make gashes in' (MT) Israelite territory making attacks on their northern border and regaining land east of Jordan which had been so often the area of contention between them. *Aroer* may be modern Khirbet 'Arā'ir, four kilometres east of the Medaba to Kerak road on the north bank of the Wadi Meyīb (River Arnon), the traditional southern limit of Israel (Dt. 2:36). We know too little of the history of Moab to question the reliability of these statements, and Moab itself could have been weak at this time. The region was certainly regained by the days of Jeroboam II (2 Ki. 14:25).

34. The *other events* would include Jehu's submission to Shalmaneser III of Assyria in 841 BC (Black Obelisk Inscriptions; *IBD*, p. 242). *All his achievements*; *cf.* 1 Kings 10:6. The phrase usually refers to warfare. Some have argued that Jehu regained Moab for Israel.

35–36. It is not usual for the historian to place the length of reign at the end. His intention may be to underscore the start of the long dynasty (*cf.* v. 30).

---

[1] J. R. Vannoy in *NIV Study Bible* (London: Hodder & Stoughton, 1985), p. 542.

IV. THE HISTORY OF JUDAH AND ISRAEL TO THE FALL OF THE NORTHERN KINGDOM (2 Ki. 11:1 – 17:41)

The history continues with Judah and with the line of David almost extinguished through its association with the Baal-allied northern regime. There, despite a temporary resurgence under Jeroboam II, Israel is gradually weakened by Assyrian pressure and with the fall of Samaria ceases to be a viable kingdom. Throughout this very disturbed period God provides his spokesmen, Isaiah and Micah to Judah and Amos and Hosea to Israel.

A. Athaliah takes over Judah (11:1–20)

Following Jehu's coup in the north, Athaliah tried to save something for Ahab's family by trying to eradicate the Davidic dynasty in Judah. It looked as if the promised line of the Messiah (2 Sa. 7:11, 16; 1 Ki. 8:25) would fail. That it did not was due to the efforts of the high priest who, with the people, renewed the covenant with God.

i. Athaliah's plot (11:1–3). *Cf.* 2 Chronicles 22:10–13; Josephus, *Ant.* ix.7. Athaliah, as Ahab's daughter, had married Jehoram (2 Ki. 8:18). By destroying 'all the royal line' (NEB) or 'stock' (JB) who had not already been slaughtered (2 Ki. 10:10–14; 2 Ch. 22:1, 8–9) she may, as queen mother, have had power in her own right to rule until a successor to the throne was elected.[1] The variants in the name Atalyah (Heb. vv. 13–18) and Atalyahu elsewhere are not indications of different sources, for such occur commonly in personal names ending -yah or -yahu in the same source. Athaliah's rule is treated as a usurpation or interruption, so the usual introduction to a normal Judean reign is omitted. The wife of the high priest *Jehosheba* (Jehoshabeath in 2 Ch. 22:11) was a daughter of Jehoram through another wife than Athaliah. She was probably the half-sister of Ahaziah and the infant Joash was her nephew. *J(eh)oash* ('Yah[weh] gave') is identical in name with the contemporary Israelite king (13:9–10, *cf.*

[1] This has now been questioned by Z. Ben-Barak (Paper read to *SBL*, Birmingham, 1988).

12:1). The name is also found in the Lachish ostraca and later Elephantine papyri. Jehosheba may have lived in the priest's quarters adjacent to the temple. Josephus (*Ant.* ix.7.1) says that the *bedroom* where the child and his nurse hid was a room where spare furniture and mattresses were stored. She *stole away* the child; the Hebrew *gānaḇ* means to 'kidnap' (Gn. 40:15; Dt. 24:7) and occurs in the eighth commandment, 'you shall not steal' (Ex. 20:15). The child was *about to be murdered* — by such a narrow margin the lamp of David (see on 1 Ki. 11:36; Ps. 132:17) was almost extinguished. But God had promised that he would never fail to provide an heir to David (Ps. 89:36).

ii. Jehoiada's plan (11:4–8). Jehoiada took the army company commanders, probably of the royal guard, the royal bodyguard and the royal escort into his confidence when he *made a covenant with them* (NEB 'agreement', REB 'compact') under oath. The Carites were mercenaries from Caria in southwest Asia Minor and may be identified with the Kerethites in the royal bodyguard of David (2 Sa. 20:23; *Karî*). The account in Chronicles (2 Ch. 23:1) names the commanders and the recruitment of Levites and heads of families ('clans'). The plan was for the five companies of priests, including two that had gone off duty after a week's service and the one on duty, all to be in the temple together without suspicion at a major Sabbath festival. Meanwhile the guards from the royal palace (leaving that clear, v. 13) and others would be able to protect the young king at his public appearance.

6. The *Sur Gate* may be identical with the Foundation Gate in the outer temple court (2 Ch. 23:5 reads *y^esôḏ* there) rather than take this as an error for Horse (*sûs*) Gate (*cf.* vv. 16, 19). The Talmud (Erubin 22c) defines it as the east gate of the temple court where the unclean were turned back. The text has after *the temple* a reference here to Massah, taken by some to be a proper name of a location but omitted by LXX, RSV, NEB, *cf.* 'to be a barrier' (RV). The AV 'that it be not broken down' is based on a Jewish commentary, as is 'from destruction' (Rashi). Other unlikely suggestions include 'relieving one another' (Gray) or 'warding off the people' (Keil). *The gate behind the guard* is not locatable, but it must be remembered that the temple and palace complexes were adjacent, with many guarded doors between them.

iii. The plot as carried out (11:9–12). The groups of priests were supported by the army, whose commanders, to avoid suspicion and in accordance with custom, entered the temple unarmed. The men were drawn up in ranks with the royal escort (*rāṣîm*) and their officers armed from the weapons already in the temple itself. Some of those had been dedicated there by David as spoils of war (2 Sa. 8:7–8) some were replacements for lost articles (1 Ki. 14:26–28). The spear (MT is singular, but *cf*. 2 Ch. 23:9, plural) could have been a royal symbol or standard. There were thus sufficient arms to preclude an attack on the young king. The guard formed a semi-circle outside the temple building and the altar in the courtyard from south to north (v. 11).

This chapter includes a unique and complete account of the installation of a king in Judah. Following the anointing, a characteristic of the charismatic kings of the 'Davidic tradition',[1] the crowning is followed by a formal covenant ceremony in the temple. This takes the form already made traditional in the Mizpah covenant (1 Sa. 10:17–25). The monarchic covenant is made by the LORD's representative Jehoiada who anointed Joash amid public acclamation (v. 12). The covenant had a political aspect between king and people, and also a religious aspect, being between God (Yahweh), king and people (v. 17).[2]

The coronation ceremony (as now known also from the detailed ceremony recorded for several ancient Near Eastern kings)[3] took place in stages, first in an inner sanctuary and then as a presentation to a wider group of representatives outside. In Judah the *crown* (*nēzer*), the covenant and perhaps the anointing, were unique. Saul had been crowned and given an armlet (2 Sa. 1:10;[4] so RSV emends here). Some interpret the text to say that as well as the crown the *covenant* or 'testimony' (AV, MT *'ēdût*) was put 'over' or 'upon him' since both are governed by 'he gave'. This could affirm that the divinely chosen king was not an absolute monarch, but as Yahweh's anointed was under the law. The full meaning of the term

---

[1] Z. Weisman, 'Anointing as a Motif in the Making of the Charismatic King', *Biblica* 57, 1976, pp. 378–398.

[2] Z. Ben-Barak, '*The Manner of the King*' and '*The Manner of the Kingdom*' (PhD Hebrew University, Jerusalem, 1972), pp. 200–232.

[3] D. J. Wiseman, *Nebuchadrezzar and Babylon* (Oxford: British Academy, 1985), pp. 19–21.

[4] S. Yeivin, '*Eduth*', *IEJ* 24, 1974, pp. 17–20.

here is not sure. *Covenant* may well indicate a copy of the ten commandments and the Mosaic covenant, especially the regulations regarding the obligations of kingship (Dt. 17:14–20; 1 Sa. 10:17–25). The covenant promises made to David (2 Sa. 7:12–16) could have been included if this is taken to be a formal agreement drawn up for the occasion, but this is not proven. Most translations therefore add to the Hebrew text a verb, *e.g.* 'gave' (AV) or *presented him with* (NIV, NEB) a copy of the covenant terms (*'ēḏûṯ*; 'the warrant', NEB). This is the basis for the British custom of presenting the monarch with a copy of the Bible during the coronation service. Others have attempted to interpret the word as 'head cover' or an ornament like the winged disk.[1]

12. They *proclaimed him king, i.e.* Jehoiada, the priests and the representatives of the people (*cf.* 2 Ch. 23:11). On *anointed* see 1 Kings 1:34, 39; on the acclamation *Long live the King!* see also 1 Kings 1:25; 2 Kings 9:13; *cf.* 1 Samuel 10:24.

iv. The death of Athaliah (11:13–16). *Cf.* 2 Chronicles 23:12–15. This passage has been judged to be from a separate source because of seeming divergencies (but see on vv. 1, 20). The assembly of *the people* who ratified the accession were joining with the *guards* (these were the 'royal escort') in acclamation when Athaliah emerged. The seven-year old king Joash (v. 21) was *standing by the pillar* (MT *'ammûḏ*) near the temple entrance (2 Ch. 23:13; Ezk. 46:2), probably the pillars Jachin and Boaz taken as covenant symbols (see 1 Ki. 7:21). A precise location is required here rather any rereading of the text to 'on a *dais*' or 'platform' (NEB *'ōmēḏ*) or to 'his place' (*'om^eḏô, cf.* 2 Ch. 34:31); nor are 'singers' (*šārîm, cf.* 2 Ch. 23:13) necessary here instead of *officers* or 'captains' (*śārîm*).

14. *All the people of the land* (*'am hā'āreṣ*) has been much discussed. It is a Judean concept with no precise definition.[2] These folks had some judicial authority (2 Ki. 21:9; Je. 36) and were represented in relation to the appointments of, or by, the king (*cf.* 2 Ki. 14:21; 21:24). They were not solely property owners or the proletariat (hence NEB 'populace'); nor

---

[1] S. Yeivin, *ibid.*; S. Dalley, 'The god Ṣalmu and the winged disk', *Iraq* 48, 1986, p. 92.

[2] E. W. Nicholson, 'The Meaning of the Expression עם הארץ in the Old Testament', *JSS* 10, 1965, pp. 59–66.

were they a sacral community (Gray). They certainly were
people of the land, including farmers.

15. The priest ordered Athaliah to be escorted out to avoid
defiling the holy house of God. *Between the ranks* is preferable
to AV 'without the ranges' or NEB 'outside the precincts'. The
word (MT *šᵉdērôṯ*, as Akkad. *sidirtu*) is used of an orderly rank
or row. This was to ensure that no-one should try to break
through to rescue or follow Athaliah.

16. The horse-gate was at the rear of the palace (*cf*. 2 Ki.
23:11; Je. 31:40; Neh. 3:28). The ramp leading up into a
stable yard is depicted on Assyrian reliefs from Nineveh.

v. The renewal of the covenant (11:17–20). As earlier with
David (2 Sa. 5:3; 7:8–16), and later with Josiah (2 Ki. 23:3), an
essential part of the return of God's people to true worship
and service was the renewal of the covenant (Ex. 24). The king
and people must now bind themselves to be, and to act as, the
people of God (Dt. 4:20; 27:9–10). The heart of this covenant
is that Yahweh will be their God and they his holy people (Dt.
14:2), a truth which is applicable not only to faithful Jews but
also to Christians (2 Cor. 6:16; Heb. 8:10; 1 Pet. 2:10).

The *covenant* was reaffirmed when it had been broken (*cf*.
Ex. 34, the golden calf; 2 Ki. 23, Manasseh) or after foreigners
had been married (Ezr. 10:3). It was also renewed at times of
change in national leadership, by Joshua (Jos. 8:30–35); David
(1 Ch. 11:3); Hezekiah (2 Ch. 29:10) and here and at moments
of major national moment (1 Ki. 8; Je. 34:8; 2 Ch. 15:12).

The essential requirement of a covenant between *king and
people* was for the king to bind himself to rule according to
God's law. This is omitted in 2 Chronicles 23:16 (but *cf* 1 Ki.
12:12; 2 Ki. 23:3). It was not just a political, as opposed to a
religious, covenant but was also a public commitment to carry
out the covenant obligations.

18. The obligation to serve Yahweh alone necessitated the
destruction of Baalism, its places of sacrifice (*altars*), and all
representational images or *idols* including doubtless the
Asherah poles. The historian would view this as the counterpart of the abolition of Baal worship in Samaria (10:17–18).
His comment on this was that they smashed it 'rightly' or
'completely' (MT *hêṭēḇ*, NIV *to pieces*) perhaps linking it with his
commendation of a godly ruler 'doing the right' (see Introduction, pp. 48–49). *Mattan's* name could have been 'Gift (of

Baal)' but not necessarily so (Je. 38:1), for Mattaniah is 'Gift of Yah(weh)' (*cf*. Mattanah, Nu. 21:18).

20. There was no opposition from dissident elements in the city of Jerusalem, for 'the city made no move' (JB) and all *was quiet*. This verse must be read as pluperfect (*Athaliah had been slain*) and there is no need to see here an account of her death differing from verse 16.

B. Joash of Judah (11:21 – 12:21)

i. Summary of reign (11:21 – 12:3). *Cf.* 2 Chronicles 24. The historian follows his usual pattern with the introduction (11:21 – 12:3) giving details of accession, synchronism with Israel, length and place of reign, king's mother's name and assessment. The latter was that *he did right* but it is qualified as only initially and not completely. Before the concluding formulae (vv. 19–20) we are given only two selected items; the repair of the temple (vv. 4–16) and temple tribute paid to Hazael. Both are of special interest to our historian, the latter as punishment for Joash's apostasy. This account needs to be read in conjunction with that of the Chronicler (2 Ch. 24).

1. The MT begins chapter 12 with 11:21. *Joash* as the name for the Judean king is so read by NIV for the fuller 'Jehoash' (RSV) to differentiate him from the king of Israel bearing the same name (13:10–25). As a *seven year old* he needed a tutor who may well have given advice in competition with Athaliah. The *forty year* reign (835–796 BC) is not a general span (as Jdg. 5:31; 8:28), but realistic (see on 1 Ki. 11:42). His father's marriage to *Zibiah* ('Gazelle') may have been to gain tribal support on the Negeb border with Edom.[1]

2. Joash *did what was right* (see Introduction, pp. 48–49) *all the years* or 'so long as' (NEB) Jehoiada helped him (so 2 Ch. 24:2). The older man was respected for this and was eventually buried among the kings (2 Ch. 24:15–16). When the priest became old and Joash independent, the king, alas, followed evil ways (2 Ch. 24:17–27). The benefit of an experienced spiritual advisor may be seen by Joash's departure from the faith when Jehoiada's influence is removed.

3. Joash's life is evaluated with qualifications, *cf*. Asa (1 Ki. 15:14) and Jehoshaphat (1 Ki. 22:43) where the worship of

---

[1] S. Yeivin, 'The Divided Kingdom', *WHJP* IV.1, p. 150.

Yahweh at high places opened the door to divergence from true worship because of pagan practices performed at these sites (*cf.* 1 Ki. 3:2–3).

ii. Temple repairs (12:4–16). The maintenance of the main national temple was the responsibility of the king, for the temple served also as a chapel royal. All ancient Near Eastern monarchs record their care for such shrines. Joash, whether from poverty or design, transferred executive responsibility to the temple priests. Much work was needed on the 124-year-old building following the depredations of Athaliah and her son's actions in breaking up the temple of Yahweh and transferring the objects to the shrines of Baal (2 Ch. 24:7).

4. The normal temple income was from: (i) daily sacred dues received (RSV, JB, 'holy things', NEB 'holy gifts', NIV *sacred offerings*); (ii) poll-tax assessment of half a shekel for each registered male in the census list (Heb. *'ōḇēr*; as in Ex. 30:11–14; *cf.* Mt 17:24); (iii) payments for vows taken (Lv. 27:1–25); (iv) voluntary gifts or 'the money which comes upon a man's heart to bring' (MT; *cf.* Lv. 22:18–23; Dt. 16:10), *i.e.* given spontaneously.

5. These monies were also received by the priests from those who (according to 2 Ch. 24:5) collected them from all the towns of Judah. The official concerned may have been a 'business assessor' (Gray) rather than 'his acquaintance' (RSV, Heb. *makkārô*, vv. 6, 8), which could be interpreted as a class of temple official (Ugar. *mkrm*) or someone 'who did business' (Akkad. *makāru*). NIV renders *one of the treasurers*, and NEB, on the basis of post-biblical Hebrew, 'from his own funds' (which is unlikely). Originally the priests received all the revenue and used it to maintain the temple services and carry out necessary repairs.

Lack of zeal by the priests (2 Ch. 24:5) and perhaps lack of supervision by the ageing Jehoiada (who was to die aged 124) led Joash, now aged thirty (v. 6), to make new arrangements (vv. 9–16) for making good the repairs needed (v. 7, *damage*, 'breaches' AV). There seems also to be concern over possible mishandling of financial affairs which ever brings shame on God's house. Joash's transfer of responsibility to the whole people may have been directed to making the temple self-supporting and to get all the people involved in sharing in provision for God's work. The priests now relinquish both the collection of funds and the management of repairs on the fabric (vv. 7–8).

The breach between Jehoiada and Joash may have occurred about this time.

9. The location of the collection-box (MT 'box' or *chest*; Heb. *ʾᵃrôn*, v. 10; 'ark', AV) has been much discussed. It seems to have been put beside the main altar at its right side as seen from the entrance. Yet verse 9 (and 2 Ch. 24:8) implies that it was outside at the temple doorway. This has led to the suggestion that there was a threshold altar.[1] Others (JB and LXX Alexandrinus) read 'beside the pillar', *i.e.* by the Jachin column at the main entrance into the temple. Yet others seek to amend the text.

10–12. Three priests or groups of doorkeepers (2 Ki. 22:4, 8; *cf.* 25:18) were responsible for seeing that all gifts went into the box. The supervision and counting of the gifts was a combined operation of temple and state. The designation high priest is said to have originated with the second temple, but the earlier existence of a primate, as here, is attested in other cultures (*e.g.* Ras Shamra *rb khnm*, *cf.* 2 Ki. 25:18).

The *royal secretary* was not a fiscal officer and his presence implies that the palace had direct control of temple finances equally with clerical authorities. Since coinage did not become common until after the fifth century BC the silver objects and fragments were the *money* (RSV, NIV, Heb. 'silver').[2]

They *counted the money . . . and put it into bags*. This rendering of RSV, NIV transposes the verbs to make sense since the first verb (*ṣārar*, Heb. v. 11) was understood to be 'to wrap'. There is no word in MT for 'the bags' though the Chronicler reads *wayyāṣurū* as *wayeʿārû* 'they emptied it' (2 Ch. 24:11). A different verb *ṣrr* (Akkad. *ṣurrūru* 'to pour out') or *ṣûr* (= *ṣrr*, 'to melt') would make good sense. Silver was commonly melted down into ingots, so NEB 'they melted down the silver . . . and weighted it'. It was then readily available for payments and purchases. For the craftsmen see on 1 Kings 5:13–18.

When the people were assured that the money would really be used for the purpose for which it was given, they

[1] W. McKane, 'A Note on II Kings 12:10 (EVV 12:9)', *ZAW* 71, 1959, pp. 260–265.

[2] As in seventh-century Assyria, V. Hurowitz, 'Another Fiscal Practice in the Ancient Near East: 2 Kings 12:15–17 and a Letter to Esarhaddon (LAS 277)', *JNES* 45, 1986, pp. 289–294.

responded generously and so similar arrangements were continued by Josiah (22:3–7).

13–15. The prohibition of using the precious metal for ornamental and ritual objects rather than the fabric may imply some earlier misuse. It happened that there were extra funds after the essential repairs had been completed, which were then put to this decorative use (2 Ch. 24:14). The giving of block grants to the foremen depended on their *honesty* (Heb. 'faithfulness'). Our use of money is always a test of faithfulness.

16. Income from *guilt offerings* ('āšām, Heb. v. 17) used to make restitution or atone for offences against others (Lv. 4:5), and *sin offerings* to atone for sins against God, was left to the priests (Lv. 5:16; 6:5; Nu. 5:7–10). Such sacrifices were known and offered before the time of the Exile.

iii. Annalistic details (12:17–21). There is no extra-biblical source for these events. Assyrian pressure may have been off Aram now, allowing Hazael to raid, via a weakened Israel, as far as Gath. Such swift movement can be compared with Shalmaneser III's expedition in 841 BC which was met by Jehu (*cf*. 10:34).

The historian in Kings emphasizes the punishment and in Chronicles the sin that caused it. An Aramean group defeated a large Judean army (2 Ch. 24:24) and had to be bought off. Joash was badly wounded at this time and this was taken as evidence of divine displeasure (2 Ch. 24:25). The location of *Gath* is not known, for excavations at Tell el 'Areini, about thirty kilometres northeast of Gaza, failed to find evidence of Gath, one of five principal Philistinian cities. Other possible sites to its south have been suggested. See Map, *IBD*, p. 543.

The *other events* of the reign (vv. 19–21) are given in greater detail in Chronicles (2 Ch. 22:10 – 24:27). The murder of Joash by his *officials* (v. 21) or servants implies that it may have been the result of disaffection following the defeat by Hazael. It was more likely direct revenge on Joash for having stoned to death Jehoiada's son Zechariah in the temple after he had criticized the king. The location could be a garrison or other site at the *Millo* at the east of Jerusalem (1 Ki. 9:15; 11:27 *cf.* Jdg. 9:6). *On the road down to Silla* is omitted by LXX. NEB assumes it to be the descent to the Kidron Valley, others interpret Silla as 'ramp' (Heb. *mᵉsillâ*). The MT gives variants for one identical name for the two assassins, which is possible, both being distinguished by their patronymics. RSV, NEB read 'Jozachar', or with Chronicles (2 Ch. 24:25–26) take them to be Zabad and Jehozabad (again variants of a single name), sons of Ammonite and Moabite women who murdered Joash in his bed. It is noteworthy that he was buried in the City of David but not in the royal mausoleum (2 Ch. 24:25).

C. Jehoahaz of Israel (13:1–9)

The history continues through a period when the Northern Kingdom was sorely pressed by the Aramean state of Damascus (*cf.* v. 22). The main reason for this was that for a while Assyrian attention was diverted from the west both by campaigns on its northwest and eastern frontiers at the end of Shalmaneser III's reign, and by a great revolt in Nineveh and other Assyrian centres noted in the Eponym Chronicle for the years 827–822 BC. His successor Shamshi-Adad V (823–811 BC) had to win control nearer home and for a time the Assyrian domination of the west lapsed. This was Hazael's opportunity to harass Israel. The historian recounts the reign of Jehu's son within his given framework, with the introduction (vv. 1–2) followed by the oppression of Aram (v. 3) and the provision by God of a deliverer ('saviour') (vv. 4–6) retold in terms reminiscent of God's similar action at times of weakness and oppression under the 'Judges' (Jdg. 3:9, 15). After a note on the resultant weakness of Israel's army (v. 7), the narrative is ended with the normal details of the concluding formulae (vv. 8–9).

1. The *twenty-third year* (of the forty-year rule) *of Joash . . . of Judah* can be compared with his first year falling in the seventh year of Jehu (12:1), who died after twenty-eight years in Jehoash of Israel's twenty-second year. There is therefore no need to suspect different reckonings between the two kingdoms, Jehoahaz' reign therefore began in this twenty-third year.

2–3. For the sins of *Jeroboam* see on 1 Kings 12:26. Jehu's reformation was short-lived. The Hebrew 'all the days' need not imply 'continually' (RSV) or 'without intermission' (Gray) but rather 'for some years' (NEB) or possibly *for a long time* (NIV). Hazael's action was one of 'squeezing' Israel (see v. 22). Hazael may have died during this reign, for his son

Ben-Hadad (III) began to reign about 806 BC. God's anger aimed to discipline not destroy. He never abandons his people yet never ceases to express his displeasure at their erring ways (Rom. 9:22; 13:4–5).

Though commonly ascribed to a later editor, verses 4–6 are essential to explain the turning of God's anger away through prayer (Heb. *ḥillâ*, 'to beseech'; AV 'besought' rather than entreat the favour of God or 'tried to placate him', JB, NEB). The LORD's answer to these, as to many, prayers was not immediate but given in the following reign (vv. 22, 25).

5. The *deliverer* was not Elisha, nor even Jehoash (vv. 17, 19, 25), nor Jeroboam II who was later to roll back the oppressors (14:25–27), but Adad-nirari III of Assyria who in 802 and 796 BC marched back to the Mediterranean and took heavy spoil en route (see on v. 10). That the Israelites *lived in their own homes* does not necessarily imply that earlier they had been driven to the hills (Gray). Rather to 'dwell in tents' (MT: the tent being 'home', 1 Ki. 8:66) means they were undisturbed. God gave them peace round about.

6–7. Not only did the Israelites fail to turn away from Jeroboam's sins (for this see on 1 Ki. 12:31), but each one is held responsible for his own sin (Heb. 'walked', *i.e.* 'lived' is singular, *cf.* NIV *they continued in them*). The Asherah-pole remained standing in Samaria just as it had been set up there by Ahab (1 Ki. 16:33) but not noted as removed by Jehu (2 Ki. 10:27–28). Human defences are always weak and the depreciated state of Israel's army given here contrasts starkly with its contribution of but part of its resources (two thousand chariots and ten thousand men) to the coalition opposing Assyria at the Battle of Qarqar in 853 BC.

8. This concluding formulae is repeated in 2 Kings 14:15. It is not possible to state which of these is the original.

D. Jehoash of Israel (13:10–25)

i. Summary of reign (13:10–13). An Assyrian stela found at Tell Rimah, northern Mesopotamia, dated to the reign of Adadnirari III records his campaigns against Syria in 805–802 BC. Among the rulers bringing tribute he claims 'Jehoash the Samaritan' (*Yu-'a-su Sa-mer-ri-na-a*) by this also noting that the dynasty of Omri (*bīt Humrī*) had passed away. Some date this reference as 796 BC, but this is by no means sure.[1] The same Assyrian ruler dominated Damascus taking spoil from *Mar'i* (= Ben-Hadad III) whom he refers to in the previous line of the same stela by his Syrian name of Mar'i (see Additional Note on Hazael, p. 214).

This reign is entered here only with reference to its introductory (vv. 10–11) and closing formulae (vv. 12–13).

10. The *thirty-seventh* year (as MT) need not be changed to thirty-ninth (as some MSS and NEB) to coincide with 13:1, 14:1, since that includes a possible two year co-regency of Joash with his father in 789–796 BC.

12–13. These verses are repeated in 2 Kings 14:15–16 and are perhaps used here to make the record of this reign, without any detail (the war with Amaziah is given later in 14:8–14; 2 Ch. 25:17–24), conform to the historian's pattern. Some wish to delete it because of variants. But these may be deliberate, since Jeroboam 'sat on his throne' (NIV *Jeroboam succeeded*) could indicate that he deliberately took over the throne (*cf.* the Assyrian annals '*x* sat on the throne', implying a take-over, legitimate or not, compared with 'they caused *x* to sit on the throne' following the usual election procedure). 14:16 has the normal formula.

ii. The closing events of Elisha's life (13:14–21). 14. This final reference to Elisha after a ministry of more than sixty years does not give details of his terminal illness or its location. By contrast with Elijah, he was 'sick' rather than suffering. The visit provides a glimpse of the close relationship there should be between king and prophet. It is generally interpreted that the statement '*My father* . . .' is the word of the king anxious at the loss of the one who was a true prophet. Elisha was more of a protection to Israel than its army, though it would be unusual for the king to use the exact phrase employed by Elisha to Elijah (2 Ki. 2:12). It could be that these are the words of the dying prophet anticipating death.

15–19. A test of faith. There is no sure indication of the use of sympathetic or creative magic in the Old Testament, nor would such action be expected of Elisha. It is rather a symbolic action, like that of Joshua thrusting with a spear at Ai (Jos. 8:18). Similarly the shooting of arrows by Jonathan was a pre-arranged signal to David and no mere belomancy (1 Sa.

[1] S. Page, 'A Stela of Adad-nirari III and Nergal-ereš from Tell al Rimah', *Iraq* 30, 1968, p. 141, l. 8; *POTT*, pp. 145–146.

20:20–22). The act of Elisha in placing his hands on those of the king could be symbolic of unity of purpose or aim rather than of Yahweh's blessing on the coming war. The prophecy of victory over Aram at Aphek awakens memory of the earlier great victory for Israel there (1 Ki. 20:26–30). This attack on Aphek (Tell En Gev) may be marked by destruction level II there.[1] The extent of victory is limited by man's failure to persevere, so firing arrows into the ground only three times (perhaps using only half a quiver full) meant that Joash himself would not obliterate the enemy. It was left to Jeroboam to gain control of them (14:25, 28).

20–21. Elisha in death is claimed to possess the miraculous powers Elijah had in life (2 Ki. 4:32–37; 1 Ki. 17:21–24). This story must not be judged post-exilic on the basis of its unique character of because it is linked with a reference to the patriarchal covenant (v. 23). Also it is mere conjecture to assume that because Elijah had not died something unusual had to be recorded to Elisha's passing. 'His body prophesied when he was dead. As in his life he did wonders so in his death his deeds were marvellous' (Sirach 48:13–14).

Note the long gaps between periods of such miraculous manifestations in Scripture. As here, they appear to occur in greater number at times of national or church weakness. This was perhaps a symbol of the need for God's people to come to life again.

iii. A note on Israel – Aram relations (13:22–25). 23. This links the history with verses 3, 7, and emphasizes the LORD's *covenant* relation with his people in terms of his dealing with their ancestors. It would remind the hearer or reader of the covenant's clear provisions forecasting exile if his requirements were broken and yet of the promise of forgiveness and restoration when they turned from their evil ways. The former was to be fulfilled less than a century later when he let them go into exile from Samaria (2 Ki. 17:14–23).

Such punishment by banishment *from* the *presence* of God had been long foretold since Adam (Gn. 3:23) and the possibility reiterated (1 Ki. 8:47). Meanwhile God's long-suffering compassion and grace (*yāḥān*, 'shower mercy') and *concern* for his people would give time for repentance without which his

[1] *IEJ* 11, 1961, p. 193.

judgment must inexorably fall, though it was not his will that any should perish. His dealing with people in the time of Noah illustrates this (Gn. 6:13; *cf.* 7:11; 1 Pet. 3:20; 2 Pet. 2:5). On the human side the reluctance of Aram to invade Israel could be in part explained by the pressure Adad-nirari of Assyria was imposing on Damascus (see Additional Note on Hazael, p. 214),

To this day is evidence that this record predates the exile in Babylon (see Introduction, p. 57).

Millard has suggested that the deliverance of Israel from Aramean oppression at this time may have resulted from the request by Zakkur of Hamath and 'Anah of Assyria to intervene against Bar-Hadad, son of Hazael, of Aram.[1]

24. The last reference to Hazael in extra-biblical texts is 838 and the latest to his son Ben-Hadad III (as *mar'i*) is 806 BC.

25. *The towns* recovered by Jehoash were probably west of Jordan (*cf.* 1 Ki. 20:34), since those east of Jordan were lost in Jehu's time (10:32–33) and not regained until Jeroboam did so (14:25). The defeat inflicted by Jehoash (Heb. here has the variant Joash) *three times* is recorded to show the fulfilment of the promise of verses 18–19.

E. Amaziah of Judah (14:1–22)

i. Summary of reign (14:1–7). The history continues in a way that well illustrates the author's freedom to arrange his sources according to his plan. The introduction with the normal data for a ruler in Judah (vv. 1–6) is followed by a brief report on the campaign against Edom (v. 7) and then continues the Jehoash narrative, from an Israelite viewpoint and, probably using a northern source, relating that king's invasion of Judah (vv. 8–14), after which the end of Jehoash's rule is given (vv. 15–16). Finally, additional details of Amaziah's life and assassination after Jehoash's own death are given (vv. 17–21). Many commentators see here the work of later revisers concentrating each on individual preconceptions such as reference to the ancestors (v. 3), the law of Moses (v. 6) or prophetic fulfilment (v. 25, DtrP), but the narrative stands well as a whole. It is noteworthy that throughout the historian

---

[1] For the Stela of Zakkur see now A. R. Millard, 'Israelite and Aramean History', *TynB* 41, 1990, pp. 273–274, *cf.* p. 264; 'The Homeland of Zakhur', *Semitica* 39, 1989, pp. 60–66.

here favours Amaziah against his Israelite contemporary.

1–2. The chronology fits if it includes a twenty-four year co-regency with his son Azariah, beginning *c.* 791 BC (v. 21, *cf.* 15:1–2). That would not be unduly long in relation to the fifty-two years reign attributed to Azariah. Some try to read 'nine' for *twenty-nine years*, but verse 17 is against this. In common with entries for Judah, his mother's name *Jehoaddin* (MT *Kᵉtîb*, and Gk.) is given (see Introduction, p. 47). Some Versions and Josephus (*Ant.* ix.9.1) read this with 2 Chronicles 25:1 as *Jehoaddan* 'Yah(u) has given delight' (NIV mg.).

3. Though the evaluation is of a king who did *what was right* the exception *but not* (MT *raq*, 'only') carries the reader back to David (who did the right 'except in the case of Uriah the Hittite', 1 Ki. 15:5) and 2 Chronicles 25:14–16 reminds us that Amaziah did not break free from pagan involvement. His faithful following of the LORD fell short of that of his predecessors Asa and Jehoshaphat (1 Ki. 15:11, 14; 22:43).

4. *The high places . . . were not removed.* See 1 Kings 15:14.

5–6. It seems that Amaziah had to struggle to gain control much as Solomon had done (*cf.* 1 Ki. 2:46, though the verb there is 'firm, settled' and here 'strong'). He eventually put to death his father's assassins (2 Ki. 12:20), which was common Near Eastern practice which all king's vassals and officials swore under oath to effect (*e.g.* Vassal-Treaties of Esarhaddon 672 BC ll. 302–315). Assyrian practice also treats the whole family as responsible. However, in contrast the humanizing tendency of the law is now followed in not putting children to death for their father's sin (singular, as Dt. 24:16). The reference to the *Book of the Law of Moses* is no later Deuteronomistic addition, but is the necessary explanation which would have been drawn at the time for such unusual behaviour. Those who follow the law of God will be distinctive.

7. The note from the archives on Judah regaining the control of Edom lost in the reign of Jehoram (8:20–22) does not give the detail available in 2 Chronicles 25:12 which implies that the *ten thousand* was the number killed, *i.e.* a whole army contingent (*cf.* 2 Ki. 13:7). The *Valley of Salt* was the perennial battlefield south of the Dead Sea in the northern Arabah. Here David had defeated Edom (2 Sa. 8:13; 1 Ch. 18:12; Ps. 60 title). *Sela* ('Rock') was not Petra, the Edom capital eighty kilometres south of the Dead Sea, but probably Silʿ, northwest of Buseirah, which commanded the King's

Highway.[1] Renaming a captured place as at *Joktheel* implied control over it. Such instances are rare in Israel, *e.g.* Canaanite Laish changed to Dan after occupation (Jdg. 18:29) and Kenath to Nobah (Nu. 32:42).

ii. Israel fights Judah (14:8–16). This Israelite account is used by the author without giving the background. Following hs victory over Edom, Amaziah had taken over captured Edomite deities and incorporated them in the cult in Jerusalem and thus incurred prophetic disapproval which foreboded judgment (2 Ch. 25:14–15). It could be also that mercenaries not required in the Judean army for the Edom venture had themselves raided Samaria or Israel (2 Ch. 25:13–24). In the historian's way of portraying his subject's major doings he, unusually here, does not describe them but clearly shows that he believed that Amaziah erred through pride following the victory (v. 10).

8. The call to *come, meet me face to face* was no mere call to a personal meeting, though 'face to face' includes this and is commonly used of a challenge to an encounter with God (Gn. 32:30; Ex. 33:11; Dt. 5:4 and in 1 Cor 13:12) NEB paraphrases 'to propose a meeting' (REB 'a confrontation'). The suggestion that it was a proposal for a treaty sealed by a marriage alliance depends on the fable which follows. Such a proposition would have taken Judah back to the Joram – Ahaziah situation (8:27) and is unlikely. It is more likely to be a challenge to war, for such a taunt often occurs in the initiation of conflict (1 Sa. 17:4ff).

9. The fable – a story not founded on fact but allied to parable and allegory – is found in many ancient literary collections, usually with examples of animals, trees and plants, as here. Some relate to inter-city quarrels. One, a form of proverb-riddle, occurs in a thirteenth century BC letter from Ras Shamra in which the kings of Carchemish and Ugarit correspond.[2] The form may be compared to Jotham's fable (Jdg. 9:8–15) and for other examples see possibly Isaiah 10:15; Ezekiel 17:3–8; 19:1–9. Jehoash views himself as the

---

[1] J. R. Bartlett, 'The Moabites and Edomites', *POTT*, p. 253 n. 55. Iron Age remains have been found here.

[2] J. Nougayrol, 'Textes Sumero-Accadiens des Archives et Bibliotheques privées d'Ugarit', *Ugaritica V*, 1968, pp. 108–109 No. 35; *cf.* D. Daube, *Ancient Hebrew Fables* (Oxford: Oxford University Press, 1973).

strong cedar and Amaziah as the little thistle easily trodden upon.

10. Success in Edom 'has gone to your head' (NEB). 'Boast in your triumph' but don't take me on too, gives a more vivid sense than *Glory in your victory*. Both the fable and its explanation are confirmed by the cautionary reply of Jehoash against 'engaging in strife' (Heb. *gārâ, cf. ask for trouble*) which would result 'in disaster' (NEB) to the Judean king and people. The Chronicler implies that Amaziah's failure to listen was made part of the chain of causes which God allowed to work to his downfall (2 Ch. 25:20).

11. This *Beth Shemesh* (Tell er-Rumeilah) lies about thirty-two kilometres west of Jerusalem (1 Ki. 4:9) near the border with Dan (Jos. 15:10; 1 Sa. 6:9) *in Judah, i.e.* distinguished from the place of the same name in Naphtali. Beth-Shemesh (destruction level IIc) may have been looted at this time by Jehoash.

13–14. The attack on Jerusalem. No details are given as to where, or for how long, the king was held captive. It could be that at this time his son was appointed acting regent (v. 21).

The layout of Jerusalem at this time is unknown, but the *Ephraim Gate* would be in the north wall (Neh. 12:39) corresponding to the modern Damascus (Shechem) Gate, and the *Corner Gate* lay beyond the 180 m. breach to the northwest (Je. 31:–38; Zc. 14:10). It is nowhere stated precisely what was looted from the temple at this time and little may have been left since Hazael (2 Ki. 12:17–18), as earlier Shishak (1 Ki. 14:–25–26), had pillaged it.

The *hostages* (v. 14; the Heb. phrase *bᵉnē hataᵃrubôt* occurs only here and in the parallel 2 Ch. 25:24) were hardly pledges for war indemnity (scarcely recorded in Old Testament times) but rather high ranking officials taken as a guarantee for future loyal behaviour. It could be that if temple officials were among them, this was the situation in which some temple singers, exiled to the north and longing to be back in God's house, composed such psalms as 42–43.

15–16. The concluding formulae for Jehoash's reign may be re-inserted here (see on 13:12–13) to remind the reader of his reprieve after disaster.

iii. The end of Amaziah (14:17–22). The connection back to his own record (v. 7) is made with verse 17. The concluding formulae, begun in verse 18, are interrupted by the record of the plot against Amaziah. The conspirators' names are not given, but appear to originate in the capital since Amaziah first fled to *Lachish* (modern Tell ed-Duweir, 55 kilometres southwest of Jerusalem[1]). Yeivin has suggested that Azariah (Uzziah) might have been involved since he did not punish the plotters.[2]

21–22. The election of Amaziah's son Azariah may refer to an earlier time when 'all the people had taken Azariah, when he was sixteen years old and had made him king' while Azariah had been a prisoner. If translated as 'had taken' this 'flashback' would link this to the fuller story of his reign in 15:1. The choice appears to be of a popular election (*cf.* 2 Ki. 11:14). The presence of Judah in *Elath*, at the northwest of the Gulf of Aqaba, is attested by a seal inscribed 'belonging to Jotham' found at Tell el-Khaleifeh.[3] That ancient fortified port was of immense importance to Judah then, as it is to Israel today. It maintained a trade with south Arabia which resulted in a south Arabian seal found at Bethel.[4] Control of the port of Elath seems to have soon been lost *c.* 730 BC to Aram, who later let it revert to the control of their allies Edom (16:6).

F. Jeroboam II of Israel (14:23–29)

The historian shows his selectivity by giving remarkably little space to this most illustrious, long reigning (793–753 BC) and prosperous king of Israel. Jeroboam, the fourth king of the dynasty of Jehu, followed up the victories of Jehoash over Ben-Hadad III of Aram (2 Ki. 13:25). He was able to carry on Jehoash's aggressive policy of expansion because the campaigns of Adad-nirari III had broken the heart of the Aramaean coalition and the Assyrians had now turned to

---

[1] This identification is confirmed, but see queries raised by G. I. Davies, 'Tell ed-duweir: not Libnah but Lachish', *PEQ* 117, 1985, pp. 92–98.

[2] S. Yeivin, 'The Divided Kingdom', *WHJP* IV, p. 160.

[3] Edomite seal *lytm*; N. Avigad, 'The Jotham Seal from Elat', *BASOR* 163, 1961, pp. 18–22; *cf.* N. Glueck, 'The Third Season of Excavation at Tell Kheleifeh', *BASOR* 79, 1940, pp. 13–15, Fig. 9; Seal 'Jotham son of Eliezer' in P. Bordreuil and A. Lemaire, 'Nouveaux sceaux hébreux et araméens', *Semitica* 29, 1979, p. 75, pl. IV. 7.

[4] R. L. Cleveland, 'More on the South Arabian Clay Stamp found at Beitîn', *BASOR* 209, 1973, pp. 33–36.

campaigning in Urartu (Armenia) leaving Jehoash, whom they record as a vassal or tribute-paying servant of Assyria (see on 2 Ki. 13:10), free to become a powerful force in the area and to restore the northern boundary of Israel to what it had been in the days of David.

The resultant prosperity, however, which ended in the wrong use of power in luxury and the oppression of the poor, was denounced by the contemporary prophets, especially Amos (2:6–7; 8:4–6); Isaiah (3:18–26; 5:8–13) and Micah (2:2). They saw the state's security as false (Am. 6:1–8) and behind it all an empty religious ritual (Am. 5:21–24).[1]

Assyria grew weaker under Ashur-dan III (772–754 BC), a situation which may provide much of the background for this reign.[2] Freedom from outside interference brought advances reflected in the tax returns described in the ostraca from Samaria[3] which show the economy as producing an increasing royal income. The personal names they recorded thereon show an advance in apostasy in that for every eleven personal names compounded with Yah seven now include Baal.

The form of the history is regular. The introduction (vv. 23–24) is followed by diverse notes about the expanding boundaries (v. 25) and the divine deliverance allowed Israel under Jeroboam (v. 26). While commentators ascribe these notes to different redactors they may well be information available from different contemporary, including prophetic, sources (see Introduction, p. 44). The conclusion of the reign follows in verses 28–29.

23. *The fifteenth year of Amaziah* is compatible with verses 1 and 17, and with 15:1, if a co-regency between Jeroboam and Jehoash is allowed. This would then be the beginning of this sole reign, the whole *forty-one years*, including such a co-regency, lasting *c.* 793–753 BC.

25. The newly re-occupied region included that formerly held by Aram-Damascus *from Lebo-Hamath* marking the northern border of Israel with the kingdom of Hamath, *i.e. Lebo* (Labweh) in the Lebanese Beqa' valley running between the Lebanon and Anti-Lebanon ranges. This was historically the ideal northern boundary of Israel (Nu. 13:21) as in the time of

---

[1] J. Bright, *A History of Israel* (London: SCM Press, [2]1981), pp. 238–248.
[2] M. Haran, 'The Rise and Decline of the Empire of Jeroboam ben Joash', *VT* 17, 1967, p. 279; D. J. Wiseman, 'Jonah's Nineveh', *TynB* 30, 1979, p. 46.
[3] *DOTT*, pp. 204–208; *ANET*, p. 321.

David and Solomon (1 Ki. 8:65). The southern boundary was the *Sea* (brook) *of the Arabah*. If this is identified with the 'brook of the Willows' (*ᵃrāḇîm*, Is. 15:7, RSV) or the Valley of Salt (see (v. 7) then Jeroboam dominated Moab and the entire length of the King's Highway.[1] This success is confirmed by Amos 6:13–14.

This expansion was prophesied and so the prophet *Jonah* is named as the author and encourager of Israel's action. Amos is not mentioned because his message was critical of the spiritual state of the nation. 'Jonah belonged to the tradition of Elisha rather than Amos.'[2] He also undertook a foreign mission to the heartland of Israel's coming enemy, Assyria. While most deny the book of his name as written at this time, there is growing evidence that the days of Ashur-dan III form a true background to his work in Nineveh.[3] *Gath Hepher* in Zebulun (Jos. 19:13) just north of Nazareth (at ez-Zurra' or al-Meshed) was Jonah's birthplace (*cf.* Jon. 1:1).

26–27. After the suffering caused by Aram (10:32–33; 13:3–7), Moab (13:20), and Ammon (Am. 1:13), God now gave a period of grace to give opportunity for repentance. See on 13:23. Yet continued apostasy was leading inevitably to final judgment (Am. 4:2; 6:14) and 'Israel used the time of her respite to weave the rope with which she was soon to be hanged'.[4]

Verses 26–27 are an explanation of verse 25.

28. The *other events* of Jeroboam's long reign and *all he did* include extensive building work at Tirzah, the repair of the great gate and local governor's palace with large buildings with stone foundations. At Megiddo the large grain storage pit (7 m deep × 11.4 m wide) capable of holding 12,800 bushels of grain is attributed to his work. The sixty-three inscribed sherds from Samaria, if dated to his reign and not to Menahem, record the prosperity which enabled imports of oil and wine from neighbouring crown-estates to maintain a high income from taxes on these and other items.

---

[1] Y. Aharoni, *The Land of the Bible: A Historical Geography* (London: Burns & Oates, ²1979), p. 344; B. Oded, 'The Historical Background of the Syro-Ephraimite War Reconsidered', *CBQ* 34, 1972, p. 158.

[2] Jones, p. 515.

[3] D. J. Wiseman, 'Jonah's Nineveh', *TynB* 30, 1979, pp. 29–51; for a review of current views see now T. D. Alexander in D. W. Baker *et al.*, *Obadiah, Jonah and Micah* TOTC (Leicester: IVP, 1988), pp. 77–81.

[4] Robinson, p. 133.

God uses various hands to bring in his salvation, *cf.* 13:5. The Hebrew of part of this verse, 'To Judah for Israel' (MT) leads to various interpretations. Jeroboam's authority extended to Hamath and Damascus where Ahab had first held an economic toe-hold (1 Ki. 20:34). Either these 'had belonged to Judah' (RSV) or, more likely, had belonged to *Yaudi* (so NIV). A state *Y'dy* is named in an Aramaic text from Sam'al (Zenjirli) in which there is a reference some take to be to 'Azariah of Judah', but it would be an unusual coincidence for there to be two similarly named rulers and territories (*Azriyau* ᵐᵃᵗ*Yaudaia*) at this same time.[1]

29. The accession of *Zechariah* fulfils the prophecy that there would be four generations in Jehu's line (10:30). For the reign of Azariah of Judah see 15:8–12.

The history of Israel and Judah is continued with the theological purpose uppermost. Thus for Azariah (Uzziah), the greatest Judean king after David, only brief space is given to say that he continued to 'do the right' in the Davidic tradition. This one chapter covers approximately fifty years in which the reigns of two Judeans (*c.* 790–732 BC) and five Israelite kings are reviewed.

At this time it must be assumed that Judah now shared in the prosperity of Israel before the pressure Assyria was to exert had begun to be felt. The pattern of introduction with evaluation of reign, brief historical comment and concluding notes on the end of the reign are given for each ruler in turn.

G. Azariah of Judah (15:1–7)

The Chronicler (2 Ch. 26) gives important additional data for this reign.

1. On the chronological relation with Jeroboam see Introduction, p. 31. Again the historian is dating by the accession-year system and the synchronism can be best explained by taking Azariah as co-regent with his father Amaziah for twenty-four years, thus marking the year in which he *began* his sole reign *c.* 767 BC. His official part years each counted as a regnal year, *i.e.* he had been co-regent *c.* 791/0–767 BC as his son Jotham was to be regent during part of this reign (15:33; *c.* 750–740 BC).

[1] H. Tadmor, 'Azriyau of Yaudi', *Scripta Hierosolymitana* 8 (Jerusalem: Magnes Press, 1961), pp. 232–271.

Azariah ('my help is Yah(weh)') is unlikely to be a throne-name. His other name Uzziah is as frequently used of him here in Kings (vv. 13, 30, 32, 34) and elsewhere in the Old (except 1 Ch. 3:12) and New Testaments (Mt. 1:8–9) including the Prophets (Is. 1:1; 6:1; 7:1; Ho. 1:1; Am. 1:1; Zc. 14:5). Uzziah ('my strength is Yah(weh)') is of a known variant type of personal name (*e.g.* Azare-el – Uzzi-el, 1 Ch. 25:4, 18).

3–5. As is usual when a favourable evaluation (*did what was right in the eyes of the LORD*) is made, some qualifying statements are given. The Chronicler adds other failings to that of not removing the hill shrines (on this see 1 Ki. 3:2–4). Azariah's disease was taken to be God-inflicted, as was sickness in Bible times. The 'dreaded skin disease' (GNB), or *leprosy* (AV, NIV; see on 2 Ki. 5:3) was a punishment for unlawfully usurping the priestly function of burning incense on the temple altar (2 Ch. 26:16–21; *cf.* Lv. 13:46). Since he then could not undertake royal public functions he 'lived in a house on his own, relieved of all duties' (GNB). The *separate house* (RSV, NIV) is a word (Heb. *bēṯ haḥopšîṯ*) which is difficult to interpret, indeed the Greek only transliterates it. It may be related to 'freedom' from slavery (Ex. 21:3, 5; Dt. 15:12; Je. 34:9–11 as in Ugar. *ḥpṯ*; Akkad. *ḥupšu*) or from taxes or civil obligations (1 Sa. 17:25). There is no evidence to link it with words for a place of isolation (JB 'he lived confined to his room'), but more likely he lived as a king 'in freedom at home'. A fine small royal building southwest of Jerusalem at Ramat Rahel is thought by Aharoni, its excavator, to be the place to which the king went. Similar buildings, also made of stone, are known from earlier periods at Samaria and Megiddo.

In Uzziah's absence Jotham his son served both as the major palace administrator ('he who is over the house', see on 1 Ki. 4:6) and as governor of *the people of the land*. The latter denotes either his position as head of the judiciary and senior counsel or as being responsible for all the administration.[1]

6. The other events and doings of Azariah can be gleaned from 2 Chronicles 26:6–15. He warred successfully against the Philistines, controlled the Arabs in Transjordan and received tribute from ther Ammonites. His fame spread to the very border of Egypt through his control of the Negeb by establishing a series of 'watchtowers in the desert', one of

---

[1] See H. Reviv, 'The Structure of Society', *WHJP* V, p. 144.

which was at Qumran over which the later settlement was built.[1] Elat was rebuilt and Ezion Geber enlarged about this time which, with the good relations with the Arabs, enhanced trade. Jerusalem was fortified and given modern defence artillery with the army reorganized and re-equipped. Economically all was well, but when Uzziah became famous and very powerful his pride led to unfaithfulness and to his fall (2 Ch. 26:8, 15–16). Yet at the very time of his death the LORD called Isaiah to an initial or new vision of himself (Is. 6:1; Jn. 12:41).

7. There is no discrepancy in the burial account with 2 Chronicles 26:23 which refers to his resting place with the fathers as in the *field of burial* belonging to the kings. Since he was a leper, he was not buried in the royal mausoleum but *near them* in the City of David. A first-century AD Aramaic inscription records that he was later reburied – 'here we brought the bones of Uzziah – do not open'.[2] For the reign of Jotham see verses 32–38.

H. Zechariah of Israel (15:8–12)

The death of this last king of the dynasty of Jehu (v. 12) saw the end of the Northern Kingdom proper. In the last twenty years six rulers were to follow each other, but only one was to die naturally. Anarchy, rivalry and regicide led to terminal bloodshed which fulfilled Hosea's prophecies (1:4). The customary introduction (v. 8), evaluation of the reign as evil (v. 9) are followed by details of the assassination (v. 10) which rendered detail of the normal concluding formula, *e.g.* burial, inapplicable.

8. The apparent discrepancy with 14:23 and 15:1 can be explained if (i) a co-regency of Azariah with his father is allowed, and (ii) Zechariah's *six months* spanned two separate years (753–752 BC), *cf.* 1 Kings 22:51.

9. On the *sins of Jeroboam* 'who led Israel into sin' (NEB, referring the relative particle to Jeroboam rather than to the sin, as RSV) see on 1 Kings 12:26–33; 13:33–34.

10. *Shallum, son of Jabesh*, may be taken as 'a man of Jabesh'.

[1] R. de Vaux, 'Installation Israélite, Fouilles de Khirbet Qumran', *RB* 63, 1956, pp. 535–537.
[2] E. L. Sukenik, 'Funerary Tablets of Uzziah, king of Judah', *PEQ* 63, 1931, pp. 217–220; *IBD*, p. 1615.

The place of a conspiracy is occasionally given (v. 25, *cf.* 1 Ki. 15:27) but not invariably (v. 30). Thus the NIV *in front of the people (qābāl 'ām, cf.* NRSV 'in public') though an unusual grammatical form, may be possible. There is little support (LXX(L)) for the differing reading (RSV) 'in Ibleam' (Heb., *bᵉyiblᵉ'ām*) though it appeals since there Jehu's dynasty itself began with an assassination (2 Ki. 9:27).

12. For the fulfilment of God's promise see 2 Kings 10:30.

I. Shallum of Israel (15:13–16)

The brief reign of this usurper lasted one month until rival factions contending for the throne assassinated him. Insufficient detail is given to determine whether this was a resurgence of the older tribal factions or a protest against any possible revival of the hereditary principle of succession.

13. On *Uzziah* (Azariah) see verse 2. *One month*, Heb. 'a month of days', is possibly a full month.

14. *Menahem* ('comforter') may have been a garrison commander at *Tirzah* the capital of Israel before Samaria was founded (1 Ki. 14:17; 15:21, 33). For his reign see verses 17–22. *Son of Gadi* is a name meaning 'my luck' (*cf.* Gadiyahu), rather than related to the tribe of Gad. There is no reference to Shallum as 'a son of a nobody' in the Assyrian annals as is implied by some commentators (Jones, Gray).

16. *At that time* (Heb. *'āz*, 'then') introduces additional data from an annal. The action by Menahem (on whose rule see verses 17–22 below) against the inhabitants of Tiphsah is unparalleled for brutality by any Israelite. Here it may mark the increasing influence of the surrounding nations (*cf.* 2 Ki. 21:2,6). It was a foreign practice inflicted on the Israelites themselves by Aram (2 Ki. 8:12), Ammon (Am. 1:13) and Assyria (Ho. 13:8). Some find this possible if *Tiphsah* (MT, NIV) is identified with the distant Thapsacus on the west bank of the River Euphrates. This important 'fording-place' (Heb. *tipsaḥ*) was on the boundary of Solomon's kingdom (1 Ki. 4:24). Though the political situation might allow it to be located there, there is no other evidence for an Israelite raid so far to the northeast. For this reason some follow a rare Greek rendering here of 'Tappuah' (RSV; LXX(L)). This was on the Ephraim border (Jos. 17:8) south of Shechem and not far from Tirzah at modern Sheikh Abu Zarad. If this reading is accepted it implies intense rivalry for the throne. Others think it may be an unknown place whose inhabitants supported Shallum (*cf.* JB 'Tappush').

J. Menahem of Israel (15:17–22)

Menahem took over just before Tiglath-pileser III of Assyria (745–727 BC) began renewed operations in the west in a series of campaigns from 743 BC onwards which culminated in the first major direct contact of Assyria with Israel. The Assyrian policy was initially to leave a state on its borders independent, though requiring substantial annual payment for this privilege. Thereafter the state might be made a vassal, which entailed having an Assyrian official at court as a watchdog on the ruler's attitudes. This usually left the local king on the throne but in the event of any infringement the Assyrians would invade, exact special payments, and increase the annual tribute. Eventually Tiglath-pileser, who reorganized the whole administration, and his successors sub-divided Syro-Palestine into Assyrian provinces directly responsible to the Assyrian capital. Menahem maintained his position by harsh methods (v. 16) until, near the end of his reign (752–742/1 BC), Tiglath-pileser (Pul) made an approach and was paid to support Menahem. This formed the major entry in annals recording the life of this king of Israel (vv. 18–20), the introductory (vv. 17–18) and concluding details (vv. 21–22) following the historian's usual pattern.

17. Menahem is named in the Assyrian annals (*me-ni-hi-im-me* ^{al}*sa-me-ri-na-a*).[1] They were aware that he was not related to any dynasty (*i.e.* that he was not of the dynasty of 'the house of Omri', Bit-Humri). The name occurs in a composite list of tribute payers between 743 and 738 BC. Between 745 and 740 the Assyrians annually marched west as far as Arpad to receive tribute and this action falls early in this period.[2]

19–20. *Pul* (Assyr. *Pulu*) is the personal name Tiglath-pileser used in 729 BC when assuming the throne of Babylon.

[1] Annals of Tiglath-pileser III, p. 150; *ANET*, pp. 282–284; *DOTT*, pp. 54, 57. The name *mnḥm* is also written on an ostracon from Nimrud *c.* 700 BC (J. B. Segal, 'An Aramaic ostracon from Nimrud', *Iraq* 19, 1957, p. 140).

[2] For a new stela from Iran with variant names of tribute-bearers in which Menahem is listed see D. Levine, 'Menahem and Tiglath-pileser: A New Synchronism', *BASOR* 206, 1972, pp. 40–42; E. R. Thiele, *The Mysterious Numbers of the Hebrew Kings* (Grand Rapids: Zondervan, ^{3}1983), pp. 126–128.

It occurs also in 1 Chronicles 5:26, *cf.* Poros in Ptolemy's Canon. *A thousand talents of silver* represents three million shekels, about thirty-seven tons or 'thirty-four thousand kilogrammes' (GNB). At *fifty shekels* a head, which was the current price of a slave in Assyria,[1] it needed sixty thousand payers to buy off (redeem) the threat. The sum was *exacted*, the money coming from the leading class (*gibbôrē haḥayil*) who would otherwise have had to furnish men of war. 'All the men of rank' (JB) is less interpretative than *wealthy* or 'rich men' (GNB), the sums paid by individuals would not have been unduly oppressive. This levy doubtless enabled Menahem to appoint his son Pekahiah as successor, for the fear of any Assyrian return would have prevented any rebellion.

K. Pekahiah of Israel (15:23–26)

Of this brief reign the historian records the introductory (vv. 23–24) and concluding formulae (v. 26) with a report of the conspiracy (v. 25) which leads on to his successor Pekah. Pekahiah seems to have followed his father's pro-Assyrian policy which led to his ousting.

The chronological data, *fiftieth year of Azariah*, is consistent within the chapter (vv. 8, 13, 17, 27). *Pekahiah* ('Yah[weh] has opened [the eyes/the womb]') is a name which occurs on a Palestinian seal (*pkhy*).[2] His assassin may have been his commander-in-chief (on Heb. *šālîš* 'third man', *chief officer* see 1 Ki. 9:22). Some think him leader of a Gileadite faction which was against Pekaiah as representing hereditary kingship.

The place of the murder is obscure. *Argob and Arieh* could be personal names, as NIV, the names of the guard units,[3] or even place names (*cf.* 1 Ki. 4:13; Dt. 3:4); RSV omits, taking them to be displaced from verse 29. One possible suggestion is that they refer to gateway figures of an eagle (*'rgb*) and lion (*'ryh*). Sennacharib was cut down between protective figures according to Ashurbanipal's account.[4] Such detail here would be unusual.

---

[1] D. J. Wiseman, 'The Nimrud Tablets, 1953', *Iraq* 14, 1952, p. 135 n. 1.
[2] D. Diringer, *Le iscrizioni antico-ebraiche palestinesi* (Firenze Universita degli studi di Firenze 1934), p. 353.
[3] S. Yeivin, 'The Divided Kingdom', *WHJP* IV. 1, p. 174.
[4] M. J. Geller, 'A New Translation for 2 Kings XV. 25', *VT* 26, 1976, pp. 374–377.

L. Pekah of Israel (15:27–31)

The introduction and evaluation of the reign as evil (vv. 27–28) is followed by two historical extracts relating to the first Assyrian invasion into Israel and to the first deportation of Israel into exile (v. 29). Then follows the overthrow by Hoshea and the murder of Pekahiah (v. 30) and the standard concluding formula (v. 31).

The wider historical background is important. Pekah's anti-Assyrian stance led Tiglath-pileser of Assyria in 734 BC to march as far as Gaza to cut off any hope of Egyptian assistance (as later 2 Ki. 17:4; *cf*. Ho. 7:11; 12:1). Its king Hanunu fled for a time to Egypt and the Assyrians maintained control of the coastal route by setting up a province *Du'ru* (Dor) to watch the Philistia-Sharon region. In 733/2 the Assyrians conquered Gal'za, Abilakka which is near Samaria (*Bīt-Humria*) and the wide land of Damascus (*Bīt-Haza'ili*) to its entire extent. 'I added these to Assyria and appointed my own officials as governors over them' (Assyrian annals).[1] the cuneiform texts show how Assyria overran north Galilee (v. 29) and incorporated it into the provincial system (with *Magiddu* = Megiddo as its centre) as well as Gilead (*Gal'za*). This was to be the beginning of the elimination of Israel as an independent state. The Assyrian invasion may have been the result of the appeal to them for help by Ahaz or Judah (see on 16:7).

27. *Fifty-second year of Azariah* is consistent with verse 23; 15:8. The Hebrew texts omit *and he reigned*, but this can be supplied on the basis of the regular formulae. *Twenty years* of reign is often considered impossible by comparison with Assyrian records.[2] This view is, however, usually based on a presumed late date of 738 BC for Menahem's tribute, now known to be *c*. 743 BC (see on v. 17). The solution, rather than deletion of *twenty* here and in verse 30 without manuscript support, may be that the first twelve years of Pekah overlapped both Menahem by ten years and Pekahiah by two years and that those were not counted. Pekah's 'reign' would then

[1] *ANET*, pp. 272, 283; D. J. Wiseman, 'Two Historical Inscriptions from Nimrud', *Iraq* 13, 1951, pp. 21–24; 'A Fragmentary inscription of Tiglath-pileser III for Nimrud', *Iraq* 18, 1956, pp. 117–129.
[2] Jones, p. 528; J. Reade, 'Mesopotamian Guidelines for Biblical Chronology', *Syro-Mesopotamian Studies* 4/1, 1981, pp. 5–6; Thiele's idea that Pekah began his reign in Gilead when Menahem ruled in Samaria before later taking control of the whole kingdom is unsupported.

be from 752 BC, with his 'sole' reign beginning in 740. On this view Pekah would have been a rival to the two overlapping contemporaries much as Zimri, Tibni and Omri had been (1 Ki. 16:15–24).

29. *Tiglath-Pileser: cf.* 16:7, 10 (more correctly anglicized as Tiglath-pileser, *cf.* Assyr. *Tukulti-apil-ešar(ra)*) with the Tilgath-pilneser of 1 Chronicles 5:6, (26); 2 Chronicles 28:20 explicable as inner-Hebrew variations.[1] On the historical background see above. *Ijon* (Tell ed-Dibbîn), *Abel Beth Maacah* (T. Avel Bet Maakha) fourteen kilometres to the south, and *Hazor* (T. el Qedaḥ) were a line of fortified towns on the direct road south into Israel. These had been taken by the Arameans responding to an earlier call for help from Judah (1 Ki. 15:19–20). At Hazor a destruction level (VA) revealed a potsherd inscribed *lpqḥ smdr* ('For Pekah, semader[-oil]', *IBD*, p. 1181). The Assyrians moved west up the valley to *Kedesh* (Abu Qedes, near Megiddo rather than Tell Qades northwest of Lake Huleh) and to *Janoah* (Yanuḥ, north-east of Acco), thus cutting northern Israel off from possible Aramean aid. So all *Galilee* and *Gilead* were now lost and Israel was pressed back into the 'Ephraim' hill-country.

Deported the people. This first reference to the practice of removing leaders and selected experts into exile shows that the next step had now been taken towards making Israel a vassal-state. Some action had provoked the Assyrian Tiglath-pileser III who records 'From Israel (Bīt-Humria) . . . I led off its inhabitants and possessions to Assyria' (Annals). Deportation served as a punishment to rebels, weakening possible centres of resistance, as well as warning of further exile for continuing offenders.[2] It was to be expected as a punishment for any deviation from a covenant-treaty made with the Assyrians or Babylonians.

30. *Hoshea* ('Saviour') is also named in the Annals of Tiglath-pileser: 'they overthrew Pekah (*pa-qa-ha*) their king so I set Hoshea (*a-ú-si-'i*) as king over them. I received from them as tribute 10 talents of gold and 1,000(?) talents of silver and brought them back to Assyria'.[3] While Kings implies a popular

---

[1] A. R. Millard, 'Assyrian Royal Names in Biblical Hebrew', *JSS* 21, 1976, p. 7.

[2] B. Oded, *Mass Deportation and Deportees in the Neo-Assyrian Empire* (Wiesbaden: Reichart, 1979), pp. 41–59.

[3] *ANET*, p. 284.

revolution the Assyrian chronicler emphasizes their part in the change.

31. *Other events* included Pekah's attack on Jerusalem (v. 37; 16:5–9; Is. 7:1).

M. Jotham of Judah (15:32–38)

Cf. 2 Chronicles 27:1–9. After the rapid changes in the Northern Kingdom the scene switches back to Uzziah's son Jotham who was already active in state affairs during his father's reign and illness (v. 5). The usual form of introduction (vv. 32–33) and evaluation for a worthy Judean ruler (*did* the *right*, v. 34) is hedged about by the exceptions in fully righteous living known also to his forefathers (v. 35, *cf.* v. 3; 2 Ch. 27:2). The only matter noted for his reign is some rebuilding of a temple gateway (v. 35). The concluding formulae (vv. 36–38) are interrupted by a retrospective note about the Aram–Israel (Syro–Ephraimite) incursions into Judah (v. 37). Yet, as Chronicles shows, Jotham strove to defend his small territory and his increasing power was attributed to his steadfast way of life before God. The compiler of the book of Kings surprisingly does not include this or his conquest of Ammon from which he received a large tribute over three years.

32–33. *Jotham* ('Yah[weh] is perfect') began his sole rule in Pekah's second year after ten years of co-regency, included in his sixteen regnal *years*. His mother's place of origin may be omitted on the assumption that Zadok's priestly title implied Jerusalem. 2 Chronicles 27:1 reads her name as Jerusha. A seal of Jotham found at Elat (Ezion Geber) shows a pair of bellows denoting the importance of the copper industry in the Arabah there at the time (*cf.* 14:22).

35. The rebuilt *Upper Gate* was possibly the Benjamin Gate northeast of the temple area (Zc. 14:10), *i.e.* the Upper Benjamin Gate of Jeremiah 20:2 facing north (Ezk. 9:2). The Chronicler adds other building works on an extensive wall on Ophel hill and in towns in the Judean hills with forts and watchtowers in the wooded areas as part of the anti-Syria/ Ephraim defence measures now necessary.

37. The initial moves by Rezin and Pekah against Judah are noted as an explanation of verse 35. The full hostilities did not come until the days of Ahaz (126:5–12), but Jotham, aware of the impact of the attack on Jerusalem in his father's time

(14:13), was taking no chances. *Rezin* was the last king of Aram-Damascus and is mentioned in the Assyrian annals and in Isaiah (7:1–8; 8:6; 9:11). The variant Rezon (1 Ki. 11:23–25) has been taken to imply that this was a title (*cf. rōzēn*, 'ruler') held by more than one king of Aram. Tiglath-pileser III *c.* 738 BC records the name *Ra-hi-ia-nu* (Rahyān, Razyôn, *i.e.* Rezôn, formerly misread as *Ra-ṣun-nu*), in a list before Menahem of Samaria, as bringing him tribute.[1]

N. Ahaz of Judah (16:1–20)

Cf. 2 Chronicles 28:1–27. The history moves forward to the end of the Northern Kingdom, but here with the emphasis on the idolatry and apostasy of the king of Judah who was perhaps trying to compromise, in the mistaken belief that this would produce national unity in the face of adversity. The historian does not even accord Ahaz the qualified approval he had given Amaziah (14:3), Azariah (15:3) or Jotham (15:34). Today many view Ahaz as weak rather than wicked, but the historian of Kings makes no distinction. The Chronicler adds emphasis to the record of Ahaz' apostasy.

The political background is the growing Assyrian intervention in Palestinian affairs. In 734–732 BC Pekah and Rezin may have approached Ahaz to join them before he became sole ruler in Judah after Tiglath-pileser of Assyria had campaigned as far south as the border with Egypt (*Nahal-muṣur*; Wadi el-'Arish). External circumstances led Ahaz to trust in Assyria for help against the advice of Isaiah (vv. 1–7).

The introduction (vv. 1–4) is followed by two entries; one on the Aram–Israel (often called Syro–Ephraimite) War which led to the attack on Jerusalem and to the Judean alliance with Assyria (vv. 5–9); the other on the changes in the temple furnishings which either stemmed from personal ambition or leanings towards the syuncretistic worship which was fast leading to Israel's downfall and exile. The concluding formulae are given in verses 19–20.

[1] Annals of Tiglath-pileser III. For the corrected reading of this name see B. Landsberger, *Sam'al* (Veöffentichungen der Türkischen Historischen Gesellschaft VII/16, Ankara, 1948), p. 66. n. 169; M. Weippert, 'Menahem von Israel und seine Zeitgenossen in einer Steleninschrift des assyrischen Königs Tiglath-pileser III aus dem Iran', *ZPDV* 89, 1973, pp. 26–53.

i. Summary of reign (16:1–4). 1–2. *The seventeenth year* of
Pekah as a correlation reckons from that king's reign as sole
king (15:27–31) and dates Ahaz' reign from *c.* 744/3 BC when
he was co-regent with Azariah (17:1). From 735 BC Ahaz was
senior co-regent with Jotham and sole ruler after the death of
Jotham in 732 BC.[1]

Ahaz as a personal name also occurs elsewhere on a seal
'Ashna, official of Ahaz'.[2] It is an abbreviation of the name
Jehoahaz (13:1), written by the Assyrians *Ya-ú-ha-zi* ^*māt*^*Ya-ú-da-
aia* in the list of kings from Cilicia to Gaza who paid tribute to
Assyria about 732 BC.[3] The chronology here is difficult and it
may be assumed that the *twenty years old* was his age when he
began to rule as co-regent with Jotham in 735 BC, and would
then have been about fourteen when Hezekiah was born.
There is then no need to read 'twenty-five' with LXX, Syr. in 2
Chronicles 28:1. The *sixteen years* of reign would be after the
death of Jotham (see 15:30). It is unusual that the name of the
mother of a Judean king is omitted. That he *did not do right* is a
unique evaluation of his reign and character. It may be a
sorrowful appraisal which implies that he did not take some
specific steps which would warrant the specific classification as
doing evil. On the other hand only Manasseh is more severely
berated than Ahaz.

3–4. This is the first instance where Judah imitates Israel's
apostasy (*cf.* 17:17), and this was to influence Manasseh (21:6;
23:10). He even 'caused his son to pass through fire' (AV, so
Heb.) has been interpreted as *sacrificed* (NIV) or as a burnt-
offering (RSV) – a desperate act in the face of defeat (3:27)
contrary to the Mosaic law requiring the redemption of the
first-born (Lv. 18:21; Dt. 18:10). But if taken as child sacrifice,
which is rarely attested until later, this view must be based on
an interpretation of the vow in Judges 11:31. There may be a
Canaanite practice dedicating or initiating a son to the god
Molech in a fire cult (see on 1 Ki. 11:7) which differs from

---

[1] H. G. Stigers, 'The Interphased Chronology of Jotham, Ahaz, Hezekiah
and Hoshea', *Bulletin of the Evangelical Theological Society* 9, 1966, pp. 81–90.

[2] C. A. Torrey, 'A Hebrew Seal from the Reign of Ahaz', *BASOR*, 1940, p.
27; but against this interpretation see D. Plataroti, 'Zum Gebrauch des Wortes
mlk im Alten Testament', *VT* 48, 1978, pp. 286–300.

[3] *ANET*, p. 282; *DOTT*, pp. 56–57.

child-sacrifice which was not practised in Assyria.[1] The hill-shrines were now used for the worship of both Yahweh and other local gods, and *every spreading tree* notes the widespread immoral rites practised here as in Israel (see on 1 Ki. 14:23).

ii. The Syro–Ephraimite attack (16:5–6). This followed the earlier pressure on Jotham (15:37) with a direct attack. There is no evidence that this was to force Ahaz into an anti-Assyrian coalition. The plan was to depose Ahaz and put Tab-'el on the throne (Is. 7:6) rather than to win expansion of Israelite territory.[2] Either they failed to overpower or to 'bring him to battle' (NEB) or divine intervention (MT 'they were unable to fight') means that Ahaz or his men put up no resistance and so later fell into Syrian hands (so 2 Ch. 28:5). Judah suffered heavy casualties, while Ahaz withstood the attacks (Is. 7:3) but then called for help. The statement that *Rezin ... recovered Elath for Aram* (MT, NIV) has been questioned on the basis of geography and Aram (*'rm*) has been taken by RSV, NEB as an error for Edom (*'dm* as in 1 Ki. 9:26; 22:48). However, the statement that the *Edomites* then moved into the city (AV changes this also to 'Syrians'!) makes the temporary occupation by Arameans a possibility.

iii. The appeal to Assyria (16:7–9). The use of letters by the hand of messengers in negotiations is well attested in Assyrian diplomacy. The address 'I am your servant and your son' clearly places Ahaz as the petitioning vassal and shows he was trusting in Assyria rather than in the LORD, against the advice of Isaiah (7:10–16; *cf.* Ex. 23:22). From this time Judah, whose inhabitants are here first designated men of Judah or 'Jews' (as AV), was, with minor exceptions, subservient to Assyria. According to Assyrian vassal-treaties a vassal could expect help against any of the overlord's enemies who might attack him. The Chronicler adds that at this time Edom and Philistia were attacking Judah (2 Ch. 28:20–21) and views this embassy to Assyria as being 'most unfaithful to the LORD' and

---

[1] A. J. McKay, *Religion in Judah under the Assyrians, 732–609 B.C.* (Society for Biblical Theology, 26, 1973), pp. 39–41; M. Cogan, *Imperialism and Religion: Assyria, Judah and Israel in the Eighth and Seventh Centuries BCE* (Missoula: Montana; SBL Mon. 19, 1974), pp. 77–83.

[2] As B. Oded, 'The Historical Background of the Syro-Ephraimite War Reconsidered', *CBQ* 34, 1972, pp. 153–165.

as 'promoting wickedness in Judah'. The intervention was bought at a heavy price. The temple and treasury reserves were depleted (*cf.* 12:18; 14:14) to send a 'bribe' (so NEB, *šōḥaḏ*) which was accepted by the Assyrians as tribute (see v. 1).

Tiglath-pileser's seizure and capture of Damascus is also recorded in his annals for 733–732 BC which refer to the city as 'the house of Haza'el (*Haza'ili*)'. Deportation was a method much used by the Assyrians at this period to quell opposition (see on 15:29). The return to *Kir* in Elam (Is. 22:5–6) is taken to be the fulfilment of prophecy (Am. 1:5; 9:7). There is no support for Gray's identification of *qîr* ('the city') with Nineveh.

iv. Ahaz makes innovations in the temple (16:10–18). This may come from ancient temple records (note the references to King *Ahaz*). Vassal kings met at Damascus to bring tribute to their Assyrian overload. '(Jeho)ahaz of Judah' is named with those rulers of Ammon, Moab, Ashkelon, Edom and Gaza who brought their gifts in 734 BC.[1] Panamuwa of Sam'al is named at this same meeting according to the stela of his son Bar-Rekub.

It has been questioned whether *the altar* represented Judah's new status, for there is no evidence of the imposition of such symbols in a vassal's national temple though there is of an Assyrian stela or royal image being placed there. The historian would perhaps have been expected to have inveighed against such a devastating public move away from Yahwism. Others interpret this as an aesthetic preference for a Syro–Phoenician or Aram type altar (so 2 Ch. 28:23) reused for Yahweh worship. In any event it implied drastic change in the ritual rather than emphasizing Judah's subordinatiuon to a higher political power. The reason for the change of position substituting the new stone(?) altar set on steps (v. 12, 'went up' *cf.* NIV, *approached*) for the original Solomonic bronze altar is not clear.

Ahaz seems to have been delayed in Damascus long enough for the altar to have been made. He then acted as Solomon had at the dedication of the temple (1 Ki. 8:62–4) offering the full range of sacrifices.

Verse 13 is the *locus classicus* for such rites, the *burnt offering*

[1] *DOTT*, pp. 56–57 (*Ya-ú-ha-zi (māt)Ya-ú-da-a-a*).

(*'ōlâ*) being totally consumed and the *grain* or 'cereal' *offering* (*minḥâ*) and libation or *drink offering* (*nesek*) of oil and wine, as produce of the land, being poured out (Num. 15:5–12). The culmination was the 'peace' (against JB, 'sacrifice', communion or *fellowship*) offering (*šᵉlāmîm*) shared by priest and worshippers. Ahaz acting as priest dedicated the new altar for purposes which it could be argued were essentially right but in a manner not commanded by God. The result was the temporary closure of the temple following the institution of a new ritual (2 Ch. 28:24). This continued the basic sacrifices (vv. 15–16) of the perpetual *morning* and *evening* offerings (Ex. 29: 38–42; Nu. 28:2–8); the institution of special royal offerings (known only from later sabbath and festival practice, Ezk. 46:12) and communal offerings. All this may well represent the insinuation of a practice of trying to be 'all things to all people' and deities.

15. The use of the *bronze altar* for *seeking guidance* or 'to inquire by' (RSV) is not clear as there is no derogatory comment about it. The Hebrew *baqqēr* means 'to examine for defect' and Jewish tradition interprets this as the proper examination of sacrificial animals. It is, however, an unusual term to use of searching animal entrails for omen guidance, a practice condemned by Deuteronomy 18:10–12. Others interpret the use of this altar to be for the king's exclusive personal use ('as for the altar of bronze I shall see to that' JB).

17. Ahaz needed precious metal for replenishing the treasury and perhaps for payment of a further annual tribute. He therefore cut up the *side panels*, 'borders' (NASB) or 'frames' (RSV) of the ten mobile basins (*cf.* 1 Ki. 7:27–33) and replaced the bronze base of the vast 'Sea' laver with stone (*cf.* 1 Ki. 7:23–25). All this to get hold of metal which was primarily dedicated to the worship and glory of God alone.

18. Other building changes are difficult to interpret. 'The structure' (NEB), 'covering/foundation of the seat' (LXX; Heb. *mûsak*) may have been a 'covered way' (used) 'for the Sabbath' (RSV following Jewish exegetes; *cf.* NIV *Sabbath canopy*). Some think this may have been a covered colonnade used by the priests. The private royal passageway from the palace to *outside* (*hᵃḥîṣônâ*) the building was apparently changed about (MT *hēsēb*; RSV changes to 'removed', *hēsîr*). All these changes are said to have been made 'from before the face of the king of Assyria' (MT), perhaps 'because of' (RSV) the installation of an alien royal statue. Most interpret these actions as carried out by a vassal *in deference* to the king of Assyria, but that is not the only interpretation possible.

v. Concluding formula for Ahaz' reign (16:19–20). For the reign of *Hezekiah* see 18:1–20; 21.

O. Hoshea and the fall of Israel (17:1–41)

The historian reviews the reign of Hoshea (vv. 1–2) and uses annalistic sources to cover the detail of the fall of Samaria (vv. 3–6). This goes to the heart of the theology of Kings, for he now summarizes events leading up to the division of the nation (vv. 7–17) and then shows how the Israelites had repeatedly refused to return to their covenant allegiance to God (Yahweh, vv. 21–23). The same fate as had befallen Israel will now come upon Judah (vv. 18–20). The explanation given is that God allowed this as retribution for the nation's sin against him. Israel had repeatedly rejected the LORD and the prophet's warnings of judgment to come had failed to move them to keep their spiritual obligations. So the covenant curse foretold by Moses (Dt. 28:49–68; 31:16 ff.) was now to fall on Judah, so *all the people of Israel* (here Israel and Judah) are rejected (v. 20).

Some commentators see various strands of comment throughout this chapter, but all such could be explained as the expected 'Deuteronomistic' historian's understanding of the nation's disregard for the law and its movement towards a non-Yahwistic religion. Commonly verses 7–17 have been taken as by one commentator and vv. 18, 21–23 by another with verses 19–20 added after the fall of Jerusalem,[1] but that would be just the time the historian of Kings would have been at work himself (see Introduction, p. 53).

i. The occasion of the exile (17:1–6). 1–2. *Hoshea* ('Salvation') see 15:30. For the chronology see Introduction, p. 33. He seems to have been made a vasssal of Assyria *c.* 732/1 but not recognized as sole king in Israel till *c.* 730.[2] Another possibility

---

[1] Jones, pp. 542–545; J. MacDonald, 'The Structure of 2 Kings xvii', *Glasgow University Oriental Society Transactions* 23, 1969/70, pp. 29–41.

[2] R. Borger and H. Tadmor, 'Zwei Beiträge zur alttestamentlichen Wissenschaft auf Grund der Inschriften Tiglatpilesers III', *ZAW* 94, 1982, pp. 244–249.

is that here the accession is synchronized with that of Ahaz of Judah, whereas in 15:30 it was with his father Jotham and that this double synchronism may be evidence for a co-regency.[1] *Nine years, i.e.* 732/1–724/3 BC. The unusual qualification of his 'evil' reign as *not like the kings of Israel* cannot be that he had no time for religious matters (as Gray, p. 641), since others with shorter reigns are condemned in severer terms. He seems not to have inaugurated or continued the anti-Yahwistic practices for which Israel itself is condemned (vv. 7–21).

3. *Shalmaneser V* (Assyr. *šulman-ašaridu*) succeeded Tiglath-pileser III as the king of Assyria (727–722 BC) to whom Hoshea *had been vassal* (see on 15:30). It is not clear if when Shalmaneser *came up* to Hoshea it was to receive his *tribute* (or 'gift') during an Assyrian campaign against Phoenician cities (Josephus, *Ant.* ix.14.2) or more likely it was to attack him (Heb. *'ālāw*, 'upon him' *cf.* 1 Ki. 25:1). However, Hoshea soon failed to make his annual peace statement and pay tribute necessary to mark his continuing loyalty, and appears to have sought an alliance with Egypt (Ho. 7:11).

4. This was treachery in Assyrian eyes for 'no man can serve two masters'. The identity of *So, king of Egypt* is uncertain. Hebrew *sô'* may be an abbreviation of the name of the Libyan Osorkon IV (*c.* 727–716 BC), for the suggested equation with Sib'e, an Egyptian general whom Sargon II says he met at Raphia, is based on a misreading of the name for Siwe. Others reading that name as Rē'e think that person could have been acting for Osorkon.[2] Chronologically the king cannot be the later pharaoh Shebaka, nor is the equation So = Sais (*s'w*; as NEB), a Delta town held now by Tefnakte (726–716 BC), likely since it requires it to be mistakenly taken to be a royal name.[3] Hoshea may have been *put in prison* (*i.e.* 'arrested', NEB; *cf.* Je. 33:1; 36:5; 37:4) when outside Samaria.

5–6. The subsequent siege of Samaria is well documented by Assyrian annals in 724/3–722/1 BC. The *king of Assyria* is not specifically named (but *cf.* 18:9–11) and this may reflect the statement by the Assyrian Shalmaneser V that he took the city, while his successor, Sargon (II, *cf.* Is. 20:1) makes the same

[1] Cogan and Tadmor, p. 195.
[2] R. Borger, 'Das Ende des ägyptischen Feldherrn Sib'e = Sô', *JNES* 19, 1960, pp. 49–50.
[3] H. Goedicke, 'The end of "So, King of Egypt"', *BASOR* 171, 1963, pp. 64–66.

claim in his first year. Samaria was well fortified and the three-year siege could have been carried out by both, including operations in all the surrounding territory (v. 5). Few of Shalmaneser's records just before his death in 722/1 are extant. Sargon claimed 'the men of Samaria with their king were hostile to me and consorted together not to carry out their vassal obligations or bring tribute to me, so they fought me . . . I clashed with them and took as booty 27,280 people with their chariots and their gods in whom they trusted. I incorporated 200 chariots into my army. The rest of the people I made to dwell within Assyria. I restored the city of Samaria and made it greater than before.'[1] So Samaria was made capital of an Assyrian province under an Assyrian district-governor.

The deportees were taken to *Halah*, possibly Halahhu east of Haran (so AV) near the River Balikh (LXX) or to Calah; to *Gozan* (Tell Halaf) on the River Habur,[2] and to places in Media recently occupied by Sargon, where his annals contain several references to deportations there. Many Israelites settled there (v. 23), but this section forms no basis for any theory of the survival of 'the lost tribes of Israel' in exile, where they would have formed small village communities and from which some went into the Assyrian army.[3]

ii. The reasons for Israel's exile (17:7–18). This typically 'Deuteronomistic' account of God's dealings with his people brings together all the lessons to be learned from failure to keep to the Sinai covenant (v. 7, *cf.* Ex. 20:3) following the basic redemptive act (*brought them out of Egypt*) which made them his people. Their sin is shown (vv. 7–9a) by (a) worship of other gods; (b) following pagan (Canaanite) practices; and (c) the introduction of non-Yahwistic ritual and customs by *the kings of Israel*: Jeroboam I (1 Ki. 12:28–33); Omri (16:25–26); Ahab (16:30–34); Jehu (2 Ki. 10:31) and now Jeroboam II (14:24).

[1] C. J. Gadd, 'Inscribed Prisms of Sargon II from Nimrud', *Iraq* 16, 1954, pp. 179–180; *cf. ANET*, p. 284; *DOTT*, p. 54.
[2] Texts from Tell Halaf name one Halbišu from Samaria as there, also others with names compounded with *-yau*, B. Oded, *Mass Deportation and Deportees in the Neo-Assyrian Empire* (Wiesbaden: Reichart, 1979), p. 79.
[3] I. M. Diakonoff, 'The cities of the Medes' in M. Cogan and I. Epha'al, *Ah! Assyria, Scripta Hierosolymitana* 33 (1991), pp. 13, 20, takes these to be in the Kar-Kašši (Harhar) region.

9. This indictment is enlarged with specific reference to the sin of building high places (see on 14:4) in the smallest to largest inhabited localities (Heb. *'îrîm*; MT from watch tower to fortified city). So the practice of worshipping the LORD (Yahweh) and local deities together (syncretism) spread. This was associated with places of sacrifice (*sacred stones*), *Asherah* (fertility) *poles* or symbols, and probably sexual rites under *every spreading tree*, including ritual prostitution (1 Ki. 14:24; Ho. 4:13–14).

11. These were *wicked things* against God's specific denunciations made in the law and were acts which always make God *angry*. To provoke God *to anger* is a recurrent theme in Kings (vv. 11, 17).[1]

12. The making and worship of *idols* is prohibited in the decalogue (Ex. 20:4; Dt. 5:8) and led to the great sin of Jeroboam in the specific case of the two bull-calves at Bethel and Dan (vv. 12, 16; 1 Ki. 12:28–30). Worse still was the rejection of the prophetic warnings to turn away from such breaking of the unique law of God given at Sinai (vv. 12–13, 15; 1 Ki. 13:1–3).

13–15. Both kingdoms were warned by their own prophets who proclaimed that deviation from the law was the result of obstinacy ('stubborn', stiff-necked; Dt. 10:16; Je. 7:24) which leads to 'no faith, no stability' (Is. 7:9). A lack of response (obedience) to God's word shown in infidelity to the LORD's words (v. 15) always leads to *worthless* objectives sought by 'worthless lives' (REB), pursuing empty phantoms such as the bull-calves at Bethal and Dan (1 Ki. 14:15), and so themselves becoming empty (v. 15, NEB).

16–17. Other sinful ways listed include an interest in astrology and astral deities (*cf.* Am. 5:26), a practice clearly forbidden to Israel in Deuteronomy 4:19; 17:3 but later reintroduced into Judah by Manasseh (2 Ki. 21:3, 5), and abolished for a time by Josiah (23:4–5, 12, *cf.* Ezk. 8:16). Equally sinful was the dedication of children to the god Molech (v. 17, see on 1 Ki. 11:5), possibly divination (the Heb. *qāsam* as in Pr. 16:10, 'fateful decision') and *sorcery* condemned in Deuteronomy 18:9–13 (the Heb. *niḥēš* may mean use of snake-charmers, *cf.* Gn. 44:5; 1 Ki. 20:33; looking for signs or

[1] Such provocation often occurs with idolatry. See also 1 Ki. 14:9, 15; 15:30; 16:2, 7, 13, 26, 33, 22:53; 2 Ki. 21:6, 15; 23:19. Note the variety in Chronicles (2 Ch. 28:25; 33:6).

fortune-telling). These forms of 'taking the omens' ascribe to heavenly bodies the powers which are inherently to be found only in God their creator.

18. This verse is often separated from the preceding text on the basis that this is the only reference here to the fall of the Northern Kingdom, but that is not specifically said and it may refer back to verse 7. Only *Judah* retained its tribal integrity.

iii. Sin and retribution in Judah (17:19–20). For that kingdom also is guilty of Israel's sins (*cf.* 16:3–4). The mention of *plunderers* is reminiscent of 2 Kings 24:2, but see also 10:32–33; 13:3, 20.

iv. A further summary of Israel's sin (17:21–23). Punishment was the fulfilment of prophecy. The LORD took the action but the nation brought judgment on itself (1 Ki. 11:11, 31). For Jeroboam's *great sin* see 1 Kings 12:26–32; 13:33–34. Again the warnings of the prophets are stressed as preceding the final exile.

v. Samaria resettled (17:24–28). The introduction of alien religions into the already mixed beliefs and practices of the Samaria region is now related in order to explain the origin of the Samaritans, who were long to be at odds with the people of Judah.

23–24. Sargon II tells how he 'settled people of the many lands I had conquered into Hatti' (Syro-Palestine).[1] It was Assyrian practice to make such colonists as free as possible locally yet with direct dependence on Assyria. Esarhaddon of Assyria (681–669 BC) and Ashurbanapli (669–627 BC) continued the same policy (Ezr. 4:2, 9–10). Following campaigns in Syria and Babylonia in 721–709, peoples were transferred in substantial numbers.[2] Some came from *Cuthah* (Kutha; Tell Ibrahim, eight kilometres northeast of Babylon) captured by Sargon in 709 BC, and 'Cuthites' would remain a term of abuse for Samaritans for many centuries. Others came from Assyrian provinces in Syria itself, *Avva* being perhaps Kefr 'Aya on the Orontes (*cf.* Ivvah, 19:13; Is 37:13) rather than 'Ama in Elam, captured by Sargon in 710 BC. *Hamath* on the Orontes was sacked by the Assyrians in 720 (see 18:34).

---

[1] *ARAB II § 4.*   [2] B. Oded, *op. cit.*, p. 79.

Sepharvaim, because of its deities, may be Sibraim near Damascus (Ezk. 47:16) rather than Sippar in Babylonia, which had also been attacked about this time. The Sabara'im of the Babylonian Chronicle is a name for Samaria itself and so cannot apply. The absorption of these new elements, including their religious beliefs, took time, for *when they first lived there, they did not worship the* LORD (vv. 25, 28), and indeed they never did totally (v. 33).

26. The incursion of *lions* was interpreted as divine retribution (*cf.* Lv. 26:21–22). They were known in that area and the Jordan valley until the last century (*cf.* 1 Ki. 13:24; 20:36; Am. 3:12), and their movements were the subject of ominous speculation. The memory of this event, however, was such that the Samaritans were later called 'proselytes of the lion'.[1]

27. Every god had his own custom, ritual or 'established usage' (NEB) which, if flouted, could bring disaster, so priests who knew it were brought in. Sargon also followed the policy of instructing deportees in the cult of local deities, according to a Khorsabad inscription.[2]

28. *One* (or certain) *of the priests* could have included one versed in the golden calf cult from Bethel (1 Ki. 12:28–31). This activity flourished because no prophet had yet been sent to call these folk to repentance (2 Ki. 17:13). Later the Samaritans would follow the Mosaic law and monotheism. This is the only Old Testament mention of 'Samaritans' as such.

vi. The colonists' differing religious practices (17:29–41).

30. *Succoth Benoth* could be a place ('booths') for prostitution (as MT, LXX) or for worship of a Babylonian goddess (Banītu as an epithet of Ishtar/Astarte). Since the name of a deity is expected, Zēr-banit (Marduk's consort) has been suggested and Succoth compared with Sakkut (Saturn) in Amos 5:26. *Nergal* was the god of war, death and pestilence at his principal shrine at Cutha, his symbol being a lion. *Ashima* is possibly the '*šm* of the Elephantiné papyri or the Ashima idol named in Amos 8:14.

31. The god *Adrammelech* has the same name as one of Sennacherib's murderers now known to be Arda-mulišši (see

---

[1] F. F. Bruce, *Commentary on the Book of Acts* (London: Marshall, Morgan & Scott, 1965), p. 177, n. 18.

[2] S. M. Paul, 'Sargon's Administrative Diction in II Kings 17.27', *JBL* 88, 1969, pp. 73–74.

on 19:37), meaning the servant of Milki. Anu-milki is possibly 'the God Anu is ruler'. But these deities, like *Nibhaz* and *Tartak*, are otherwise unknown. Their devotees *burned* (so Heb.) their *children*, in contrast to verse 17, 'made to pass through fire'; NIV *sacrificed*. All these false worshippers are served by a non-regulated priesthood (v. 32), none of whom would know God's special covenant requirements (1 Ki. 12:31).

34–40. This is a purely syncretistic worship by non-Yahweh-fearers (vv. 34, 36, 39) without governing *ordinances* (vv. 34, 37), so leading to different customs and practices (vv. 34, 38). Such unfaithfulness to the great covenant between God and his own people contrasts with the law and order which should characterize them. The language and style is thoroughly 'Deuteronomistic' in condemning the Samaritan form of mixed worship. Worship of the LORD must be faithful and exclusive, never part of paganized worship (vv. 37–40). Those who do not do this do not in fact worship God, whatever they profess.

41. For *to this day* see Introduction, p. 57. If *grandchildren* is here taken literally it would have a bearing on the possible dating of this section of the history some seventy years later.

V. THE HISTORY OF JUDAH TO THE FALL OF JERUSALEM (2 Ki. 18:1 – 25:30)

The last part of the history concentrates on Judah alone after the fall of Israel (amaria). It focuses in detail on Hezekiah who, encouraged by Isaiah, resisted the Assyrians (18:1 – 20:21) and on Josiah's reforming reign (22:1 – 23:30), emphasizing the Deuteronomic ideal and selecting data which minimizes the anti-Assyrian intrigues and the drastic reduction in power suffered by the loss of Judean territory. Yet it notes these very failures, similar to those condemned in Israel, which were to bring the house of David into exile after the fall of Jerusalem (ch. 24–25). This history needs to be read in conjunction with 2 Chronicles 29–32 which provides more detail, and with Isaiah 36–39 (a parallel text to 2 Ki. 18–20). Archaeological evidence, including the contemporary Assyrian annals, corroborates the events from another viewpoint.

The flashback to the fall of Samaria (vv. 9–11), repeated

from 17:3–6, has as the theological explanation for it (v. 12) the historian's desire to heighten the difference between the 'successful' early reign of Hezekiah and the apostate final years of the Northern Kingdom. Judah did not go to the help of Samaria, for Hezekiah adopted a policy of non-alignment with Assyria. Similarly he did not side with Philistia when Ashdod fell in 712 BC, but following the unrest in Assyria on Sennacherib's accession there in 705 BC and rebellion by Luli of Tyre and Sidon against the new king, Hezekiah's own plans for expansion (18:8) were interpreted as anti-Assyrian moves or leading the way to ties with Egypt.

The history of Hezekiah (18:1 – 20:21) brings together material from different sources, including the annals of Judah (and probably that account of the fall of Samaria (18:9–12). Details of Sennacherib's attack on Judah (18:13–16) and the demand for the surrender of Jerusalem (18:17 – 19:37) correspond with the Assyrian records. The prophetic tradition emphasizes Isaiah's distinctive role in affairs, in the healing of Hezekiah (20:1–11) and in the reception of Merodach-baladan's embassy (20:12–19).

Many argue that the narrative shows signs of two versions being amalgamated, *e.g.* 18:17 – 19:7 and 19:9b–35, despite overall agreement, as is the case with extra-biblical sources. There is no proof that they should be classed as 'popular anecdotal tradition' rather than as the edited history they purport to be. Others consider references to the divine commandment (18:6–7) or references to cult reform (v. 4) to be the work of different editors, one of whom takes a positive view of the Judean dynasty (and is designated source DtrG). He is revised by another particularly interested in the law and the king's obedience or disobedience to it (DtrN). This interpretation implies complete ignorance of the law of God before Josiah's day, which is unproven (see p. 20).

A. Hezekiah of Judah (18:1 – 20:21)

i. His early years (18:1–12). The usual introductory formula (18:9–11) is followed by an account of the fall of Samaria (18:9–11) which repeats 17:3–6 with only minor changes and with the addition of a theological comment. Its position here may be to place this crucial event in the context of Hezekiah's new reign as a contrast to the history of the Northern

Kingdom which ends with these verses. The selection of the major episodes of Hezekiah's rôle in the deliverance of Jerusalem following faith in God (18:17 – 19:37), and a fatal failure in that faith in conspiring with the Babylonians who were themselves to bring Judah to its knees (20:12–19), highlights the historian's emphasis. His reign ends with the customary concluding formulae (20:20–21).

1–3. *The third year of Hoshea, i.e.* 729/8 BC in which year Hezekiah became co-regent with Ahaz. His sole reign began in 716/6 BC. Compare this with verse 13 where his *fourteenth year* as sole ruler (716/5–687/6 BC) is a date (701 BC) verifiable from Sennacherib's annals. Hezekiah was *twenty-five years old* when he became king in his own right. *His mother's name* Abi (MT) is an abbreviation of Abijah (2 Ch. 29:1). *He did . . . right . . . just as his father David had done* is the same qualification of character and life as given of Asa (1 Ki. 15:11), Jehoshaphat (1 Ki. 22:43) and Josiah (2 Ki. 22:2). Behind this lies the influence of Isaiah, who encouraged him to reopen the temple which had been closed by Ahaz (2 Ch. 28:24; 29:3) and to clean up the worship in Jerusalem (2 Ch. 30:14). His action is interpreted as good (*cf.* 2 Ch. 19:3), as was the influence of the prophet Micah on him (Je. 26:18–19).

4. The motivation for reform was twofold. Firstly, there was a desire for unity in face of the Assyrian threat. The Chronicler tells how Hezekiah issued a challenge to all Israel (2 Ch. 29:5–11) which resulted in a national Passover celebration and contributions to the temple (30:21–27) and its repair (v. 16), with the reorganization of its services and servers (31:11–21). Secondly, the aim of restoring the old Davidic and Solomonic kingdom and centring power at Jerusalem might well have been involved, as well as personal piety and political expediency.[1] His zeal in destroying high places dedicated to Baal (*cf.* 12:3; 14:4; 15:4, 35; 17:9) could have become known to Sennacherib (v. 22). Those who try to make this reform an editorial anticipation of that of Josiah fail to appreciate that 'doing the right' itself required an act of reformation (see Introduction, p. 48). For the *high places*, see Additional Note (pp. 82–83), 1 Kings 3:2; *sacred stones*, 1 Kings 14:23; and

---

[1] E. W. Nicholson, 'The Centralization of the Cult in Deuteronomy', *VT* 13, 1963, pp. 383–389; H. Reviv, 'The History of Judah from Hezekiah to Josiah', *WHJP* IV.1, p. 194; M. Weinfeld, 'Cult Centralisation in Israel in the Light of Neo-Babylonian Analogy', *JNES* 23, 1964, pp. 202–213.

Asherah poles, 1 Kings 14:15. The *Nehushtan* (a name from *nāḥāš*, 'snake' and *nᵉḥōšeṯ*, 'piece of bronze') was still the revered symbol of a bronze snake which represented life to the faithful in Moses' day (Nu. 21:4–9) rather than a Jebusite symbol taken over by Zadok in Jerusalem. Such snake-emblems seem to have become increasingly venerated (*e.g.* a standard found at Hazor. *IBD*, p. 1421). So Hezekiah had turned it from an object of false worship into scrap-metal.

5. Hezekiah's character is given as one who *trusted in the LORD* (v. 5), *held fast* and followed him (v. 6), with the result that the LORD was with him (v. 7) and granted him victory (v. 8). He was unique among kings of Judah since David in this respect, as Josiah was to be in observance of the Mosaic law (23:25).

7. One result was success (AV 'prospered') in everything, which was granted to his demonstrated faith and hard work and despite his diversions and difficulties.

8. The defeat of *the Philistines* reversed the loss of territory to Ahaz (2 Ch. 28:18–19), who had become an Assyrian vassal. Hezekiah sought for independence, but his deposition of Padi of Ekron and alliance with Sidqa of Ashkelon was, according to the Assyrian annals, taken to be anti-Assyrian action. *Gaza* remained loyal to Assyria.

9–11. The fall of *Samaria* repeats 17:3–6 (see above). *The Assyrians took it* (v. 10, Heb. 'they took') may reflect the part played by both Sargon II and Shalmaneser V in this event, see on 17:3–6.

The comment of verse 12 would be appropriate for the 'Deuteronomistic' author of this history. Contrast the attitude of the Northern Kingdom to God with that of an *obedient* Israel, *obey . . . not to violate, i.e.,* keep the *covenant,* do all . . . the LORD commands . . . listen . . . act (Ex. 24:7; Dt. 7–9).

ii. Opposing Sennacherib's threats to Jerusalem (18:13 – 19:37).

a. Sennacherib's campaign in Judah (18:13–16). This king's third campaign (701 BC) was directed via Phoenicia, where Luli of Sidon then fled to Cyprus and was replaced by Ethbaal, and down into Philistia where Sidqa was captured along with Beth-Dagon, Joppa, Ben-Barak, and Azor. The Ekronites were punished for their opposition to the king Padi who was held by Hezekiah in Jerusalem. According to Sennacherib's

annals the forces of the king of Egypt came out as far as Eltekeh[1] and were defeated in open battle. Sennacherib claimed tribute about this time from the rulers of Sidon, Arvad, Gebal (Byblos), Ashdod, Ammon, Moab and Edom.

Following the fall of Timnah (Tell el-Baṭashi) and Ekron (Khirbet el-Muqanna‘) the Assyrian king turned on the heartland of Judah. He had cut off the valley of Sorek and Elah as a possible route into or out of Judah. Sennacherib claimed that the rebel Hezekiah (*Hezaqiau* 'the Jew'; *Yaudāya* could also be taken as 'the Judean') had been 'shut up in Jerusalem his royal capital like a bird in a cage'. Among the captured were 200,150 persons and '46 of his strong walled towns and countless small villages in the vicinity'. Meanwhile Jerusalem itself was closely besieged.[2] See map opposite.

Judah was thus diminished in area and its outlying towns given over to Ashdod, Ekron and Gaza, while the annual tribute levied was considerably increased. Sennacherib turned to Jerusalem from his headquarters near *Lachish* (Tell ed-Duweir), which is depicted on the palace-reliefs from Nineveh as successfully besieged. Hezekiah had pleaded guilty (v. 14) and released Padi, but he had to pay a heavy cost: *three hundred talents of silver* (eleven tons) and *thirty talents of gold* (one ton). In Judah silver appears to have been more valuable than gold. The Assyrian annals record the receipt of '30 talents of gold and 800 talents of silver'.[3] The difference could be due to different scales of weight, but this is unlikely. If not a misreading of the digits in the Assyrian scribal notes then the silver stripped from the temple (v. 15) could have been added in the total, for the details of treasures taken from the temple are meticulously recorded (*cf.* 12:10, 18; 14:14; 16:8; 1 Ki. 7:51; 14:26; 15:18). Sennacherib implies that it took time to collect this payment.

16. The *doorposts* (Heb. *'ōmᵉnôṯ* only here) possibly 'doorframes' (NEB).

b. Sennacherib threatens Jerusalem (18:17–37). See also Isaiah 36–37; 2 Chronicles 32. This is a parallel account of the

---

[1] Tell esh-Shallaf, about 3 km north of Jabneh and 40 km southwest of Jerusalem.
[2] D. Luckenbill, *The Annals of Sennacherib* (Chicago: Chicago University Press, 1924), pp. 29–34, ii. 37 – iii. 49; *ANET*, pp. 287–288; *DOTT*, pp. 66–67.
[3] *Cf.* D. Luckenbill, *op. cit.* iii. 41–49 (*DOTT*, p. 67, *cf. ANET*, p. 288).

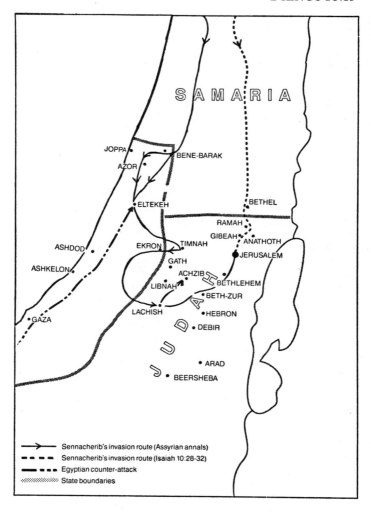

Assyrian Attack on Hezekiah, 701 BC

text already given to support the historian's case for Hezekiah's resistance based on trust in God, prayer and the prophetic promise of deliverance. Some seek to discern two sources here: (i) 18:18 – 19:9a; 19:36–37 and (ii) a more theological overview in 19:9b–33. But both viewpoints could have been incorporated according to the historian's purpose. There is nothing here which cannot be reconciled with the Assyrian annals, which refer to one attack on the city and make no reference to any capture of it. This view now prevails over theories of a second, later attack (*c.* 689 BC) devised to answer the supposedly inappropriate extreme youth of Tirkhakah of Egypt who intervened. New sources, however, indicate that he was at least twenty in 701 BC.

17. The *aqueduct* where the surrender was demanded is the precise place where Isaiah had called on Ahaz to trust the LORD, not Assyria, for deliverance (16:5–10; Is. 7:1–17). The *Upper Pool* (*cf.* Is. 7:3) cannot now be precisely located, but was probably the spring of Gihon east of the city from which the aqueduct, partly underground, watered the fields down to the lower pool (Birket el-Hamrā).[1] See also 20:20 and 2 Chronicles 32:30 for Hezekiah's other irrigation works, including the Siloam tunnel, which enabled the city to withstand the siege. The participants in the parley for surrender were Assyrian high officials: (i) the *supreme commander* (Heb. *tartān*; Akkad. *turtan, cf.* Is. 20:1 (NRSV), 'commander-in-chief'); (ii) the Rabsaris (*rab sārîs*) may be the chief of the royal close advisors (Akkad. *rab ša rēši*) a *chief officer* (*cf.* REB); (iii) the *rab-šāqē* (NRSV 'Rabshekah', probably not the *field commander*) was the title held by an Assyrian provincial governor. This was a powerful team to confront Judah's own high-ranking officials.

18. *Eliakim* 'who was over the palace' administration, see on 1 Kings 4:6, was a son of Hilkiah. This was a common name (*cf.* vv. 26, 37).[2] *Shebna* the Scribe at one time held Eliakim's position as well as that of 'treasurer' or the senior palace administrator ('Prime Minister'), and was condemned by

---

[1] Y. Shiloh, 'City of David, Excavation, 1978', *BA* 42, 1979, pp. 165–171; D. Bahat, 'The Fuller's Field and the "Conduit of the Upper Pool"', *EI* 20, 1989, pp. 253–255 (Heb. pp. 203–204), thinks it to be the conduit running down from the Bethesda pools to water Upper Ophel. This was in speaking distance of the city walls.

[2] The seal reading 'Hanan son of Hilkiah the priest' could refer to the Hilkiah named here or in 22:12 (J. Elayi, 'Le sceau du prêtre Ḥanan, fils de Hilqiyahu', *Semitica* 36, 1986, pp. 42–46).

Isaiah for his halting faith. The name of Shebna also occurs on seals.[1] Nothing else is known about *Joah* as recorder (Heb. *mazkîr*, *cf*. Sa. 8:16).

The negotiations were a masterpiece of deception and psychological warfare. The main Assyrian spokesman appealed on behalf *of the great king* (v. 19) over the head of the king to the people themselves, as the Assyrians had done at the siege of Babylon in 731 BC.[2] The argument aimed to undermine the Judeans' trust, in that (i) Jerusalem had no military might or skill to resist (vv. 20, 23); (ii) Yahweh could not save Jerusalem, any more than had the gods of cities already taken by the Assyrians (vv. 32–36); (iii) Egypt's help would be unreliable (vv. 20–21) and (iv) The Assyrian conquest had been sanctioned by God (Yahweh, v. 25). This was largely true, for Judah's army was a conscript force of infantry with few cavalry. The Assyrians appear aware of Isaiah's words calling them 'the rod of God's anger' (Is. 10:5–11) and emphasizing Egypt's weakness (v. 21, *cf*. Is. 30:1–5).

22. Hezekiah's reforms may not have been universally popular and the negotiators trade on this and try to split the oposition. Corroboration that the reforms were by Hezekiah and not Josiah is found in the dismantling of the altar at Beersheba at this time.[3]

26. This accounts for their insistence on speaking in the current Judean dialect (Heb. *y^{e}hûdît*, the 'Jew's language', v. 28; *cf*. Neh. 13:24) rather than in the diplomatic *Aramaic* (*^{a}rāmît*) used in Assyrian court documents at this time.[4] There are details in Assyrian records of officials speaking such local

---

[1] A contemporary seal from Lachish (*lšbn' 'ḫ'b*), S. H. Hooke, 'An Israelite Seal from Tell Duweir', *PEQ* 66, 1934, pp. 97–98, pl. VII, *cf*. seal impression on a *lmlk* jar handle (*lnr' šbn'*), Y. Aharoni, *Excavations at Ramat Rahel, Seasons 1959 & 1960* (Rome: Centro di studi semitici, 1962), pp. 16 f., pl. 6. 2; and on a jar (*lšnbn' šhr*), C. C. McCown, *Tell en-Naṣbeh I* (Berkeley and New Haven: Palestine Institute of Pacific School of Religion and ASOR, 1947), pp. 160–162, pl. 57, 9–12. Shown also in D. J. Wiseman, *Illustrations from Biblical Archaeology* (London: IVP, 1958), p. 59; *IBD*, p. 1431.

[2] H. W. F. Saggs, 'The Nimrud Letters, 1952', *Iraq* 17, 1955, pp. 23–24 (ND. 2632); H. Tadmor, 'On the use of Aramaic in the Assyrian Empire: Three observations on a relief of Sargon II', *EI* 20, 1989, pp. 249–252 (Hebrew) discusses a relief from Khorsabad showing an Assyrian officer standing on a siege-machine and holding a scroll as he addresses defenders on the wall.

[3] Y. Aharoni, 'The Horned Altar of Beer-sheba', *BA* 37, 1974, p. 6.

[4] See D. J. Wiseman, *Nebuchadrezzar and Babylon* (Oxford: British Academy, 1985), pp. 1–2.

languages, some of them being native exiles (see on 17:5).

27–32. The Assyrians appeal on the basis of fear and favour. The threat is that there would be a long damaging siege if they do not capitulate (v. 27), with the blame for it put on Hezekiah (v. 29). The power of *the great king*, an Assyrian royal title, elsewhere used only of the LORD God (Ps. 47:2; Mal. 1:14; Mt. 5:35), is emphasized (vv. 28, 29). The appeal is to *make peace with me* (NIV, NEB, MT). The use of 'blessing' for a treaty relationship, usually 'peace' (*šālôm*), occurs only here and may denote making a gesture of compromise in order to enjoy an idyllic life of peace and prosperity in their own land (v. 31, *cf.* 1 Ki. 4:25; Mic. 4:4; Zc. 3:10). Exile was a constant threat to all minority groups in the ancient Near East, and references to it in the Old Testament should not always be interpreted as written during the major post-Judean exile, for the example of the exile from Samaria was fresh in their minds.[1]

33–35. Isaiah was to counter this taunt of the inability of their national God to save them from the hand of Assyria and answer it by the fact that Yahweh is the true and living God, who cannot be equated with non-gods (Dt. 4:35, 5:7), and who actually did save the city (*cf.* 19:31–36; 2 Ch. 32:21; Is. 10:9–11).

Hamath (v. 34) had been taken over by Sennacherib following its capture in 720 BC. *Arpad* (Tell Erfad, north of Aleppo); *Sephervaim and Ivvah*, see on 17:24; *Hena* is unknown but may have been in their vicinity. Some MSS (LXX(L) and Old Latin) insert 'where are the gods of the land of Samaria?' after Ivvah, but this is implied. 'Have *they* rescued Samaria?' refers to the gods of Samaria, on which see on 17:5.

36–37. The people's silence shows support of their king and was not necessarily a sign of fear, even though it marked their distress, as did the *torn clothes*, a traditional sign of mourning, perhaps here at the insults and blasphemous words spoken about God (19:4, 6; *cf.* Mt. 26:65).

c. Jerusalem's deliverance foretold (19:1–36).

i. Hezekiah seeks a word from the LORD (19:1–5). The story of Sennacherib's siege of Jerusalem continues with the first

[1] K. A. Kitchen in J. B. Payne (ed.), *New Perspectives on the Old Testament* (Waco: Word, 1970), pp. 1–2.

reference to the prophet Isaiah being consulted (vv. 1–7). He was outspokenly anti-Egyptian and anti-Assyrian (Is. 30:1–7; 31:1–9; 10:5–19). Hezekiah was moved by the circumstances to repentance (*cf.* v. 14), and his entry into the newly reopened temple may be related to a public act of fasting (*cf.* Je. 36:6–9). This need not be a mere editorial emphasis on the king's piety, for the change of attitude in verses 6–7 is explained as due to a message from God. He involved both state and religious authorities at a time of crisis (v. 2, *the secretary* and *leading priests, cf.* Je. 19:1). On Eliakim and Shebna see 18:18, 37.

The message to Isaiah (vvc. 3–5) reflects Hezekiah's view of the critical situation and the feeling of helplessness (the difficult childbirth may be a proverb, v. 4). He was aware that God had heard the blasphemy (v. 6) shown by the words of the Assyrian officials as they 'mock' (v. 4, NRSV; NIV *ridicule,* REB 'taunt') God by putting him on the same level as no-gods. Words spoken against God's people are the same as speaking against God himself. For this both the speaker and the one who sent him will be held to account. For Hezekiah God is alive (*living*) in contrast to the no-gods (18:33–35). He counted on Isaiah the prophet as a man of prayer like Moses (Ex. 32:31–32; Nu. 14:13–19) and Samuel (1 Sa. 7:8–9; Ps. 99:6; Je. 15:1).

The doctrine of *the remnant* (vv. 4, 30) left by God's grace through times of trial was demonstrated by Isaiah, whose son was named Shear-Jashub, 'remnant will return' (Is. 7:3; 37:30–32). Israelites fled to Judah so that in one sense Judah also included the remnant of Israel to carry on God's name and work.

ii. Isaiah's reply to Hezekiah (19:6–7). The answer comes with divine authority (*This is what the LORD says*) and is consistent with God's word through the ages to his people in distress: *Do not be afraid* (*cf.* 1 Ki. 17:13; 2 Ki. 6:16). The spokesman for God is saying what God himself always said (*cf.* Gn. 15:1; Mt. 10:26; 14:27; Rev. 1:17; 2:10). It is God also who moves men's minds and hearts, here using a rumour to divert the enemy's attack. This could be either the approach of Tirhakah with his Egyptian forces (vv. 8–9) or the disturbances in Syria which later led to Sennacherib's death.

The view that *Tirhakah* (Egypt. *Taharqa*; Assyr. *Tarqu*) was too young to lead the combined Nubian (Cush) and Egyptian forces has now been shown to be incorrect, as he was more than twenty years old and later became king of the 25th Dynasty (*c.* 690–664 BC). That he is here named 'King of Kush' has been explained as due to someone writing before 680 BC who was aware of his opposition to Sennacherib who named him in his annals (ii. 80) during his long reign, using his well-known title. At this time Tirhakah was the army commander-in-chief for his brother Shebitku, king of Egypt, who died *c.* 691 BC.[1] Though Sennacherib defeated a confederation at Eltekeh (*altaqū*), he did not capture the Egyptian king, who may well have come back. There is no need to posit a second invasion of Judah by the Assyrians *c.* 686 BC, since Sennacherib's annals do not mention this.

7. Isaiah's prophecy (vv. 20–34) covers the withdrawal by the Assyrians both from Judah and Jerusalem (v. 8) and foretells Sennacherib's murder twenty years later in 681 BC, taken to be the punishment for his blasphemy against Yahweh.

iii. Another message to Hezekiah from Sennacherib (19:8–13).

8. Sennacherib attacked *Libnah* (between Gath and Lachish; possibly Tell Burnaṭ)[2] with the intention of preventing the Egyptians from reaching Jerusalem. The Assyrian reliefs from Nineveh show Judeans being taken into exile from Lachish at this time.

9–10. This second message (*again sent*) to Hezekiah comes from a different source than 18:19–35, but does not contradict it. The MT 'turned and sent' (*cf.* Is. 37:9) stresses the repetition and the scroll 1QIsa (and Gk.) reads 'when he heard (*cf.* v. 7) he sent'. There are variants, and the letter may show Sennacherib's increased arrogance, and perhaps haste under pressure, rather than, as some would have it, mere theological reflection by a later editor. Note the precise Assyrian letter form: '*Say to* . . .' The argument still depends on the belief that God cannot save the city. How can 'you be (so) deluded by your god?' (REB).

11–12. The list of city-states put to the ban (Heb. *ḥērem*;

---

[1] K. A. Kitchen, *The Third Intermediate Period in Egypt (1100–600 B.C.)* (London: Aris & Phillips, 1972), pp. 154–158; Supplement 1986, p. 557, *contra* M. F. L. Macadam, *Temples of Kawa* I (London: Oxford University Press, 1949), pp. 18–20, considers that Taharqa was not born until *c.* 709 BC.

[2] Y. Aharoni, *The Land of the Bible: A Historical Geography* (London: Burns & Oates, [2]1979), p. 439.

'exterminated' or destroyed completely, RSV) reminds the reader that it was not only Israel who used this method in warfare (see Nu. 21:2–3; Jos. 6:21).

Gozan (Tell Halaf) was captured by Assyria in 809 BC (*cf.* 17:6); *Rezeph* is possibly Rezafeh northeast of Damascus, taken *c.* 841 BC; *Eden* is the Assyrian province of Bīt-Adīni south of Harran, of which *Tel Assar* (*cf.* Is. 37:12) may be one town, possibly Tell Assur or Tell Bassar southeast of Raqqa on the River Euphrates. All these were notable examples of Assyrian triumphs in an area known to the people of Palestine. On the other places in verse 13 see on 17:24, 18:34.

iv. Hezekiah's prayer (19:14–19). Cf. Isaiah 37:14–20. The historian notes that not only the prophet but the ruler prays (*cf.* v. 1). To *spread out* a parchment or papyrus letter can be compared with the contemporary Mesopotamian practice of placing letters in the temple to be read by the god. These were usually pleas for help, including deliverance from sickness as well as reports on factual situations.[1] The prayer is addressed to God as creator and king, alive, unique and still ruling. The plea is that the suppliant may be heard and the situation seen by God.

15. *Enthroned between the cherubim, i.e.,* present with his people, see on 1 Kings 6:23–28 (*cf.* Ex. 25:18; 1 Sa. 4:4). The inspiration for this may come from the temple and possibly from Isaiah's experience (Is. 6:1). *You alone are God,* for his rule was considered to be universal as the creator of all.

18. Once it is recognized that idols are merely *fashioned by men's hands* (Dt. 4:28; Acts 17:29), then they can be seen as *no-gods* and unable to do anything (Is. 44:9–11; Je. 10:3–10). The futility of such deities (Ps. 115:3–8; 135:15–18) is a recurrent theme in Isaiah's teaching (2:20; 40:19–20; 41:7; 44:9–20).

19. The plea *deliver us* ('save us', RSV) can only be answered if asked for God's glory. *That you alone, O LORD, are God* has been called a 'standard recognition formula' but need not be classified as post-exilic on the basis of supposed frequent use

[1] W. W. Hallo, 'Royal correspondence of Larsa: a Sumerian prototype for the prayer of Hezekiah', in B. L. Eichler *et al.* (eds.), *Kramer Anniversary Volume* (Kevelaer: Butzon & Bercker, 1976), pp. 209–224; *JAOS* 53, 1968, pp. 75–80; N. Na'aman, 'Sennacherib's "letter to God" on his campaign in Judah', *BASOR* 214, 1974, pp. 25–39.

in Ezekiel, where the precise phrase is not used (*cf.* Is. 37:16, 20; Neh. 9:6). This is the basis for asking God to vindicate his ways to man.

v. Isaiah's prophecy (19:20–34). Cf. Isaiah 37:21–35. Isaiah's reply consists of separate messages to Sennacherib (vv. 21–28) and Hezekiah (vv. 29–31). Though some argue that these are later insertions, others think they were added not long after the composition of this whole narrative (18:17 – 19:37).[1] The collection of sayings is relevant to the situation of Assyrian arrogance against God.

God's reply to Sennacherib (19:21–28). The enemy, not God, is now mocked in a poetic 'taunt-song' with its characteristic metre. There are some parallels between the contents of these songs (*e.g.* vv. 28, 33).

21. Jerusalem and its inhabitants are personified as defence-less as a *virgin daughter*. To shake or 'wag the head' (RSV; NIV *toss*) is a gesture of derisory contempt (Ps. 22:7; Je. 18:16).

22. *The Holy One of Israel* is a characteristic Isaianic phrase (1:4, *etc.*, *cf.* Ps. 71:22; Je. 50:29; 51:5).

23. The Hebrew here is difficult. To have *ascended the heights* may be compared with the boasts in Assyrian annals to reach inaccessible mountainous regions where none has been before. NEB 'I have mounted my chariot ... gone high up in the mountains' adds 'and done mighty deeds' (not MT, but in a few LXX MSS). To *cut down . . . cedars* was the object of many military expeditions to the Lebanon ranges. *Remotest parts* or 'farthest corners' (REB) or *heights*, 'densest forest' (RSV;·'most luxurious forest', REB) is emended from MT 'forest of his Carmel'.

24. 'All the rivers of besieged places' (*māṣār*, AV) may be nearer the MT than '*I have dried up all the streams of Egypt*', since Egypt (*miṣrayîm*) is not in the Hebrew text. Apart from Herodotus' reference to Sennacherib reaching Pelusium (II. 141) there is no other statement that the Assyrians now entered Egypt, so most take this as boastful exaggeration. But since the text has 'streams of a fortress' (*māṣôr*) others seek for another location such as an unlocated Miṣṣôr (El Amarna letters) or less likely, Muṣri.[2]

25. This is a picture of complete destruction, with fortified

---

[1] R. E. Clements, *Isaiah 1–39* (London: Marshall, Morgan & Scott, 1980), p. 285.
[2] H. Tawil, 'The problem of Ye'ōrē Maṣôr', *JNES* 41, 1982, pp. 195–206.

cities trampled down into *piles of stones* or 'heaps of rubble' (NEB, REB; *cf.* Is. 37:26, 1QIs^a).

26. This symbolizes fragile weakness, 'short of hand' (MT, *cf.* Is. 50:2), *drained of power*. The simile of grass on a roof scorched before it is grown up or 'before the east wind' (REB, *cf.* Is. 37:27) follows 1QIs^a scroll.

27. The same text adds 'rising up' before 'sit down' (NIV *stay*) in 1QIs^a on Isaiah 37:28 (*cf.* Ps. 139:2).

28. The Assyrian practice of leading foreign princes captive with a ring or *hook in* the *nose* is depicted on Esarhaddon's stela at Zenjirli showing him holding Tirhakah of Egypt and Ba'alu of Tyre (*ANEP*, p. 447).

God's reply to Hezekiah (19:29–34). The picture of the recovery of the land within two full years after the Assyrian invasion is taken as a message of hope for survivors (*a remnant*). The sign (*'ôt*, a word used in Is. 7:11) is that the existing stored and standing crops destroyed in about March or April will only leave *what grows by itself* (REB 'self-sown grain'). The word (*sāpiaḥ*) refers to seed left during a sabbatical year (Lv. 25:5, 11). The Assyrian army may have left only about October, when it would be too late to expect a further crop. However, by the *third year* all will have recovered.

30. The doctrine of *the remnant* – though the word here (*p^{e}lêṭat*) is not that used in Isaiah (7:3, *š^e'ār*) where he names his son Shear-Jashub ('The remnant will return') – is prominent in both Old and New Testaments. It refers to those kept for future redemption (Is. 10:20–22; 11:11, 16; Mi. 4:7; Rom. 11:5). Since many Israelites fled to Judah at this time, there is a sense in which Judah became the remnant of Israel.

31. *The zeal of the LORD Almighty will accomplish this* applies here to the miraculous act of the deliverance of Jerusalem, as in Isaiah. Isaiah 9:6–7 uses this phrase of the birth of a unique deliverer-king to rule David's kingdom.

Verses 32–34 continue verse 21 as the prophet's answer to Hezekiah. This does not contradict Sennacherib's annals, which state that he used earth-ramps and siege equipment, mines and other works against the towns of Judah (including Lachish), but in Jerusalem where he shut up Hezekiah, he set up an encircling group of watch-posts (*halṣu*) to prevent anyone entering or leaving the city (*contra ANET*, p. 288, translation 'earthwork'). There is then no need to consider verses 32–33 to be an exaggeration or to refer to a second attack.

33. 'This is the very word of the LORD' (NEB) translates the two Hebrew words ($n^{e^{,}}um\ yhwh$) *declares the LORD*, which always authenticate a prophecy. The repetition of ideas in verse 33 (*cf.* v. 28) could be for emphasis, just as verse 34 underscores the theological significance of the defence of Jerusalem. Such a purpose is prominent throughout Hezekiah's reign and does not involve any view of the inviolability of the capital in general. For the special relation shown by '*for my sake and for the sake of David*', v. 34, see 1 Kings 11:12–13. Jeremiah later argued that those who traded on this prophecy as meaning that the temple in Jerusalem would never be taken were superstitious and presumptuous (Je. 7:1–15).

vi. Sennacherib's retreat (19:35–36). Cf. Isaiah 37:36–38; 2 Chronicles 32:21–22. The location of the Assyrian camp is not given, for the king himself may not have been at Jerusalem but possibly to the southwest (Libnah?). Herodotus (II.141) tells of an Assyrian retreat after mice had eaten through the leather thongs of military equipment at Pelusium in northeast Egypt. This has been interpreted as bubonic plague. But this incident is possibly different from that at Jerusalem, of which insufficient detail is given for any positive identification of the cause for the withdrawal. For the *angel of the LORD* as causing death or disease see 1 Chronicles 21:12–15, 30 (*cf.* Ex. 12:12, 29–30). The ancients attributed disease to the 'hand of God'. This has been thought to be a bacillary dysentery which had a three-day incubation period.[1] Chronicles implies that the leaders were also affected (2 Ch. 32:21). The numbers could be interpreted as 'a hundred and eighty-five officers' who died (*cf. a hundred and eighty-five thousand men*). *When the people got up the next morning – there were all the dead bodies!* (NIV) makes more sense than 'when they arose next morning, behold they were all dead corpses'! (AV). Herodotus' story is significant in that Egyptian tradition (Herodotus II.141) also referred to divine intervention saving Egypt from Sennacherib in 701 BC. Sennacherib's return to his capital Nineveh is confirmed by his annals (iii.47–48).

d. The death of Sennacherib (19:37). The Assyrian king some years later (hence *one day*) was killed by his son on 20th

[1] D. J. Wiseman, 'Medicine in the OT World', in B. Palmer (ed.), *Medicine and the Bible* (Exeter: Paternoster Press, 1986), p. 25.

Tebet of his twenty-third year (681 BC). A neo-Babylonian letter says that there was a conspiracy (as Babylonian Chronicle) led by an older son Arda-muliŝŝi (so Adrammelech, Berossus *Adramelos*, Ardamuzan). The conspirators fled to Hanigalbat in Urartu (Ararat) and eventually a younger son Esarhaddon ruled Assyria (681–668 BC), *cf*. Ezra 4:2.[1] A later account of the murder by Ashurbanipal implies that the assassination took place between the guardian figures at the temple entrance. *Nisroch* may be a rendering of the name of the national god Assur (*cf*. LXX Esdrach, Asorach) rather than of the god Nusku (*nswk*).

2 Chronicles 32:23 adds a note of the international recognition accorded Yahweh and Hezekiah for this successful resistance against Assyrian power.

iii. Other incidents in Hezekiah's reign (20:1–21). The account of this king ends with two incidents, Hezekiah's sickness (vv. 1–11) and a visit from an embassy sent by Merodach-baladan of Babylon (vv. 12–19, the same order as followed by Isaiah 38–39) and the customary concluding formulae (vv. 20–21). The emphasis is on Hezekiah as the recipient of divine favour, despite the role of Isaiah in pointing up his failings. Three prophetic oracles are given (vv. 1, 4–6, 16–18) and some see these as a collection of independent traditions. Note that verses 1–8 use the personal name Hezekiah (*ḥizqiyāhû*) and verses 9–11 Yehezekiah (*yᵉḥizqiyāhû*). Those who disallow predictive prophecy (vv. 16–18) make some sections *post-eventum* (after 587 BC) and seek to trace a developing theology producing differing editorial hands.[2] However, the author of Kings himself could well have been reflecting on these events about that time.

a. Hezekiah's illness (20:1–11). *Cf*. Isaiah 38; 2 Chronicles 32:24–26. *In those days* is a general statement, but the embassy from Merodach-baladan would presumably have taken place before his exile in 702 BC. The historian links the illness with the siege of Jerusalem (v. 6). The king was 'dangerously ill'

---

[1] S. Parpola, 'The Murder of Sennacherib', in B. Alster (ed.), *Death in Mesopotamia* (Copenhagen: Akademisk Forlag, 1980), pp. 171–182.

[2] R. E. Clements, *op. cit.*, pp. 277–297; P. Ackroyd, 'Interpretation of the Babylonian Exile; a study of 2 Kings 20, Isaiah 38–39', *Scottish Journal of Theology* 27, 1974, pp. 329–352.

(NEB) and *at the point of death,* and this is not contradicted by the later treatment of a mere symptom (v. 7) or by his swift recovery. For interventions by a prophet in terms of illness see also 1 Kings 17:17–24; 2 Kings 4:22 ff.; and for his advice to *put your house* (family affairs) *in order* before death, *cf.* 2 Samuel 17:23. The Hebrew *ṣiwwâ* means to 'give commands' and here and in 1 Kings 2:1 some interpret this as 'give your last charge' (NEB 'instructions') on the basis of a later Arab. *waṣā*. It may include the requirement to name a successor. The additional fifteen years of life allowed Hezekiah time to train his son Manasseh as his co-regent. The prophetic assertion *you are going to die* (typical of ancient medical prognosis) will be changed by prayer (*cf.* Am. 7:1–3, 4–6). There are contemporary Assyrian and Babylonian prayers to the gods 'for the lengthening of my days and the multiplying of my years'.[1]

Divine sovereignty does not render prayer in sickness inappropriate, for prayer and God's answer are both part of his plan (*cf.* 1 Ki. 21:29; Ezk. 33:13–16; Jas. 5:15–16).

3. This is no mere emphasis on Hezekiah's piety, for he wept and repentance is mentioned in 2 Chronicles 32:26. The words used in prayer, that Hezekiah had *walked* (lived) *faithfully,* done *good in your* (the LORD's) *eyes* and been 'loyal in your service' (REB) are typical of Kings and Deuteronomy. The LORD looks in favour on those who faithfully serve him (*cf.* 2 Sa. 22:21).

4. The prophet had just left the palace when God sent him back. He was responsive to God's call. The *middle court* (MT *Q'rē,* the text as read; *ḥāṣēr,* 'court') lay between the palace and temple (as in 1 Ki. 7:8), though MT Kethib (the text as written) has *middle city* (*hā'îr*), whence presumably REB 'the citadel'. The title *the leader* or 'the prince' (MT *nāgîd,* not in Is. 38:5) was a link between Hezekiah and David (1 Ki. 1:35). Since God orders everything (Eph. 1:11), he alone can say *I will heal you* (Is. 57:18; Je. 33:6) as the ultimate healer (Ex. 15:26; *cf.* Acts 9:34). Such a belief does not preclude the use of proven medicines or doctors (v. 7).

5–6. *On the third day* ('the day after tomorrow') implies 'very soon' rather than as sometimes traditionally and literally interpreted of the resurrection (Mt. 12:40). The third day terminates the conventional period of hospitality or a visit. The

---

[1] D. J. Wiseman in B. Palmer, *op. cit.,* p. 40.

importance of giving thanks in God's house is stressed (*cf.* Lk. 17:14, 16–17). Here going *up to the temple* may have been for that purpose (Lv. 14:2). Our times are in God's hands (Ps. 31:15) and any lengthening of life is by his special blessing. Hezekiah was granted an added *fifteen years*; since he died *c.* 686 BC this promise can be dated from about the time of the siege of Jerusalem. His recovery was then also symbolic of the recovery of Jerusalem (as in v. 6). On the care of God for his city and dynasty (but not necessarily their inviolability) see 19:34. *For the sake of David* as promised initially (2 Sa. 7:15–16) and often reiterated, see 19:34; 1 Kings 11:13; Acts 2:30.

7. This is a rare example of a prophet as healer. *The poultice of figs* rather than 'cake of figs' (RSV; 'fig plaster', REB) is influenced by the known occurrence and use of the term (*dᵉbelet*) in medical texts (Ras Shamra 55:28; 56:33), where a raisin-poultice was used to cure a horse! In Isaiah (38) the cure follows Hezekiah's psalm of thanksgiving (omitted here and 2 Ch. 32). If there is significance in this, it means that he had faith to believe the prophet's word before it happened.

8–11. The sign of healing. This miraculous sign (so 2 Ch. 32:24) is also an integral part of Isaiah 38:1–8 and cannot be dismissed as later prophetic 'legend'. A sign to authenticate a prophet's word that it is God who is acting is not uncommon. It was natural ('a light thing' MT) for the shadow to move forward, so this reversal of the natural order by regression would be more significant and less unmistakable than a rapid advance.[1] The degrees or *steps* have best been interpreted as 'upper chamber' or 'sundial'.

An upper chamber (reading *ᵃliyat* with Qumran 1QIaᵃ in Is. 38:8) was used perhaps for celestial observations for guiding decisions. Ahaz may have introduced such practices in the temple area.[2] The story is not 'clearly legendary' (Jones) or a reference to a solar eclipse. Such authenticating phenomena are also noted in Joshua 10:12–14. A sundial (v. 11) was known in Babylon (Herodotus II. 109) and in Egypt was marked by the shadow on steps or *stairway* (as NIV; MT *maᵃlôt*; see *IBD*, p. 1567) leading from east to west and perhaps miraculously lit up.[3]

---

[1] *Cf.* B. Ramm, *The Christian View of Science and Scripture* (London: Paternoster Press, 1955), pp. 110–112.

[2] S. Iwry, 'The Qumran Isaiah and the end of the Dial of Ahaz', *BASOR* 147, 1957, pp. 27–33.

[3] B. Ramm, *op. cit.*

2 KINGS 20:12–19

b. Envoys from Merodach-baladan (20:12–19). 12.
Merodach-Baladan (MT Berodach-baladan, Heb. *b* and *m* are a common labial variant) was Marduk-apla-iddinna II, the Chaldaean king of Babylon in 721–710, and for six months in 703/2 BC. *Son of Baladan* is likely to be the common Babylonian name Bel-iddin (revocalized MT *bēlʾᵃdan* fits with Aramaic notations on cuneiform tablets *bl⁽ʾ⁾dn*).[1] Sending *letters and a gift* by envoys was the normal Babylonian diplomatic procedure. The timing of the embassy may have been before or during Merodach-balan's second period on the throne (see above). Hezekiah 'paid attention' to the messengers (MT *šmʿ*), whereas Isaiah 39:2 'gladly' follows Greek and Vulgate in reading 'rejoiced' (*śmḥ*).

According to Josephus (*Ant.* x.2.2) the purpose of the visit was to secure Hezekiah as an ally in an anti-Assyrian coalition, but this is not stressed here. The Babylonians were already challenging their Assyrian overlords and Isaiah was consistently against alliance with any world-powers of the day.

13. Hezekiah was not 'overly hospitable'; such display in *storehouses* of precious objects (RSV 'treasure-house', REB 'treasury', Heb. *bēt nᵉḵōt*; only here and Is. 39:2; Akkad. *bīt nakkamāti*) was common to impress potential allies. For Hezekiah's wealth see 2 Chronicles 32:27. The extent of that account implies this was before the payments to Sennacherib in 701 BC (18:15–16). The *spices* and 'fragrant aromatic oil' (NEB) indicates good trade with central Arabia. The *armoury* may have been the House of the Forest of Lebanon where Solomon had stored the state treasures (*cf.* 1 Ki. 10:16–17).

14–19. Isaiah's reply. The prophet wisely established the facts before passing judgment. His statement makes it clear that the royal treasures will be taken to Babylon and that Hezekiah's descendants (RSV 'sons', v. 16) will go there also. Most commentators view this as a much later comment and do not give weight to the fact that Babylon's attitude is already known and Jerusalem will suffer the same fate as Samaria if it continues in sin. Another special deliverance cannot be counted upon.

The word of the LORD ... is good (v. 19) could only be a formal reaction to the oracle. Here for Hezekiah it is interpreted as peace and security while he is alive. Hezekiah may

[1] A. R. Millard, 'Baladan, the Father of Merodach-Baladan', *TynB* 22, 1971, pp. 125–126.

288

have been accepting God's word submissively rather than just with relief at the postponement of judgment, though such it was. God's word is open to differing interpretations as good or bad according to the recipient's life and attitude.

c. Concluding formulae (20:20–21). These standard elements in the history take as an example Hezekiah's water-supply tunnel running from Gihon (Virgin's Spring) to the Upper Pool (Birket Silwan) west of Ophel and to the Old (Lower) Pool in Jerusalem (*cf.* Is 22:11). This tunnel, found in 1880, was cut for 643 metres to cover a direct distance of 332 metres to enable the defenders to fetch water within the protective walls even during a siege. An inscription in cursive Hebrew of the early eighth century BC details the work:

> When (the tunnel) was driven through while (the quarrymen were swinging their) axes, each man towards the other and, while there was still 3 cubits to be cut through (there was heard) the voice of a man calling to his fellow, for there was a crevice(?) on the right . . . and when the tunnel was (finally) driven through, the quarrymen hewed each towards the other, axe against axe. Then the waters flowed from the Spring to the Pool for 1,200 cubits and the height of the rock above the head(s) of the quarrymen was 100 cubits.[1]

The additional detail in 2 Chronicles 32:30 (Sirach 48:17) may, however, confuse the tunnel with a conduit along the lower surface of the hill with sluices designed to water the royal gardens below, perhaps the work of Ahaz (18:17).[2]

21. Hezekiah was buried on the sloping hill where the tombs of David's descendants were cut (2 Ch. 32:33). This was because the royal Iron Age burial caves north of the city were full by this time and hereafter no Judean kings were buried in the rock-hewn caves there.[3] On *Manasseh* see 21:1–17.

---

[1] For the text, *cf. DOTT*, p. 210; *ANET*, p. 321. A facsimile is given in *IBD*, pp. 1452–1453; for the tunnel (height varying 1–3.5 m. and width *c.* 60 cm.) see also *ANEP*, nos. 275, 744.

[2] Y. Shiloh, 'City of David, Excavations 1978', *BA* 42, 1979, p. 168.

[3] A Kloner, 'The Cave of the Kings', *Levant* 18, 1986, p. 129. He places these tombs to the north of the Damascus Gate (in modern St Etienne) and dated to the late Iron Age by their very fine cutting.

B. History of reigns (21:1–26)

i. Manasseh of Judah (21:1–18). *Cf.* 2 Chronicles 33:1–20;
Josephus, *Ant.* x.3.1–4. Though Manasseh had the longest reign of any king of Israel or Judah, the historian concentrates on his religious apostasy, which contrasts with the good of his predecessor Hezekiah and successor Josiah. His selection of events is no distortion, for the fuller picture by the Chronicler conveys the same message.

Manasseh was born after Hezekiah's illness (20:6) and lived during the height of Assyrian power which, under Esarhaddon (681–669 BC) and Ashurbanipal (669–627 BC) controlled as far west as Upper Egypt, and from 671 onwards Judah was a steady and stable vassal of the Assyrians, allowing them free passage on the coastal route. Manasseh is named in Assyrian annals (*Menasi* or *Minse*, king of Yaudi) among twelve rulers of Palestine who brought tribute in kind to their overlord.[1] There is, however, no evidence that the Assyrians forced any vassal to change his religious policy except in so far as he had to acknowledge his overlord's god as the one who would exact revenge for any infringement of a covenant-treaty, a copy of which would have to be laid up in the temple. Manasseh's sin in reversing his father's purification of the cult (18:3–5) and in reverting to Ahaz' practices (16:3) would have been his own decision. This may have been encouraged by a pro-Assyrian or pro-Egyptian party gaining the ascendency.

a. Summary of reign (21:1–9). **1.** The introductory formulae (vv. 1–2) give a reference to when Manasseh became a ruler (MT 'in his governing') as co-regent from 696/5 or earlier (sole ruler 687/6 – 642/1 BC) for a total of *fifty-five years*. His name means, 'he made to forget (the loss of an earlier child)'. His mother *Hephzibah*, 'my delight is in her' (*cf.* Is. 62:4).

2–3. Manasseh's sins were considered to be the worst of all the kings of Judah and led to the judgment of exile on the whole people (v. 12; 24:3). They were 'Canaanite' practices specifically forbidden by the Mosaic law. The abhorrent *detestable practices* (RSV, AV 'abominations') were all idolatrous (*cf.* 1 Ki. 14:24), reversing those removed by Hezekiah (2 Ki.

---

[1] Also an Assyrian letter (K1295) of this time mentions 'gold from Beth-Ammon and Moab, silver from Edom and 10 mana of silver from the inhabitants of Judah' (*ANET*, p. 301; *DOTT*, p. 75).

18:3–5) and returning to those practised by Ahaz (2 Ki. 16:3). The hill shrines (*high places*) had been destroyed by Hezekiah (18:4; *cf.* 2 Ch. 31:1), while *altars* and *an Asherah pole* (the symbol of the Astarte mother-goddess cult) had been introduced by *Ahab* (1 Ki. 16:32–33). The aggravated sin lay in their now being introduced into the very temple precincts. Manasseh was 'the Ahab of Judah' and the antithesis of the great David. Astral worship of the *starry hosts* of heaven was practised throughout Palestine (as was that of the 'Queen of Heaven', Je. 7:17–18, etc.).

4. Yahweh's exclusive *Name*, denoting his character and presence, must always dominate worship of him (see 1 Ki. 8:16–19; Ex. 20:24). Since two temple courtyards are not named in 1 Kings 6, some regard this as an interpolation from Ezekiel's inner and outer courts (Ezk. 40:19). It may refer, however, to the 'middle court' of 20:4.

6. On *sacrificed his own son in the fire* compare the Hebrew 'made … pass through fire', rather than RSV 'burned his son as an offering' which presupposes child sacrifice, see on 16:3. For 'soothsaying' (RSV) or *sorcery* see on 17:17 and on 'augury' (RSV) or *divination* (MT *niḥēš* may imply chanting or even snake-charming). *Mediums*, 'ghosts' and *spiritists* imply acknowledgement of powers of revelation other than God. These are all ancient practices forbidden in Moses' time (Lv. 19:26; Dt. 18:10–14). There is no evidence that the Deuteronomic prohibitions against these practices were only composed at a later period.

The strong comments by the historian and the ensuing prophetic pronouncements in verses 7–15 are taken by many critics to be a later explanation of the destruction of Judah. But the language is consistent with that employed throughout this book. The unique expression 'graven image' (RSV) or *carved Asherah pole* (*cf.* 2 Ch. 33:7, 'image of the idol') may imply the importation of a sumptuous idol into the temple. This section (vv. 8–15) uses typical Deuteronomistic phraseology, for the people are linked with Manasseh's sin. No nation can sin apart from popular consent or acquiescence. The leader is the most responsible.

9. The Greek adds 'evil in the eyes of the LORD'. The nations the LORD destroyed at the entry to the land left a residual legacy of temptation to follow their ways (1 Ki. 14:24; Dt. 12:29–31).

b. God's word to Manasseh (21:10–15). God warns through more than one messenger. *His servants* here also are *the prophets* whose official status gained them access to the court (as 2 Ch. 33:18).

11. On *more evil than the Amorites* see 1 Kings 21:26.

12. The *disaster on Jerusalem* refers to the final sack of Jerusalem in 587 BC, re-echoed in the words of Jeremiah (19:3). Note also the use of *God of Israel* which occurs thirty-two times in Jeremiah. The *measuring and plumb lines* used in construction (Is. 44:13) will mark the careful work of complete destruction (Is. 34:11; Am. 7:7–9) as had been experienced by Israel (*house of Ahab*). To wipe a dish and turn it *upside-down* to drain signified the depopulation of the land (*cf.* Je. 51:34).

14. On *the remnant* see 19:4, 30–31. God will give over the sinner to judgment at the hands of his enemies (Dt. 1:27; 2 Ki. 13:3; 17:20).

15. *Because* adds another reason for punishment to verses 12–14. People, like prince (v. 6), provoke God.

c. Further events and concluding formulae to reign (21:16–18). **16.** To *shed innocent blood* implies oppression against the young, innocent and godly (*cf.* 2 Ki. 24:3–4). The uncorroborated Jewish tradition (*The Ascension of Isaiah*) says that Isaiah was sawn in half during the reign of Manasseh (*cf.* Heb. 11:37). Others interpret it as the liquidation of opponents.[1]

17–18. The concluding formulae refer the reader to other sources. 2 Chronicles 33 adds details of the religious practices (vv. 1–9), the work of rebuilding the wall of Jerusalem (v. 14) and (an aspect omitted by the author of Kings) Manasseh's abduction to Babylon, perhaps to appear in some Assyrian victory celebration there (648 BC?), which was followed by his repentance and release and acknowledgment that Yahweh is indeed the God (vv. 11–16). There is as yet no external evidence for this episode or for Manasseh's removal of foreign deities and altars in and around Jerusalem (2 Ch. 33:15–16). Ahlstrom, who thinks Kings gives us a distorted picture of this reign, argues that Manasseh recovered territory lost by Hezekiah and reorganized the administrative and religious

---

[1] H. Reviv, 'The History of Judah from Hezekiah to Josiah', *WHJP* IV. 1, p. 199; B. Oded, in J. H. Hayes and J. M. Miller (eds.), *Israelite and Judean History* (London: SCM Press, 1977), p. 452.

2 KINGS 21:19 – 22:1

systems accordingly, with emphasis on local worship centres.[1]

The burial in the *palace garden of Uzza*, not necessarily a contraction of Uzziah or of some Arabian deity Uzza (Venus), was probably due to the lack of space in the royal mausoleum (see on 20:21).

ii. Amon of Judah (21:19–26). The historian gives us only the introductory formulae (vv. 19–22), brief details of the conspiracy and assassination (vv. 23–24) and the concluding formulae of this brief two year-reign (vv. 25–26). This king followed his father's apostasy (vv. 20–22) and suffered the fate which had befallen similar wayward kings in Israel. It had been assumed that his mother's name, *Meshullemeth*, and her place of origin, indicates that she was an Arab. But the identification of such names is not certain. *Jotbah* is possibly Jotbathah, north of Aqaba (Nu. 33:33; Dt. 10:7).

20. *Did evil* (see Introduction, p. 49). It is noteworthy that in a long life his father's influence seems to have encouraged the son to replace yet again the idolatry which Manasseh had removed. This view is reinforced by reference to its existence in Josiah's reign (23:5–7, 12).

23–24. There is no record of Assyrian intervention in this reign and the conspiracy against Amon may have stemmed from a pro-Egyptian political group rather than from religious motives.

26. On the *people of the land* see 11:14. On the *garden of Uzza* see verse 18. On *Josiah* see 22:1ff.

C. Josiah's reign and reformation (22:1 – 23:30)

Cf. Chronicles 34–35. The historian devotes much space to the last godly king of Judah before the exile. Though the contemporary prophet Jeremiah is not mentioned, he commended Josiah (Je. 22:15–16) and the prophet Zephaniah (1:1) was at work in this reign.

The structure of the history follows the normal pattern, with an introduction (22: 1–2) and notes on historical highlights, notably the temple repairs (vv. 3–7) and the discovery of the Book of the *Law* (vv. 8–10) with the king's response to it. Next there is the answer by the prophetess Huldah when

[1] G. W. Ahlstrom, *Royal Administration and National Religion in Ancient Palestine* (Leiden: E. J. Brill, 1982), pp. 75ff.

consulted (vv. 14–20), in two prophecies, one concerning the fate of Jerusalem (vv. 15–17), the other the favour to Josiah in avoiding the final fall of the city (vv. 18–20). The reading of the book publicly resulted in both a reaffirmation of the divine covenant (23:1–3) and a series of acts of reformation based on its teachings (vv. 4–25). Throughout and at the end the historian stresses the statement and fulfilment of prophecy (vv. 26–27). The closing formulae for the reign are given (vv. 28–30).

The Chronicler (2 Ch. 34–35) appears to present a two-stage sequence of events: (i) the purification of religious practices in Judah, Jerusalem and Naphtali in Josiah's twelfth year, and (ii) a continuing reformation stimulated by the discovery of the Book of the Law in the eighteenth year. But this may be a presentation to fit in with the Chronicler's particular emphases.[1] Those who follow this interpretation link the first action with the death of Ashurbanipal of Assyria, *c.* 627 BC, which encouraged Judah to work towards independence during the uncertainties which dogged the succession in both Assyria and Babylonia. Others see the increasing influence of anti-Assyrian groups in Judah straining to break away, or they interpret the narrative in two strands: (i) the first stage of reform after the discovery of the book (22:3 – 23:3), and (ii) reforms made without any specific reference to the law book (23:4–20). This latter understanding is unlikely in view of the coherent picture of the references to the language and theology of Deuteronomy throughout and of the previous history of reforms in Judah. Most view the reforms as spurred on by the discovery of the scroll.

It may not be possible to determine the precise nature of the Book of the Law (*cf.* Introduction, p. 20). Those who once argued that it was written *ad hoc* here in Josiah's reign cannot explain the Levitical changes and other 'out of date' descriptions, so make it a late 'pious fraud'. Similarly those who would see the book as the complete Pentateuch must assume that only parts were read publicly with full comprehension twice in a single day. This also indicates that if it was the present book of Deuteronomy, only the legal corpus and curses (*i.e.* without the introduction, chs. 1–11, and epilogue, 31–34) may have been in the rediscovered copy. However, since the historical

[1] H. G. M. Williamson, *1–2 Chronicles* (London: Marshall Morgan & Scott, 1982), pp. 397ff.

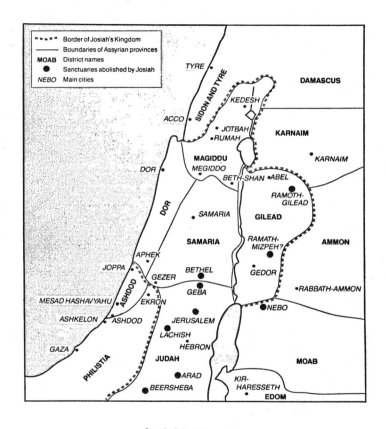

Josiah's Kingdom

background is essential to its interpretation, the whole scroll could well have been found complete. The identification with Deuteronomy rests on the dependence of some of Josiah's actions on the book (*e.g.* 23:9, *cf.* Dt. 18:6–8; and the impact of the prophecies predicting exile; the support Dt. 17:14 gives to nationalistic aspirations, *etc.*).

An increasingly held view is that Deuteronomy was a product of priests who fled from the Northern Kingdom before the fall of Samaria. This requires the hypothesis that originally it referred to the Shechem sanctuary and had to be revised to relate to a centralized worship at Jerusalem alone. Suggestions that the book was placed in the temple by this reform group and that the story of the discovery was a later interpretation, or that it was composed in the time of Hezekiah to support his reforms, are unsubstantiated hypotheses.

Many argue that Deuteronomy has original older elements going back to Moses (*Urdeuteronomium*). The view taken here is that the history and covenant with the law was written down soon after its compilation, not later than the period of the Judges or the early monarchy. The relation of God and his people in covenant terms was an on-going tradition (see Introduction, pp. 18ff.). The book of Deuteronomy may well have been lost for a generation and not been read during the reigns of Manasseh, Amon and the early days of Josiah.

i. Summary of reign (22:1–3b). 1. The reign of *Josiah* ('Yah-[weh] has given', *cf.* the name Joash, 12:1), 640/39 – 609 BC, is fixed by the date of his death during the march of Necho II to support the Assyrian king at Harran in 609 BC (Babylonian Chronicle).[1] *Jedidah* means 'Beloved'. *Bozkath* lay between Lachish and Eglon (Jos. 15:39).

2–3a. *He did what was right* (see on 1 Ki. 15:11, *cf.* Dt. 17:19), as had his ancestor David, and so was given the same unqualified approval as Hezekiah (18:3). *Eighteenth year* (622/1 BC): he had begun to serve God at sixteen and to purge the land at twenty years old (2 Ch. 34:3). The work of repairing the temple – customarily a responsibility of all ancient Near

[1] 17th year of Nabopolassar, D. J. Wiseman, *Chronicles of Chaldaean Kings (626–556 B.C.) in the British Museum* (London: British Museum, 1956), p. 63; A. K. Grayson, *Assyrian and Babylonian Chronicles* (Locust Valley, New York: J. J. Augustin, 1975), p. 95, l. 61.

Eastern kings – may have awaited the outcome of the death of Ashurbanipal of Assyria (*c.* 627) and the subsequent Scythian raids.

ii. Temple repairs and the finding of the law book (22:3b–20).

a. The temple repairs (22:3b–7). Cf. Chronicles 34.8–13. These followed the method adopted by Joash, including a public collection (12:4–16).

3b. Shaphan, the *Secretary* of State (MT *sōp̄ēr*) rather than REB 'adjutant-general', is given his full patronymic to distinguish him, as this was a common name (*cf.* 2 Sa. 8:17; 2 Ki. 25:22, Je. 36:11). For his office see on 1 Kings 4:3. Others were sent with him (2 Ch. 34:8).

4. *Hilkiah* ('Yah(weh) is my portion'), referred to as *high priest* in Jerusalem (*cf.* 12:10), now possibly an established office, was the last to hold the position before his successor was executed by the Babylonians before the exile (2 Ki. 25:18–21). The money was 'reckoned up' (RSV) or got *ready* (Heb. *tmm* means 'made up', 'complete'). There is no need to emend to 'melt down' as NEB (see on 12:10). For the supervisors see the names in 2 Chronicles 34:12–13.

5–7. These verses may well have been derived from temple records, as also for 12:9–15.

b. The discovery of the law book (22:8–10). This is introduced without undue surprise. *The Book of the Law* was readily recognized as such. It could have been found in the box when the silver was 'poured out' (2 Ch. 34:14). Note that it was first read personally (v. 8), then to the king (v. 10; MT 'in it'; NIV *from it* implies an abstract), and then publicly to the people (23:2). On the *Book of the Law* or *Covenant* (23:2) see above. When introduced to the king it is referred to as *a* book (or scroll, *sēp̄er*), the king not yet being aware of its specific nature, but verse 11 may be against such an interpretation.

c. The enquiry (22:11–14). The king's response to the word of God is contrition and remorse (grief for his and the nation's sin), for *he tore his* (official) *robes* (*cf.* 18:37). Contrast this reaction with that of Jehoiakim later (Je. 36:24). He may well have heard the sections of Deuteronomy which detailed the curses for failing to keep the covenant, resulting in exile (28:15–26; 29:25–28). Verse 11 introduces the king's response (vv. 11–13). This contrasts with the theory that the structure here is alternatively patterned on 'he sent ... he commanded ...' and that verse 11 concludes the section consisting of verses 3–11 (Lohfink).

12. This is an official delegation asking for interpretation not by divination but through a spokesman of God. The reply was needed both by the king and by the people of Judah. Both must act in accord. *Ahikam* son of Shaphan was a priest who helped Jeremiah (26:24) and the father of Gedaliah, later the governor of Judah (2 Ki. 25:22; Je. 39:14). *Acbor* ('mouse') was the father of Elnathan (Je. 26:22; 36:12). *Asaiah* was 'the royal official' (*'eḇed hammeleḵ*), a term common on administrative seals from Judah. This is better than reading *the king's attendant*, 'servant' (AV, NRSV) or 'minister' (Gray).

13. The word of God has always to be seen as relevant and to be applied (*concerning us* NIV, RSV, has the implication of 'against' (*'al*), or 'upon us', so NEB 'laid on us').

d. The prophecy of Huldah (22:14–20).

The identity of *Huldah* as the person asked to explain the words cannot be known and is unimportant in that she obviously had the authority to speak for God and interpret the scroll. Some suggest that Jeremiah was absent at the time or not yet fully recognized (this is unlikely because of his family connections); that Zephaniah was little known, or that a prophetess would be more sympathetic (! *cf.* Deborah, Jdg. 4:4–5) or give a more favourable prophecy as the wife of a temple official. *Shallum* as *keeper of the* (temple?) *wardrobe* (*cf.* 2 Ki. 10:22) may have been an uncle of Jeremiah (32:6). The *Second District* or 'Mishneh quarter' of Jerusalem was a 'second' New Quarter (Zp. 1:10, *cf.* Ne. 3:9, 12) built to the northwest of the original Jerusalem (not 'college', as AV, based on later secondary meaning of Heb. *mišneh*).

15. *The man* (one) *who sent you to me, i.e.* the one who recommended you come to me, rather than stressing the king as a mere man. The true prophet's word is always with authority, *This is what the LORD says*. The reply is in two parts, one each for the king and for the people.

16–17. The message about Jerusalem is based on the scroll. The phraseology is typical of Deuteronomy and Jeremiah.

This place is Jerusalem. *Everything written* or 'all the words of the scroll' (RSV), *i.e.* the curses (2 Ch. 34:24), looks back to Leviticus 26:14–46; Deuteronomy 28. Many critics see evidence for later reworking of these verses, but in the light of remembered repeated experiences (*e.g.* the fall of Samaria) this need not be supposed to be written up after the fall of Jerusalem in 587 BC.

18–19. The reply to the king links up with his situation at the time of the request (*cf.* v. 11). Faithfulness to God is ultimately rewarded.

20. *Buried in peace* is not contradicted by Josiah's death in battle and subsequent burial, *cf.* 23:29–30. Sometimes an early death can be God's blessing in preventing our having to endure further heart-rending disaster. *I will gather you to your fathers*, *cf.* 1 Kings 1:21. Here it is deliberately stated to be God's act.

iii. Josiah renews the covenant (23:1–3). One immediate response to the finding of the Book of the Law was Josiah's act of leadership. As a basis of unity and action he called upon the nation's members to return to the old covenant and publicly accept its obligations, which would then mark them out as the exclusive people of God and reaffirm the covenant as the law of the land. This, with the celebration of the Passover, was to be influential in the development of both Judaism and Christianity.

The ceremony compares with the basic Mizpah covenant (1 Sa. 8:11–17; 10:25) and the renewal of the covenant at Shechem (Jos. 24), both of which marked turning points in Jewish history.[1] The participants (v. 2) included those of every status (2 Ch. 34:30 later substitutes 'Levites' for *prophets*). All are essential for total commitment, with Josiah, to follow the LORD as he takes the lead in the tradition of Moses (Dt. 1:3; Ex. 24:3–8), Joshua (Jos. 8:34; 24) and Samuel (1 Sa. 7:6; 12:18–25), followed later by Ezra (Neh. 8:2). The covenant renewal (*cf.* Dt. 29) has at its heart the written *Book of the Covenant* (first called this here, *cf.* v. 8 used by some technically of Ex. 20–23), a term applied widely to Deuteronomy.

3. The King stood *by the pillar* as Joash had done (2 Ki. 11:14); 'on the dais' NEB (*cf.* Neh. 8:4). The word (*'ammûḏ*)

---

[1] Z. Ben-Barak, '*The Manner of the King*' and '*The Manner of the Kingdom*' (PhD Hebrew University, Jerusalem, 1972), pp. 49–68, 197ff.

may simply denote 'a standing place', the royal station in the ritual. The people 'gave their allegiance' (JB) to the covenant and thus pledged themselves (lit. 'stood', NRSV 'joined in') in ratification of the Deuteronomic command *to follow the LORD.* For this they stood (literally), and both symbolically (Je. 34:18) and verbally (saying 'Amen', Dt. 27:11:26) gave their assent. Such periodic communal confession is essential to the life of God's people.

iv. The purification of national worship (23:4–20). The historian in Kings and the Chronicler (2 Ch. 34–35) present a possible different order of events and many argue that 23:4–20 is a list of undated reforms, some of which may include action taken before the discovery of the Book when the reform could have already begun. Among these are the centralization of worship in Jerusalem[1] with the attendant fiscal requirements that tithes be paid to the central palace, a practice possibly confirmed by the widespread distribution of inscribed jars and handles (*lmlk*) at this time.[2] The aim may have been to make the temple function more as a 'central sanctuary' and less as a 'royal chapel'.

4. The king acted in a firm manner (*ordered, cf.* 22:12; 23:21). On the *high priest* see on 12:10 (*cf.* 2 Ki. 25:18; Je. 52:24 'the chief priest'). The *priests next in rank* is preferable to 'the deputy high priest' (NEB, but the Heb. is plural) or to 'priests of the second order' (RSV), since such orders are not attested elsewhere. Temple *doorkeepers* were a long-standing profession in ancient temples and would include lower grades of priests (*cf.* 2 Ki. 12:9). Action was taken to remove all objects introduced into the Jerusalem temple itself for the worship of *Baal* and his consort *Asherah,* the Canaanite (Syro-Phoenician) deities whose introduction in the time of Jeroboam and Ahab had led Israel astray. *All the starry hosts* of heaven included all deities associated with their heavenly representations seen in the heavens (as most of them were), together with astral worship and astrological practices. These idols, many with wooden cores (Is. 40:20), were burned

---

[1] G. Wenham in C. Brown (ed.), *History, Criticism and Faith* (London: IVP, 1976), pp. 36–38.
[2] W. E. Clayburn, 'The Fiscal Basis of Josiah's Reform', *JBL* 92, 1973, pp. 11–22; N. Na'aman, 'Sennacherib's Campaign to Judah and the date of the *lmlk* Stamps', *VT* 29, 1979, pp. 61–86.

outside the holy city so that it would not be further defiled.

The fields of the Kidron Valley (Heb. *šaḏᵉmôṯ*; NEB 'open country')
were on 'level land' or 'terraces' (*šāḏam*), though some prefer
the LXX 'lime kiln' (*miśrᵉpôṯ*), but this requires emendation of the
text. The distribution of the ashes *to Bethel* is no mere 'absurd
intrusion' by a later editor, for Josiah set out to expand his
borders (see on v. 19 below) and here may have aimed to
desecrate Bethel as the place which originated the false worship
of the golden calves (1 Ki. 12:28–29) but long before taken by
Assyrian or other conquerors (Hos. 10:5–6). Bethel also
marked the southern border of the former Northern Kingdom, now the Assyrian province of Samaria, and so was a clear
challenge to the weakening Assyrian masters.

5. Similarly, the purge extended to neighbouring Judah,
where he 'caused the pagan priests to cease'. The type of
officiant (Heb. *kᵉmārîm*, Akkad. *kumru*)[1] denotes the worship
of pagan deities (*cf.* Zp. 1:4; Hos. 10:5). Unlike those at work
in Judah (v. 8), these priests were not brought into Jerusalem.
The *starry hosts* and *constellations* (Heb. *mazzālôṯ*, Akkad. *man-
zaltu*) are terms used both for the object in the heavens
represented by the image and for the stand on which it was
set. The signs of the Zodiac are not attested elsewhere by this
time.

6. On the *Asherah* see on 1 Kings 14:15. Since the symbolic
wooden pole could be burned and pulverized (Heb. *dqq*) the
scattering of the ashes over peoples' graves (JB 'common
burying ground') served to despise both the god and its
worshippers (*cf.* Je. 26:23). These Asherah symbols had been
reintroduced by Manasseh (21:7) and perhaps not fully
removed after his repentance (2 Ch. 33:15), following the
earlier purge by Hezekiah (18:4). Amon also appears to have
brought others in (21:21; 2 Ch. 33:22).

7. For 'cult-prostitutes' (RSV; AV 'sodomites') see 1 Kings
14:24. The word is masculine (*qᵉḏēšîm*), so most translate *male
(shrine) prostitutes* (NIV, NEB), though the word may generally
refer to both sexes (*cf.* Dt. 23:17; Gn. 38:21–22). The Hebrew
word basically denotes 'holy, set apart', here clearly for non-
Yahwistic purposes. It is generally assumed that these persons
were associated with a fertility cult, but there is no specific
evidence for this or for the nature of the activities for which

---

[1] *CAD* K 534–535.

they are always condemned.[1] The *quarters* or houses (*bāttê*) of
the shrine prostitutes may rather be interpreted as the 'hang-
ings' (RSV) or 'woven-garments' (*bāttîm*; Akkad. *bittu* of wool)
which were used by the priests or statues or to denote the
'plaited cord' round the head as worn by Babylonian women
prostitutes.[2]

8–9. These verses may refer to the work done outside
Jerusalem (*cf.* vv. 4–5). For the *high places* see on 1 Kings 3:3.
Geba to Beersheba denotes the north and south boundaries of
Judah by their administrative and cult centres, as in 1 Kings
15:21.[3]

The *shrines at the gates* (NIV mg *high places*) are otherwise
unknown and NEB 'of the demons' (*haśśᵉ'îrîm*; 'satyrs') requires
a change from MT 'gates' (*haśśᵉ'ārîm*; *cf.* 2 Ch. 11:15; Lev.
17:7). Yadin has suggested that this refers to a high place
destroyed by Josiah found at Beersheba.[4] The redundancy
among the clergy was solved by their being given provisions,
as required by Deuteronomy 18:6–8, but here perhaps on the
scale for those priests with physical defects (Lv. 21:16–23).[5]

10–11. The purge extended to rarer deviations in worship.
Topheth or 'fire-place' was associated with Molech (Ugaritic
mlk) worship and the practice of passing males and females
through fire (NIV *sacrifice*). It was located in the rubbish tip
area of the *Valley of (Ben) Hinnom* west and south of Jerusalem
which gave its name to Gehenna (*Gē'*, 'valley', *Hinnom*; Greek
and Latin 'place of Torment'). The use of the word 'burn' has
made some commentators compare this with Phoenician practices of child-sacrifices, but this is rarely attested elsewhere in
the biblical world. See on 1 Kings 11:5 (*cf.* Dt. 12:31; 2 Ki.
17:31; Je. 7:31; 19:5).

The evidence for the solar cult in Jerusalem rests on this
passage and the models of *horses*, some with solar disks on

[1] M. Weinfeld, 'The Worship of Molech and the Queen of Heaven and its
Background', *UF* 4, 1972, pp. 133–154.

[2] Herodotus I. 199.

[3] A. J. McKay, *Religion in Judah under the Assyrians, 732–609 B.C.* (Society for
Biblial Theology, 26, 1973), p. 105.

[4] Y. Yadin, 'Beersheba: The High Place destroyed by King Josiah', *BASOR*
222, 1976, pp. 5–17.

[5] G. J. McConville, 'Priests and Levites in Ezekiel', *TynB* 34, 1983, pp. 5–8,
considers that this passage is not a blanket condemnation of country priests.
He does not think these verses can be used to argue that they 'were pressing a
Levitical claim to serve at the Jerusalem sanctuary because the reform had
deprived them of their living'. The priests of the high places were not Levites.

their forehead, found east of Ophel and at Hazor and other sites.[1] The quarters where Nathan-Melek, the officer in charge (Heb. *sārîs*; 1 Ki. 22:9; NEB 'eunuch'), was located is uncertain. The *court* (*parwār*) has been rendered 'precincts' (RSV) which were west of the temple, or, on the basis of 1 Chronicles 26:18 (*parbār*), 'colonnade' (REB). Rabbinic Hebrew interpreted this as 'suburbs'.

12–13. For altars on the roof used for astral worship compare the upper room of Ahaz (20:11) and Manasseh (21:3, *cf.* Je. 19:13; 32:29; Zp. 1:5 for contemporary activity) and for the *two* courts see 2 Kings 21:4–5. The action taken about the altars is unclear; *smashed them* (*cf.* on v. 15) follows the LXX, *cf.* NEB change to 'pounded them to dust' for the strange Hebrew 'broke them in pieces from there'. The pagan places of worship east of Jerusalem had been initiated to placate Solomon's foreign wives (1 Ki. 11:5–11). The *Hill of Corruption* (*har hammašḥît*, 'mount of the Destroyer', *cf.* 1 Ki. 11:7) at the southern end of the Mount of Olives (modern Jebel Batm el Hawa) is changed by NEB by a play on words, *i.e.* olive oil, to 'Mount of Oil' (*hammišḥâ*), but this is unnecessary.

15. Mention of *the altar at Bethel* marks Josiah's extension of authority northwards rather than being the work of a later editor (DtrP) anxious to weave in a commentary on fulfilled prophecy. Its destruction (vv. 15–17) emphasizes the reformation work outside Jerusalem. Since burning a high place seems difficult, though it might be an abbreviation for burning (bones) on it, NEB changes to 'broke its stones in pieces' (*i.e.* reading *wayyᵉšabbēr 'eṯ ᵃḇānāw* for *wayyiśrōp 'eṯ habbāmâ*).

16. The prophecy given in 1 Kings 13:1–2 is shown to have been fulfilled. The longer Greek text is followed by NEB '. . . thus fulfilling the word of the LORD announced by the man of God when Jeroboam stood by the altar at the feast. But when he caught sight of the grave of the man of God who had fulfilled these things he asked . . .'

17. The 'monument' (NEB; Heb. *ṣîyûn*) was a conspicuous landmark (Je. 31:21), as were other tombstones (*cf.* 'marker' in Ezk. 39:15).

19. Josiah is again said to have moved into the Assyrian province of *Samaria*. This with the references to Bethel (vv. 4,

[1] Y. Yadin, 'The Third Season of Excavation at Hazor, 1957', *BA* 21, 1958, pp. 46–47; K. M. Kenyon, 'Excavations in Jerusalem, 1967', *PEQ* 100, 1968, pp. 97–109.

15, 19) and the claim to control Manasseh, Ephraim, and Simeon as far as Naphtali (2 Ch. 34:6-7, possibly a later idealized picture) gives a good growing view of Josiah's extended kingdom. This is reinforced by archaeological evidence of the period from Arad, where he strengthened the fort, the inscribed Hebrew texts of the archive of Eliashib,[1] En-Gedi on the west Dead Sea shore, Meṣad Hashavyahu[2] and that of the *lmlk* sealings. A few interpret the list of districts given in Joshua 15:21-63 as reflecting the consequent administrative reorganization of this time.[3] See Map. on p. 295.

20. He *slaughtered all the priests* in the northern high places which were a cause of the defection of Israel (*cf.* 1 Ki. 13:2; 18:40; 2 Ki. 10:18-25).

v. The Passover celebrated (23:21-23). *Cf.* 2 Chronicles 35:1-9. The uniqueness of this passover may lie in the act of the Levites slaying the lambs centrally rather than by families as in Hezekiah's passover (2 Ch. 30:2-3, 17-20), perhaps the first to be held since that at Gilgal (Jos. 5:10-12). Here also the day of the Feast of Unleavened bread is linked with it (2 Ch. 37:17; Dt. 16:1-8). The Passover was a communal act (Ex. 12:21-27; 23:15-17).

vi. Further reforms and deferred judgment (23:24-27). **24-25.** The removal of Manasseh's innovations involving both the occult (see on 2 Ki. 21:6, and condemned in Dt. 18:11) and the use of personal or *household gods* (*tᵉrāpîm*, Gn. 31:19) which might be used for divination (*cf.* Jdg. 17:5) or false purposes (1 Sa. 19:13-16) wins the historian's added approval (*cf.* 2 Ki. 18:5 and Dt. 6:4-5). The term *law of Moses* (1 Ki. 2:3) is not necessarily a later synonym for the law as a whole. Josiah was commended for keeping the law in these major ways (*cf.* Dt. 6:5).

26-27. If, as some critics wish, the prophetic element is to be removed, what is left here does not make sense. Judgment is postponed but not removed by reformation. The language

[1] Y. Aharoni, 'Arad: Its inscription and Temple', *BA* 31, 1968, pp. 5-10.

[2] J. Naveh, 'A Hebrew Letter from the Seventh Century BC', *IEJ* 10, 1960, pp. 129-139.

[3] *Cf.* G. Ogden, 'The Northern Extent of Josiah's Reform', *Australian Biblical Review* 26, 1973, pp. 26-34.

about the choice of the temple and Jerusalem has been used earlier in 1 Kings 8:16; 2 Kings 21:4, 7, 13.

vii. The closing formula (23:28–30). *Cf.* 2 Chronicles 35:20–27. This section adds data about Josiah's clash with Egypt and subsequent death, both considered as outstanding events of his reign. Assyrian control in the west was effectively ended by 631/0 BC and Megiddo appears to have been an Egyptian, not Assyrian, base from 646 BC. Archaeological evidence shows that the sole fortification there (Level II, Area C) was probably Egyptian.[1] Thus Necho II warned Josiah that the Egyptian army was en route to a 'fortified base' (possibly Carchemish, 2 Ch. 35:20–22) and thence to *help* (rather than AV 'against') Ashur-uballit who had fallen back west to Harran following the sack of Nineveh by Medes and Babylonians in 612 BC. Josiah's plan to block the Egyptian advance by the Wadi 'Ara pass near *Megiddo* (Magiddu), rather than a more southerly Magdol near Ashkelon on the Egyptian border (the Magdalus of Herodotus ii.159), failed. At this time Necho II held Gaza and sacked Meṣad Hashavyahu (Yabne Yam). He failed, however, to reach Harran in time in 610/9 BC and four years later was defeated by the Babylonians at Carchemish. It could be that the capture of Harran and the appearance of a new pharaoh emboldened Josiah to act. The Chronicler interprets Josiah's death as due to his failure to heed Necho's warning 'from the mouth of God' (2 Ch. 35:22), but the anti-Egyptian *people of the land* of Judah supported him and chose as his successor a younger son *Jehoahaz* considered as less pro-Egyptian than his older brother Eliakim (Jehoakim, v. 34).

D. The last days of Judah (23:31 – 25:30)

The historian concludes his history with abbreviated summaries of the last five kings; Jehoahaz (23:31–35) as an introduction to the reign of Jehoiakim (23:36 – 24:6); Jehoiachin (24:8–17); and Zedekiah (24:18–20) as leading on to the fall of Jerusalem and the exile (25:1–21). Two appendices are added

[1] A. Malamat, 'Josiah's Bid for Armageddon', *Journal of the Ancient Near Eastern Society of Columbia University* 5, 1973, pp. 267–280; A. C. Welch (*ZAW* 43, 1925, pp. 255–260) put forward the idea that what happened at Megiddo was 'not so much a battle as a court-martial'.

which give information to those in the Babylonian diaspora: (i) the history of Judah under Gedaliah and the exile into Egypt (25:22–26) and (ii) the release of Jehoiachin (25:27–30).

The kings are given the customary introductory formula but not closing data (except for Jehoiakim), since they all finished as prisoners of war in the lands of Egypt or Babylon in which they had trusted rather than in God (Yahweh). Much of this data stems from the personal knowledge of the historian (*e.g.* 25:1–12, 18–26 with vv. 22–26) and could well be related to Jeremiah's memoirs (Je. 40–41). Others seek here for various editors (called R[edactor] or R[eviser] or Exilic) because of the 'negative tone',[1] but this does not differ from other comments found throughout the sorry tale of the failure of God's people.

i. Jehoahaz of Judah (23:31–35). Necho II, after defeating Josiah, moved north to Harran. He had summoned his pro-Egyptian successor in Judah, Jehoahaz, to Riblah, whence he took him to Egypt.

31. *Jehoahaz* ('Yah[weh] had seized') was probably a throne-name, for his personal name was Shallum (Je. 22:11; 1 Ch. 3:15). The practice of primogeniture was overriden in view of his older brother (Eliakim) showing anti-Egyptian tendencies.

His mother *from Libnah* (presumably recovered to Judah by Josiah, *cf.* 2 Ki. 8:22) was so designated to distinguish her father from the prophet Jeremiah.

32. Judgment on a three-month period of responsibility as *evil* is understandable (for his failings, *cf.* Je. 22:13–17), as had been said of the six months in office of Zechariah (2 Ki. 15:9), and as can be inferred of an earlier Shallum who ruled only for one month (2 Ki. 15:13–15). Jehoahaz was *put in chains* and 'removed from the throne of Jerusalem' (NEB, 2 Ch. 36:3).

33. *Riblah* on the River Orontes, thirty-four kilometres south of Homs, was an Egyptian garrison fort guarding the main road into the Beqa' valley. Nebuchadnezzar later made it his headquarters (2 Ki. 25:6, 20).

The tribute levied may have been a one-off payment, silver (3¾ tons) being of more value to Egypt than the gold (34 kg.).

34. The change of name from *Eliakim* ('God has established') to *Jehoiakim* ('Yah[weh] has established') was to mark

---

[1] M. Weippert, 'Die "deuteronomistichen" Beurteilungen des Königs von Israel und Judades Problem der Königsbücher', *Bib* 53, 1972, pp. 301–339.

his new allegiance (*cf.* 2 Ki. 24:17) rather than as a spiritual concession to Yahweh worship. The Egyptians doubtless claimed that Yahweh was on their side.

35. To meet the payment the *people of the land,* as anti-Egyptian, were taxed much as Menahem had done earlier in meeting an extraordinary foreign claim (2 Ki. 15:19–20).[1] Yet at the same time Jehoiakim was wasting resources on the construction of a new palace by forced labour (Je. 22:13–19).

ii. Jehoiakim of Judah (23:36 – 24:7). *Cf.* 2 Chronicles

36:5–8. The introduction (vv. 36–37) indicates that Josiah also controlled Rumah in the Megiddo area. The significant background to this reign (609–657 BC) was the invasion by Nebuchadnezzar king of Babylon (605–562 BC). His name means 'Nabu has protected my offspring' (Babylonian *Nabû-kudurri-uṣur,* hence the common writing of his name as *Nebuchadrezzar* used by Jeremiah and contemporaries).[2] Nebuchadnezzar's father Nabopolassar had defended Harran in 609 BC from a counter-attack by Ashur-uballiṭ, the last king of Assyria. In the following years he had countered Egyptian advances from Carchemish on the River Euphrates, until after his death on 15 August 605 BC his son Nebuchadnezzar II had defeated the Egyptian garrison at the Battle of Carchemish and chased them westward. The Babylonians gained the Hamath area. According to reliable details in the Babylonian Chronicle, Nebuchadnezzar received all the kings of Hatti (Syro-Palestine) who came before him with their tribute in the next year.[3]

Whether Jehoiakim became a vassal of Babylon then or when the Babylonians returned in 603 BC is not known. It was probably the earlier occasion for, following a rebellion in Babylonia, Nebuchadnezzar met the Egyptians in open battle in 601 BC. The Babylonians were forced to return home to re-equip and this seems to have emboldened Jehoiakim to rebel as a *vassal* after three years (24:1, *c.* 603–601 BC). The

[1] A. Malamat, 'The Last Years of the Kingdom of Judah', *WHJP* IV. I, p. 207.

[2] D. J. Wiseman, *Nebuchadrezzar and Babylon* (Oxford: British Academy, 1986), pp. 2ff.

[3] D. J. Wiseman, *Chronicles of Chaldaean Kings (626–556 B.C.) in the British Museum* (London: British Museum, 1956), pp. 19–28. See also 'Babylonia 605–539 B.C.' in *The Cambridge Ancient History* III/2 (Cambridge: Cambridge University Press, 1991), p. 231.

Babylonians were in no position to send a punitive force of their own at once, so they encouraged neighbouring vassals to join in on raids on Judah. For the *Babylonians* ('Chaldaeans', RSV) and *Arameans* see Jeremiah 35:1, 11, and for Moab and Amon, Zephaniah 2:8–10.[1]

2–4. This section gives the historian's theological view of the history. *The LORD sent.* His actions through human agents were part of his judgment on sin. History is the fulfilment of the LORD's plan (*cf.* 2 Ki. 21:12–15), and this interpretation can be argued to be the overall aim of the historian of Kings, not necessarily only that of a later re-editor (*e.g.* a DtrP = 'Deuteronomistic Priestly' Source).

Shedding *innocent blood* (v. 4), as in 2 Kings 21:16, was both a 'cruel act of tyranny' (Je. 22:17) and deliberate breaking of God's law. This the LORD is *not willing to forgive* (AV, NRSV 'pardon') according to Deuteronomy 29:20 (*cf.* Gn. 9:5). We will always require the special gift of forgiveness, even when our sins have been forgiven for Christ's sake, to forgive others also (Ps. 130:4; Lk. 7:47; Col. 3:13).

5–6. The closing formulae make no reference to the burial of Jehoiakim, whose death occurred about December 598 before the first capture of Jerusalem by Nebuchadnezzar. 2 Chronicles 36:7 implies that he was taken to Babylon, but Jeremiah 22:19 tells how he was thrown unmourned outside Jerusalem, perhaps by a pro-Babylonian group who gave him the unceremonial burial of 'an ass'. The tradition that he was buried in the garden of Uzza (see 2 Ki. 21:26) stems from a Greek translation of 2 Chronicles 36:8.

Among his *other events* was the reintroduction of idolatrous ('detestable') things (2 Ch. 36:8). This is the last reference to the official *annals of the kings of Judah* (see Introduction and 1 Ki. 14:29 for the first reference) which presumably ended with the siege of the capital city.

7. This note underlines the final Egyptian incursion after their defeat at Carchemish when the Babylonians reached, and defended, the southern border of Judah.[2] The Egyptians were untrustworthy people. Neither the king Adon (of an unspecified city) appealing for help in a letter to the pharaoh in 604 BC,[3] nor Jehoiakim, nor Zedekiah later, received the

---

[1] Wiseman, *Chronicles of Chaldaean Kings*, pp. 29–31.
[2] Josephus, *Ant. Jud.* x. 6, says the same.
[3] Wiseman, *Nebuchadrezzar and Babylon*, pp. 25–26.

help for which they asked. The *Wadi of Egypt*, Nahal-muṣur, modern Wadi el-'Arish (1 Ki. 8:65), marked the border with Egypt south of Gaza. Some scholars think that here ended the original Book of Kings, the remainder being a series of appendices.

iii. Jehoiachin of Judah (24:8–17). This reign (597 BC) is recorded also in 2 Chronicles 36:9–10; Jeremiah 29:2; 1 Esdras 1:41–44; Josephus, *Ant.* x.6.3; 7.1 and continued in 2 Kings 25:27–30.

8. *Jehoiachin* (Heb. *yᵉhôyāḵîn*, 'Yah[weh] confirms'; Baby. *Yaukîn*) was probably the throne-name of Jeconiah (so Heb. 1 Ch. 3:16; Je. 24:1, 'Yah[weh] is firm'), abbreviated also to Coniah (Je. 22:24; Heb.). The name occurs as *ykyn* on contemporary jar-handles.[1] He ruled three months and ten days (2 Ch. 36:9), most of this during the Babylonian siege of Jerusalem. *Eighteen* years old is more reliable than 'eight' (as some Heb. MSS, 2 Ch. 36:9). *Elnathan* was the son of Acbor (Je. 26:22).

9. The evaluation as *evil* lies behind Ezekiel 17:12–24. For his father's sin, *cf.* 23:37; Jeremiah 22:24–30.

The first capture of Jerusalem (vv. 10–17) as recorded here agrees well with the Babylonian Chronicle which says that 'in Nebuchadnezzar's seventh year in Kislev (November/December), the Babylonian king called up his army and marched to the land of Hatti (Syro-Palestine). He besieged the city of Judah (Jerusalem) and on the second day of the month Adar he seized the king and captured the city.'[2]

12. Nebuchadnezzar came up from Riblah probably to accept Jehoiachin's surrender, the siege taking from sometime after December 598 when the army had set out from Babylon till the day of the capture of Jerusalem on 15/16 March, 597 BC. Nebuchadnezzar's *eighth year* began on 13 April and this date agrees with 'at the turn of the year', *i.e.* the spring (2 Ch. 36:10, NEB). Prisoners and spoil need not have been taken away immediately.[3] According to the same Babylonian Chronicle, Nebuchadnezzar 'appointed there a king of his own

---

[1] W. F. Albright, 'The Seal of Eliakim and the Latest Preexilic History of Judah, with Some Observations on Ezekiel', *JBL* 51, 1932, pp. 77–106.

[2] Wiseman, *Chronicles of Chaldean Kings*, pp. 72–73; A. K. Grayson, *Assyrian and Babylonian Chronicles* (Locust Valley, New York: J. J. Augustin, 1975), p. 102.

[3] Nor would this be evidence of a different dating system (as A. Malamat, 'The Last Years of the Kingdom of Judah', *WHJP* IV. I, p. 211).

choice (lit. 'heart', *i.e.* Mattaniah/Zedekiah) and, taking vast tribute, brought it to Babylon'. This extra-biblical record thus attests the beginning of the Exile. Verses 13–14 therefore need not be a summary by the editor including data of the final sack of the city ten years later. Jehoiachin 'went out' (MT) *i.e. surrendered.* The numbers of deportees given may be either general for 'a large number' (*ten thousand*) or the seven thousand fighting men plus a thousand skilled workers (v. 16), plus others unspecified. In the light of Jeremiah 52:28 some interpret the figures either as of deportation in two stages, 3,023 and 7,000 or as 3,023 from Jerusalem and 7,000 from Judah. The aim was to remove all *leading men* (v. 15) including administrators and religious leaders, 'all the men of substance' (NEB, REB 'foremost'; RSV 'men of valour') who would provide ablebodied and skilled men who could organize further resistance.

15–16. Jehoiachin's captivity (*cf.* vv. 27–30) fulfilled the prophecy of Jeremiah (22:24–27). His presence in Babylon is attested by tablets listing oil and barley supplies to him, his family and five sons in 592–569 BC and naming him as 'Yaukin king of the Judeans'.[1]

17. Nebuchadnezzar chose Mattaniah the third son of Josiah (1 Ch. 3:15) and like his brother Jehoahaz an antiEgyptian, to succeed him. He was thus *Jehoiachin's uncle* (2 Ch. 36:10, Heb. using 'brother', *i.e.* 'relation'). The change of name from *Mattaniah* ('Gift of Yah[weh]', Je. 1–3) to *Zedekiah* ('Yah[weh] is righteous' or 'Righteousness of Yah[weh]') may have been given to stress that Yahweh's act against Jerusalem was justified judicially rather than merely to emphasize Zedekiah's status as a vassal (2 Ki. 23:14).[2]

iv. Zedekiah of Judah (24:18–20). See also 2 Chronicles 36:11–14; Jeremiah 39:1–10; and the almost verbatim repetition in Jeremiah 52.

This king (597–587 BC) inherited a much reduced Judah, for the Negeb was lost (Je. 13:18–19) and the land weakened by the loss of its experienced personnel. There were both a pro-Egyptian element and false prophets among the survivors (Je. 28–29; 38:5). Nonetheless Jeremiah continued to advise about the rebellion against Babylon being stirred up by outsiders (Je. 27), and yet he supported Zedekiah. The historian

---

[1] Wiseman, *Nebuchadrezzar and Babylon*, pp. 81–83.
[2] *Contra* A. Malamat, *op. cit.*, p. 213.

considered Yahweh as the true king and Jehoiachin still 'King of the Jews' rather than as head of the Jewish exiles.

He visited Babylon (Je. 51:59) and maintained contact with exiles there (Je. 29:3), perhaps to allay any suspicions Nebuchadnezzar may have held about his loyalty, yet in 589 BC he rebelled, perhaps encouraged by pharaoh Psammetichus II (Psamtik) who was now on the throne of Egypt and had visited the Phoenician coastal cities *c.* 592. His successor Apries (Hophra) in 589 was collaborating with Koriah the commander-in-chief of Judah.[1] Since Zedekiah called together diplomatic representatives of Tyre and Sidon, Edom, Moab and Ammon, but significantly not from the Philistinean cities, to Jerusalem (Je. 27:1–11), these may have encouraged him to rebel in 595/4 BC, the year in which Nebuchadnezzar faced a rebellion at home.

Zedekiah's *evil* (v. 19) is fully explained in 2 Chronicles 36:12–14. (i) He was not willing to listen to God's word through Jeremiah; (ii) he broke an oath made in Yahweh's name as a vassal of Babylon; (iii) he was unrepentant and failed to restrain leaders and priests from defiling the temple with the reintroduction of idolatrous practices. The historian again adds his theological reasons for the exile (interpreted as *'thrust from* God's *presence'*). The history is explained in terms as much of divine action as that of men. No specific mention is made here of Zedekiah's call for Egyptian help from Hophra. Tyre rebelled and was besieged for thirteen years.[2] Ammon appears to have joined Zedekiah in rebellion, but this did not make an effective coalition against the might of Babylon.

v. The fall of Jerusalem (24:20 – 25:21). *Cf.* Je. 39:1–10; 52:4–27; 2 Ch. 36:17–20. The writer now centres on the major event of Zedekiah's reign, namely his rebellion against Babylon which brought the final judgment on the ruling house in Judah, on its capital city and on the temple in Jerusalem. This is mainly a factual record drawn from state records, temple lists and personal observation. The historian could be aware of the sources used in parallel records of this

[1] Lachish Letter (*ANET*, p. 322); K. S. Freedy and D. B. Redford, 'The Dates in Ezekiel in Relation to Biblical, Babylonian and Egyptian Sources', *JAOS* 90, 1970, p. 480.
[2] Wiseman, *Nebuchadrezzar and Babylon*, pp. 26–29, favours the years 580–573 BC for this.

same event.[1] Since the Jeremiah account follows the note 'thus far are the words of Jeremiah' (51:64), several see here a record made by Baruch, Jeremiah's scribe,[2] though an earlier account of this same event (v. 18, vv. 1–12 in Je. 39:1–10) could stem from his master Jeremiah rather than, as Noth suggests, what 'appears to be' a summary of the later parallel passages. Most scholars take 2 Kings 25 to be a reliable historical record. The absence of theological comment (as in the other accounts) may be explained in part by the selection of items to lead to the conclusion that 'Judah went into exile away from the land' (25:21), thus fulfilling the prophecy last reiterated in Josiah's reign (23:27) that the evil done since the time of Manasseh would result in exile. Indeed, exile was the expected outcome of breaking Yahweh's covenant (Dt. 28:36; Lv. 26:33) and no less that of the covenant-treaty entered into as a vassal of Babylonia but now neglected.[3] The lesson of Samaria's fall and exile should have been learned.

a. The fall of the city (25:1–7). 1. The siege began *c.* 15 January, 588 BC. *Cf.* Jeremiah 39:1; 52:4; Ezekiel 24:1–2 for *ninth* year. The one and a half year siege may be due to (i) Nebuchadnezzar's absence at Riblah and concern with containing the Phoenician sea-ports and, (ii) his watchfulness against Egypt's potential intervention on behalf of Zedekiah (Je. 37:5, 11).
2–3. The Babylonians relied initially on tight control using 'watch-towers' (NEB, 'siege-towers', REB; Heb. *dāyēq*) rather than *siege works* (RSV, NIV), allowing those who wished to leave to do so (*cf.* v. 11; Je. 38:19; 39; 9), but starving out the city (Je. 38:2–9).

[1] *E.g.* 2 Ki. 24:18–25:21 used in Je. 52:4–27; 2 Ch. 36:17–20; 25:1–12 in Je. 39:1–10; 2 Ki. 25:22–26 in Je. 40:7–9; 41:1–3, 16–18.
[2] The seal of Baruch inscribed 'Berechiah, son of Neriah, the scribe' (*lbrkyhw bn nryhw hspr*) was found with those of other persons named in Je. 36 (*e.g.* Jerahmeel), probably indicating that he was also a state official who was working for the prophet Jeremiah (N. Avigad, 'Jerahmeel and Baruch', *BA* 42, 1979, pp. 114–117).
[3] *Cf.* D. J. Wiseman, *The Vassal-Treaties of Esarhaddon* (London: The British School of Archaeology in Iraq, 1958), p. 52, ll. 292–295, 'If you transgress the treaty you will be giving your land to be ruined and your people to be carried off as prisoners.'

4. The city was then breached to the north,[1] rather than NEB 'thrown open' (REB 'capitulated'), for the enemy incursion was fiercely resisted and this enabled some to escape through the southeast double wall overlooking the Kedron (*cf.* for this double wall Is. 22:11). The intention might have been to continue resistance in the Judean hills and then join with Bealis of Ammon by fleeing via the Arabah rift valley and south of the Dead Sea. It seems that the army scattered to avoid capture; some link the prophecy of Obadiah 2–14 about Edom to this time.

6. Despite this incident, Nebuchadnezzar was known as 'a just king'[2] and 'spoke with him (according to) law' (MT, *cf.* NEB 'he pleaded his case before him') and so the *sentence was pronounced on him.* The execution of the royal heirs was to wipe out the possibility of future claim to the throne or rebellion (*cf.* 2 Ki. 10:1–17). This also fulfilled Ezekiel's prophecy that Zedekiah would be taken to Babylon but not see it (Ezk. 12:13). Blinding prisoners was a rare occurrence (*cf.* Jdg. 16:21), for most were put to work. If Zedekiah had heeded the prophet's word he would have saved both Jerusalem and himself (Je. 38:14–28), for he was to die in Babylon (Ezk. 12:14).

b. The destruction of the temple (25:8–21). More attention is paid to the temple than to the city, for it was the symbol of God's presence and glory now departed. The final assault was led by Nebuzaradan (Nabû-zēr-iddina), named in Nebuchadnezzar's 'court-list' found at Babylon as a senior official (Chancellor, *rab nuhatimmu,* lit. 'Chief Baker'; *cf.* Heb. *rab ṭabbāḥîm,* lit. 'Chief Butcher'). The precise month dates given from here onwards (vv. 8, 27) follow the Babylonian calendar with the year beginning in Nisan (March/April). The temple fell a week after the breakthrough (7th or 10th Ab. *c.* 5 August, 587) and the whole city fell about a month later. Those who believe Judah used an autumnal (Tishri) new year dating make this 586 BC.[3]

---

[1] A. Malamat, 'The last years of the Kingdom of Judah', *WHJP* IV. I, p. 220; *cf.* references to the Middle and Benjamin Gate (Je. 38:7; 39:3; Ezk. 12:12 'hole in the wall').

[2] Wiseman, *Nebuchadrezzar and Babylon,* pp. 99–101.

[3] *E.g.* A. Malamat, 'The last Kings of Judah and the Fall of Jerusalem', *IEJ* 18, 1968, p. 150. Against this, such a year dating beginning then is denied by D. J. A. Clines, *Australian Journal of Biblical Archaeology* 2, 1972, pp. 9–34; 'The Evidence for the Autumnal New Year in Pre-exilic Israel Reconsidered', *JBL* 93, 1974, pp. 22–40.

The sacking of the city, temple, palace *and all the houses* (v. 9) is qualified by *every important* (*gādôl*) *building*. NEB reads *gādôl* (NRSV 'great'; REB 'notable's') as 'the mansion of Gedaliah' without justification. For the complete destruction of the city see also Jeremiah 39:8; 52:12–14; Ezekiel 33:21; Nehemiah 2:13; and of the temple 2 Chronicles 36:19; Jeremiah 52:13. Archaeological evidence for the siege is accumulating, with weapons found in the upper city,[1] and burned buildings and fallen masonry on the 'Ophel' hill which was later abandoned (*cf.* Neh. 2:13 ff.).[2] Elsewhere many towns and villages in Judah ceased to be inhabited.[3]

11. The classes of exiles given include deserters and the rest of the 'multitude' (RSV, MT *hehāmôn*), *populace* which some read as 'artisans' (NEB by reading *hā'āmôn*, *cf.* Je. 52:15). These general terms may in part account for the difficulty in interpreting the precise numbers (*cf.* 24:16).

12. The unskilled left behind were employed as vinedressers. The area north of Jerusalem (Mizpah, Gibeon, Mozah) and nearby estates, Tell Beit Mirsim, Beth-Shemesh and Ramat Rahel were left to supply wine for the Babylonian forces and court. Seals mentioning these places found in excavation attest the supply.[4] The 'ploughmen' (RSV, 'labourers' NEB, MT *yōgᵉbîm* only here and Je. 52:16) is best read as *fields* (NIV, Vulg., without change of consonants, *yᵉgēbîm*).

13–17. The details of the temple fittings as broken up for transport to Babylon may well be taken from a separate list (Je. 52:17–23, *cf.* 1 Ki. 7:15–45). For the *bronze . . . Sea cf.* 1 Kings 7:23–26; the absence of reference to the bronze bulls supporting them is explained by their earlier removal by Ahaz (2 Ki. 16:17).

The Babylonians prized gold more than silver (v. 15, *cf.* 18:14–15). There are some unexplained variants in this list, with the capitals on the pillars Jakin and Boaz (1 Ki. 7:15–22) given measurements differing here by three cubits. This could

---

[1] N. Avigad, 'Jerusalem, the Jewish Quarter of the Old City, 1975', *IEJ* 25, 1975, p. 26.
[2] Y. Shiloh, *Excavations at the City of David I* (= *Qedem* 19, Jerusalem, 1984), pp. 1–31.
[3] Wiseman, *Nebuchadrezzar and Babylon*, p. 38.
[4] J. N. Graham, '"Vinedressers and Plowmen"; 2 Kings 25:12 and Jeremiah 52:16', *BA* 47, 1984, pp. 55–58.

be either a different reading of the list or possibly change due to repair (*cf*. Je. 52:22).

The list of those executed at Riblah (vv. 18–21) conforms to the common practice of removing resistance leaders and possible future rebels. A similar act is depicted on the Lachish relief of Sennacherib. *Those still in the city* (v. 19) may mean that some tried to hide while others had fled.

18. *Seraiah*, here first designated 'chief priest' (23:4; a common title in Chronicles and Ezra), had a son Jehozadak, whose grandson was Ezra, taken to Babylon (Ez. 7:1–5). *Zephaniah*, grandson of Hilkiah, was the deputy high priest (25:18; Je. 52:24) and possibly the priest named in Jeremiah 21:1. The mention of the five senior priests may indicate their responsibility in the anti-Babylonian movement.

19. The state officials included the military commander (18:17, *sārîs;* NEB 'a eunuch who was in charge of the fighting men'). The *royal advisers* as 'five men who saw the king's face' (Heb.) were those who had access to the king's presence and as such formed 'the king's council' (RSV). The secretary to the commander-in-chief was a high position (*cf*. NEB 'adjutant-general'). The sixty involved in *conscripting the people of the land* could be major landowners or a token group (NEB 'the people') rather than provincial notables (Gray).

21b. The comment on Judah going into captivity *away from her land* is considered by most to be the end of the original Book of Kings.

vi. Gedaliah, Governor of Judah (25:22–26). This is again an abbreviated account (*cf*. Je. 40:7 – 41:9), the author perhaps aware that the details were given elsewhere. This appendix aimed to show (i) how the Babylonian nominee Gedaliah, who had Jeremiah's support, was rejected and with that no representative of the House of Judah was left in the land; (ii) those who stand out as a minority must be prepared for danger, death and difficulty in the pursuit of any policy of resistance.

22. *Gedaliah* was supported by Babylonian officials (v. 24) according to current practice whereby an overlord ensured the loyalty of his appointee. At Lachish he was well known as a member of Zedekiah's court, the son of Ahikam, a pro-Babylonian helper of Jeremiah (Je. 26:24) and grandson of Shaphan, who had participated in Josiah's reform (22:12). The seal of Gedaliah (*lgdlyh* 'who is over the house') has been found at Lachish.[1] Family influence can prepare a person for a crucial role. Gedaliah had the reputation of being gentle and generous (Josephus, *Ant.* x.9.1) and his enemies played on this.

23. Jeremiah 40:7 states that the men were still in the open country (as refugees) when they heard the news (this is not in MT here). *Mizpah* (probably Tell en-Nasbeh fourteen kilometres north of Jerusalem) was originally an important administrative centre (1 Sa. 7:5; 1 Ki. 15:22). *Ishmael*, who is named on two contemporary seals,[2] was trusted by Gedaliah despite Jeremiah's warnings against him (Je. 40:14). His grandfather Elishama had been Jehoiakim's Secretary of State (*cf.* v. 25; Je. 36:12), but his loyalty now lay with the pro-Ammonite faction. Ishmael was resisted by *Johanan* (Je. 41:11–18). *Seraiah* is distinguished from the high priest of the same name by the addition of a family name and his family origin near Bethlehem (*cf.* for the Netophathites, 1 Ch. 9:16; Ne. 12:28). The official agate seal of Jaazaniah (inscribed *y'znyh*, 'official of the king') was found at Tell-en Nasbeh (Mizpah).[3] It is noteworthy that a cache of inscribed sealings has been discovered in Jerusalem[4] (the papyrus to which they were fixed is now lost), including that of 'Baruch son of Neriah, the scribe', which may indicate the dispersal of the state officials named in Jeremiah 36.

24. Gedaliah swore *an oath* as part of his undertaking official duties as governor, or gave his word in God's name that loyalty would ensure safety. He urged acceptance of the judgment God had inflicted on Judah by maintaining a pro-Babylonian policy. *Settle down in the land* peaceably was also Jeremiah's message to the exiles (29:4–7). When it is recognized that a foreign ruler has been the divine agent for punishment, such passive resistance is all the more powerful.

25–26. The story of Gedaliah's assassination here is brief compared with that in Jeremiah 40:13 – 41:15 which shows that men from Shechem, Shiloh and Samaria were also killed. Such anti-Babylonian direct action inevitably produced reprisals and the people were justly fearful of the

[1] Illustrated in *IBD*, p. 545.
[2] D. Diringer, *Le iscrizioni antico-ebraiche palestinesi* (Florence: Universita degli studi di Firenze, 1934), pp. 203, 310.
[3] *IBD*, p. 725; *ANEP*, p. 276.
[4] N. Avigad, 'Jerahmeel and Baruch', *BA* 42, 1979, pp. 114–117.

Babylonians. The prophet Jeremiah was forced reluctantly into exile in Egypt where Apries (Hophra) was king (24:20). He argued that they were acting against God's word by leaving (Je. 42:7 – 43:7). The Babylonian reaction came in 582/1 BC when Nebuzaradan took away a further 745 Judeans into Babylonian exile and Judah was temporarily made part of the province of Samaria (Je. 52:30; Josephus, *Ant. Jud.* x.9.7). The story ends with Judah under Samaria, the old Northern Kingdom which had been the first of God's people to be taken into exile. The Samaritans were to be constant opponents of the Jews.

vii. Appendix: Jehoiachin's release (25:27–30). This second appendix is added to remind the reader that while Jehoiachin was still in Babylon as the representative of David's dynasty God still preserved his people. Some see this as intended to end the history on a hopeful note, perhaps even of 'Messianic revival'. The absence of reference to Jeremiah need not be explained as due to his viewpoint being unacceptable to the 'Deuteronomist historian' or that the story originated in Babylon where Jeremiah's account was unknown. As in the earlier appendix, the author could have been Jeremiah or a close associate in contact with exiles in Babylon (*cf.* Je. 52:31–34; *cf.* 40:7 – 43:7).

27. *The thirty-seventh year of the exile.* Jews throughout the diaspora reckoned years by Jehoiachin's captivity (Ezk. 1:2). Jehoiachin's improved circumstances can be accurately dated from Babylonian texts which show that *the twenty-seventh day of the twelfth month* of the year, when Nebuchadnezzar's successor *became king* (Bab. *reš šarrūti*), fell on 22 March/4 April 562/1 BC. *Evil-Merodach* (Heb. *ʾⁿwîl mrdk*) is an exact transcription (not vocalization) of the Babylonian Awēl-Marduk, who succeeded his father Nebuchadnezzer in October 562 and reigned till 560 BC when, having managed affairs 'in a lawless and outrageous fashion', he was murdered by his brother-in-law Nergal-šarra-uṣur (Neriglissar), who took the throne.

This act of clemency to Jehoiachin was later taken to be a deliberate reversal of his father's policy rather than any amnesty[1] at the time of accession or at a New Year Festival. 'To

---

[1] D. J. Wiseman, *Cambridge Ancient History* III/2 (Cambridge: Cambridge University Press, 1991), pp. 240–242; *Nebuchadrezzar and Babylon*, pp. 102, 113–115; R. H. Sack, *Amel-Marduk; 562–560 BC* (Wiesbaden: Butzon & Bercker, 1972), p. 25.

raise the head of a person' (MT) denotes more than *released* or 'showed favour' (NEB), since it includes a change of status and pardon (*cf*. Gn. 40:13, 20). The Babylonian ration texts dated to 592–568 BC show that already Nebuchadnezzar had granted Yaukīn his support.

28. To 'eat at the king's table' was to receive regular allowances of barley, oil, meat and clothing which were not necessarily used only at the palace. Texts show that such favours were promulgated; the benefits included residence and land sufficient to maintain the royal family in return for loyalty to the donor.[1]

The change of status is here marked by a higher position (*seat*) at ceremonial functions. (On 'come up higher' see Lk. 14:10.) This resulted from an agreement (MT, 'spoke good (things) with him') rather than just generally *spoke kindly to him*.

The ending of this appendix does not assert that Jehoiachin was only now an approved vassal or was finally designated the official king of Judah. It indicates that God protects his own and that this is not the end of the story. The history of God's dealings with his people continued then as now.

[1] Wiseman, *Nebuchadrezzar and Babylon*, p. 83; *cf*. 1 Ki. 4:27; 11:18–19. On eating at the king's table see also 2 Sa. 9:7; 19:33; 1 Ki. 2:7.